JavaServer Pages™

fast&easy® web development

Aneesha Bakharia

PRIMA TECH

A DIVISION OF PRIMA PUBLISHING

A Division of Prima Publishing

Prima Publishing, colophon, and Fast & Easy are registered trademarks of Prima Communications, Inc. PRIMA TECH is a trademark of Prima Communications, Inc., Roseville, California 95661.

Publisher: Stacy L. Hiquet

Associate Marketing Manager: Heather Buzzingham

Managing Editor: Sandy Doell

Acquisitions Editor: Emi Smith

Project Editor: Cathleen D. Snyder

Technical Reviewer: Michelle Jones

Copy Editor: Gabrielle Nemes

Interior Layout: Shawn Morningstar

Cover Design: Prima Design Team

Indexer: Sharon Hilgenberg

Proofreader: Randall Clark

ISBN: 0-7615-3428-8

Library of Congress Catalog Card Number: 00-111676

Printed in the United States of America

00 01 02 03 04 DD 10 9 8 7 6 5 4 3 2 1

This book is dedicated to my grandmother, Rada Bakharia, and my parents, Abdullah and Juleka Bakharia.

Acknowledgments

I would like to thank:

- **My Grandmother**, who took care of me before I started school.
  My Mum for taking care of me even though I'm all grown up now.
  My Dad for sending me to my first computer course.

- My family (**Kulsum, Hajira, Shaida, Julie, Celine, Zaeem, Ebrahem, Rashid, Cassim, Anne**, and **Judy**) for their encouragement and support.

- **Emi Smith** (Acquisitions Editor) for her continued support, dedication, and enthusiasm.

- **Cathleen Snyder** (Project Editor) for her guidance, inspiration, direction, and flexibility. She has been 100% approachable during the development of this book.

- **Gabrielle Nemes** (Copy Editor) and **Michelle Jones** (Technical Editor) for their excellent feedback and refinements.

- **Shawn Morningstar** (Layout Tech), **Sharon Hilgenberg** (Indexer), **Randall Clark** (Proofreader), and **Jason Haines** (CD-ROM Producer).

- **Tracy Williams** for giving me the opportunity to write professionally.

- **Madonna** for making great music to listen to while writing.

About the Author

Aneesha Bakharia is a freelance Web Developer and author. She is fluent in C++, Java, JavaScript, ASP, JSP, HTML, XML, and Visual Basic. Aneesha specializes in creating dynamic database-driven Web sites. She has a Bachelor of Engineering in Microelectronic Engineering and has various postgraduate qualifications in multimedia, online course development, and Web design. In her spare time, she is a keen Madonna fan. She can be reached via e-mail at bakharia@squirrel.com.au.

Contents

Introduction

Thanks for purchasing *JavaServer Pages Fast and Easy Web Development*! Dynamic database-driven Web sites are all the buzz at the moment. Web sites that were once static have been transformed into service-oriented Web applications. As a Web developer, you need to acquire new skills to remain competitive and provide your clients with cutting-edge solutions. You have made a wise choice in selecting JavaServer Pages (JSP) as your tool to develop dynamic database-driven Web applications.

Using JSP, you can leverage the power of Java, a modern object-oriented programming language. Processing forms, sending e-mail messages, displaying dynamic content retrieved from a database, tracking user activity, and parsing XML will all soon be simple exercises. The creation of portals, forums, online campuses, and e-commerce enabled applications is now within your reach.

JSP caters to the modern Web site, where visual presentation is just as important as database integration and programming. JSP separates content from presentation, and allows Web designers and programmers to work independently toward a common goal.

JavaServer Pages offers many advantages when compared to other competing technologies, such as Active Server Pages (ASP), ColdFusion, and PHP. JSP does not restrict you to a particular vendor or platform. Additionally, many cross-platform application servers support both JSP and servlets. Applications built with JSP are also completely scalable. This is extremely handy because you can never accurately predict the popularity of a Web site.

Who Should Read This Book?

JavaServer Pages Fast and Easy Web Development is definitely not like other JSP books. This book takes a totally visual approach to teaching JSP, and includes step-by-step instructions for building compelling Web sites. You hold in your hands one of the few JSP books on the market that assumes no prior knowledge of Java or programming.

The book is aimed at the first-time JSP user, who is already familiar with HTML. As a novice user, you will find valuable information about object-oriented programming in Java; getting started with JSP; processing forms; sending e-mail messages; working with cookies, sessions, JavaBeans, servlets, XML, and tag libraries; and accessing databases. Web developers, graphic designers, and programmers will all find the practical JSP examples useful. Make no mistake, this book will provide you with the hands-on experience that you require to be a proficient JSP developer.

What You Need to Get Started with JSP

The CD-ROM that accompanies this book has everything you need to build and test your JSP applications locally. Allaire JRun Developer Edition is the ideal application server to get you started. You will need to download the JDK (*Java Development Kit*) from Sun's Web site (http://java.sun.com/products/jdk/1.2/index.html). Your JSP code can be written in Notepad, but tools like Forte and JRun Studio will improve your productivity. Chapter 2, "Getting Started," will help you configure your local server.

Conventions Used in This Book

You will find several special elements that will make using this book easier.

TIP

Tips tell you about new and faster ways to accomplish a goal.

NOTE

Notes delve into background information regarding a given topic.

CAUTION

Cautions warn about pitfalls and glitches in an application or procedure.

1

Introducing JavaServer Pages

This chapter introduces JavaServer Pages (JSP). You will gain insight into how the Web has evolved and the benefits that JSP brings to the creation of dynamic Web applications. In this chapter, you'll learn how to:

- Determine the advantages of working with JSP
- Recognize the type of applications that can be built using JSP
- Work with JSP

An Overview of JavaServer Pages

Over the past decade, we have all been witnesses to an information revolution. The Internet has had a substantial impact on the way people interact with information, shop, and communicate. The Web itself is still evolving. I remember a time when every Web page was *static*, meaning that the Web sites contained information that had to be manually updated. Static Web sites certainly did nothing to entice the user to return. These days, Web sites have evolved into highly interactive service-oriented applications. In fact, you probably purchased this book because you want to develop dynamic Web applications.

Creating dynamic, database-driven Web sites is by no means a simple and straightforward task. There are numerous server-side scripting languages available, and it is up to you to select the one that will allow you to compete commercially. You might have already heard of Active Server Pages (ASP), PHP, ColdFusion, servlets, and Perl. JSP merits your attention because it includes several features that most other server-side scripting languages lack. JSP is easy to learn, robust, scalable, and cross-platform.

To truly understand the power and flexibility of JSP, you need to take a good look back at using traditional CGI (*Common Gateway Interface*) scripts to build a Web application. CGI scripts reside and are executed on a Web server. The actual script could be written in just about any programming language; common CGI languages included Perl, C++, Visual Basic, and even Java. The biggest disadvantage to using CGI was that it placed a tremendous load on your Web server. Basically, a CGI script was treated like an actual program when it was executed. Each time a request was made to the server, a new process was started. Each request usually involved loading another instance in memory, passing the relevant parameters, performing the required tasks, and then closing the application. The Web server could, therefore, process only a limited number of requests simultaneously.

CGI scripts also did not offer much flexibility in terms of design and layout because the entire Web page had to be generated using print statements. Each time the layout of the page changed, it was necessary to update and test the code. CGI scripts that contained complex HTML were long and hard to debug. As you can imagine, editing dynamic pages was certainly a tedious task.

It was difficult to reuse the code contained in CGI scripts because it included both the presentation and programming logic. Code had to be copied and edited before it was used to perform the same task on a different page. And, of course, the code had to be tested before it was implemented each time.

This is where JSP came to the rescue. JSP lets you separate your Java code from the HTML code that is used to visually render the page in a Web browser. Java code is actually embedded in the HTML-coded Web page. You can combine HTML markup that incorporates text, headings, lists, tables, links, and images with Java code to generate dynamic content. When a Web browser requests a JSP page, the Java code is executed and the generated HTML code is sent back to the browser. Code can also be stored in reusable components known as JavaBeans.

These days, almost all Web applications are large and fairly complex in nature, and are developed by a team of professionals. Separate team members are likely responsible for the design and programming of the Web site. JSP enables the graphic designer to change the layout of the Web page without disturbing the programming logic that makes the page dynamic. More importantly, JSP pages can still be edited in your favorite Web page design and layout software.

The following applications can be created with JSP:

- Shopping carts
- Portals
- Discussion forums
- Rotating banner advertisements
- Employee directories
- Electronic postcards

How Do JavaServer Pages Work?

A JSP page is just like any other HTML file. It contains HTML formatting tags and can include client-side JavaScript, Flash animations, and Java applets. A JSP page, however, also includes Java code and must have a .jsp file extension. The extension simply indicates that the file should be executed before it is sent to the Web browser.

Java statements must be placed within <% and %> tag delimiters. Only code placed within these delimiters will be executed as Java code.

The steps below outline how a JSP page is processed.

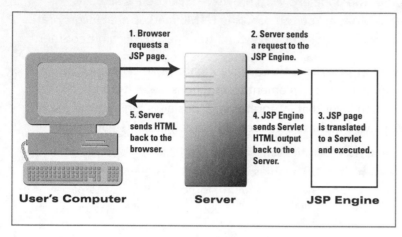

1. A Web browser requests a JSP page from a Web server. This could occur because the user has typed the address of the page or clicked on a link.

2. The Web server determines that a JSP file is being requested by looking at the file extension. The JSP file is translated to a special Java class known as a servlet. (In other words, the source code for a servlet is generated.) This only occurs the first time that a JSP page is requested. The servlet is then compiled. If a JSP file has been updated, a new servlet will be generated.

3. The Servlet is then executed and the resulting HTML output is sent to the Web browser.

4. The Web browser receives the generated HTML code and displays the page. Dynamic content is displayed in the browser without the need for the user to install any additional software.

The Advantages of Using JSP

While JSP is extremely powerful and capable of creating complex Web applications, it is also very easy to learn. JSP offers numerous advantages over other server-side technologies.

- **JSP leverages the power of Java**. Java is an object-oriented programming language supported by a complete range of APIs, all of which are available to a JSP file. Java is also robust, threaded, scalable, secure, and cross-platform.

- **JSP simplifies Web development**. JSP separates business and presentation logic. This makes it easier to create and maintain dynamic pages. JSP also includes numerous implicit objects that aid the Web development process. These implicit objects allow you to retrieve and process data submitted in a form, track users, and send output to a Web browser.

- **JSP is not limited to a particular platform or vendor**. Many application servers that run on a variety of platforms support JSP. BEA WebLogic, Allaire JRun, IBM WebSphere, and Apache Tomcat are just a few of the application servers that currently support the JSP specifications. JSP does not tie you to a specific platform or operating system.

- **JSP is an integral part of Java 2 Enterprise Edition**. Java 2 Enterprise Edition (J2EE) ensures that enterprise application servers implement transactions, security, and persistence. JSP is the presentation layer that integrates with business logic stored in JavaBeans and servlets. JDBC (Java Database Connectivity), JavaMail, JAF (Java Activation Framework), JTS (Java Transaction Server), EJB (Enterprise JavaBeans), and XML (Extensible Markup Language) are all part of the J2EE specifications and can, therefore, easily be incorporated in a JSP page.

- **JSP is extensible**. It is very easy to create custom JavaBeans—you only need to know a few basic object-oriented programming techniques. JavaBeans are components that can easily be reused in other JSP pages. You can also create tag libraries.

Making the Transition from ASP to JSP

Conceptually, JSP is similar to ASP. Both are normal HTML pages that use a set of special tags to mark the start and end of the embedded code segments. They both also use similar object models to retrieve data from the user and to send back a response.

ASP can be written in either VBScript or JScript, which are both scripting languages. JSP, on the other hand, is programmed with Java—a full-blown object-oriented language. While Java is more powerful and ideally suited to Web development, it is harder for the novice programmer to learn. You will also find that many JSP books neglect to cover the basics of programming in Java. This book addresses that problem by introducing Java programming constructs in the context of developing Web applications.

Web applications built in ASP are limited to the Windows platform and Internet Information Server (IIS). ASP can be ported to the Unix platform, but you need to purchase additional software. Only core ASP features are available on the Unix platform.

Table 1.1 lists some of the similarities and differences between JSP and ASP.

Table 1.1 Comparing JSP and ASP

	JSP	ASP
Platform	Linux, Unix, Windows 98, Windows NT, and Windows 2000	Windows 98, Windows NT, and Windows 2000
Web/Application Servers	Apache Tomcat, BEA WebLogic, IBM WebSphere and Allaire JRun	Personal Web Server (PWS) and Internet Information Server (IIS)
Language	Java	VBScript and JScript
Components	JavaBeans and Enterprise JavaBeans (EJB)	COM
Database Support	JDBC-compliant databases	ODBC-compliant databases

2

Getting Started

Building Web applications with JSP won't seem like such a daunting task once you actually get started. Taking that first bold step is the hardest part of learning anything new. You will need to set up a test environment for your JSP development and embed some basic Java code in a Web page. Overcoming these hurdles will boost your confidence. When you complete this chapter you'll be ready to take on the rest of this book. In this chapter, you'll learn how to:

- Install and configure the Java Development Kit (JDK)
- Install JRun Developer Edition
- Select an appropriate JSP editor
- Write your first JSP page

Installing the Java Development Kit

The Java Development Kit (JDK) is required before you can build anything using the Java programming language. The JDK is available at no charge and can be downloaded from the Sun Microsystem's Web site. You will need to download and install the JDK before you install a JSP application server. All application servers require the JDK before JSP applications can be deployed. The JDK comes with tools to compile and execute Java applications. The javac compiler will be used in Chapter 9, "Using JavaBeans," and Chapter 17, "Working with Servlets." In both of these chapters, Java code must be compiled into a class file.

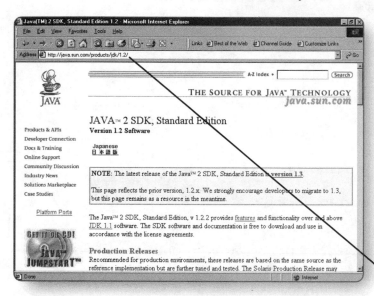

1. Download the latest version of the JDK from Sun's Web site.

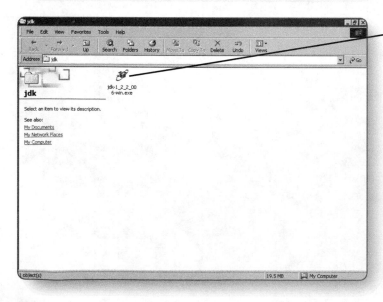

2. Double-click on the JDK installation file. The JDK setup will start.

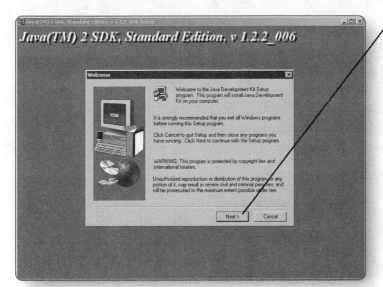

3. Click on Next. The Software License Agreement will be displayed.

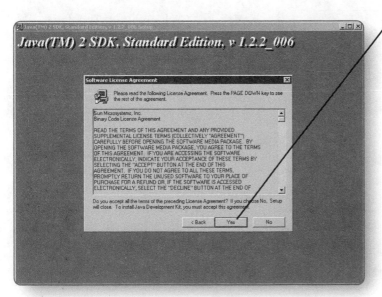

4. Click on Yes after reading the License Agreement. The Choose Destination Location dialog box will open.

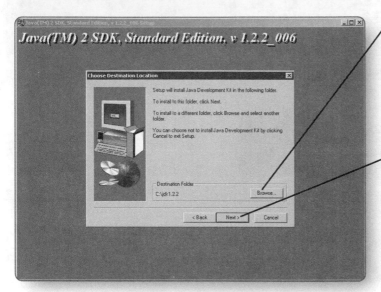

5. Click on Browse to set the installation directory. The default destination is usually a safe bet.

6. Click on Next. The Select Components dialog box will open.

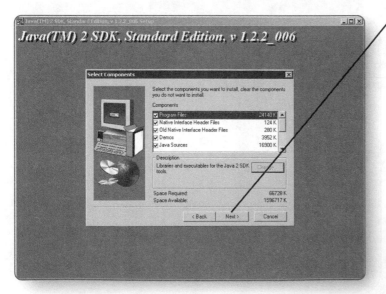

7. Click on Next. The Java Runtime Environment dialog box will open.

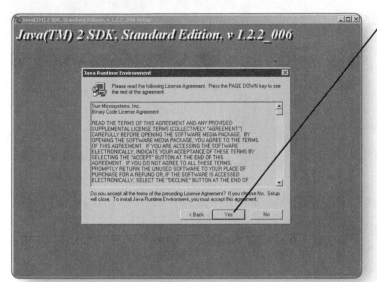

8. Click on Yes after reading the License Agreement. The Choose Destination Location dialog box will open.

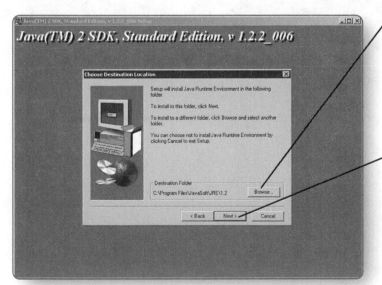

9. Click on Browse to set the installation directory. The default destination is usually a safe bet.

10. Click on Next. The installation process will start, and files will be copied to your hard drive.

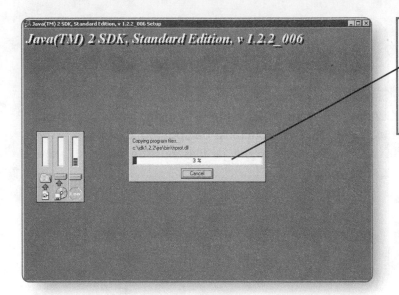

NOTE
The progress bar will indicate the percentage of files that have been copied to your hard drive.

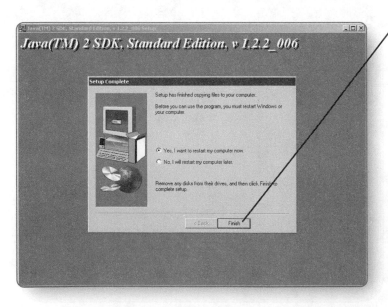

11. Click on Finish. Your computer will restart.

Setting the CLASSPATH Variable

The CLASSPATH environment variable stores the location of third party classes that are not part of the core Java 2 platform. The javac compiler and Java applications use the CLASSPATH variable. Each time you install a new extension, the CLASSPATH variable must be updated. Classes are stored in .jar files. The path to the .jar files must be included in the CLASSPATH variable.

As an example, the servlet.jar file is installed with your application server. The path to the servlet.jar file must be present in the CLASSPATH variable before a servlet can successfully be compiled.

Setting the CLASSPATH Variable in Windows 95/98

The CLASSPATH variable is defined in the autoexec.bat file if you use Windows 95 or 98 as an operating system. The autoexec.bat file is located in the root directory of your hard drive.

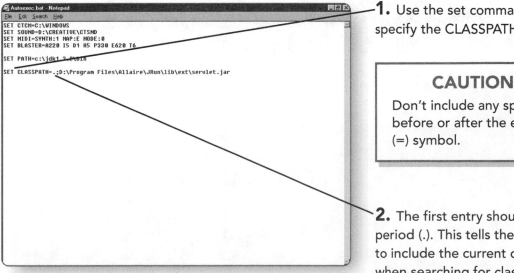

1. Use the set command to specify the CLASSPATH variable.

CAUTION
Don't include any spaces before or after the equals (=) symbol.

2. The first entry should be a period (.). This tells the compiler to include the current directory when searching for classes.

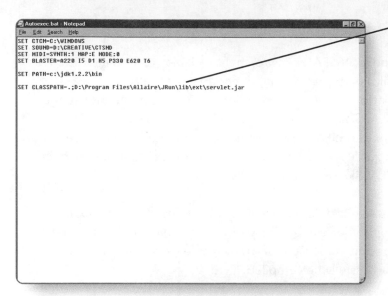

3. You must include the full path, which must begin with a drive letter.

NOTE

Use a semicolon to separate paths.

Setting the CLASSPATH Variable in Windows 2000/NT/Me

Windows 2000, Me, and NT are more sophisticated and allow you to set the CLASSPATH variable in a user-friendly dialog box.

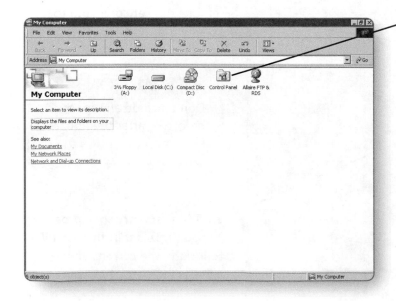

1. Double-click on the Control Panel folder. The contents of the folder will be displayed.

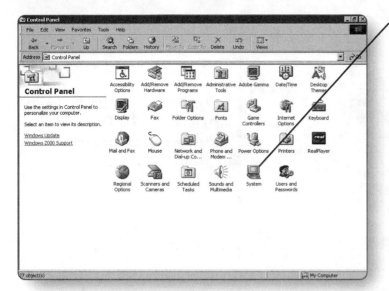

2. Double-click on the System icon. The System Properties dialog box will open.

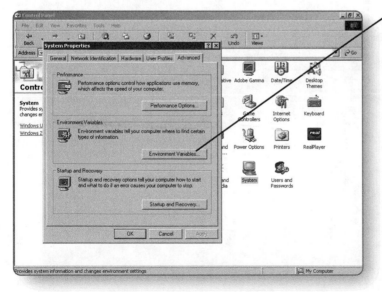

3. Click on Environment Variables. The Environment Variables dialog box will open.

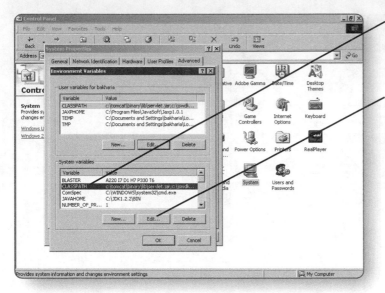

4. Click on the CLASSPATH variable. The variable name will be selected.

5. Click on Edit. The Edit System Variable dialog box will open.

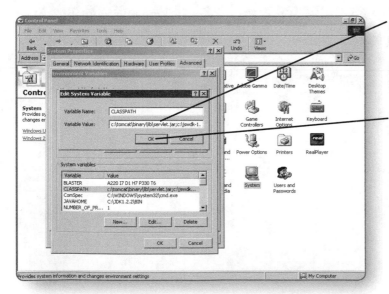

6. Add the full path to the .jar file to the list of paths. Use a semicolon to separate each path.

7. Click on OK. The Edit System Variable dialog box will close.

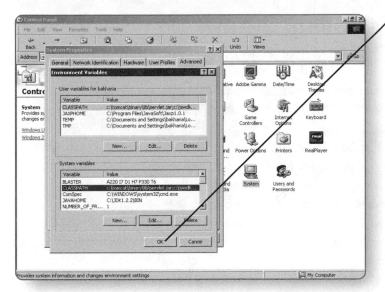

8. Click on OK to close the Environment Variables dialog box.

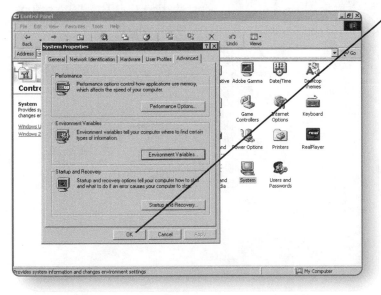

9. Click on OK to close the System Properties dialog box.

Installing JRun Developer Edition

There are many application servers that are compliant with the JSP 1.1 specification. You are by no means restricted to any one platform or application server. However, Allaire's JRun Developer Edition is the ideal choice for beginners. It is not only easy to install and configure, it is also free. JRun Developer Edition contains the full JRun Server feature set and is not time-limited. The catch is that it can only handle five simultaneous Web browser requests. This will not have any impact if you run JRun locally. It can run as a stand-alone Web server or integrate with Microsoft Personal Web Server, Netscape Enterprise Server, or Apache. A copy of JRun Developer Edition is on the CD-ROM included with this book.

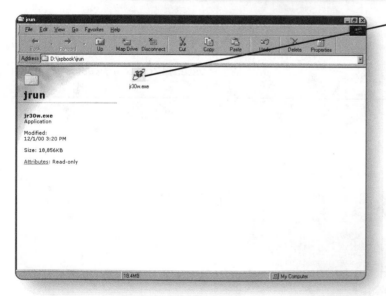

1. Double-click on the JRun installation file. The JRun setup program will start.

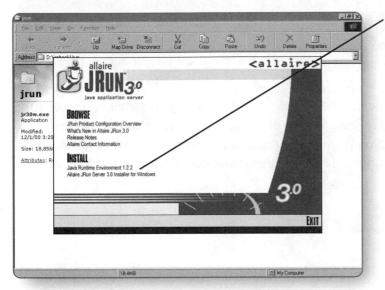

2. Double-click on Allaire JRun Server 3.0 Installer for Windows. The Setup dialog box will open.

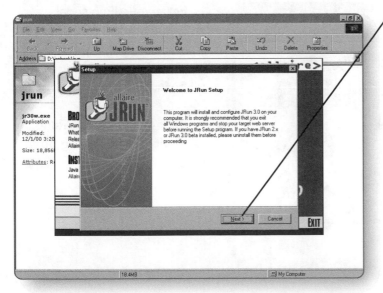

3. Click on Next. The JRun License Agreement will be displayed.

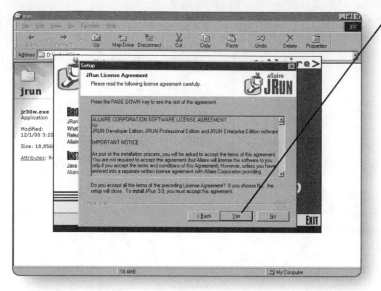

4. Click on Yes after you have read the License Agreement. The JRun Product Serial Number dialog box will open.

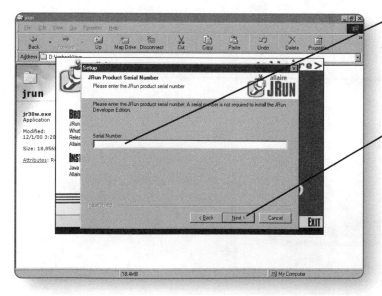

5. Enter your JRun serial number, if you have purchased JRun. If you don't enter a serial number, JRun Developer Edition will be installed.

6. Click on Next. The JRun Installation Folder dialog box will open.

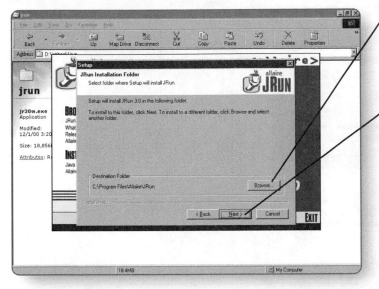

7. Click on Browse to set the installation directory. The default destination is usually a safe bet.

8. Click on Next. The Setup Type dialog box will open.

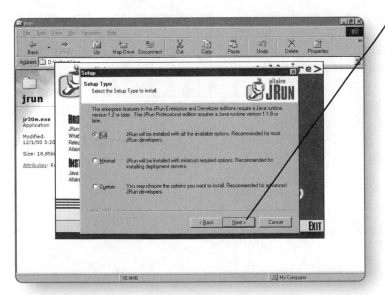

9. Click on Next. The Select Program Folder dialog box will open.

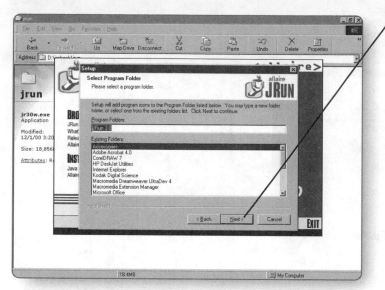

10. Click on Next. The installation will begin copying files to your hard drive.

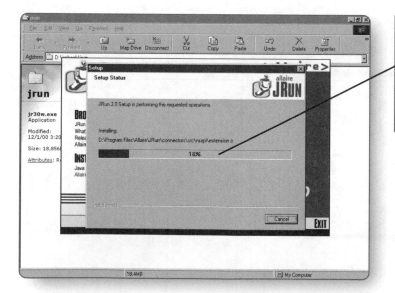

NOTE

The progress bar will indicate the percentage of files that have been copied to your hard drive.

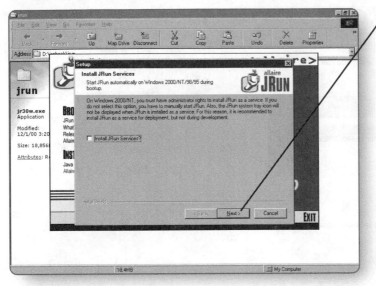

11. In the Install JRun Services dialog box, click on Next. The Select a Java runtime dialog box will open.

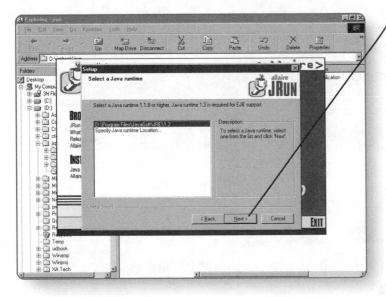

12. Click on Next. The JRun Management Console dialog box will open.

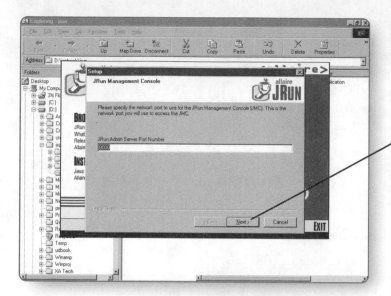

NOTE

The JRun Admin server will run on port 8000.

13. Click on Next. The JRun Management Console Admin Account dialog box will open.

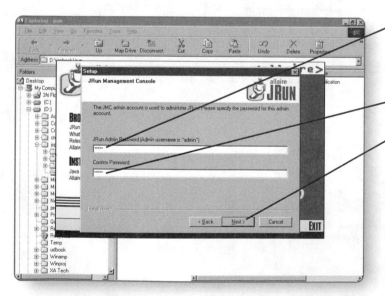

14. Enter a password. An asterisk will be displayed for each character that you enter.

15. Enter the password again.

16. Click on Next. The JRun Product Information dialog box will open.

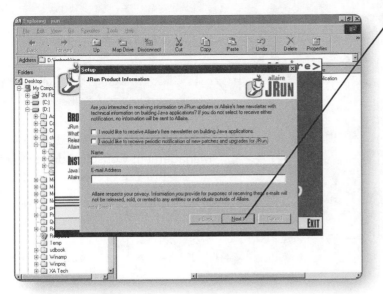

17. Click on Next. The JRun Setup Complete dialog box will open.

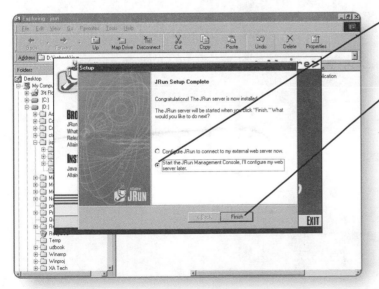

18. Select the second option to run JRun as a stand-alone server.

19. Click on Finish. The setup program will close. The JRun Application Management console will load in your default Web browser and prompt for your user name and password.

NOTE

The user name for the Admin server is "admin."

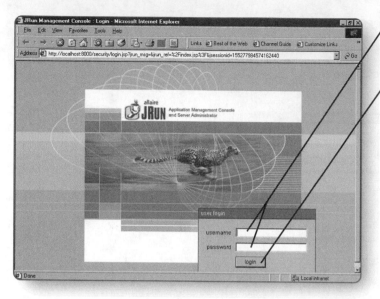

20. Enter the admin user name and password.

21. Click on login. The JRun Quick Start window will appear.

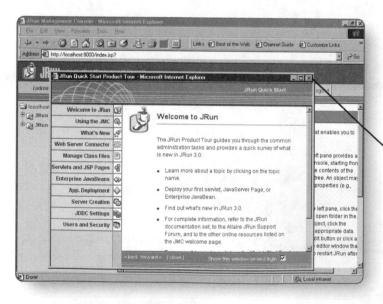

22. Click on the close button. The JRun Management Console window will appear.

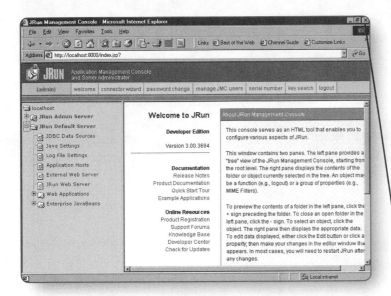

NOTE

You will need to use the console to configure JRun. The default setting will work fine in the first instance. Consult the JRun documentation for more information.

23. Click on the close button to close the JRun Management Console.

Selecting a JSP Editor

A JSP page is really just HTML code interspersed with Java code. All you really need to create JSP applications is a text editor—even Notepad will suffice. However, using a JSP-specific editor will improve your productivity immensely.

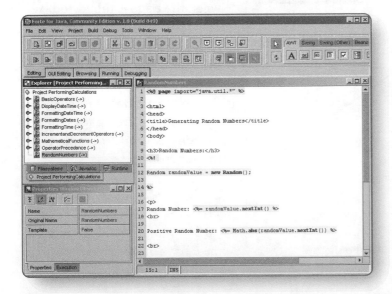

Forte is an excellent Integrated Development Environment (IDE) for all your Java development needs. The Community Edition is available free of charge from http://www.sun.com/forte/ffj. All of the code included in this book was written in Forte.

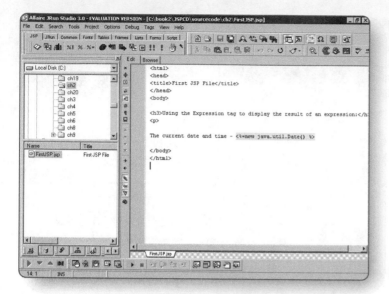

Allaire JRun Studio is based on the popular HomeSite HTML editor. A 30-day evaluation copy of JRun Studio is on the CD-ROM that accompanies this book.

Writing Your First JSP Page

With everything set up and ready to go, you can finally have some fun. This example inserts some simple Java code that displays the date in a Web page. The Java code must be placed within the <%= and %> delimiters. Code placed within this special tag will be executed when the page is requested. The output generated by the code will then be displayed in the Web page.

1. Create a new file with a .jsp extension. All Web pages that include Java code must have this extension.

2. Insert opening and closing <HTML>, <HEAD>, and <BODY> tags. A JSP page must have valid syntax.

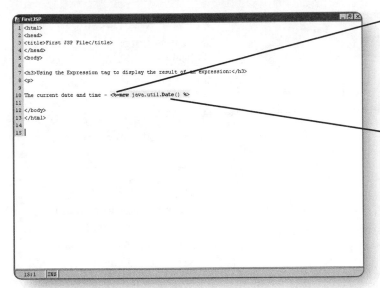

3. Type **<%= %>** at the position where the date must be displayed. Your Java code will only be executed if it is placed within this tag.

4. Type **java.util.Date()** between the <%= and %> delimiters. This Java statement will create a date object that stores the current date and time.

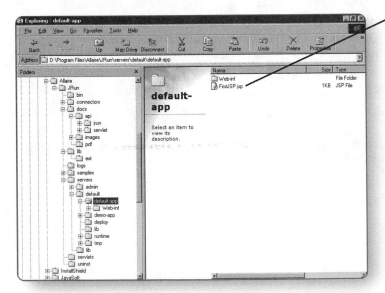

5. Save the JSP page in the Web publishing directory of your default Web server. If you're using JRun, save the file to the JRun installation directory, in the \servers\default\default-app folder.

6. Open a Web browser.

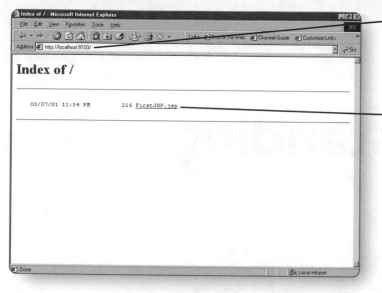

7. Type **http://localhost:8100** and press Enter. The contents of the root folder on your Web server will be displayed.

8. Click on the file name of the JSP file that you created.

NOTE

Localhost is the domain name of your local computer. Your domain name could vary depending upon the workgroup settings on your computer. The http://127.0.0.1 IP address can also be used to access a local Web server. The default JRun server is installed on port 8100. Other JSP application servers might run on port 8080. The home directory path is mapped to the domain name assigned to your computer. When a browser requests a URL, the file is retrieved from the Web publishing directory, which can store complex folder structures. All files placed in this folder can be accessed through a Web browser.

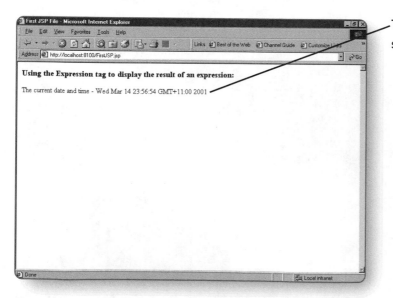

The JSP page will be displayed, showing the date and time.

3

Understanding JSP Basics

JSP has certainly revolutionized the creation of dynamic Web applications. You can now leverage the power of Java to create cross-platform Web applications that are both robust and scalable. JSP allows you to separate HTML and programming logic. This makes updating both the layout and dynamic components of your Web site a much simpler process. There are numerous JSP tags that enable you to embed Java code within a Web page. In this chapter, you'll learn how to:

- Use the Expression, Declaration, and Scriptlet tags
- Comment your code
- Work with implicit variables

Using the Expression Tag

An expression is any valid Java code that returns a value. The Expression tag evaluates an expression, converts the result to a string, and then prints it to the JSP page. It can also be used to print the results returned by methods. The Expression tag is defined by the <%= and the %> delimiters. You could also pass the expression to the out.println method to achieve the same result. In fact, the Expression tag is really just a shortcut for calling the out.println method.

1. Type **<%=** at the position where you want to insert the result of an expression. The <%= delimiter indicates the beginning of an Expression tag.

2. Type the expression that must be evaluated and printed to the page.

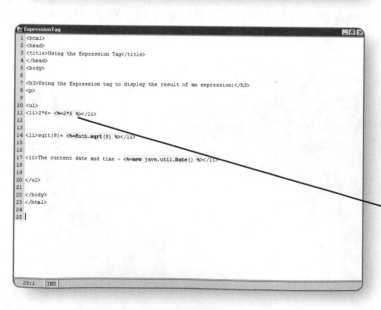

NOTE

It isn't necessary to include a semicolon at the end of the expression.

3. Type **%>** after the expression. This marks the end of the Expression tag, thus closing it.

Using the Declaration Tag

The Declaration tag is used to declare variables and methods that can be accessed by Java code embedded within the same JSP page. A Declaration tag is marked using the <%! and %> delimiters.

Variables store data in memory so that the data can be easily reused when performing calculations. All variables must be declared as either a string or an integer because Java is a strongly-typed language. It has primitive data types to create both integer and string variables. The syntax for declaring variables of different types is outlined in Table 3.1.

Table 3.1 Declaring Variables	
To	**Use**
Declare an integer	int variablename;
Declare a string	String variablename;

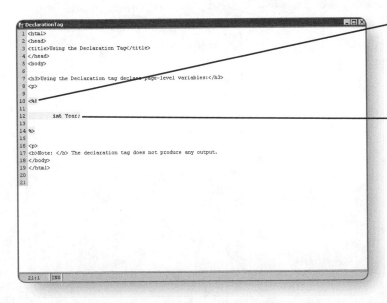

1. Type **<%!** to open the Declaration tag. The <%! delimiter indicates the beginning of the Declaration tag.

2. Type the data type keyword of the variable that needs to be declared. A variable can be declared as an integer or a string.

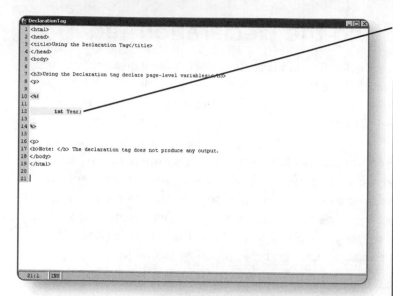

3. Type the name of the variable.

NOTE

Here are some simple rules that must be followed when naming variables:

- Variables must start with a letter, underscore (_), or the symbol $.

- Variables are case sensitive. (Uppercase letters are different from their lowercase counterparts.)

- No spaces can be used.

- A variable declaration must end with a semicolon.

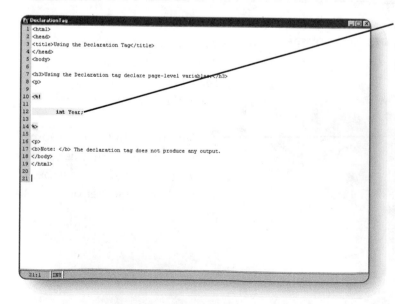

4. Type a semicolon after the variable name. Each declaration must end with a semicolon.

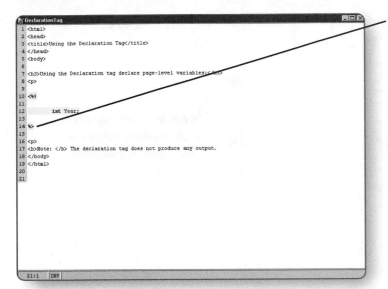

```
DeclarationTag
1  <html>
2  <head>
3  <title>Using the Declaration Tag</title>
4  </head>
5  <body>
6
7  <h3>Using the Declaration tag declare page-level variables:</h3>
8  <p>
9
10 <%!
11
12        int Year;
13
14 %>
15
16 <p>
17 <b>Note: </b> The declaration tag does not produce any output.
18 </body>
19 </html>
20
21
```

5. Type **%>** after the declaration. This will end the Declaration tag.

> **NOTE**
> Declaration tags produce no output.

Declaring Integer Variables

Integers are used to store numeric data and are declared with the keyword int. There are four standard types of integers, all of which can hold both positive and negative values. Table 3.2 describes the range of values that a particular type can store.

Table 3.2 Integer Data Types

Integer Type	Range of Values
byte	– 128 to +127
short	–32,768 to +32,767
int	–2,147,483,648 to +2,147,483,647
long	–9223372036854775808 to +9223372036854775807

When developing JSP pages, you will often use the int type. Here's how to declare integer variables, assign values, and print their contents.

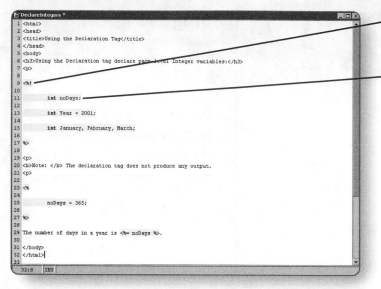

1. Type **<%!** to open the Declaration tag.

2. Type **int** followed by the variable name and a semicolon. This declares a single variable as an integer.

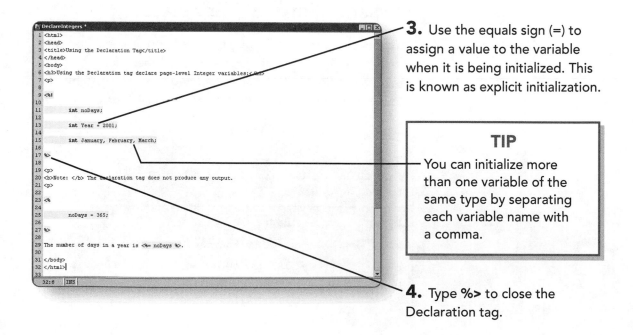

3. Use the equals sign (=) to assign a value to the variable when it is being initialized. This is known as explicit initialization.

TIP

You can initialize more than one variable of the same type by separating each variable name with a comma.

---

4. Type **%>** to close the Declaration tag.

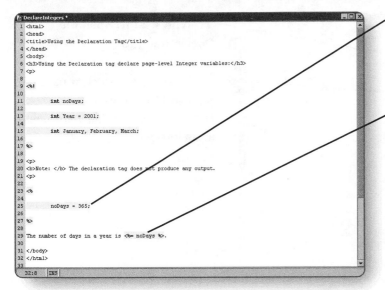

```
DeclareIntegers *
1  <html>
2  <head>
3  <title>Using the Declaration Tag</title>
4  </head>
5  <body>
6  <h3>Using the Declaration tag declare page-level Integer variables:</h3>
7  <p>
8
9  <%!
10
11         int noDays;
12
13         int Year = 2001;
14
15         int January, February, March;
16
17  %>
18
19  <p>
20  <b>Note: </b> The declaration tag does not produce any output.
21  <p>
22
23  <%
24
25         noDays = 365;
26
27  %>
28
29  The number of days in a year is <%= noDays %>.
30
31  </body>
32  </html>
33
32:8   INS
```

5. Type = to assign a value to a variable. The value must be placed on the right side of the equals sign.

6. Use the Expression tag to print the value of a variable to the JSP page.

NOTE

Integers only store whole numbers. You will need to use the float and double integer types to store decimal values such as float interestRate = 7.25.

Declaring String Variables

A string is comprised of words and characters and must be enclosed in quotation marks. Java does not have a primitive string data type. A string is not a basic type like an integer, Boolean, or character; a string is an object that has its own class. The String class provides methods for string manipulation. In Chapter 5, "Working with Strings and Arrays," you will learn to concatenate and search strings. This chapter is only concerned with using the Declaration tag to declare and initialize string objects.

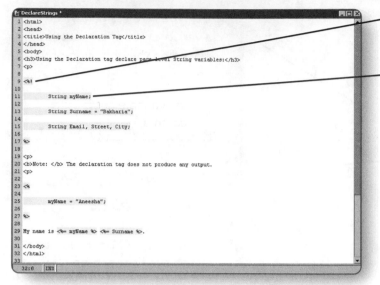

1. Type **<%!** to open the Declaration tag.

2. Type the string class name followed by the variable name and a semicolon. This initializes a single variable as a string object.

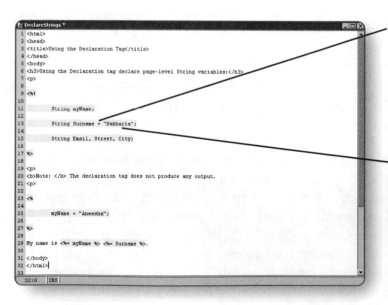

3. Use = to assign a value to the variable when it is initialized. This is known as explicit initialization.

NOTE

The value assigned to a string must be enclosed in quotation marks.

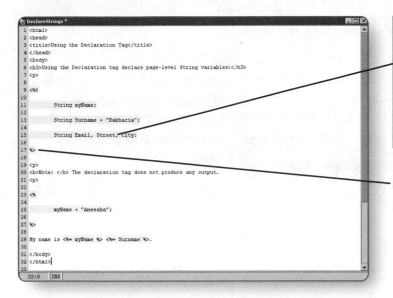

```
1  <html>
2  <head>
3  <title>Using the Declaration Tag</title>
4  </head>
5  <body>
6  <h3>Using the Declaration tag declare page-level String variables:</h3>
7  <p>
8
9  <%!
10
11        String myName;
12
13        String Surname = "Bakharia";
14
15        String Email, Street, City;
16
17  %>
18
19  <p>
20  <b>Note: </b> The declaration tag does not produce any output.
21  <p>
22
23  <%
24
25        myName = "Aneesha";
26
27  %>
28
29  My name is <%= myName %> <%= Surname %>.
30
31  </body>
32  </html>
33
```

TIP

You can initialize more than one variable of the same type by separating each variable name with a comma.

4. Type %> to close the Declaration tag.

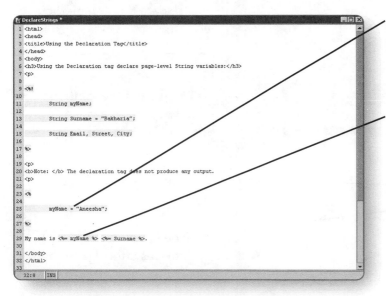

```
1  <html>
2  <head>
3  <title>Using the Declaration Tag</title>
4  </head>
5  <body>
6  <h3>Using the Declaration tag declare page-level String variables:</h3>
7  <p>
8
9  <%!
10
11        String myName;
12
13        String Surname = "Bakharia";
14
15        String Email, Street, City;
16
17  %>
18
19  <p>
20  <b>Note: </b> The declaration tag does not produce any output.
21  <p>
22
23  <%
24
25        myName = "Aneesha";
26
27  %>
28
29  My name is <%= myName %> <%= Surname %>.
30
31  </body>
32  </html>
33
```

5. Type = to assign a value to a variable. The value must be placed on the right side of the equals sign.

6. Use the Expression tag to print the value of a variable to the JSP page.

Declaring Methods

A method stores a group of Java statements that you can execute from more than one location in your JSP page. This saves you from repeating the same code and allows you to update the code in a central location. You can call a method as many times as you like. A method can accept arguments and return a result to the code from which it was called, providing greater flexibility. In the following example, a method is declared to calculate percentages.

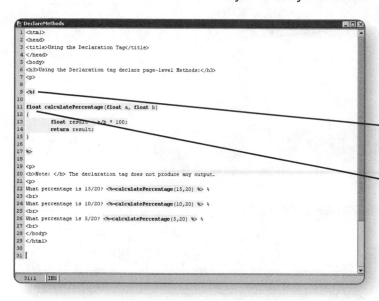

1. Type **<%!** to open the Declaration tag.

2. Type the keyword for the type of data that the method will return.

NOTE
Type **void** if the method will not return a value.

---

3. Type the name of the method.

4. Type opening and closing parentheses after the method name.

5. Declare the arguments that the method can accept.

NOTE

A method can accept multiple arguments. A comma must separate each argument. Parentheses must always follow the method name even if there are no arguments to declare.

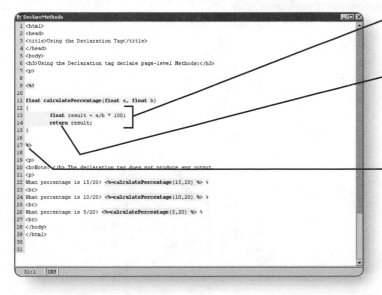

6. Insert the reuseable code within braces.

7. Type the keyword **return** before the value or variable to be passed back to the calling method code.

8. Type **%>** to close the Declaration tag.

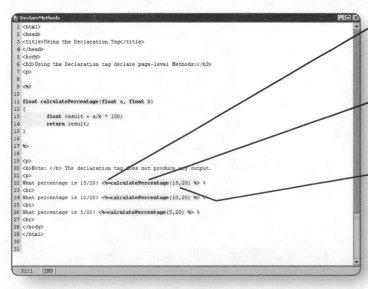

9. Use the Expression tag to print the result returned by the method.

10. Type the method name between the Expression tag delimiters.

11. Pass the parameters to the method in the order that they were declared.

Using the Scriptlet Tag

The Scriptlet tag allows Java to be mixed with HTML to produce dynamic content. Java code must be embedded within the <% and %> tag delimiters. Each language statement must end with a semicolon.

```
1 <html>
2 <head>
3 <title>Using Scriptlets</title>
4 </head>
5 <body>
6
7 <h3>Embedding Java code within a Web page</h3>
8 <p>
9
10 <%
11
12 for (int i=1;i<7;i++)
13 {
14
15     out.println("<H" + i + ">The size of H" + i + "</H" + i + ">");
16     out.println("<br>");
17
18 }
19
20 %>
21
22 </body>
23 </htal>
24
25 |
```

1. Type **<%** to indicate the beginning of the Scriptlet tag.

2. Type the applicable Java code after the <% delimiter.

NOTE

There is no need to be concerned if you don't feel comfortable writing your own Java code. As this book progresses, you will learn all the skills you require. In particular, Chapter 4, "Performing Calculations," Chapter 5, "Working with Strings and Arrays," and Chapter 6, "Loops and Decisions," will introduce Java programming constructs.

```
1 <html>
2 <head>
3 <title>Using Scriptlets</title>
4 </head>
5 <body>
6
7 <h3>Embedding Java code within a Web page</h3>
8 <p>
9
10 <%
11
12 for (int i=1;i<7;i++)
13 {
14
15     out.println("<H" + i + ">The size of H" + i + "</H" + i + ">");
16     out.println("<br>");
17
18 }
19
20 %>
21
22 </body>
23 </htal>
24 |
25
```

3. Use the out.println method to generate HTML, if required.

4. Type **%>** to close the Scriptlet tag.

In this example, HTML is passed to the out.println method. If you need to modify the HTML code, you must do so by hand. This will probably present a problem if the out.println method is being used to print complex and lengthy HTML code. A more practical solution is to separate the HTML and Java codes. You can then use the Expression tag to write any dynamic content. This creates a template that can easily be edited in any HTML editor that supports JSP.

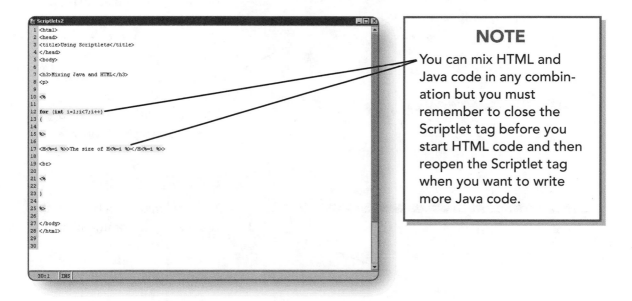

```
1  <html>
2  <head>
3  <title>Using Scriptlets</title>
4  </head>
5  <body>
6
7  <h3>Mixing Java and HTML</h3>
8  <p>
9
10 <%
11
12 for (int i=1;i<7;i++)
13 {
14
15 %>
16
17 <H<%=i %>>The size of H<%=i %></H<%=i %>>
18
19 <br>
20
21 <%
22
23 }
24
25 %>
26
27 </body>
28 </html>
29
30
```

NOTE

You can mix HTML and Java code in any combination but you must remember to close the Scriptlet tag before you start HTML code and then reopen the Scriptlet tag when you want to write more Java code.

Commenting Your Code

Comments are used to document your code. You can use comments to explain code that is difficult to understand as well as the inner workings of any algorithms that are used. Comments provide an important communication tool between you and the programmer who will update and maintain the code at a later date.

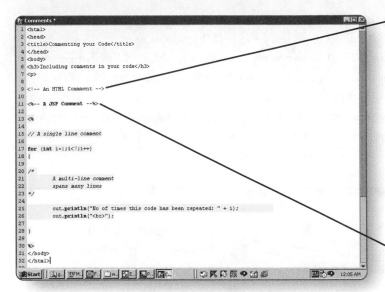

An HTML comment is enclosed within the <!-- and --> delimiters. HTML comments aren't displayed in a Web page, but they are included in the generated HTML source code. This can easily be accessed by anyone who views the source code in a Web browser. You should not place any sensitive information in HTML comments.

JSP comments are enclosed within the <%-- and --%> delimiters. JSP comments are not sent to the Web browser.

The // delimiter can be used to create a single comment line in a Scriptlet tag.

A multi-line comment can be placed within the /* and */ delimiters.

Using Implicit Variables

The JSP specification defines several implicit variables that are not necessary to declare. Implicit variables or objects (as they are sometimes known) can only be used within scriptlets and expressions. They provide a simplified way to access the Servlet API. You can use these variables to write response headers, retrieve posted form data, track sessions, and handle exceptions.

The request, response, session, and exception implicit variables will be covered comprehensively. Table 3.3 describes the purpose of each implicit variable and the chapter that explains its use.

Table 3.3 Implicit JSP Variables

Implicit Variable	Purpose	Covered In
Request	Retrieves all the information that is sent from a Web browser to a Web server	Chapter 10, "Retrieving Information from a User"
Response	Sends information back to the Web browser	Chapter 13, "Creating Interactive Web Pages"
Session	Stores and retrieves session information for each visitor to your Web site	Chapter 14, "Persisting User Information"
Exception	Provides an exception-handling mechanism	Chapter 8, "Handling Exceptions"

4

Performing Calculations

Most Web applications use data entered by a user or stored in a database to perform calculations. Java has a range of built-in methods and operators that will help you implement complex mathematical expressions. E-commerce relies upon the ability to dynamically calculate the total cost of products purchased, including sales tax and postage. Business applications also need to record the date and time when a particular transaction occurred. In this chapter, you'll learn how to:

- Perform addition, subtraction, multiplication, and division
- Use the Math class to perform trigonometric and numerical functions
- Generate random numbers
- Display the current date and time in a user-friendly format

Performing Basic Mathematical Operations

In Chapter 3, "Understanding JSP Basics," you learned to declare and assign values to variables. You will now learn how to use variables, constants, and operators (+, =, *, /) to create basic arithmetic expressions.

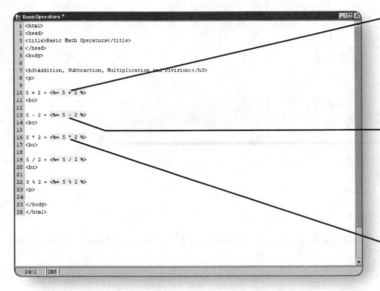

1. Type **+** between two values or variables and use the Expression tag to print the result to the Web page. The + operator performs addition.

2. Type **–** between two values or variables and use the Expression tag to print the result to the Web page. The – operator performs subtraction.

3. Type ***** between two values or variables and use the Expression tag to print the result to the Web page. The * operator performs multiplication.

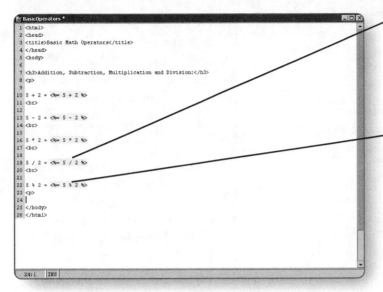

4. Type **/** between two values or variables and use the Expression tag to print the result to the Web page. The / operator performs division.

5. Type **%** between two values or variables and use the Expression tag to print the result to the Web page. The modulus operator returns the remainder when integer arithmetic is performed.

NOTE

Although the expressions in these examples all use constant values, you can easily use variables.

Changing the Order of Precedence

Multiplication and division always take precedence over addition and subtraction when an expression is calculated. You can, however, force parts of an expression to be calculated first with the aid of parentheses.

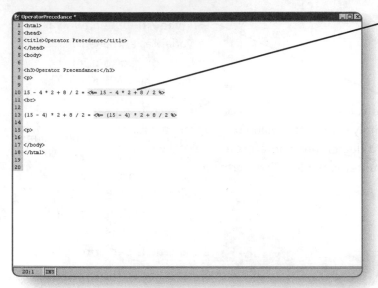

1. Type an expression that includes addition, subtraction, multiplication, and division. Use the Expression tag to print the result to the Web page.

NOTE

Multiplication and division are always performed before addition and subtraction. This is how the example expression will be calculated.

15 - 4 * 2 + 8 / 2
= 15 - 8 + 4
= 7 + 4
= 11

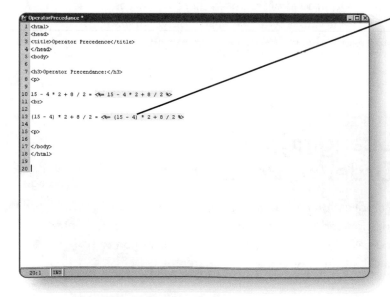

2. Place parentheses around values that need to be calculated first. Parentheses change the order of precedence.

NOTE

With the addition of parentheses, this is how the example expression will be calculated.

(15-4) * 2 + 8 / 2
= 11 * 2 + 4
= 22 + 4
= 26

Using Increment and Decrement Operators

The increment operator (++) provides a shortcut to increase the value of a variable by one. The decrement operator (– –) simply subtracts a value of one from a variable. The increment and decrement operators are helpful when used with loop counter variables. The increment operator will be used extensively in Chapter 6, "Working with Decisions and Loops," when for loops are introduced.

NOTE

The increment and decrement operators only require a single variable. They are known as unary operators for this reason.

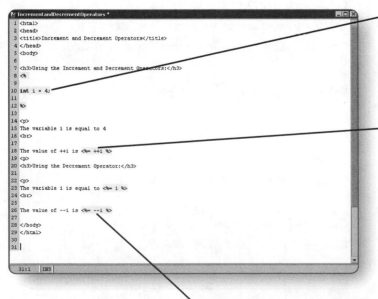

1. Assign an initial integer value to a variable. This variable will be used to illustrate the increment and decrement operators.

2. Type the increment operator (++) before the variable name and use the Expression tag to print the result to the Web page. The variable will be incremented by one before it is displayed.

3. Type the decrement operator (– –) before the variable name and use the Expression tag to print the result to the Web page. The variable will be decreased by one before it is displayed.

Working with Mathematical Functions

The Math class provides a variety of methods that can be used to perform mathematical functions. The Math class includes methods for generating random numbers, calculating square roots, and performing trigonometric functions. Mathematical constants such as Pi and logarithmic E are also included in the Math class as read-only variables. These methods are stored in the java.lang package and are automatically available in your JSP code.

Table 4.1 shows some mathematical, trigonometric, and numeric functions and their purposes.

Table 4.1 Mathematical, Trigonometric, and Numeric Functions

Method	Purpose
Mathematical Functions	
sqrt(value1)	Calculates the square root
pow(value1,value2)	Calculates value1 raised to the power of value2
exp(value1)	Calculates e raised to the power of value1
log(value1)	Calculates the natural logarithm (base e) of value1
Trigonometric Functions	
sin(value1)	Calculates the sine of value1
cos(value1)	Calculates the cosine of value1
tan(value1)	Calculates the tangent of value1
asin(value1)	Calculates the arc-sine of value1
acon(value1)	Calculates the arc-cosine of value1
Numeric Functions	
abs(value1)	Calculates the absolute value of value1
max(value1,value2)	Returns the larger of the two values
min(value1,value2)	Returns the smaller of the two values
round(value1)	Rounds value1 to the nearest integer

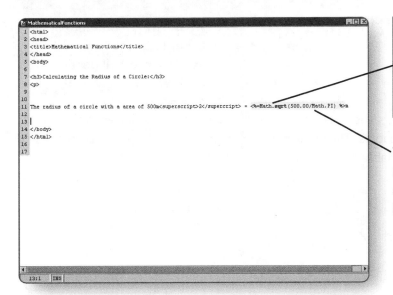

NOTE

You need to type **Math** followed by a period and the method name.

This example uses the sqrt method to calculate the radius of a circle that has an area of $500m^2$.

Generating Random Numbers

Random numbers will help you add an element of unpredictability to your Web site. You can retrieve a random number and display a corresponding image, tip, or greeting. You must first create a random object and then call the nextInt method to return a random number.

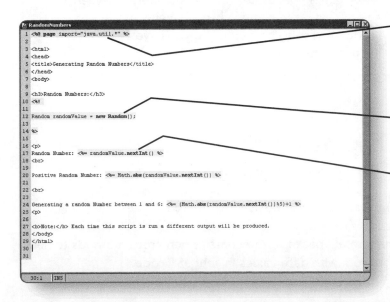

1. Use the import page directive to import the java.util package. The Random class is located in this package.

2. Create a random object instance.

3. Call the nextInt method. The nextInt method will return a random number anywhere within the full range of integer values. Be aware that the nextInt method can return a negative number.

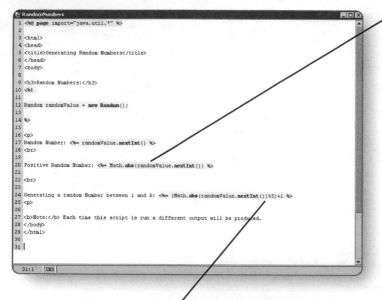

```
 1 <%@ page import="java.util.*" %>
 2
 3 <html>
 4 <head>
 5 <title>Generating Random Numbers</title>
 6 </head>
 7 <body>
 8
 9 <h3>Random Numbers:</h3>
10 <%!
11
12 Random randomValue = new Random();
13
14 %>
15
16 <p>
17 Random Number: <%= randomValue.nextInt() %>
18 <br>
19
20 Positive Random Number: <%= Math.abs(randomValue.nextInt()) %>
21
22 <br>
23
24 Generating a random Number between 1 and 6: <%= (Math.abs(randomValue.nextInt())%5)+1 %>
25 <p>
26
27 <b>Note:</b> Each time this script is run a different output will be produced.
28 </body>
29 </html>
30
31 |
```

4. Pass the generated random number to the abs method. This will convert all generated numbers from negative to positive.

> ### NOTE
> In most circumstances, you need to generate a random number that falls within a given range.

5. Use the modulus operator to calculate the remainder between a positive random number and the maximum random number that you require. Add one to this result.

> ### NOTE
> This example generates random numbers between 1 and 6. This could come in handy when you want to randomly display an image and you have a set of six images from which to select.

Displaying the Current Date and Time

The Date class can be used to create an object that represents the current date and time. The Date class is part of the java.util package and contains numerous methods to help you work with date values in your JSP code.

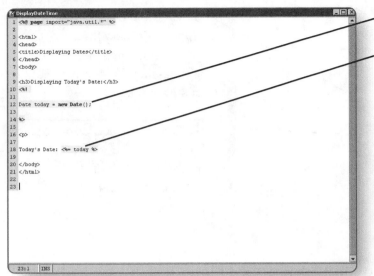

1. Create a date object.

2. Use the Expression tag to print the date to the Web page. The date will be displayed in the default format, for example: Wed Jan 31 22:29:32 GMT+10:00 2001.

Formatting the Date

Java allows you to display the date in numerous user-friendly formats. The DateFormat class is part of the java.text package. This package must be imported before you can change the format of a date.

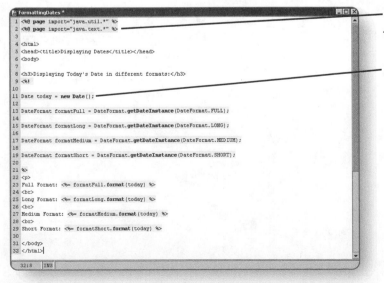

1. Use the import page directive to import the java.text package.

2. Create a date object.

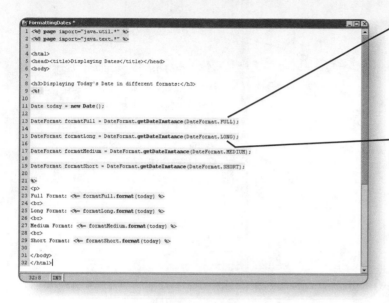

3. Create a DateFormat object by calling the getDateInstance method and passing DateFormat.FULL as a parameter.

4. Create a DateFormat object by calling the getDateInstance method and passing DateFormat.LONG as a parameter.

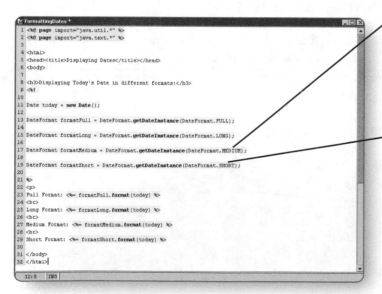

5. Create a DateFormat object by calling the getDateInstance method and passing DateFormat.MEDIUM as a parameter.

6. Create a DateFormat object by calling the getDateInstance method and passing DateFormat.SHORT as a parameter.

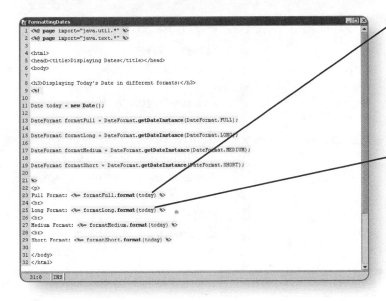

7. Pass the current date as a parameter to the format method of the formatFull object. This will display the full date, for example: Wednesday, 31 January 2001.

8. Pass the current date as a parameter to the format method of the formatLong object. This will display the long date, for example: 31 January 2001.

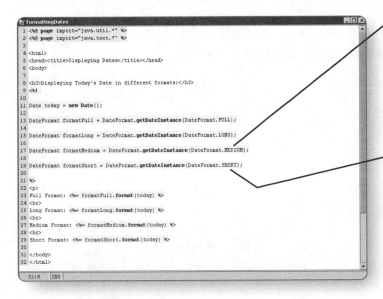

9. Pass the current date as a parameter to the format method of the formatMedium object. This will display the medium date, for example: 1/31/2001.

10. Pass the current date as a parameter to the format method of the formatShort object. This will display the short date, for example: 1/31/01.

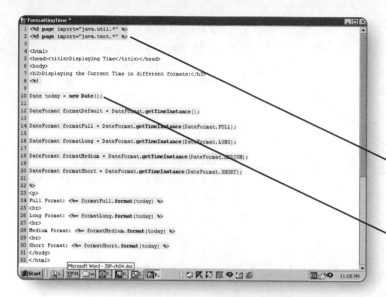

Formatting the Time

The DateFormat class can also be used to format the current system time in different formats.

1. Use the import page directive to import the java.text package.

2. Create a date object.

3. Create a DateFormat object by calling the getTimeInstance method and passing DateFormat.FULL as a parameter.

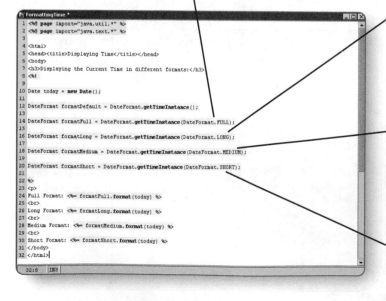

4. Create a DateFormat object by calling the getTimeInstance method and passing DateFormat.LONG as a parameter.

5. Create a DateFormat object by calling the getTimeInstance method and passing DateFormat.MEDIUM as a parameter.

6. Create a DateFormat object by calling the getTimeInstance method and passing DateFormat.SHORT as a parameter.

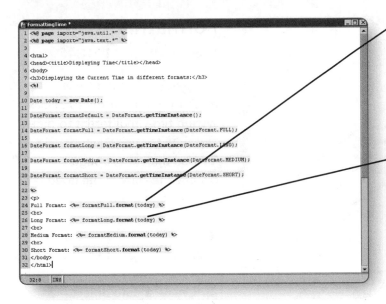

```
FormattingTime *
1  <%@ page import="java.util.*" %>
2  <%@ page import="java.text.*" %>
3
4  <html>
5  <head><title>Displaying Time</title></head>
6  <body>
7  <h3>Displaying the Current Time in different formats:</h3>
8  <%!
9
10 Date today = new Date();
11
12 DateFormat formatDefault = DateFormat.getTimeInstance();
13
14 DateFormat formatFull = DateFormat.getTimeInstance(DateFormat.FULL);
15
16 DateFormat formatLong = DateFormat.getTimeInstance(DateFormat.LONG);
17
18 DateFormat formatMedium = DateFormat.getTimeInstance(DateFormat.MEDIUM);
19
20 DateFormat formatShort = DateFormat.getTimeInstance(DateFormat.SHORT);
21
22 %>
23 <p>
24 Full Format: <%= formatFull.format(today) %>
25 <br>
26 Long Format: <%= formatLong.format(today) %>
27 <br>
28 Medium Format: <%= formatMedium.format(today) %>
29 <br>
30 Short Format: <%= formatShort.format(today) %>
31 </body>
32 </html>

32:8    INS
```

7. Pass the current time as a parameter to the format method of the formatFull object. This will display the time in the full time format, for example: 07:48:26:15 PM PST.

8. Pass the current time as a parameter to the format method of the formatLong object. This will display the time in the long time format, for example: 07:48:26 PM PST.

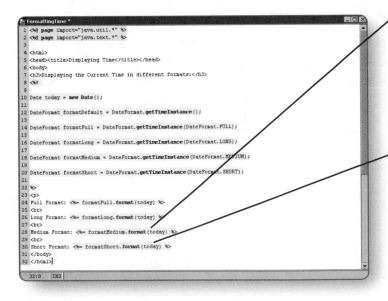

```
FormattingTime *
1  <%@ page import="java.util.*" %>
2  <%@ page import="java.text.*" %>
3
4  <html>
5  <head><title>Displaying Time</title></head>
6  <body>
7  <h3>Displaying the Current Time in different formats:</h3>
8  <%!
9
10 Date today = new Date();
11
12 DateFormat formatDefault = DateFormat.getTimeInstance();
13
14 DateFormat formatFull = DateFormat.getTimeInstance(DateFormat.FULL);
15
16 DateFormat formatLong = DateFormat.getTimeInstance(DateFormat.LONG);
17
18 DateFormat formatMedium = DateFormat.getTimeInstance(DateFormat.MEDIUM);
19
20 DateFormat formatShort = DateFormat.getTimeInstance(DateFormat.SHORT);
21
22 %>
23 <p>
24 Full Format: <%= formatFull.format(today) %>
25 <br>
26 Long Format: <%= formatLong.format(today) %>
27 <br>
28 Medium Format: <%= formatMedium.format(today) %>
29 <br>
30 Short Format: <%= formatShort.format(today) %>
31 </body>
32 </html>

32:8    INS
```

9. Pass the current time as a parameter to the format method of the formatMedium object. This will display the time in the medium time format, for example: 07:48:26 PM.

10. Pass the current time as a parameter to the format method of the formatShort object. This will display the time in the short time format, for example: 07:48 PM.

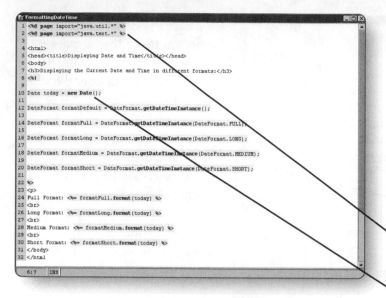

Formatting the Date and Time

The getDateTimeInstance method of the DateFormat class is used to format both the date and time to the required style. This is handy if you want to display the current date and time simultaneously.

1. Use the import page directive to import the java.text package.

2. Create a date object.

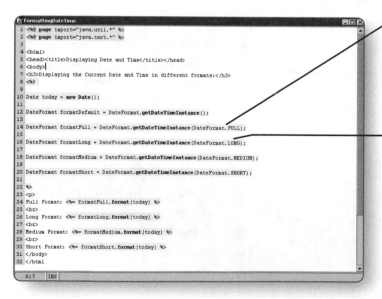

3. Create a DateFormat object by calling the getDateTimeInstance method and passing DateFormat.FULL as a parameter.

4. Create a DateFormat object by calling the getDateTimeInstance method and passing DateFormat.LONG as a parameter.

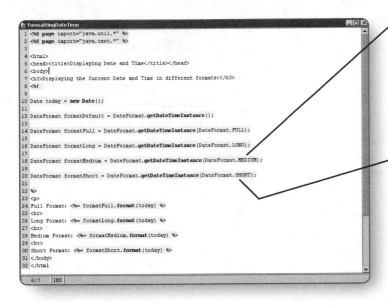

```
FormattingDateTime
 1 <%@ page import="java.util.*" %>
 2 <%@ page import="java.text.*" %>
 3
 4 <html>
 5 <head><title>Displaying Date and Time</title></head>
 6 <body>
 7 <h3>Displaying the Current Date and Time in different formats:</h3>
 8 <%!
 9
10 Date today = new Date();
11
12 DateFormat formatDefault = DateFormat.getDateTimeInstance();
13
14 DateFormat formatFull = DateFormat.getDateTimeInstance(DateFormat.FULL);
15
16 DateFormat formatLong = DateFormat.getDateTimeInstance(DateFormat.LONG);
17
18 DateFormat formatMedium = DateFormat.getDateTimeInstance(DateFormat.MEDIUM);
19
20 DateFormat formatShort = DateFormat.getDateTimeInstance(DateFormat.SHORT);
21
22 %>
23 <p>
24 Full Format: <%= formatFull.format(today) %>
25 <br>
26 Long Format: <%= formatLong.format(today) %>
27 <br>
28 Medium Format: <%= formatMedium.format(today) %>
29 <br>
30 Short Format: <%= formatShort.format(today) %>
31 </body>
32 </html>

6:7    INS
```

5. Create a DateFormat object by calling the getDateTimeInstance method and passing DateFormat.MEDIUM as a parameter.

6. Create a DateFormat object by calling the getDateTimeInstance method and passing DateFormat.SHORT as a parameter.

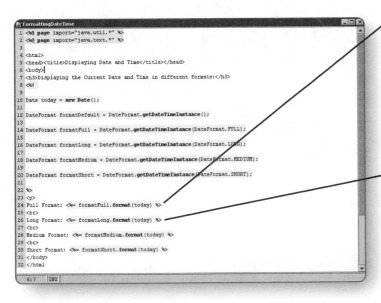

```
FormattingDateTime
 1 <%@ page import="java.util.*" %>
 2 <%@ page import="java.text.*" %>
 3
 4 <html>
 5 <head><title>Displaying Date and Time</title></head>
 6 <body>
 7 <h3>Displaying the Current Date and Time in different formats:</h3>
 8 <%!
 9
10 Date today = new Date();
11
12 DateFormat formatDefault = DateFormat.getDateTimeInstance();
13
14 DateFormat formatFull = DateFormat.getDateTimeInstance(DateFormat.FULL);
15
16 DateFormat formatLong = DateFormat.getDateTimeInstance(DateFormat.LONG);
17
18 DateFormat formatMedium = DateFormat.getDateTimeInstance(DateFormat.MEDIUM);
19
20 DateFormat formatShort = DateFormat.getDateTimeInstance(DateFormat.SHORT);
21
22 %>
23 <p>
24 Full Format: <%= formatFull.format(today) %>
25 <br>
26 Long Format: <%= formatLong.format(today) %>
27 <br>
28 Medium Format: <%= formatMedium.format(today) %>
29 <br>
30 Short Format: <%= formatShort.format(today) %>
31 </body>
32 </html>

6:7    INS
```

7. Pass the current date and time as a parameter to the format method of the formatFull object. This will display the date and time in the full time format, for example: Wednesday, 31 January 2001 07:48:26:15 PM PST.

8. Pass the current date and time as a parameter to the format method of the formatLong object. This will display the date and time in the long time format, for example: 31 January 2001 07:48:26 PM PST.

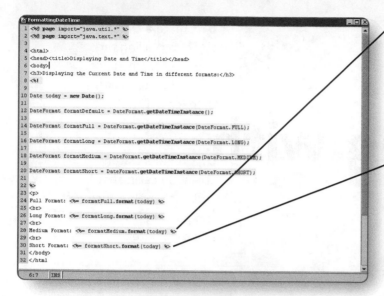

```
FormattingDateTime                                                    _ □ ×
 1 <%@ page import="java.util.*" %>
 2 <%@ page import="java.text.*" %>
 3
 4 <html>
 5 <head><title>Displaying Date and Time</title></head>
 6 <body>
 7 <h3>Displaying the Current Date and Time in different formats:</h3>
 8 <%!
 9
10 Date today = new Date();
11
12 DateFormat formatDefault = DateFormat.getDateTimeInstance();
13
14 DateFormat formatFull = DateFormat.getDateTimeInstance(DateFormat.FULL);
15
16 DateFormat formatLong = DateFormat.getDateTimeInstance(DateFormat.LONG);
17
18 DateFormat formatMedium = DateFormat.getDateTimeInstance(DateFormat.MEDIUM);
19
20 DateFormat formatShort = DateFormat.getDateTimeInstance(DateFormat.SHORT);
21
22 %>
23 <p>
24 Full Format: <%= formatFull.format(today) %>
25 <br>
26 Long Format: <%= formatLong.format(today) %>
27 <br>
28 Medium Format: <%= formatMedium.format(today) %>
29 <br>
30 Short Format: <%= formatShort.format(today) %>
31 </body>
32 </html>
 6:7    INS
```

9. Pass the current date and time as a parameter to the format method of the formatMedium object. This will display the date and time in the medium time format, for example: 1/31/2001 07:48:26 PM.

10. Pass the current date and time as a parameter to the format method of the formatShort object. This will display the date and time in the short time format, for example: 1/31/01 07:48 PM.

5

Working with Strings and Arrays

Strings store information that is crucial to the success of a Web application. Information that is entered by a user, retrieved from a database, or displayed on a Web page can be represented as a string. The Java programming language provides a rich set of string manipulation functions that can easily be incorporated within your JSP code. In this chapter, you'll learn how to:

- Combine and compare strings
- Change the case of strings
- Remove leading and trailing spaces in a string
- Search for and replace text within a string
- Store data in arrays and vectors

Working with Strings

In Chapter 3, "Understanding JSP Basics," you learned to use string variables. In Java, a string is not a native data type. A string is actually a collection of characters stored in an instance of the String class. The String class includes numerous methods for manipulating the text stored in a string object. The importance of these methods can't be stressed enough. They will be utilized throughout this book to process and validate data.

Determining the Length of a String

The length of a string is determined simply by a count of the number of characters stored in a string. Blank spaces and punctuation are included when the length of a string is calculated. You will find the length method handy when validating user input, because a length of zero usually indicates that the user has not entered any data.

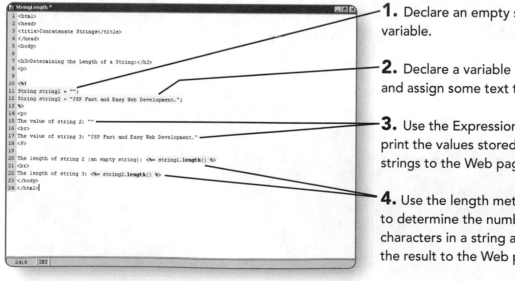

```
1  <html>
2  <head>
3  <title>Concatenate Strings</title>
4  </head>
5  <body>
6
7  <h3>Determining the Length of a String:</h3>
8  <p>
9
10 <%!
11 String string1 = "";
12 String string2 = "JSP Fast and Easy Web Development.";
13 %>
14 <p>
15 The value of string 2: ""
16 <br>
17 The value of string 3: "JSP Fast and Easy Web Development."
18 <P>
19
20 The length of string 2 (an empty string): <%= string1.length() %>
21 <br>
22 The length of string 3: <%= string2.length() %>
23 </body>
24 </html>
```

1. Declare an empty string variable.

2. Declare a variable as a string and assign some text to it.

3. Use the Expression tag to print the values stored in the strings to the Web page.

4. Use the length method to determine the number of characters in a string and print the result to the Web page.

NOTE

A length of zero will be returned if the string is blank. A string with a length of zero is known as a Null string.

TIP

The result of calculating the length of a string could also be assigned to a variable and used in calculations.

Combining Strings

The process of string concatenation involves joining strings together. The + operator is used to perform concatenation. You can use the Expression tag to print the combined string, or you can store it in a variable.

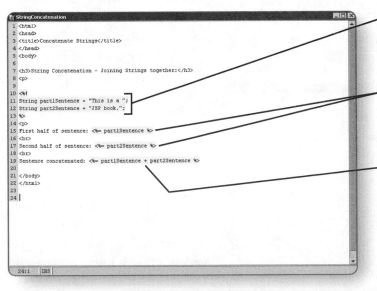

```
StringConcatenation
1  <html>
2  <head>
3  <title>Concatenate Strings</title>
4  </head>
5  <body>
6
7  <h3>String Concatenation - Joining Strings together:</h3>
8  <p>
9
10 <%!
11 String part1Sentence = "This is a ";
12 String part2Sentence = "JSP book.";
13 %>
14 <p>
15 First half of sentence: <%= part1Sentence %>
16 <br>
17 Second half of sentence: <%= part2Sentence %>
18 <br>
19 Sentence concatenated: <%= part1Sentence + part2Sentence %>
20
21 </body>
22 </html>
23
24 |

24:1   INS
```

1. Declare and assign values to the string variables that you want to combine.

2. Use the Expression tag to print the values stored in the strings to the Web page.

3. Type **+** between the two variable names and use the Expression tag to print the result.

Comparing Strings

The equals method compares one string with another and returns a true value if they are equal. The equals method is case sensitive and will only match strings that share identical capitalization. The equalsIgnoreCase method should be used if case is irrelevant.

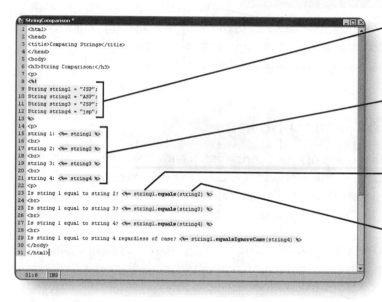

1. Declare and assign values to the string variables that you want to compare.

2. Use the Expression tag to print the values stored in the strings to the Web page.

3. Type the name of the string variable followed by **.equals**.

4. Pass the name of the string variable that is being compared to the equals method. The equals method will return a true result if the variables match.

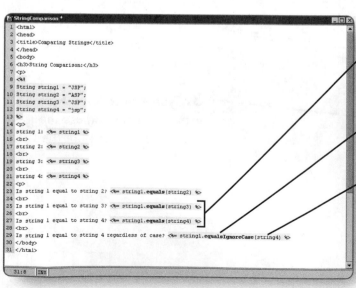

5. Repeat steps 3 and 4 for each string comparison you want to perform.

6. Type the variable name followed by **.equalsIgnoreCase**.

7. Pass the name of the string variable that is being compared to the equalsIgnoreCase method. The equals method will return a true result if the variables match.

Changing the Case of Strings

You will often need to convert a string to lowercase or uppercase before the data is printed to a Web page or stored in a database. The String class provides the toUpperCase and toLowerCase methods to accomplish this task.

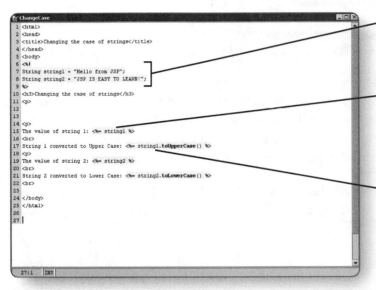

```
ChangeCase
 1 <html>
 2 <head>
 3 <title>Changing the case of strings</title>
 4 </head>
 5 <body>
 6 <%!
 7 String string1 = "Hello from JSP";
 8 String string2 = "JSP IS EASY TO LEARN!";
 9 %>
10 <h3>Changing the case of strings</h3>
11 <p>
12
13
14 <p>
15 The value of string 1: <%= string1 %>
16 <br>
17 String 1 converted to Upper Case: <%= string1.toUpperCase() %>
18 <p>
19 The value of string 2: <%= string2 %>
20 <br>
21 String 2 converted to Lower Case: <%= string2.toLowerCase() %>
22 <br>
23
24 </body>
25 </html>
26
27 |

27:1    INS
```

1. Declare the string variables that you would like to convert to either upper- or lowercase.

2. Use the Expression tag to print a string to the Web page before it is converted to uppercase.

3. Type the variable name followed by **.toUpperCase** and print the result. The toUpperCase method will convert all characters in a string to uppercase.

```
ChangeCase
 1 <html>
 2 <head>
 3 <title>Changing the case of strings</title>
 4 </head>
 5 <body>
 6 <%!
 7 String string1 = "Hello from JSP";
 8 String string2 = "JSP IS EASY TO LEARN!";
 9 %>
10 <h3>Changing the case of strings</h3>
11 <p>
12
13
14 <p>
15 The value of string 1: <%= string1 %>
16 <br>
17 String 1 converted to Upper Case: <%= string1.toUpperCase() %>
18 <p>
19 The value of string 2: <%= string2 %>
20 <br>
21 String 2 converted to Lower Case: <%= string2.toLowerCase() %>
22 <br>
23
24 </body>
25 </html>
26 |
27

26:1    INS
```

4. Use the Expression tag to print a string to the Web page before it is converted to lowercase.

5. Type the variable name followed by **.toLowerCase** and print the result. The toLowerCase method will convert all characters in a string to lowercase.

NOTE

The toUpperCase and toLowerCase methods only change the case of alphabet characters in a string. Numeric digits and symbols remain unchanged.

Removing Leading and Trailing Spaces

The trim method removes any leading and trailing spaces in a string. Information entered by a user is often padded with additional blank spaces. For example, it is a common habit for people to press the space key after typing a sentence. The trim method helps reduce errors that occur when processing data.

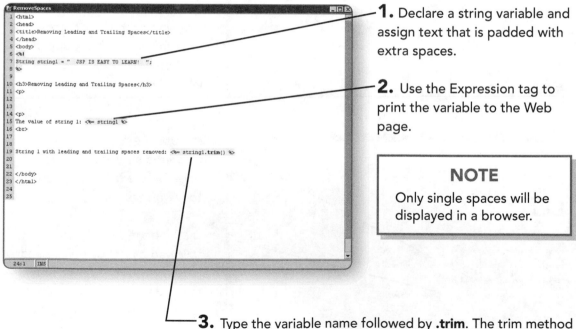

```
1  <html>
2  <head>
3  <title>Removing Leading and Trailing Spaces</title>
4  </head>
5  <body>
6  <%!
7  String string1 = "  JSP IS EASY TO LEARN!  ";
8  %>
9
10 <h3>Removing Leading and Trailing Spaces</h3>
11 <p>
12
13
14 <p>
15 The value of string 1: <%= string1 %>
16 <br>
17
18
19 String 1 with leading and trailing spaces removed: <%= string1.trim() %>
20
21
22 </body>
23 </html>
24
25
```
```
24:1    INS
```

1. Declare a string variable and assign text that is padded with extra spaces.

2. Use the Expression tag to print the variable to the Web page.

NOTE

Only single spaces will be displayed in a browser.

3. Type the variable name followed by **.trim**. The trim method will remove the leading and trailing spaces before the string is printed.

Searching for Text

The String class provides numerous methods that allow you to test for the presence of one string within another. The indexOf method searches for the first occurrence of a character, word, or sentence that is passed to it. If the string contains the portion of text, the location is returned. A value of *1 is returned if the search is unsuccessful.

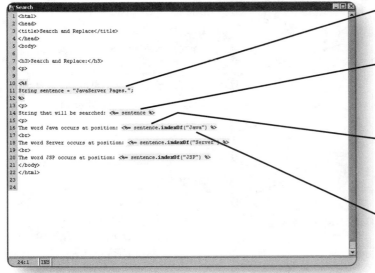

1. Declare a variable as a string and assign an initial value.

2. Use the Expression tag to print the variable to the Web page.

3. Type the name of the variable followed by **.indexOf**. This will call the indexOf method.

4. Pass the text or character for which you want to search within the string. The indexOf method will return the location if the substring is found.

NOTE

The lastIndexOf method will return the position of the last occurrence of a substring.

Replacing Characters

The replace method replaces all occurrences of a single character in a string with another character. This is useful in some situations, but usually you require a set of characters (text) to be replaced. In the next section, "Replacing Text," a method is developed that can be utilized in your JSP code to search for and replace text in a string with other text. First though, you should learn how to replace single characters.

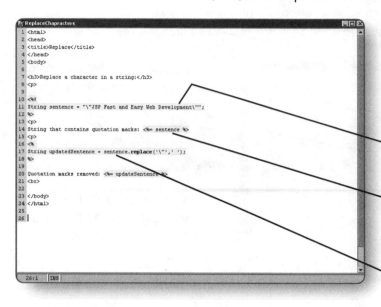

```
1  <html>
2  <head>
3  <title>Replace</title>
4  </head>
5  <body>
6
7  <h3>Replace a character in a string:</h3>
8  <p>
9
10 <%!
11 String sentence = "\"JSP Fast and Easy Web Development\"";
12 %>
13 <p>
14 String that contains quotation marks: <%= sentence %>
15 <p>
16 <%
17 String updatedSentence = sentence.replace('\"',' ');
18 %>
19
20 Quotation marks removed: <%= updateSentence %>
21 <br>
22
23 </body>
24 </html>
25
26 |
```

1. Declare a variable as a string and assign an initial value.

2. Use the Expression tag to print the variable to the Web page.

3. Type the variable name followed by **.replace**. This will call the replace method.

4. Pass the character to be replaced as the first parameter passed to the replace method.

5. Pass the replacement character as the second parameter passed to the replace method.

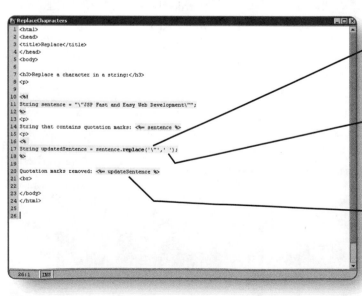

```
1  <html>
2  <head>
3  <title>Replace</title>
4  </head>
5  <body>
6
7  <h3>Replace a character in a string:</h3>
8  <p>
9
10 <%!
11 String sentence = "\"JSP Fast and Easy Web Development\"";
12 %>
13 <p>
14 String that contains quotation marks: <%= sentence %>
15 <p>
16 <%
17 String updatedSentence = sentence.replace('\"',' ');
18 %>
19
20 Quotation marks removed: <%= updateSentence %>
21 <br>
22
23 </body>
24 </html>
25
26 |
```

6. Use the Expression tag to print the result to the Web page.

Replacing Text

A method to search for and replace text in a string has been developed. The replaceSubstring method accepts three arguments: the string that must be searched, the text that must be replaced, and the replacement text.

```
ReplaceSubStrings *
1  <html>
2  <head><title>Replace Substring</title></head>
3  <body>
4  <h3>Replace a Substring in a String:</h3>
5  <p>
6  <%!
7
8  public String replaceSubstring(String originalString, String searchforText, String replacementText)
9  {
10       String leftString, rightString;
11       int startIndex = 0;
12       int foundPosition = originalString.indexOf(searchforText);
13       int searchforTextLength = searchforText.length();
14       int originalStringLength = originalString.length();
15
16       if (searchforText.length()!=0)
17       {
18            while (foundPosition>=startIndex)
19            {
20            leftString = originalString.substring(0,foundPosition);
21            rightString = originalString.substring(foundPosition+searchforTextLength,
22                                         originalStringLength);
23            originalString = leftString + replacementText + rightString;
24            startIndex = leftString.length() + replacementText.length();
25            foundPosition = originalString.indexOf(searchforText);
26            }
27       }
28       return originalString;
29  }
30  |
31  %>
32
30:1    INS
```

1. Place the replaceSubstring method within the Declaration tag on each page where you want to reuse the method.

> **NOTE**
>
> You don't need to worry about the code used to search and replace text at this point. In Chapter 6, "Working with Decisions and Loops," you will learn about the core programming constructs that make this method work—if statements and while loops.

```
ReplaceSubStrings *
15
16       if (searchforText.length()!=0)
17       {
18            while (foundPosition>=startIndex)
19            {
20            leftString = originalString.substring(0,foundPosition);
21            rightString = originalString.substring(foundPosition+searchforTextLength,
22                                         originalStringLength);
23            originalString = leftString + replacementText + rightString;
24            startIndex = leftString.length() + replacementText.length();
25            foundPosition = originalString.indexOf(searchforText);
26            }
27       }
28       return originalString;
29  }
30
31  %>
32
33
34  <p>
35  String: JSP is hard to learn.
36  <p>
37
38  Use replaceSubstring method to replace "hard" with "easy":
39
40  <%= replaceSubstring("JSP is hard to learn.", "hard", "easy") %>
41
42
43  </body>
44  </html>
45
46
44:8    INS
```

2. Call the replaceSubstring method and use the Expression tag to print the result to the Web page.

3. Pass the string that must be searched as the first parameter passed to the replaceSubstring method.

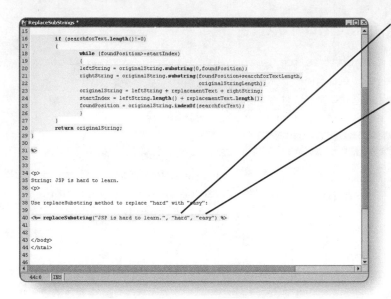

```
15
16          if (searchforText.length()!=0)
17          {
18              while (foundPosition>=startIndex)
19              {
20              leftString = originalString.substring(0,foundPosition);
21              rightString = originalString.substring(foundPosition+searchforTextLength,
22                                      originalStringLength);
23              originalString = leftString + replacementText + rightString;
24              startIndex = leftString.length() + replacementText.length();
25              foundPosition = originalString.indexOf(searchforText);
26              }
27          }
28          return originalString;
29  }
30
31  %>
32
33
34  <p>
35  String: JSP is hard to learn.
36  <p>
37
38  Use replaceSubstring method to replace "hard" with "easy":
39
40  <%= replaceSubstring("JSP is hard to learn.", "hard", "easy") %>
41
42
43  </body>
44  </html>
45
46
```

4. Pass the text to be located as the second parameter passed to the replaceSubstring method.

5. Pass the replacement text as the third parameter passed to the replaceSubstring method.

Working with Arrays

Variables can only store a single value. This is quite limiting if you are required to process and store a large amount of similar information. Arrays allow you to work with a number of variables that store the same type of data through a single variable name.

This is much more convenient than having to declare separate variables, each with a unique name. Think of an array as an ordered list. This simple table that I created in Word illustrates an example of an array.

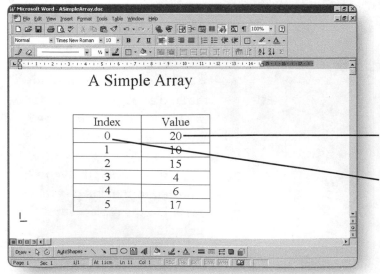

A Simple Array

Index	Value
0	20
1	10
2	15
3	4
4	6
5	17

• Each variable stored in an array is known as an element.

• An element is referenced by an index. The first element in an array has an index of 0. Elements are stored sequentially.

The size of an array is defined when the array is created and remains fixed. Since the array index starts at zero, the size of the array is always greater than the last index value by one. For example, the value stored at index 5 is actually the sixth value in the array.

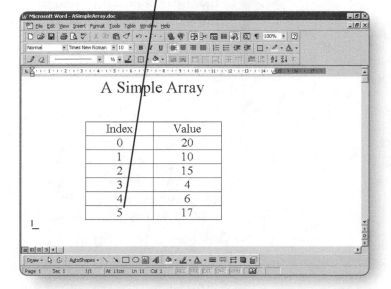

CAUTION

All values stored within an array must be of the same type. For example, you can create an array that stores strings and an array that stores integers, but not one that stores both data types.

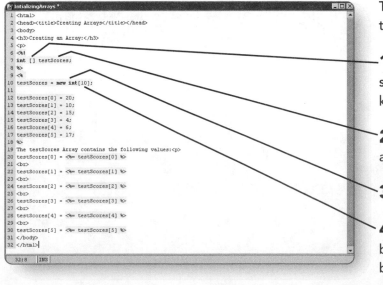

To create an array, simply follow these steps.

1. Declare an array by typing square brackets after the type keyword.

2. Type the name of the array after the square brackets.

3. Create an array object.

4. Define the size of the array by entering the size in the square brackets after the type keyword.

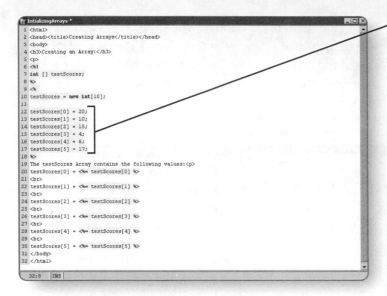

5. Assign a value to each element in the array. Individual elements are referenced with the same name, but have a different index. The index is placed after the array name in square brackets. An index always starts at zero.

NOTE

You can also create and initialize an array by assigning a list of values separated by commas, for example: int testScores = [20,10,15,4,6,17]

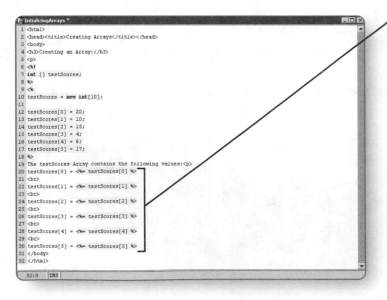

6. Retrieve the contents of an array element by referencing the element index. The Expression tag can be used to print the result to the Web page.

Processing an Array

You can easily retrieve the values stored in an array and perform calculations that involve hundreds of elements by using a few simple lines of JSP code. In the following example, you'll determine the average test score received.

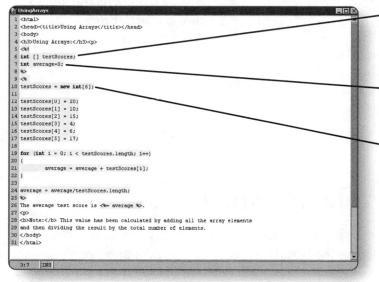

```
1  <html>
2  <head><title>Using Arrays</title></head>
3  <body>
4  <h3>Using Arrays:</h3><p>
5  <%!
6  int [] testScores;
7  int average=0;
8  %>
9  <%
10 testScores = new int[6];
11
12 testScores[0] = 20;
13 testScores[1] = 10;
14 testScores[2] = 15;
15 testScores[3] = 4;
16 testScores[4] = 6;
17 testScores[5] = 17;
18
19 for (int i = 0; i < testScores.length; i++)
20 {
21        average = average + testScores[i];
22 }
23
24 average = average/testScores.length;
25 %>
26 The average test score is <%= average %>.
27 <p>
28 <b>Note:</b> This value has been calculated by adding all the array elements
29 and then dividing the result by the total number of elements.
30 </body>
31 </html>
```

1. Declare an array variable. This variable will store the test scores received by students.

2. Declare a variable to store the average test score.

3. Create an array object.

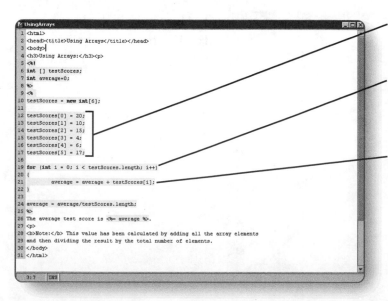

```
1  <html>
2  <head><title>Using Arrays</title></head>
3  <body>
4  <h3>Using Arrays:</h3><p>
5  <%!
6  int [] testScores;
7  int average=0;
8  %>
9  <%
10 testScores = new int[6];
11
12 testScores[0] = 20;
13 testScores[1] = 10;
14 testScores[2] = 15;
15 testScores[3] = 4;
16 testScores[4] = 6;
17 testScores[5] = 17;
18
19 for (int i = 0; i < testScores.length; i++)
20 {
21        average = average + testScores[i];
22 }
23
24 average = average/testScores.length;
25 %>
26 The average test score is <%= average %>.
27 <p>
28 <b>Note:</b> This value has been calculated by adding all the array elements
29 and then dividing the result by the total number of elements.
30 </body>
31 </html>
```

4. Assign values to each element in the array.

5. Use a for loop to increment the array index until all of the elements are referenced.

6. Add all of the test scores together and store the result in a variable.

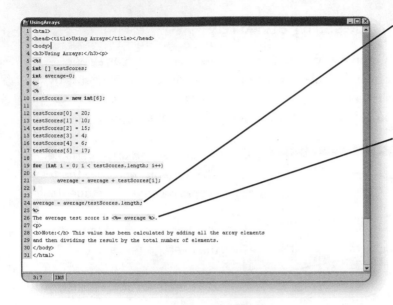

```
UsingArrays
1  <html>
2  <head><title>Using Arrays</title></head>
3  <body>
4  <h3>Using Arrays:</h3><p>
5  <%!
6  int [] testScores;
7  int average=0;
8  %>
9  <%
10 testScores = new int[6];
11
12 testScores[0] = 20;
13 testScores[1] = 10;
14 testScores[2] = 15;
15 testScores[3] = 4;
16 testScores[4] = 6;
17 testScores[5] = 17;
18
19 for (int i = 0; i < testScores.length; i++)
20 {
21          average = average + testScores[i];
22 }
23
24 average = average/testScores.length;
25 %>
26 The average test score is <%= average %>.
27 <p>
28 <b>Note:</b> This value has been calculated by adding all the array elements
29 and then dividing the result by the total number of elements.
30 </body>
31 </html>
```

7. Calculate the average test score by dividing the sum of all scores received by the number of students (in other words, the number of elements in the array).

8. Use the Expression tag to print the average test score to the Web page.

Working with Vectors

Arrays are useful, but their inability to be resized might not provide the flexibility that you require. Vectors are an alternate data structure that is similar to arrays. With a vector you can dynamically add and remove items.

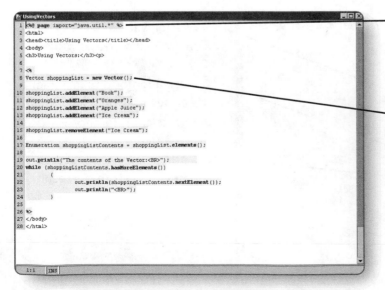

```
UsingVectors
1  <%@ page import="java.util.*" %>
2  <html>
3  <head><title>Using Vectors</title></head>
4  <body>
5  <h3>Using Vectors:</h3><p>
6
7  <%
8  Vector shoppingList = new Vector();
9
10 shoppingList.addElement("Book");
11 shoppingList.addElement("Oranges");
12 shoppingList.addElement("Apple Juice");
13 shoppingList.addElement("Ice Cream");
14
15 shoppingList.removeElement("Ice Cream");
16
17 Enumeration shoppingListContents = shoppingList.elements();
18
19 out.println("The contents of the Vector:<BR>");
20 while (shoppingListContents.hasMoreElements())
21          {
22                  out.println(shoppingListContents.nextElement());
23                  out.println("<BR>");
24          }
25
26 %>
27 </body>
28 </html>
```

1. Use the import page directive to import the java.util package. The Vector class is located in this package.

2. Create a vector object instance.

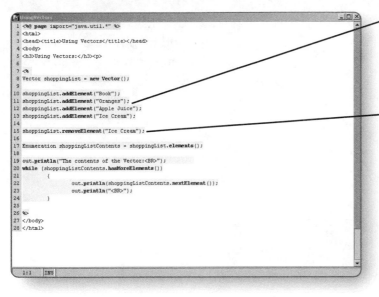

3. Use the addElement method to add an item to the vector. The item must be passed to the vector as a parameter.

4. Use the removeElement method to remove an item from the vector. The item to be removed must be passed to the vector as a parameter.

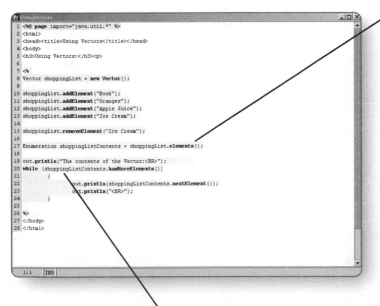

5. Use the elements method to retrieve all of the items in the vector and store the result in an enumeration object.

NOTE

An enumeration object will allow you to step item-by-item through the list of elements contained in the vector. This is handy when you need to display all of the elements in a vector.

6. Use a while loop to iterate through the items stored in the enumeration object. Use the hasMoreElements method to end the loop. It will return false when no more elements are left.

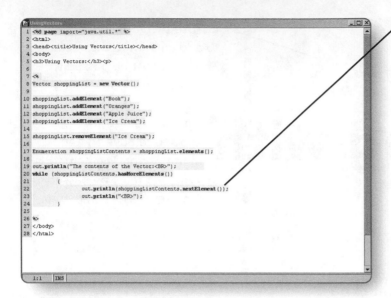

```
 1  <%@ page import="java.util.*" %>
 2  <html>
 3  <head><title>Using Vectors</title></head>
 4  <body>
 5  <h3>Using Vectors:</h3><p>
 6
 7  <%
 8  Vector shoppingList = new Vector();
 9
10  shoppingList.addElement("Book");
11  shoppingList.addElement("Oranges");
12  shoppingList.addElement("Apple Juice");
13  shoppingList.addElement("Ice Cream");
14
15  shoppingList.removeElement("Ice Cream");
16
17  Enumeration shoppingListContents = shoppingList.elements();
18
19  out.println("The contents of the Vector:<BR>");
20  while (shoppingListContents.hasMoreElements())
21          {
22                  out.println(shoppingListContents.nextElement());
23                  out.println("<BR>");
24          }
25
26  %>
27  </body>
28  </html>
```

7. Use the nextElement method to retrieve the current item and print it to the JSP page.

6

Working with Decisions and Loops

The Java code embedded in a JSP Web page doesn't have to be executed in a linear manner. It is very important that you make decisions based upon the data being processed and then execute the appropriate code. You might need to repeat execution of certain code segments, which enables you to build complex Web applications that can solve problems by making decisions and changing the flow of code execution. In this chapter, you'll learn how to:

- Use Boolean expressions
- Work with logical operators
- Work with if...else decision structures
- Use for, while, and do looping constructs to repeat the execution of code

Using Boolean Expressions

A Boolean expression is made up of two or more values that are compared to each other. Depending on the outcome of the comparison, either a true or a false value will be returned. Boolean expressions are used extensively to test for a particular condition and produce a customized response.

Table 6.1 lists the comparison operators that can be used in Boolean expressions.

Table 6.1 Boolean Operators

Comparison Operator	Title	Description
==	equal to	Compares two values and returns true if they are equal.
!=	not equal to	Compares two values and returns true if they are not equal.
>	greater than	Compares two values and returns true if the value on the left of the operator is greater than the value on the right.
<	less than	Compares two values and returns true if the value on the left of the operator is less than the value on the right.
>=	greater than or equal to	Compares two values and returns true if the value on the left of the operator is greater than or equal to the value on the right.
<=	less than or equal to	Compares two values and returns true if the value on the left of the operator is less than or equal to the value on the right.

NOTE

A Boolean expression is sometimes also referred to as a conditional statement.

One effective method for learning about comparison operators is to study examples of their use. Therefore, consider this example, which compares two integers and then displays the result. The values are compared to each other and the result is displayed on the JSP page. Results produced by all the available comparison operators are illustrated.

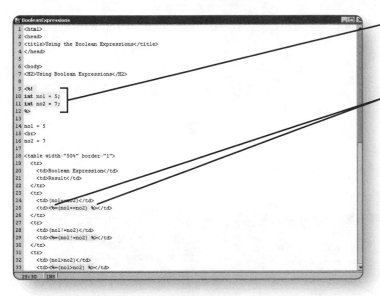

1. Declare two variables (operands) as integers and assign an initial value to each.

2. Use the Expression tags to print the result of the Boolean expression to the page.

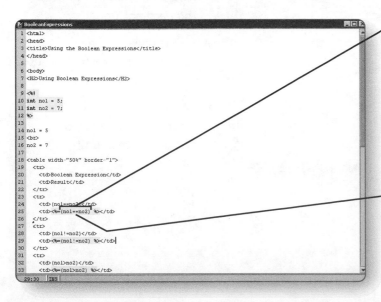

3. Type the expression between the <%= and %> delimiters. You can place the expression within a pair of parentheses. Parentheses are used to change the order in which an expression is calculated.

4. Type the comparison operator between the two operands.

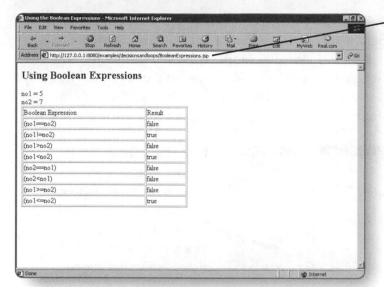

5. View the JSP page in a Web browser. The results of the Boolean expression will be displayed. In this example, a value of 5 has been assigned to no1 and a value of 7 has been assigned to no2. The test determines whether:

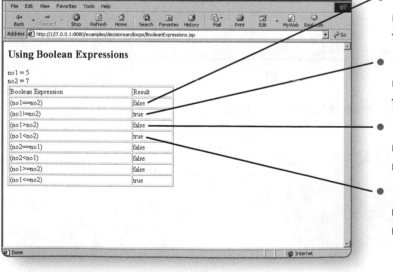

- no1 is equal to no2. This returns a false result because they are not equal.

- no1 is not equal to no2. This returns a true result because they are not equal.

- no1 is greater than no2. This returns a false result because no1 is less than no2.

- no1 is less than no2. This returns a true result because no1 is less than no2.

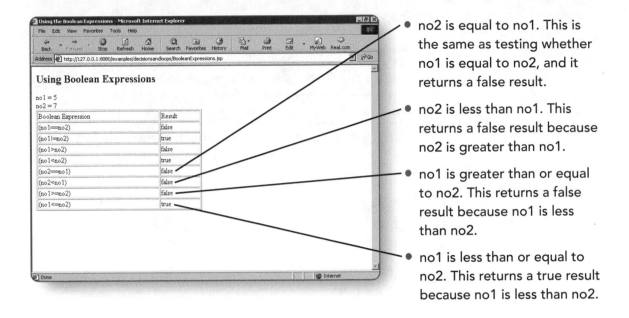

- no2 is equal to no1. This is the same as testing whether no1 is equal to no2, and it returns a false result.

- no2 is less than no1. This returns a false result because no2 is greater than no1.

- no1 is greater than or equal to no2. This returns a false result because no1 is less than no2.

- no1 is less than or equal to no2. This returns a true result because no1 is less than no2.

Using Logical Operators

Logical operators allow you to create complex Boolean expressions. Each operator returns either a true or false result. The & operator (*and*) will only return a true value when both of the expressions being evaluated are true. The | operator (*or*), on the other hand, will return true if only one of the two expressions returns a true value.

Table 6.2 lists logical expressions and their results.

Table 6.2 Results from Logical Expressions

Expression	Result
True & True	True
True & False	False
False & True	False
False & False	False
True | True	True
True | False	True
False | True	True
False | False	False

The next two figures illustrate four variables and their use when creating complex Boolean expressions consisting of both comparison and logical operators.

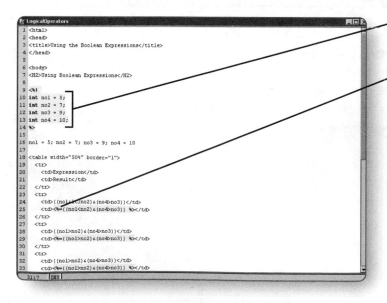

1. Declare four integer variables and assign an initial value to each.

2. Use the Expression tags <%= and %> to print the result of the Boolean expression to the page.

NOTE

You must type **&lt**, instead of **<**, if you want to display the less than sign in a Web page. The < sign indicates the start of an HTML tag and will therefore not be displayed.

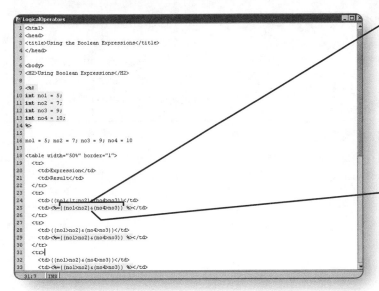

3. Type the expression between the <%= and %> delimiters. You can enclose the expression within parentheses. Parentheses are used to force the left and right sides of the expression to be calculated before the logical comparison is performed.

4. Type the logical operator between the two comparison expressions.

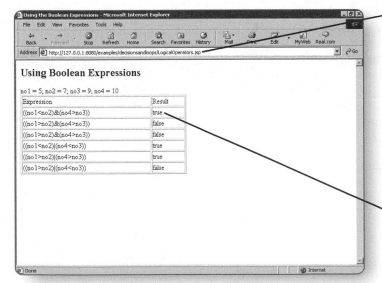

5. View the JSP page in a Web browser. The results of the Boolean expression will be displayed. In this example, a value of 5 has been assigned to no1. A value of 7 has been assigned to no2. A value of 9 has been assigned to no3. A value of 10 has been assigned to no4. The test determines whether:

- no1 is less than no2 and no4 is greater than no3. The expressions are both true, therefore a true result is returned because the & operator is used.

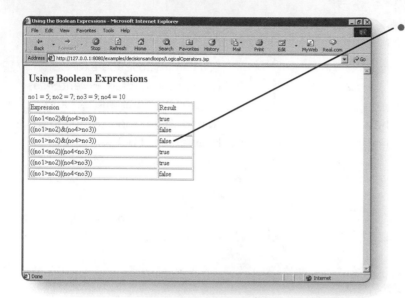

• no1 is greater than no2 and no4 is greater than no3. The left expression is false, therefore a false result is returned because the & operator is used.

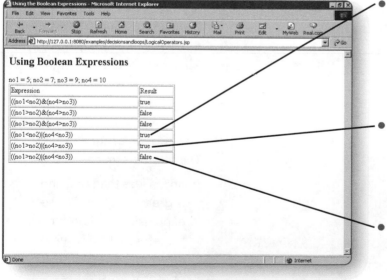

• no1 is less than no2 or no4 is less than no3. The first expression is true, consequently a true result is returned because the | operator is used.

• no1 is greater than no2 or no4 is greater than no3. The right expression is true, therefore a true result is returned because the | operator is used.

• no1 is greater than no2 or no4 is less than no3. Neither expression is true, so this will return a false result.

Using the if...else Statement

An if statement adds intelligence to your JSP applications. It is used to make simple decisions based on the outcome of an expression. The if statement is used, essentially, to decide which code should be executed and then, based on the result, to change the flow of your JSP code.

The basic structure of an if...else statement looks like this:

```
if (expression)
{
   //The if code block
   insert code to be executed if expression returns
   a true result
}
else
{
   //The else code block
   insert code to be executed if the expression
   returns a false result
}
```

The if keyword is followed by an expression that is placed in parentheses. If the expression returns a true result, the code within the if block is executed. The else statement must follow the if code block. Code within the else block is only executed when an expression is false.

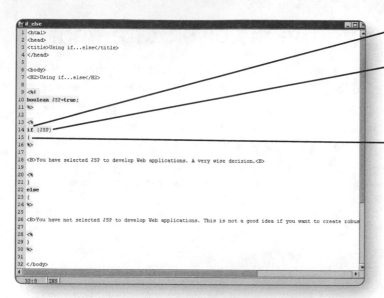

1. Type the if keyword.

2. Type an expression between the parentheses that follow the if keyword.

3. Type an opening brace. This will mark the beginning of the if code block.

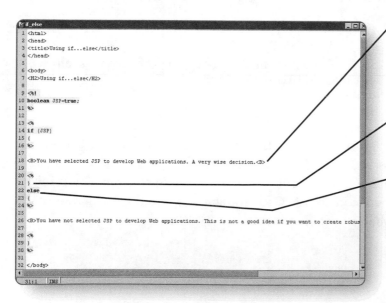

4. Type the code to be executed if the expression is true. The code can be a combination of embedded Java and HTML.

5. Type a closing brace. This will end the if code block.

6. Type the else keyword.

7. Type an opening brace. This will mark the beginning of the else code block.

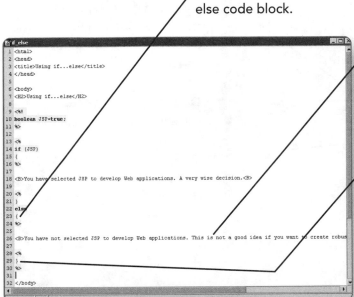

```
1 <html>
2 <head>
3 <title>Using if...else</title>
4 </head>
5
6 <body>
7 <H2>Using if...else</H2>
8
9 <%!
10 boolean JSP=true;
11 %>
12
13 <%
14 if (JSP)
15 {
16 %>
17
18 <B>You have selected JSP to develop Web applications. A very wise decision.<B>
19
20 <%
21 }
22 else
23 {
24 %>
25
26 <B>You have not selected JSP to develop Web applications. This is not a good idea if you want to create robus
27
28 <%
29 }
30 %>
31 |
32 </body>
```

8. Type the code to be executed if the expression is false. As with the if block, this code can also be a combination of embedded Java and HTML code.

9. Type a closing brace. This will end the else code block.

> ### TIP
> You can omit the else statement if there is no code to execute when the expression is false.

Using the if...else if Statement

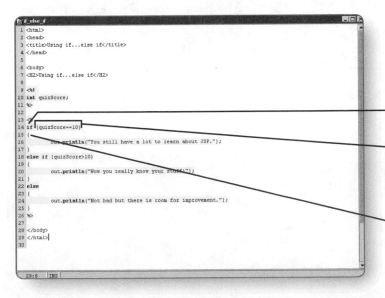

```
1 <html>
2 <head>
3 <title>Using if...else if</title>
4 </head>
5
6 <body>
7 <H2>Using if...else if</H2>
8
9 <%!
10 int quizScore;
11 %>
12
13 <%
14 if (quizScore==10)
15 {
16        out.println("You still have a lot to learn about JSP.");
17 }
18 else if (quizScore>10)
19 {
20        out.println("Wow you really know your stuff!");
21 }
22 else
23 {
24        out.println("Not bad but there is room for improvement.");
25 }
26 %>
27
28 </body>
29 </html>
30
```

An else if clause is used to test for additional conditions and then execute the appropriate code based on the result.

1. Type the if keyword.

2. Type an expression within the parentheses that follow the if keyword.

3. Type an opening brace. This will mark the beginning of the if code block.

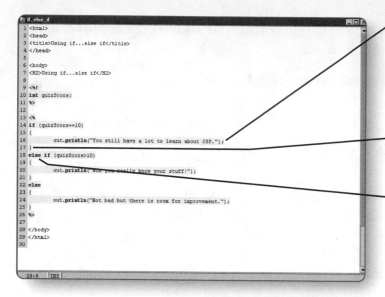

4. Type the code to be executed if the expression is true. The code can be a combination of embedded Java and HTML.

5. Type a closing brace. This will end the if code block.

6. Type **else if** followed by an expression. The expression must be placed within parentheses.

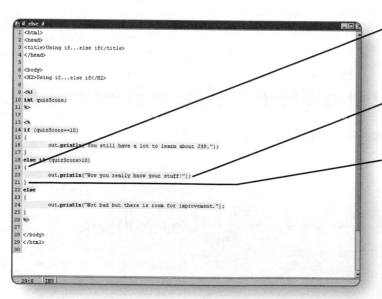

7. Type an opening brace. This will mark the beginning of the else if code block.

8. Type the code to be executed if the expression proves true.

9. Type a closing brace. This will end the else if code block.

NOTE

There is no restriction on the number of else if clauses you can include.

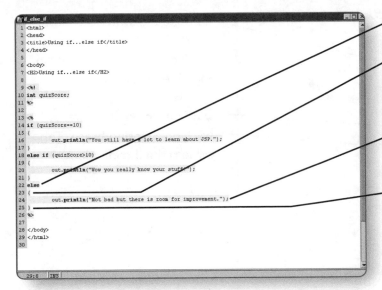

```
   if_else_if                                          [_][□][x]
 1 <html>
 2 <head>
 3 <title>Using if...else if</title>
 4 </head>
 5
 6 <body>
 7 <H2>Using if...else if</H2>
 8
 9 <%!
10 int quizScore;
11 %>
12
13 <%
14 if (quizScore==10)
15 {
16        out.println("You still have a lot to learn about JSP.");
17 }
18 else if (quizScore>10)
19 {
20        out.println("Wow you really know your stuff.");
21 }
22 else
23 {
24        out.println("Not bad but there is room for improvement.");
25 }
26 %>
27
28 </body>
29 </html>
30

   29:8    INS
```

10. Type the else keyword.

11. Type an opening brace. This will mark the beginning of the else code block.

12. Type the code that will be executed if the expression is false.

13. Type a closing brace. This will end the else code block.

TIP

The else statement can be omitted if no code will be executed when all expressions return a false result.

Using the switch Statement

A switch statement performs the same function as an if statement that includes many else if clauses. However, the switch statement is easier to implement and has a simpler syntax. A switch statement consists of an expression that is compared against test cases. If the result of the expression matches the case value, the code within the case is executed.

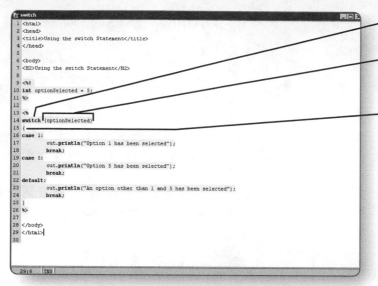

1. Type the switch keyword.

2. Type an expression within the parentheses.

3. Type an opening brace. This will mark the beginning of the switch code block.

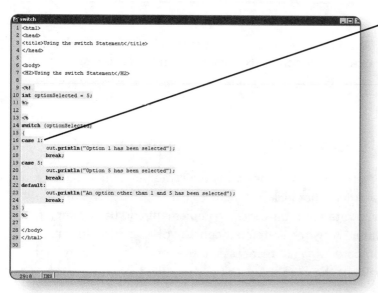

4. Type the case keyword followed by the value that must be returned by the expression to match this case. Each case statement must end with a colon (:).

NOTE

The result of the expression must be either an integer or a character.

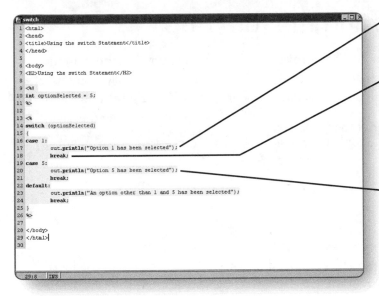

5. Type the code that will be executed if the case is matched.

6. Type the keyword break. All case blocks must end with a break statement. This will exit the switch statement, so that no other cases are tested.

7. Type all of the case blocks you require.

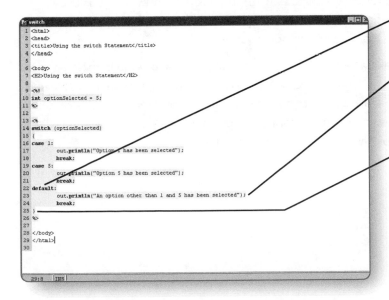

8. Type the default keyword followed by a colon.

9. Type the code that must be executed if none of the cases match the result.

10. Type a closing brace. This will end the switch code block.

Using the for Loop

The for loop provides a practical solution to repeating the execution of certain code segments. Essentially, you repeat a task until a condition becomes true. The syntax of a for loop is

```
for (loop_counter = initial_value;
➥ loop_counter<max_value; increment loop_counter)
{
    insert code to be repeated;
}
```

The for keyword is followed by parentheses. Three parameters are used to control the execution of the loop. Each of them is separated by a semicolon. The first parameter assigns an initial value to the loop counter variable—the number from which the loop will begin to count. The second parameter indicates when the loop must end, and is usually defined by a Boolean expression. The third parameter is used to increment the loop counter variable.

Take a look at the output produced by a for loop in the next few steps. The interactiveforloop.htm Web page contains an activity that allows you to alter the control parameters of a for loop and view the output produced. You should experiment with this file to quickly become familiar with for loops.

1. Open the interactiveforloop.htm file from the CD-ROM in a Web browser. (This file contains the syntax of a for loop.) You can test the loop by entering an initial value and an end value for the loop counter variable.

2. Type the initial value of the loop counter variable.

3. Type the value that will end the loop.

4. Click on Execute Loop. The results will be displayed.

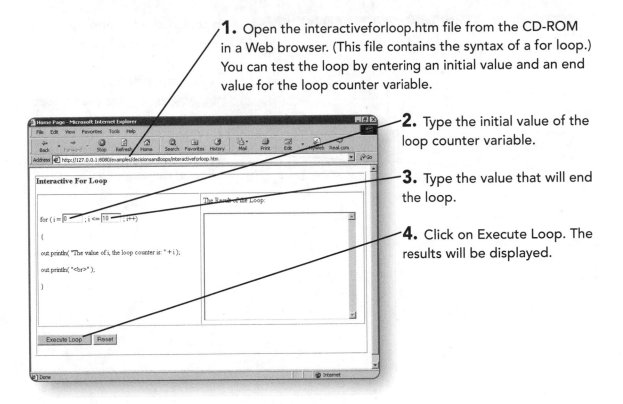

The value of the loop counter at each iteration of the loop is displayed.

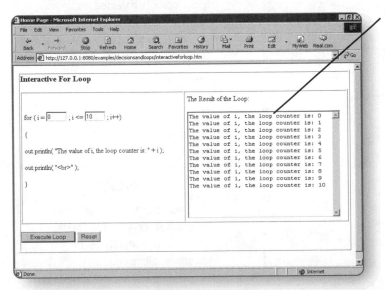

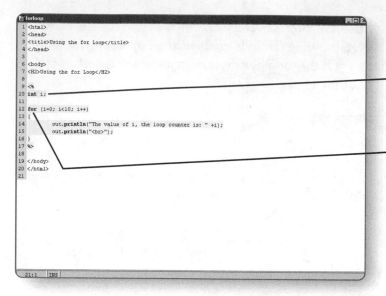

To construct a for loop, follow these simple instructions.

1. Declare a variable as an integer. This variable will be used to count repetition of the loop.

2. Type the for keyword followed by parentheses.

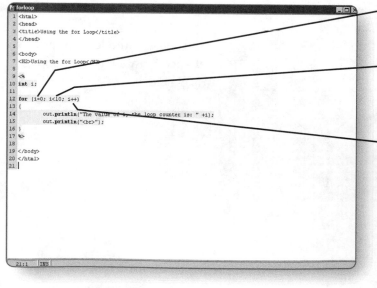

3. Assign an initial value to the loop counter variable.

4. Type a Boolean expression that will determine when the loop will end.

5. Increment the loop counter variable.

NOTE

Each control parameter passed to the for loop must be separated by a semicolon.

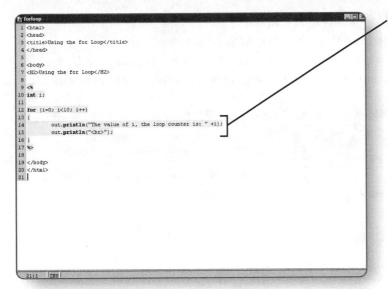

```
forloop                                          _ □ ⊠
1 <html>
2 <head>
3 <title>Using the for Loop</title>
4 </head>
5
6 <body>
7 <H2>Using the for Loop</H2>
8
9 <%
10 int i;
11
12 for (i=0; i<10; i++)
13 {
14        out.println("The value of i, the loop counter is: " +i);
15        out.println("<br>");
16 }
17 %>
18
19 </body>
20 </html>
21 |




21:1    INS
```

6. Within the braces, type the code that will be repeated.

Using the while Loop

Unlike a for statement, a while loop does not iterate until a limit is reached; instead, it continues until an expression is true. If the expression is not true when the loop starts, no code within the loop is executed.

The syntax of a while loop is

```
while (expression;)
{
   Insert the code to be executed
}
```

The interactivewhileloop.htm Web page contains an activity that will enable you to have a better understanding of the while loop. Using this file, you can change the control parameters of a while loop and view its corresponding output.

1. In your Web browser, open the interactivewhileloop.htm file from the CD-ROM. A Web page that contains the syntax of a while loop will be displayed. You can test the loop by typing an initial value and an end value for the loop counter variable.

2. Type the initial value of the loop counter variable.

3. Type the value that will end the loop.

4. Click on Execute Loop.

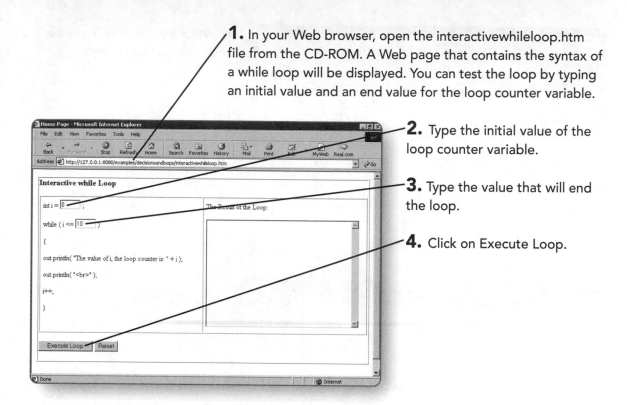

The results will be displayed.

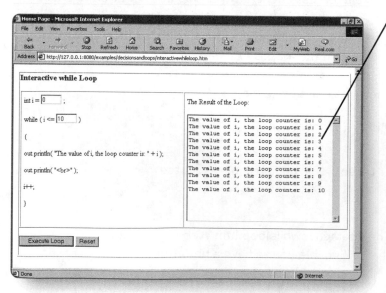

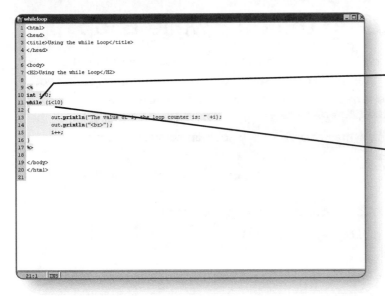

To create a while loop, follow these simple instructions.

1. Type the while keyword followed by a pair of parentheses.

2. Type a Boolean expression that will determine when the loop will end. Do not place a semicolon after the expression.

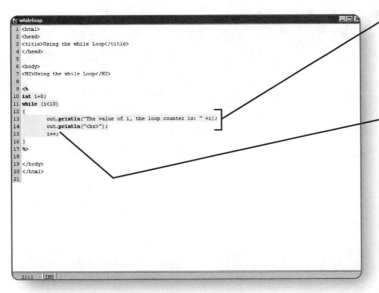

3. Within the braces, type the code that will be repeated.

NOTE

Always include a statement that will eventually cause the expression to return a true value, otherwise the loop will continue indefinitely.

Using the do...while Loop

A do loop is very similar to a while loop except that the expression is only tested after the code has been executed. This means that the loop will always be executed at least once.

The syntax of a do...while loop is

```
do
{
    Insert the code to be executed
} while (expression;)
```

An interactive activity that will allow you to control the execution of a do...while loop is available on this book's CD-ROM. This activity allows you to view the resulting output.

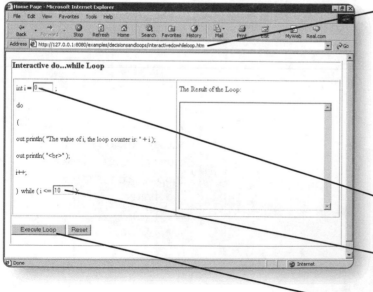

1. In your Web browser, open the interactivedowhileloop.htm file from the CD-ROM. A Web page that contains the syntax of a do...while loop will be displayed. You can test the loop by typing both an initial value and an end value for the loop counter variable.

2. Type the initial value of the loop counter variable.

3. Type the value that will end the loop.

4. Click on Execute Loop.

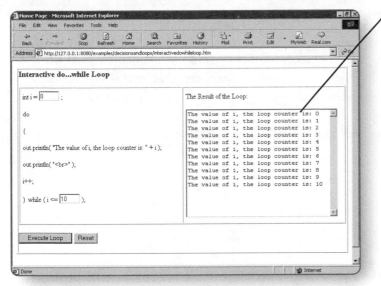

The results will be displayed.

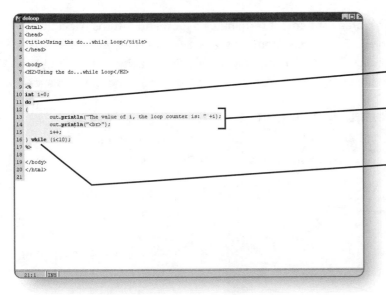

To create a do...while loop, follow these simple instructions.

1. Type the do keyword.

2. Type the code that will be repeated between the braces.

3. Type the while keyword followed by a pair of parentheses.

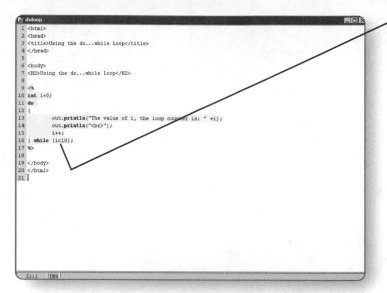

```
doloop
1  <html>
2  <head>
3  <title>Using the do...while Loop</title>
4  </head>
5
6  <body>
7  <H2>Using the do...while Loop</H2>
8
9  <%
10 int i=0;
11 do
12 {
13       out.println("The value of i, the loop counter is: " +i);
14       out.println("<br>");
15       i++;
16 } while (i<10);
17 %>
18
19 </body>
20 </html>
21 |
```

4. Type a Boolean expression that determines the end of the loop. A semicolon must be placed after the expression.

Using the break Statement

The break statement terminates a loop and returns execution to the first code statement that is present outside the loop. This book's CD-ROM includes an interactive activity that allows you to view the results produced by a break statement within a loop.

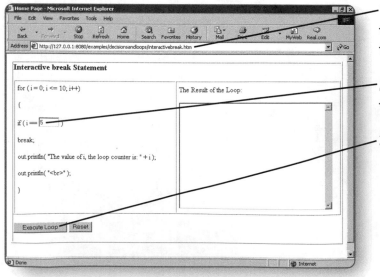

1. In your Web browser, open the interactivebreak.htm file from the CD-ROM.

2. Type the value that will terminate the loop.

3. Click on Execute Loop.

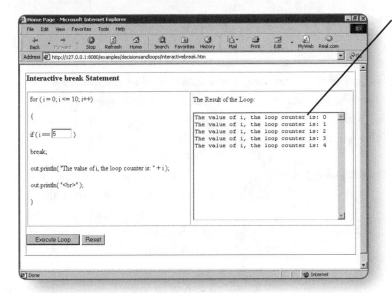

The results will be displayed.

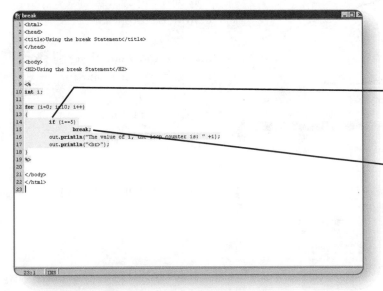

To include a break statement in a loop, follow these simple instructions.

1. Use an if statement to test for the condition that will exit the loop.

2. Type the break keyword. When the break keyword is encountered during execution, the loop will end.

Using the continue Statement

The continue statement stops the execution of the current iteration of the loop. Any code that follows the continue statement will not execute. The continue statement allows you to skip the execution of a particular iteration because of the existence of a special condition.

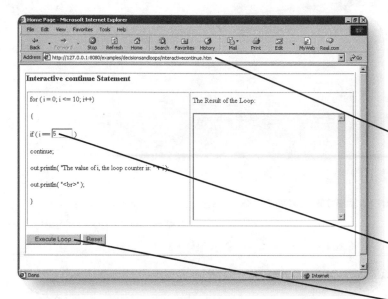

This book's CD-ROM includes an interactive activity that allows you to view the results produced by a continue statement placed within a loop.

1. In your Web browser, open the interactivecontinue.htm file. This file is a Web page that contains the syntax of a continue statement.

2. Type the value that will stop the current iteration.

3. Click on Execute Loop.

The results will be displayed.

```
continue
1  <html>
2  <head>
3  <title>Using the continue Statement</title>
4  </head>
5
6  <body>
7  <H2>Using the continue Statement</H2>
8
9  <%
10 int i;
11
12 for (i=0; i<10; i++)
13 {
14         if (i==5)
15                 continue;
16         out.println("The value of i, the loop counter is: " +i);
17         out.println("<br>");
18 }
19 %>
20
21 </body>
22 </html>
23 |
```
```
23:1    INS
```

To include a continue statement in a loop, follow these simple steps.

1. Use an if statement to test for the condition that will stop the current iteration of the loop.

2. Type the continue keyword. When the continue keyword is encountered during execution, the next iteration of the loop will begin.

7

Object-Oriented Programming

Java is a pure object-oriented programming language. You have probably already heard the *object-oriented* buzzword, but are not quite sure what it means or, more importantly, how it can be used in Web development. Conceptually, object-oriented programming is concerned with the organization and manipulation of objects that model the real world. Object-oriented programming makes it easier to build, maintain, and reuse complex applications. In this chapter, you'll learn how to:

- Create a class to define objects
- Declare instance variables
- Declare methods
- Import a class and use objects in a JSP page

What is Object-Oriented Programming?

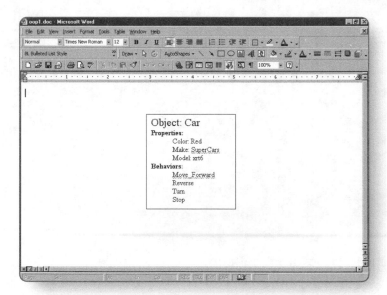

Procedural programming involves solving a problem by writing a linear sequence of instructions. This step-by-step approach to programming is not suitable when large amounts of data have to be processed in a complex manner. It is hard to associate programming code with the data that is being processed.

Object-oriented programming involves the creation and manipulation of objects. Objects model real world entities such as cars, employees, trees, and animals. An object is just like a real-world entity—it has associated properties and behaviors. A class defines both the properties of an object and the code used to manipulate these properties (in other words, behaviors). The process of integrating an object's properties and behaviors is known as *encapsulation*.

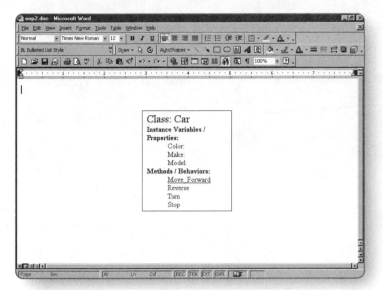

Understanding Classes and Objects

A class describes the structure of an object. The object's properties are defined in the form of instance variables. The code used to manipulate these instance variables must be placed in methods. A method is used to model the behavior of an object. An object is an instance of a class.

Instance Variables

Variables contained in a class are known as instance variables or properties. Every time an object is created, new instance variables are created. Each object will have instance variables with the same names, but the data they store will be different.

Methods

Code that has access to instance variables must be placed inside a method. A method is a function that is contained in a class. Methods have access to the data stored in object properties.

Creating a Class

A class defines the instance variables and the methods associated with an object. All classes must be named. Here is a look at the basic syntax used to create a class.

1. Type the class modifier. This is usually public and means that the class is visible to all other classes.

2. Type the class keyword.

3. Type the name of the class.

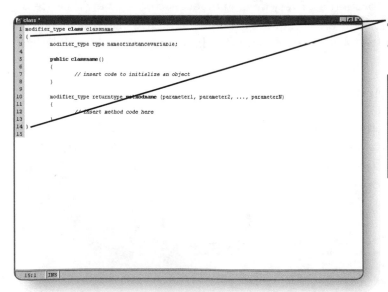

4. You must place a class block after the class name.

NOTE

A class block starts with an opening brace ({) and ends with a closing brace (}).

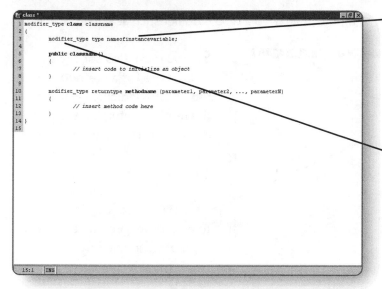

5. You must declare instance variables and methods within a class block. Declare an instance variable by typing the data type of the variable followed by the name of the variable.

6. An instance variable can have a type modifier such as public or private. A public variable or method can be accessed from other classes. A private variable or method can only be accessed from within the class.

7. A class must have a constructor method. A constructor is a public method that has no return type. A constructor is used to initialize an object when it is created.

8. A method can have a type modifier such as public or private.

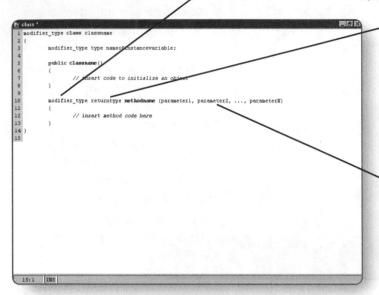

9. You must also specify a return type for a method. The return type indicates whether the method returns a string or an integer. The return type is void if the method does not return a value.

10. Parameters can be passed to a method. A comma must separate parameters.

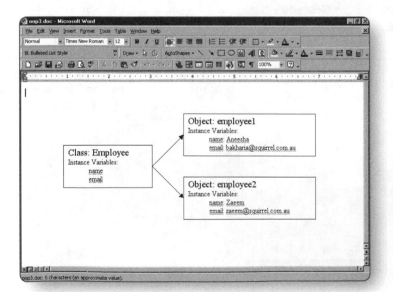

Creating an Employee Class

The next example creates a basic class to model an employee. This class needs instance variables to store the name and e-mail address of the employee, and must also have a method to display employee details.

```
Employee                                          _ □ x
1  public class Employee
2  {
3
4     public String name;
5     public String email;
6
7     public Employee()()
8
9     public String displayEmployee()
10    {
11       return (name + " (" + email + ")");
12    }
13    |
14 }

13:4   INS
```

1. Create a file with a .java extension. Source code files that contain a class must all have the same extension.

2. The file must be saved to a subdirectory on your application server. The name of this folder varies, and you should consult the appropriate documentation to identify the directory where you must place your class files. Table 7.1 lists the locations for popular JSP application servers.

Table 7.1 Class File Installation

Server	JavaBean Directory Path
Tomcat	installation_directory/webpages/WEB-INF/classes/packagename/
JSWDK	installation_directory/webpages/WEB-INF/servlets/packagename/
JRun	installation_directory/servers/servername/web-inf/classes/
Java Web Server	installation_directory/classes/
BEA WebLogic	installation_directory/classes/

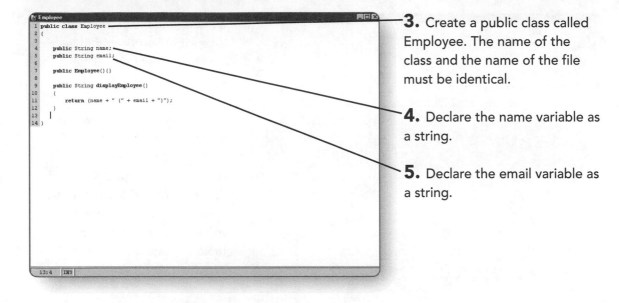

3. Create a public class called Employee. The name of the class and the name of the file must be identical.

4. Declare the name variable as a string.

5. Declare the email variable as a string.

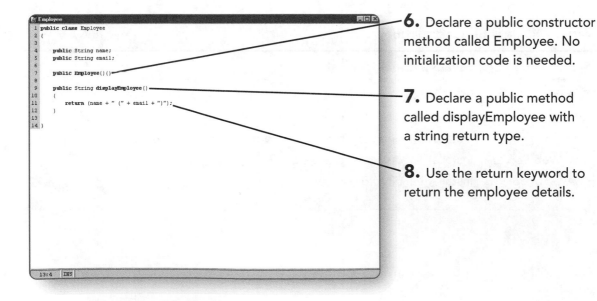

6. Declare a public constructor method called Employee. No initialization code is needed.

7. Declare a public method called displayEmployee with a string return type.

8. Use the return keyword to return the employee details.

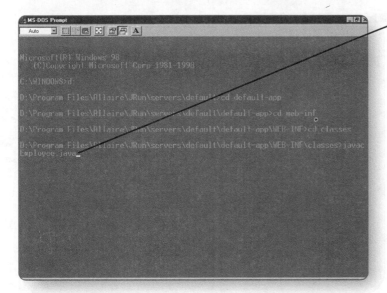

9. Use the javac compiler to compile the Employee class. A .class file will be created.

Using the Employee Class in a JSP Page

You must import a class into a JSP page using the page directive. You can create objects and call methods to manipulate the data stored in instance variables.

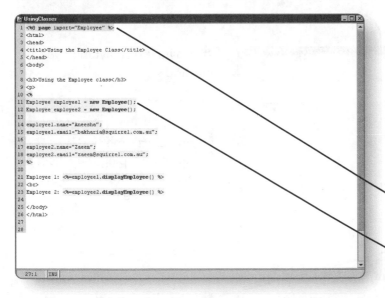

1. Use the page directive to import the Employee class.

2. Create an instance of the Employee class.

NOTE

A class instance (in other words, an object) is created by typing the class name followed by the name of the object, then using the new keyword to call the constructor method and assign the result to the object. A constructor method has the same name as the class.

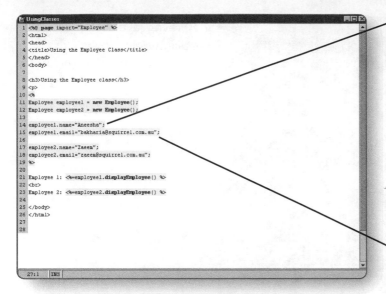

3. Set the name instance variable of the object.

NOTE

An instance variable of an object is referenced by typing the object name, a period (.), and the name of the instance variable.

4. Set the email instance variable of the object.

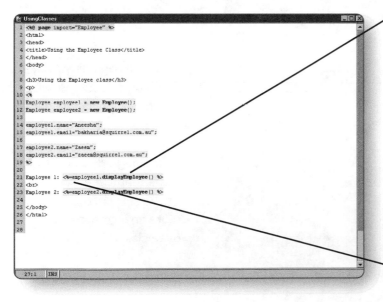

5. Call the displayEmployee method.

NOTE

An object's method is called by typing the object name, a period (.), and the name of the method. Parentheses must follow the method name.

6. Use the Expression tag to display the value returned by the displayEmployee method.

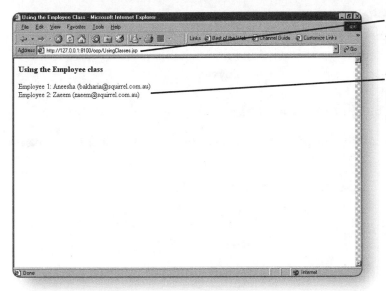

7. Preview the JSP page in a Web browser.

The instance variables of the Employee objects will be displayed.

Inheritance

Once a class is created, it can be used to define another class. This means that you don't need to create an entirely new class for each object to be modeled. You should first decide what properties your objects have in common and create a parent class from these. Other classes can then inherit the properties and methods from a parent class. A class that inherits from a parent class is known as a subclass. Organizing your classes into hierarchical relationships is important in order to create reusable code that can easily be maintained.

As an example, you could model a generic Employee class and create subclasses for the different types of employees. The Employee class would contain the fundamental characteristics of an employee. It could then be subclassed to define classes for full-time, part-time and casual employees.

The syntax for a subclass is

```
modifier_type class classname extends parentclassname
{
    instance variable declarations;
    method declarations;
}
```

In Chapter 17, "Working with Servlets," you will create a special type of class that handles Web browser requests by subclassing the HttpServlet and GenericServlet classes.

8

Handling Exceptions

It is your duty as a programmer to write bug-free applications that can deal with unexpected conditions. Nested if statements are generally used to detect abnormal conditions and handle them appropriately. However, combining program- and exception-handling code can create applications that are not robust and are hard to maintain. Java addresses this problem by supporting the try-catch error handling mechanism that does not disrupt the normal program flow. In this chapter, you'll learn how to:

- Create basic exception-handling routines
- Detect common exceptions
- Implement JSP-specific exception handling

Exceptions versus Errors

An exception is an object that is created when an error occurs while your JSP code is executing. An exception generally occurs because you have not anticipated every situation that your program needs to handle. If exceptions are not handled appropriately, your program either will be aborted or will yield incorrect results.

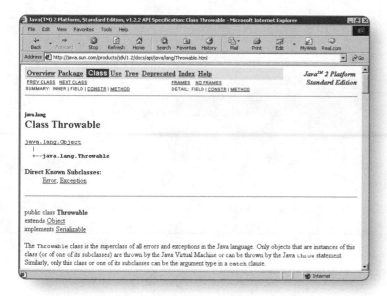

An exception object is an instance of java.lang.Throwable. The Exception subclass describes exceptions that can be caught and handled in your Web application. There is a big difference between an error and an exception. Errors are also a subclass of Throwable, but it is unlikely that your Web application will be able to recover from an error. Errors are caused by virtual machine or linkage problems. The virtual machine running out of memory is an example of an error.

Using try-catch to Handle Exceptions

Implementing exception handling in a JSP page is very easy. You need to place your program code in a try block and your exception-handling code in a catch block. The catch block must follow a try block. Placing exception-handling code in a catch block does not disturb the normal flow of your program.

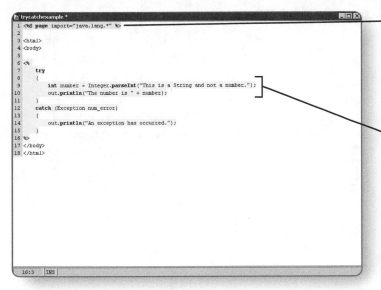

1. Use the import directive to import the java.lang.* packages. These are required to implement the try-catch exception-handling mechanism.

2. Type some code that could cause an exception within the try block. Code must be inserted within the braces. In this example, the parseInt method is used to convert a string to a number. This will throw an exception.

3. Type the class of the exception to be caught and a variable name between the parentheses of the catch statement.

NOTE

The Exception class catches all of the exceptions that can be thrown.

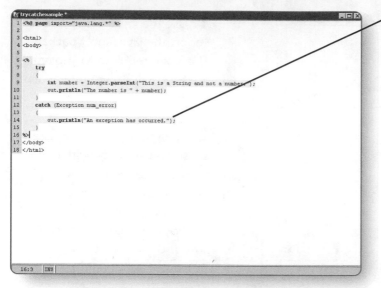

4. Type the exception-handling code within the catch block. This should include code to print an error message. In this example, a generic error message is produced because testing for a specific exception does not occur. You will learn to do this in the next section.

Catching Common Exceptions

In the previous section, a single catch block was used to handle all exceptions and produce a generic error message. It is possible to create more specific catch routines by catching subclasses of the Exception class. Table 8.1 lists some common exceptions.

Table 8.1 Common Exceptions

Exception	Gets thrown when
ArithmeticException	Invalid arithmetic has been performed
IndexOutofBoundsException	An array or string object is incorrectly indexed
IOException	Input/Output operations, such as reading to a file, fail
NumberFormatException	Numeric operations are performed on non-numeric data
NullPointerException	Object pointers are not initialized
MalformedURLException	A URL is not in the correct format

Here is an example of using a catch block to detect the NumberFormatException that is thrown when a numeric operation is performed on non-numeric data.

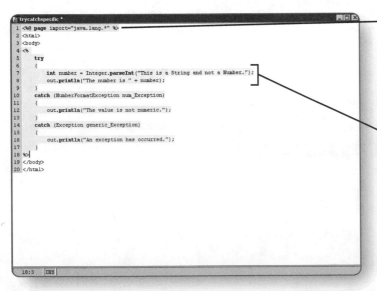

```
1  <%@ page import="java.lang.*" %>
2  <html>
3  <body>
4  <%
5      try
6      {
7          int number = Integer.parseInt("This is a String and not a Number.");
8          out.println("The number is " + number);
9      }
10     catch (NumberFormatException num_Exception)
11     {
12         out.println("The value is not numeric.");
13     }
14     catch (Exception generic_Exception)
15     {
16         out.println("An exception has occurred.");
17     }
18 %>
19 </body>
20 </html>
```

1. Use the import directive to import the java.lang.* packages. These are required to implement the try-catch exception-handling mechanism.

2. Type the code that could cause an exception within the try block. Code must be inserted within braces. In this example, the parseInt method is used to convert a string to a number. This will throw the NumberFormatException.

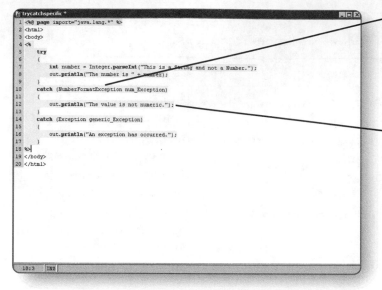

3. Type **NumberFormatException** and a variable name between the parentheses of the catch statement.

4. Place the error handling code to handle the NumberFormatException between the braces. A specific error message can now be printed.

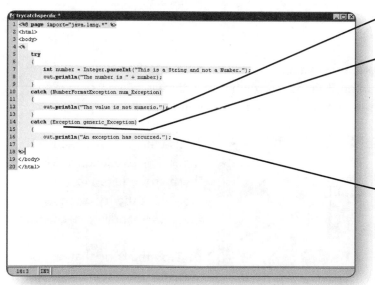

5. Create another catch block.

6. Type **Exception** followed by a variable name between the parentheses of the catch statement. This will catch all other exceptions that might occur.

7. Type your generic exception-handling code within the catch block. In this case, a generic error message will be displayed.

NOTE

You can use several catch blocks to detect different exceptions. The order of the catch blocks is important because the first block that matches the exception or a superclass of the thrown exception will be executed. The order of catch blocks must follow the class hierarchy inversely. For example, the lowest subclass should be first and the highest superclass should be last.

Creating an Error Page in JSP

The isErrorPage directive is used to define a Web page that can handle exceptions. This is known as an Error page. An Error page can display error messages generated by other pages in your Web site. You can still use try-catch blocks, but this option is easier to implement across multiple pages.

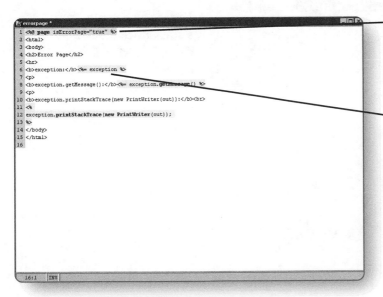

1. Set the isErrorPage directive to "true". This will generate an exception variable when the error page is requested.

2. Type **exception** between <%= and %> delimiters. This will print the contents of the exception variable to the Web page.

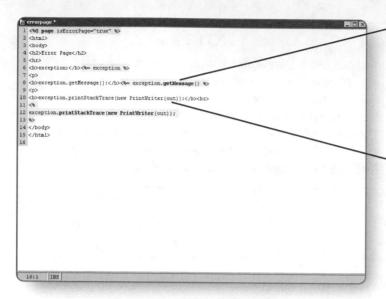

3. Type **exception.getMessage( )** between the <%= and %> delimiters. The getMessage( ) method will retrieve the error message from the exception variable.

4. Call the printStackTrace method to print the stack trace to the current output stream (in other words, the current JSP page). The stack trace will highlight where the exception occurred.

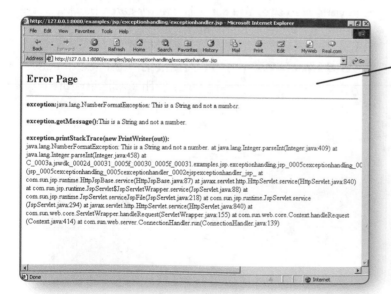

NOTE

This is an example of a stack trace that will be displayed when an exception occurs. The stack trace lists the objects and methods that were called until the exception was encountered. The stack trace will help you locate the code that caused the exception.

Specifying an Error Page for Your Web Application

The errorPage directive is used to specify the page to be displayed if an exception occurs. It can be inserted on all JSP pages that require exception handling.

1. Set the errorPage directive to the file name of the error page.

NOTE

The error page must have the isErrorPage directive set to true before you can use it.

2. Type the code that is capable of throwing an exception between <% and %> delimiters.

NOTE

There is no need to use try-catch blocks on this page. You only need to specify the error page that must be displayed when an exception occurs.

9

Using JavaBeans

JavaBeans are reusable components that can be manipulated by JSP action tags. Business logic, ideally, should be removed from a JSP page and modeled as a special class known as a JavaBean. Common functionality that is implemented as a JavaBean needs to be tested only once before it is utilized in many applications. JavaBeans remove Java code from a Web page. JSP pages can then be solely used for presentation. In this chapter, you'll learn how to:

- Create a simple JavaBean
- Use JSP tags to manipulate JavaBean properties
- Create a JavaBean that models a savings account and calculates simple interest
- Use JavaBeans to process forms

What is a JavaBean?

Think of a JavaBean as a "black box" that is capable of performing some function. You can use the black box without knowing how it actually performs the function. You need only to supply the input parameters for the output to be calculated. A JavaBean is a component that can be reused across multiple JSP pages. The use of components simplifies the development and maintenance of Web applications. Scalable Web applications can be built from a collection of existing JavaBeans that implement core functionality such as accessing a database, sending e-mail messages, and rotating banner advertisements.

Creating a Simple JavaBean

A JavaBean is essentially a class that must use a special convention for naming accessor methods. An accessor method either assigns or retrieves the value stored in an instance variable. A Bean must have

- An empty constructor. This is achieved by not including a constructor method.

- No public instance variables.

NOTE

An *instance variable* is also known as a *property*.

An instance variable xxx must be set using a method called setXxx and retrieved using a method called getXxx. A property name always starts with a lowercase letter, but when the property name is used in an accessor method, the first letter is capitalized. For example, an instance variable called message must have setMessage and getMessage methods.

TIP

You can obtain more information about the JavaBean API from http://java.sun.com/beans.

The next set of steps creates a simple JavaBean with a single instance variable that is accessed through appropriately-named getter and setter methods.

```
SimpleBean *
 1 package FEWD;
 2
 3 public class SimpleBean
 4 {
 5
 6    private String message = "Message not yet set";
 7
 8    public String getMessage()
 9    {
10       return (message);
11    }
12
13    public void setMessage(String message)
14    {
15       this.message = message;
16    }
17
18 }

17:5   INS
```

1. Create a file with a .java extension. Source code files that contain JavaBeans must all have the same extension.

2. The file must be saved to a subdirectory on your application server. The name of this folder varies, and you should consult the appropriate documentation to identify the directory where you must place your JavaBeans. Table 9.1 lists the locations for some popular JSP application servers.

Table 9.1 Installing JavaBean Classes

Server	JavaBean Directory Path
Tomcat	installation_directory/webpages/WEB-INF/classes/packagename
JSWDK	installation_directory/webpages/WEB-INF/servlets/packagename
JRun	installation_directory/servers/default/default-app/web-inf/classes/packagename
Java Web Server	installation_directory/classes/packagename
BEA WebLogic	installation_directory/classes/packagename

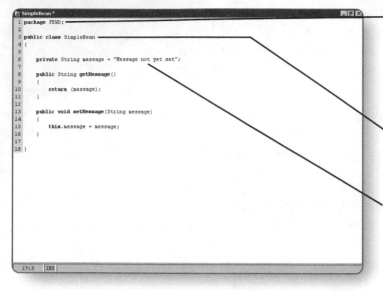

```
SimpleBean *
1  package FEWD;
2
3  public class SimpleBean
4  {
5
6       private String message = "Message not yet set";
7
8       public String getMessage()
9       {
10           return (message);
11      }
12
13      public void setMessage(String message)
14      {
15          this.message = message;
16      }
17
18 }

17:5    INS
```

3. Include the JavaBean in a package. If the JavaBean is in a package, it must be placed in a folder that has the same name as the package.

4. Create a public class. The name of the class and the name of the file must be identical.

5. Declare a private string variable and assign a default variable. This is an instance variable.

```
SimpleBean *
1  package FEWD;
2
3  public class SimpleBean
4  {
5
6       private String message = "Message not yet set";
7
8       public String getMessage()
9       {
10           return (message);
11      }
12
13      public void setMessage(String message)
14      {
15          this.message = message;
16      }
17
18 }

17:5    INS
```

6. Declare a public get method to return the instance variable. The return type must match that of the instance variable.

NOTE

All accessor methods must be declared as public.

```
SimpleBean *
1  package FEWD;
2
3  public class SimpleBean
4  {
5
6      private String message = "Message not yet set";
7
8      public String getMessage()
9      {
10         return (message);
11     }
12
13     public void setMessage(String message)
14     {
15         this.message = message;
16     }
17
18 }
```

17:5   INS

7. Declare a public method to assign a value to the instance variable. This method must be declared as void because no value is returned.

NOTE
Only a single variable can be passed to a setter method.

```
Command Prompt
Microsoft Windows 2000 [Version 5.00.2195]
(C) Copyright 1985-1999 Microsoft Corp.

C:\>cd jswdk-1.0.1

C:\jswdk-1.0.1>cd examples

C:\jswdk-1.0.1\examples>cd web-inf

C:\jswdk-1.0.1\examples\WEB-INF>cd jsp

C:\jswdk-1.0.1\examples\WEB-INF\jsp>cd beans

C:\jswdk-1.0.1\examples\WEB-INF\jsp\beans>javac SimpleBean.java
```

8. Use the javac compiler to compile the JavaBean. A .class file will be created.

Using JSP Tags to Manipulate JavaBean Properties

The JSP action tags are used to initialize and manipulate the properties of a JavaBean. The functionality contained in a JavaBean can then be implemented on numerous JSP pages.

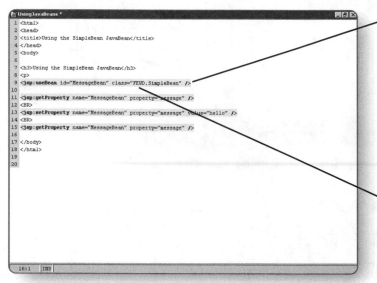

```
 1  <html>
 2  <head>
 3  <title>Using the SimpleBean JavaBean</title>
 4  </head>
 5  <body>
 6
 7  <h3>Using the SimpleBean JavaBean</h3>
 8  <p>
 9  <jsp:useBean id="MessageBean" class="FEWD.SimpleBean" />
10
11  <jsp:getProperty name="MessageBean" property="message" />
12  <BR>
13  <jsp:setProperty name="MessageBean" property="message" value="hello" />
14  <BR>
15  <jsp:getProperty name="MessageBean" property="message" />
16
17  </body>
18  </html>
19
20
```

1. The useBean tag is used to initialize a JavaBean. You need to specify

- A unique ID name for each JavaBean

- The JavaBean class name

NOTE

The package name is placed before the class name. A period separates the package and class name.

NOTE

In this example, the useBean tag instantiates a JavaBean of the class SimpleBean that is contained in the FEWD package, and associates it with the name MessageBean.

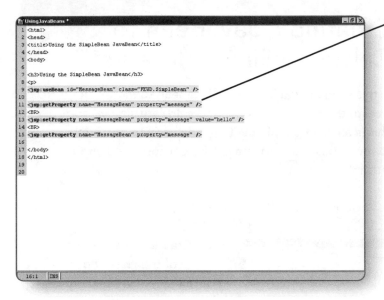

2. The getProperty action tag retrieves a property (in other words, an instance variable) and prints the result to the page. You need to specify

- The ID of the JavaBean
- The name of the property

NOTE

The getProperty tag performs the equivalent of <%= MessageBean. getMessage() %>.

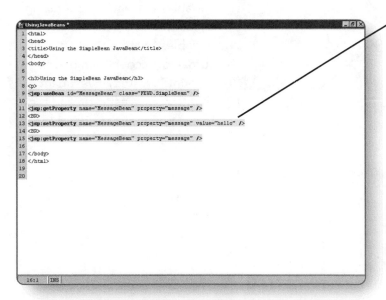

3. The setProperty action tag assignes a value to a property. You need to specify

- The ID of the JavaBean
- The name of the property
- The value that must be assigned to the property

TIP

The setProperty tag performs the equivalent of <%= MessageBean. setMessage() %>.

Creating a JavaBean to Calculate Simple Interest

In this section, you'll create a JavaBean to model an investment banking account and calculate simple interest. This is an example of how the code used to perform a common business process can be encapsulated into a reusable component.

1. Include the JavaBean in a package.

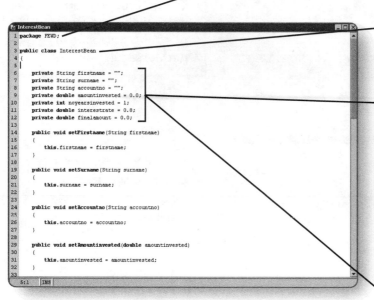

```
1  package FEWD;
2
3  public class InterestBean
4  {
5
6      private String firstname = "";
7      private String surname = "";
8      private String accountno = "";
9      private double amountinvested = 0.0;
10     private int noyearsinvested = 1;
11     private double interestrate = 0.8;
12     private double finalamount = 0.0;
13
14     public void setFirstname(String firstname)
15     {
16         this.firstname = firstname;
17     }
18
19     public void setSurname(String surname)
20     {
21         this.surname = surname;
22     }
23
24     public void setAccountno(String accountno)
25     {
26         this.accountno = accountno;
27     }
28
29     public void setAmountinvested(double amountinvested)
30     {
31         this.amountinvested = amountinvested;
32     }
33
```

2. Create a public class. The name of the class and the name of the file must be identical.

3. Declare the instance variables that make up a savings account. This includes instance variables to store the first name, surname, account number, amount invested, investment duration, interest rate, and the final amount at the end of the investment period.

4. Assign default values to the instance variables where possible.

```
InterestBean
14    public void setFirstname(String firstname)
15    {
16        this.firstname = firstname;
17    }
18
19    public void setSurname(String surname)
20    {
21        this.surname = surname;
22    }
23
24    public void setAccountno(String accountno)
25    {
26        this.accountno = accountno;
27    }
28
29    public void setAmountinvested(double amountinvested)
30    {
31        this.amountinvested = amountinvested;
32    }
33
34    public void setNoyearsinvested(int noyearsinvested)
35    {
36        this.noyearsinvested = noyearsinvested;
37    }
38
39    public void setInterestrate(double interestrate)
40    {
41        this.interestrate = interestrate;
42    }
43
44    public void setFinalamount(double finalamount)
45    {
46        this.finalamount = finalamount;
5:1    INS
```

5. Declare setter methods for each instance variable that has write access.

NOTE

You don't need to declare a setter method for the finalamount instance variable because it must be calculated.

```
InterestBean
54    public String getSurname()
55    {
56            return (surname);
57    }
58
59    public String getAccountno()
60    {
61            return (accountno);
62    }
63
64    public double getAmountinvested()
65    {
66            return (amountinvested);
67    }
68
69    public int getNoyearsinvested()
70    {
71            return (noyearsinvested);
72    }
73
74    public double getInterestrate()
75    {
76            return (interestrate);
77    }
78
79    public double getFinalamount()
80    {
81            finalamount = amountinvested * (1 + (noyearsinvested * interestrate));
82            return (finalamount);
83    }
84
85 }
5:1    INS
```

6. Declare getter methods to retrieve the values stored in each instance variable.

7. The getFinalamount method must calculate the final balance in the savings account at the end of the investment period before the finalamount property is returned. Use the following formula:

$T = P(1 + nr)$

where

T - Final amount at the end of the investment period

P - Initial amount invested

n - Duration of investment in years

r - Interest Rate per year

Using the Simple Interest JavaBean

The JSP action tags are again used to initialize the Bean and access Bean properties.

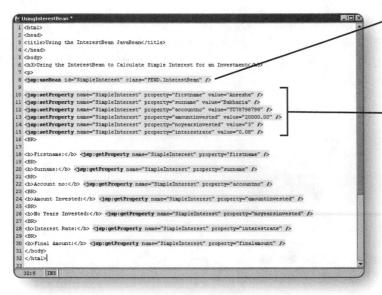

1. Use the useBean action tag to initialize the InterestBean JavaBean and assign a unique ID to it.

2. Use the setProperty action tag to assign a value to each property in the JavaBean.

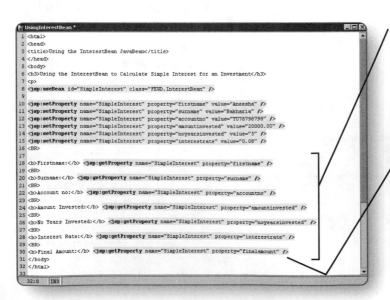

3. Use the getProperty tag to display the value of each property in the JavaBean.

NOTE

The getProperty tag will display the finalamount property after the account balance at the end of the investment period has been determined.

Understanding JavaBean Scope

The useBean action tag has an additional scope attribute, which can be set to Page, Request, Session, or Application.

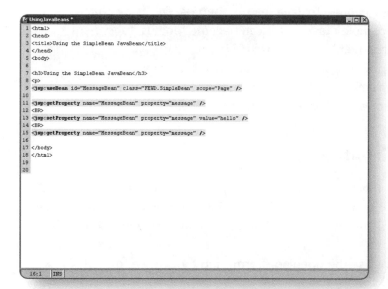

The scope of a JavaBean dictates where the Bean instance is stored. Page is the default scope attribute.

Table 9.2 details the types of JavaBean scope attributes and how they can be implemented.

A shopping cart JavaBean that is available for the duration of a session will be created in Chapter 20, "Creating an Online Store."

Table 9.2 JavaBean Scope

Scope	Definition
Page	The JavaBean instance is available to the current JSP page.
Request	The JavaBean instance is stored in the request object and is available to other JSP pages and servlets.
Session	The JavaBean instance is stored in the session object and is available to all JSP pages within the current user session.
Application	The JavaBean instance is stored within the Application context and is available to all JSP pages and servlets within the same application.

Using a JavaBean to Retrieve and Process Forms

Values to be entered into an HTML form often need to be assigned to JavaBean properties. This is by no means a complex task, but it can become tedious if there are a large number of properties in your JavaBean. JSP provides a practical solution. The setProperty action tag can automatically copy the data from form fields into JavaBean properties if both have identical names.

Creating the Form

In this form, you'll essentially create a simple interest calculator. Users are able to enter details about an investment and instantly view the amount of interest that will be earned.

1. Use the opening <form> tag to create a form.

2. Set the name attribute of the form tag by entering an appropriate name.

3. Set the method attribute of the form tag to Post.

4. Set the action attribute to specify the JSP file that uses a JavaBean to process the form.

```
InterestForm *
1  <html>
2  <head>
3  <title>An Interest Calculator</title>
4  </head>
5  <body bgcolor="#FFFFFF">
6  <p><b><font size="4">An Interest Calculator</font></b></p>
7  <form name="InterestForm" method="post" action="ProcessInterestForm.jsp" >
8    <table width="40%" border="1">
9      <tr>
10       <td width="28%">Firstname:</td>
11       <td width="72%">
12         <input type="text" name="firstname" size="40">
13       </td>
14     </tr>
15     <tr>
16       <td width="28%">Surname:</td>
17       <td width="72%">
18         <input type="text" name="surname" size="40">
19       </td>
20     </tr>
21     <tr>
22       <td width="28%">Account No.:</td>
23       <td width="72%">
24         <input type="text" name="accountno" size="40">
25       </td>
26     </tr>
27     <tr>
28       <td width="28%">Amount Invested:</td>
29       <td width="72%">
30         <input type="text" name="amountinvested" size="40">
31       </td>
32     </tr>
33     <tr>
   5:1    INS
```

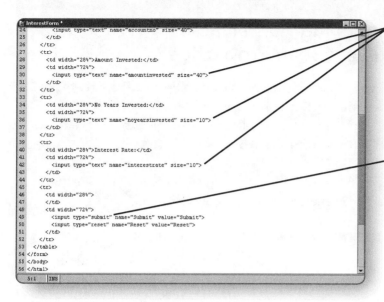

5. Create a form field for each JavaBean property you would like to set. The names assigned to the form fields must exactly match the JavaBean property names.

6. Insert a submit button. The user will click on this button to send the data to the server for processing.

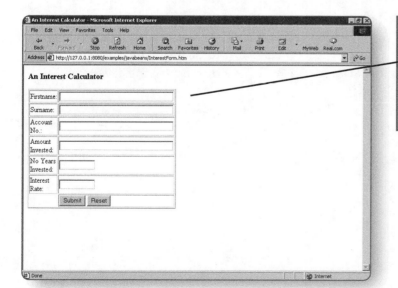

NOTE

This is what the simple interest calculator looks like when previewed in a Web browser.

Assigning Form Data to JavaBean Properties

It is no longer necessary to use multiple setProperty tags to specify every Bean property. The * wildcard is a special property variable that tells the JSP engine to retrieve form data that matches Bean properties.

1. Use the useBean action tag to initialize the InterestBean JavaBean and assign a unique ID to it.

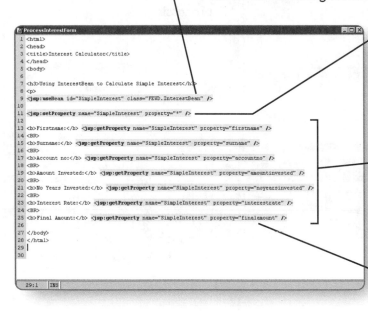

2. Use the setProperty tag to match JavaBeans properties with the appropriate form fields. This is achieved by setting the property attribute to the * wildcard.

3. Use the getProperty tag to display the value of each property in the JavaBean.

NOTE

The finalamount property will be calculated from the values entered by the user.

Using Commercial JavaBeans

The best part of using a component-based model for Web development is that you don't need to develop everything yourself. There are numerous third-party vendors that have developed JavaBeans that implement standard Web application functionality. These JavaBeans can be purchased or downloaded from the Internet. You can now build complex Web applications from a collection of customizable components. Commercial JavaBean components can drastically reduce valuable development time and maximize profits. Before you build a JavaBean, always review the commercial offerings. Table 9.3 lists some of the sites that offer commercial JavaBeans.

Table 9.3 Commercial JavaBeans

JavaBean	Purpose	Web site
BrowserHawk4J	Detects browser capabilities	http://cyscape.com/products/bhawk/javabean.asp
jspSmartSuite	Processes dates, uploads, and manages files	http://www.jspsmart.com
ImMailBean	Creates Web-based e-mail applications	http://www.imessaging.com/html/immailbean.html
easyXML	Processes XML documents	http://alphaworks.ibm.com/ab.nsf/bean/easyXML
XA dbConnection	Accesses JDBC-compliant databases	http://www.xa.com/Products.html

10

Retrieving Information from a User

Forms are fundamental to the implementation of Web applications. They provide an intuitive interface for users to enter data, which can be processed by a JSP page. Forms are central to the success of many popular dynamic applications. Online stores, surveys, and discussion forums all use forms to collect information from Web site visitors. In this chapter, you'll learn how to:

- Create HTML forms
- Retrieve and process form data
- Create a simple Web-based multiple-choice quiz
- Validate form data

Creating HTML Forms

Forms help organize the manner in which information is collected. A form is made up of a number of fields that allow users to enter data in a user-friendly and efficient manner. JSP supports the following form fields.

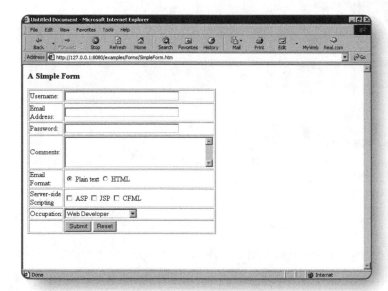

- Text entry fields
- Password fields
- Multi-line text fields
- Radio buttons
- Check boxes
- Drop-down boxes
- Hidden fields
- Submit buttons
- Reset buttons

The steps in this section assist you in creating a form that includes all of the available form fields. The <form> tag is used to define a form within a Web page. All form fields must be inserted within the opening and closing <form> tags.

TIP

Use a table to help you lay out a form. You can place the form elements and their respective labels in separate columns. Tables are also handy to perfectly align form elements with each other.

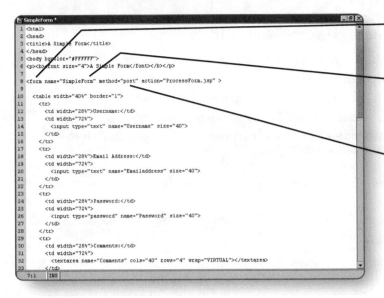

1. Use the opening <form> tag to create a form.

2. Set the name attribute of the <form> tag by entering an appropriate name.

3. Set the method attribute of the <form> tag. The method attribute specifies how data is sent to the Web server. It can either be set to Post or Get.

```
1  <html>
2  <head>
3  <title>A Simple Form</title>
4  </head>
5  <body bgcolor="#FFFFFF">
6  <p><b><font size="4">A Simple Form</font></b></p>
7  |
8  <form name="SimpleForm" method="post" action="ProcessForm.jsp" >
9
10   <table width="40%" border="1">
11     <tr>
12       <td width="28%">Username:</td>
13       <td width="72%">
14         <input type="text" name="Username" size="40">
15       </td>
16     </tr>
17     <tr>
18       <td width="28%">Email Address:</td>
19       <td width="72%">
20         <input type="text" name="Emailaddress" size="40">
21       </td>
22     </tr>
23     <tr>
24       <td width="28%">Password:</td>
25       <td width="72%">
26         <input type="password" name="Password" size="40">
27       </td>
28     </tr>
29     <tr>
30       <td width="28%">Comments:</td>
31       <td width="72%">
32         <textarea name="Comments" cols="40" rows="4" wrap="VIRTUAL"></textarea>
33       </td>
```

4. Use the action attribute to specify the JSP file that will process the form.

Post versus Get

Get is the default request method and is used if the method attribute is left blank. The Get method simply requests a Web page from the Web server. Form data is actually appended in terms of name-value pairs to the URL of the requested file. The form data is encoded to remove spaces and other special characters, and the appended form data is known as a query string. Here is an example:

```
http://www.yourserver.com/jspfile.jsp?user=Aneesha&date=9%2F7
```

A question mark (?) is inserted after the file name. Each name-value pair is separated by an ampersand (&).

The Get method should not be used if a large amount of data is being posted, because some Web servers place a restriction on the length of the query string. Usually the limit is 255 characters, but this can vary. The Get method is also not suitable if sensitive data is being submitted for processing—the data can be viewed in the URL field in a browser. Use the Get method if you would like the user to bookmark the page and return without entering data again.

The Post method sends the data back to the server in the header of the request. There is no restriction on the amount of data that can be sent. The posted form data cannot be viewed in the browser. The Post method should be used when many fields and a large amount of information must be submitted for processing. Sensitive data such as passwords and credit card details should always be sent using the Post method.

Inserting a Text Entry Field

A text input field is a single line field where the user can enter information. Any information that fits on a single line, such as a name, phone number, or e-mail address, can be entered into a text entry field.

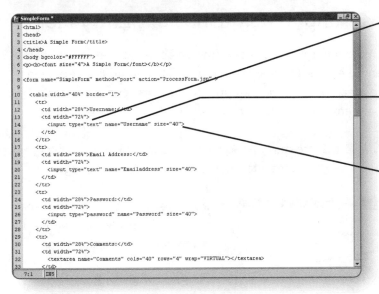

1. Set the type attribute of the input tag to text. This will insert a text entry field in the form.

2. Enter a unique name for the form field. This will be required when you retrieve the data.

3. Enter the maximum number of characters that the form field must hold. This value will depend upon the data that the user is required to enter.

Inserting a Password Field

A password field displays as asterisks the characters typed in by the user. This prevents sensitive information from being displayed in the browser window.

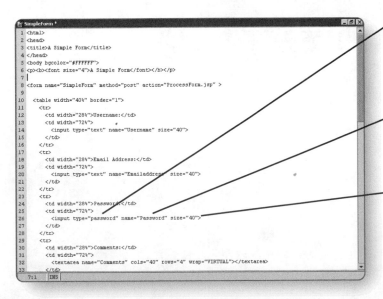

1. Set the type attribute of the input tag to password. This will insert a password entry field in the form.

2. Enter a unique name for the form field. This will be required when you retrieve the data.

3. Enter the maximum number of characters that the form field must hold. This value will depend upon the data that the user is required to enter.

Inserting a Multi-Line Text Entry Field

A multi-line text field is also known as a text area. Here, data can be entered that spans multiple lines. Multi-line text fields are ideal for gathering lengthy textual responses such as comments and descriptions.

1. Use the <textarea> tag to insert a multi-line text entry field. The <textarea> tag has opening and closing tags.

2. Enter a unique name for the form field. This will be required when you retrieve the data.

3. Enter the number of characters and rows that the form field must hold. This value will depend upon the data that the user is required to enter.

```
SimpleForm *
29    <tr>
30      <td width="28%">Comments:</td>
31      <td width="72%">
32        <textarea name="Comments" cols="40" rows="4" wrap="VIRTUAL"></textarea>
33      </td>
34    </tr>
35    <tr>
36      <td width="28%">Email Format:</td>
37      <td width="72%">
38        <input type="radio" name="EmailFormat" value="Plain Text" checked>
39        Plain text
40        <input type="radio" name="EmailFormat" value="HTML">
41        HTML</td>
42    </tr>
43    <tr>
44      <td width="28%">Server-side Scripting</td>
45      <td width="72%">
46        <input type="checkbox" name="ASP" value="Yes">
47        ASP
48        <input type="checkbox" name="JSP" value="Yes">
49        JSP
50        <input type="checkbox" name="CFML" value="Yes">
51        CFML</td>
52    </tr>
53    <tr>
54      <td width="28%">Occupation:</td>
55      <td width="72%">
56        <select name="Occupation">
57        <option>Web Developer</option>
58        <option>Systems Analyst</option>
59        <option>Programmer</option>
60        <option>Database Administrator</option>
61        <option>Graphic Designer</option>
7:1    INS
```

Inserting Radio Buttons

Radio buttons provide the user with a choice of options, but the user can only select a single option. Radio buttons must be grouped.

1. Set the type attribute of the input tag to radio. This will insert a radio button in the form.

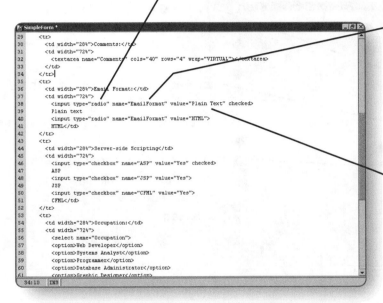

2. Enter a unique name for the radio button group. Each radio button in the group must share the same group name. The group name will be required when you retrieve the selected option.

3. Enter a unique value for each radio button in the group.

Inserting Check Boxes

Think of a check box as an on/off switch. Check boxes allow the user to either select or deselect an option. A check box is only capable of storing two values—on or off (in other words, Yes or No, or True or False). If a check box is not selected, no value is sent back to the server.

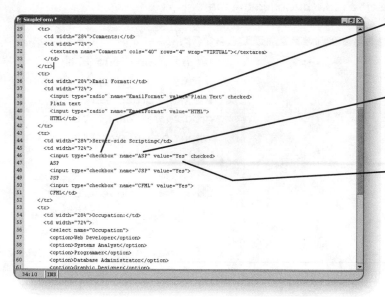

1. Set the type attribute of the input tag to checkbox. This will insert a check box in the form.

2. Enter a unique name for the form field. This will be required when you retrieve the data.

3. Enter a value for the check box. This value will be sent to the server if the check box is selected.

Inserting Drop-Down Boxes

A drop-down box is just a pull-down menu. It displays a list of choices and allows the user to make a selection.

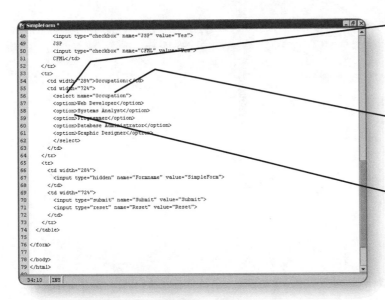

1. Use the <select> tag to insert a drop-down box. The <select> tag has opening and closing tags.

2. Enter a unique name for the form field. This will be required when you retrieve the data.

3. Use the <option> tag to insert the items that will appear in the drop-down box. The option that is selected will be posted back to the server.

Inserting Hidden Form Fields

Information stored in a hidden field is not displayed on a Web page. Users also can't edit the stored information. Hidden fields are used to store information that shouldn't be viewed by the user, but that still needs to be processed.

1. Set the type attribute of the input tag to hidden. This will insert a hidden form field in the form. Hidden form fields are not displayed.

```
SimpleForm *                                                      _ 5 X
47        JSP
48        <input type="checkbox" name="JSP" value="Yes">
49        JSP
50        <input type="checkbox" name="CFML" value="Yes">
51        CFML</td>
52     </tr>
53     <tr>
54        <td width="28%">Occupation:</td>
55        <td width="72%">
56          <select name="Occupation">
57          <option>Web Developer</option>
58          <option>Systems Analyst</option>
59          <option>Programmer</option>
60          <option>Database Administrator</option>
61          <option>Graphic Designer</option>
62          </select>
63        </td>
64     </tr>
65     <tr>
66        <td width="28%">
67          <input type="hidden" name="Formname" value="SimpleForm">
68        </td>
69        <td width="72%">
70          <input type="submit" name="Submit" value="Submit">
71          <input type="reset" name="Reset" value="Reset">
72        </td>
73     </tr>
74     </table>
75
76 </form>
77
78 </body>
79 </html>
53:10   INS
```

2. Enter a unique name for the form field. The name will be required when you retrieve the hidden value.

3. Enter a unique value for the hidden form field.

```
SimpleForm *                                                      _ 5 X
47        JSP
48        <input type="checkbox" name="JSP" value="Yes">
49        JSP
50        <input type="checkbox" name="CFML" value="Yes">
51        CFML</td>
52     </tr>
53     <tr>
54        <td width="28%">Occupation:</td>
55        <td width="72%">
56          <select name="Occupation">
57          <option>Web Developer</option>
58          <option>Systems Analyst</option>
59          <option>Programmer</option>
60          <option>Database Administrator</option>
61          <option>Graphic Designer</option>
62          </select>
63        </td>
64     </tr>
65     <tr>
66        <td width="28%">
67          <input type="hidden" name="Formname" value="SimpleForm">
68        </td>
69        <td width="72%">
70          <input type="submit" name="Submit" value="Submit">
71          <input type="reset" name="Reset" value="Reset">
72        </td>
73     </tr>
74     </table>
75
76 </form>
77
78 </body>
79 </html>
53:10   INS
```

Submitting a Form

A submit button collects all of the data in the form and sends it to the server.

1. Set the type attribute of the input tag to submit. This will insert a submit button in the form.

2. Enter a unique name for the button. This value will be displayed on the button and should, therefore, indicate the purpose of the button.

```
SimpleForm *
47        JSP
48        <input type="checkbox" name="JSP" value="Yes">
49        JSP
50        <input type="checkbox" name="CFML" value="Yes">
51        CFML</td>
52     </tr>
53     <tr>
54       <td width="28%">Occupation:</td>
55       <td width="72%">
56         <select name="Occupation">
57         <option>Web Developer</option>
58         <option>Systems Analyst</option>
59         <option>Programmer</option>
60         <option>Database Administrator</option>
61         <option>Graphic Designer</option>
62         </select>
63       </td>
64     </tr>
65     <tr>
66       <td width="28%">
67         <input type="hidden" name="Formname" value="SimpleForm">
68       </td>
69       <td width="72%">
70         <input type="submit" name="Submit" value="Submit">
71         <input type="reset" name="Reset" value="Reset">
72       </td>
73     </tr>
74   </table>
75
76 </form>
77
78 </body>
79 </html>
53:10   INS
```

Resetting a Form

A reset button restores the form fields to their default values (in other words, the values that were displayed when the form was first loaded).

1. Set the type attribute of the input tag to reset. This will insert a reset button in the form.

2. Enter a unique name for the button. This value will be displayed on the button and should, therefore, indicate the purpose of the button.

Processing a Form

JSP makes retrieving posted form data a simple process. Values entered into a form are stored in the request object.

The getParameter method must be called to retrieve the information that was entered into a particular form field.

```
ProcessForm *
1 <html>
2 <head>
3 <title>Processing a Form</title>
4 </head>
5 <body bgcolor="#FFFFFF">
6 <p><b><font size="4">A Simple Form</font></b></p>
7   <table width="40%" border="1">
8     <tr>
9       <td width="28%">Username:</td>
10      <td width="72%">
11        <%= request.getParameter("Username") %>
12      </td>
13    </tr>
14    <tr>
15      <td width="28%">Email Address:</td>
16      <td width="72%">
17        <%= request.getParameter("EmailAddress") %>
18      </td>
19    </tr>
20    <tr>
21      <td width="28%">Password:</td>
22      <td width="72%">
23        <%= request.getParameter("Password") %>
24      </td>
25    </tr>
26    <tr>
27      <td width="28%">Comments:</td>
28      <td width="72%">
29        <%= request.getParameter("Comments") %>
30      </td>
31    </tr>
32    <tr>
33      <td width="28%">Email Format:</td>
8:10   INS
```

1. Call the getParameter method of the request object.

2. Pass the name of the form field to the getParameter method.

3. Use the Expression tag to print the data that was entered into a form field.

4. Repeat steps 1 through 3 for each form field you want to display.

CAUTION

The name that you pass to the getParameter method must be identical to the name given to the form field. The getParameter method is case sensitive.

NOTE

In this example, the retrieved data has simply been displayed on a page. You could also assign the data to a variable. The data could then be analyzed and processed. As this book progresses, you will learn to store the data in a file, send it as an e-mail message, convert it to XML, or use it to update or insert new records into a database.

Retrieving Environmental Variables

Each time a browser sends information to the server, the request object stores environment variables. Environment/server variables store details regarding the file being requested, the user making the request, and the browser being used. You can easily determine the IP address of the visitor as well as which browser they're using.

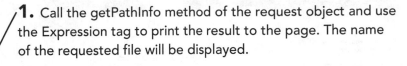

1. Call the getPathInfo method of the request object and use the Expression tag to print the result to the page. The name of the requested file will be displayed.

2. Call the getPathTranslated method of the request object and use the Expression tag to print the result to the page. The physical location of the file on the server will be displayed.

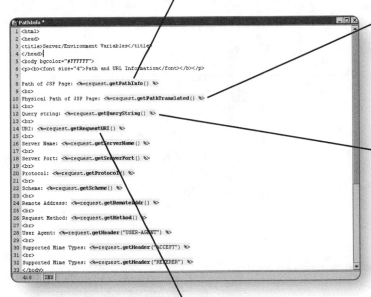

3. Call the getQueryString method of the request object and use the Expression tag to print the result to the page. The portion of the URL after the question mark (?) will be displayed.

4. Call the getRequestURI method of the request object and use the Expression tag to print the result to the page. The full URL will be displayed.

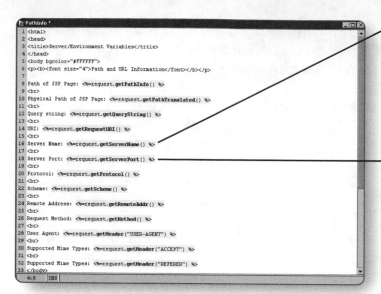

5. Call the getServerName method of the request object and use the Expression tag to print the result to the page. The domain name of the server will be displayed.

6. Call the getServerPort method of the request object and use the Expression tag to print the result to the page. The port on which the server is accepting requests will be listed.

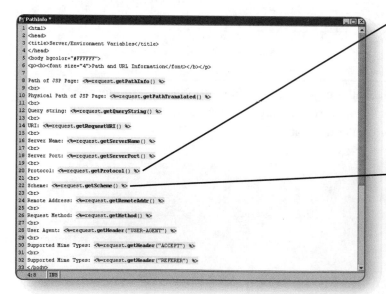

7. Call the getProtocol method of the request object and use the Expression tag to print the result to the page. The protocol that the browser used to make the request will be displayed (for example, HTTP/1.0).

8. Call the getScheme method of the request object and use the Expression tag to print the result to the page. The scheme portion of the URL will be returned.

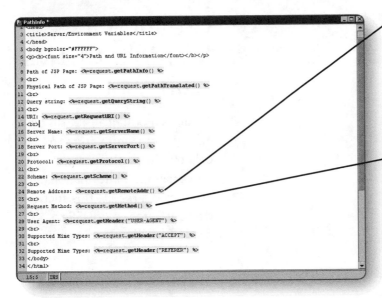

9. Call the getRemoteAddr method of the request object and use the Expression tag to print the result to the page. The IP address of the user's computer will be displayed.

10. Call the getMethod method of the request object and use the Expression tag to print the result to the page. The method used to make a request from the server will be returned. This can be either Get or Post.

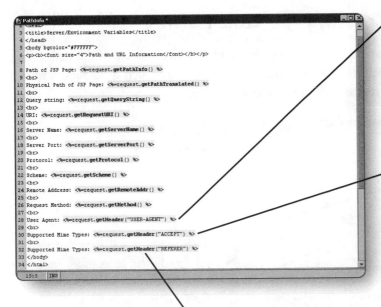

11. Call the getHeader method of the request object and use the Expression tag to print the result to the page. Pass USER-AGENT to the getHeader method. The name of the browser will be displayed.

12. Call the getHeader method of the request object and use the Expression tag to print the result to the page. Pass ACCEPT to the getHeader method. The type of files supported by the browser will be displayed.

13. Call the getHeader method of the request object and use the Expression tag to print the result to the page. Pass REFERER to the getHeader method. The URL of the page that the user visited before running the JSP page will be displayed.

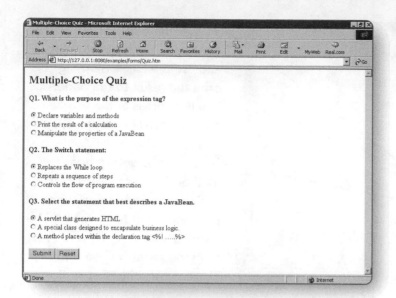

Creating a Multiple-Choice Quiz

A quiz is a practical, yet simple, example of using a form to collect information from a user, processing the information, and producing a result. This section demonstrates using JSP to grade a multiple-choice quiz.

Creating the Quiz Form

Each question in a multiple-choice quiz provides the user with a number of options, only one of which is correct. Radio buttons provide this functionality.

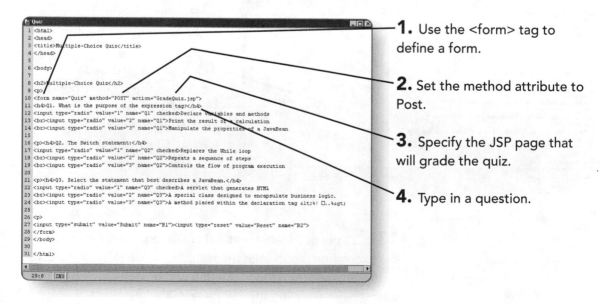

1. Use the <form> tag to define a form.

2. Set the method attribute to Post.

3. Specify the JSP page that will grade the quiz.

4. Type in a question.

5. Define a radio button group for each question. A radio button must be included for each possible answer.

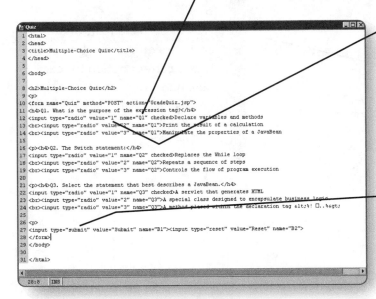

```
 1 <html>
 2 <head>
 3 <title>Multiple-Choice Quiz</title>
 4 </head>
 5
 6 <body>
 7
 8 <h2>Multiple-Choice Quiz</h2>
 9 <p>
10 <form name="Quiz" method="POST" action="GradeQuiz.jsp">
11 <h4>Q1. What is the purpose of the expression tag?</h4>
12 <input type="radio" value="1" name="Q1" checked>Declare variables and methods
13 <br><input type="radio" value="2" name="Q1">Print the result of a calculation
14 <br><input type="radio" value="3" name="Q1">Manipulate the properties of a JavaBean
15
16 <p><h4>Q2. The Switch statement:</h4>
17 <input type="radio" value="1" name="Q2" checked>Replaces the While loop
18 <br><input type="radio" value="2" name="Q2">Repeats a sequence of steps
19 <br><input type="radio" value="3" name="Q2">Controls the flow of program execution
20
21 <p><h4>Q3. Select the statement that best describes a JavaBean.</h4>
22 <input type="radio" value="1" name="Q3" checked>A servlet that generates HTML
23 <br><input type="radio" value="2" name="Q3">A special class designed to encapsulate business logic
24 <br><input type="radio" value="3" name="Q3">A method placed within the declaration tag &lt;%! □..%&gt;
25
26 <p>
27 <input type="submit" value="Submit" name="B1"><input type="reset" value="Reset" name="B2">
28 </form>
29 </body>
30
31 </html>
```

6. Set the value of each radio button group to a unique number. You will need this information when you grade the quiz.

7. Repeat steps 2 through 5 for each multiple choice question in the quiz.

8. Insert a submit button. Remember to label the button appropriately. This button will be used to submit the form.

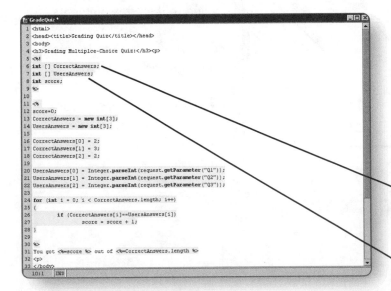

```
 1 <html>
 2 <head><title>Grading Quiz</title></head>
 3 <body>
 4 <h3>Grading Multiplce-Choice Quiz:</h3><p>
 5 <%!
 6 int [] CorrectAnswers;
 7 int [] UsersAnswers;
 8 int score;
 9 %>
10
11 <%
12 score=0;
13 CorrectAnswers = new int[3];
14 UsersAnswers = new int[3];
15
16 CorrectAnswers[0] = 2;
17 CorrectAnswers[1] = 3;
18 CorrectAnswers[2] = 2;
19
20 UsersAnswers[0] = Integer.parseInt(request.getParameter("Q1"));
21 UsersAnswers[1] = Integer.parseInt(request.getParameter("Q2"));
22 UsersAnswers[2] = Integer.parseInt(request.getParameter("Q3"));
23
24 for (int i = 0; i < CorrectAnswers.length; i++)
25 {
26        if (CorrectAnswers[i]==UsersAnswers[i])
27              score = score + 1;
28 }
29
30 %>
31 You got <%=score %> out of <%=CorrectAnswers.length %>
32 <p>
33 </body>
```

Grading the Quiz

Before the quiz is graded, you need to determine the correct responses for each question. If the user answers a question correctly, a value of one will be added to the user's score.

1. Declare an array to store the correct answer for each question in the quiz.

2. Declare an array to store the answers entered by the user.

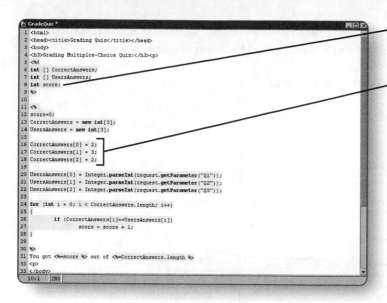

3. Declare a variable to store the user's grade.

4. For each element of the array, assign the number given to the correct option for each question.

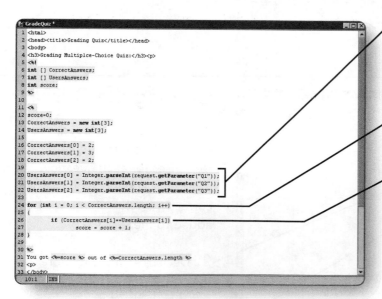

5. Use the getParameter method to retrieve the answer for each question and assign the value to the array elements.

6. Use a for loop to iterate through each question.

7. Use an if statement to compare the correct response with the response entered by the user.

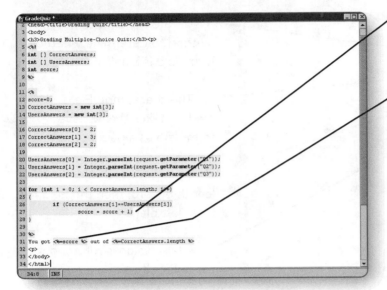

8. Add a value of one to the user's grade if the answer is correct.

9. Print the result to the Web page.

Validating User Input

Before you process data, you need to ensure that the data has been entered and is in the correct format. This will prevent errors from occurring while you process the data, and will also allow you to store valid information that can easily be reused at a later stage.

Validating Empty Fields

A form will often contain mandatory fields that must be filled out by a user. You need to detect an empty field and inform the user that the data can't be submitted until the mandatory criteria are met.

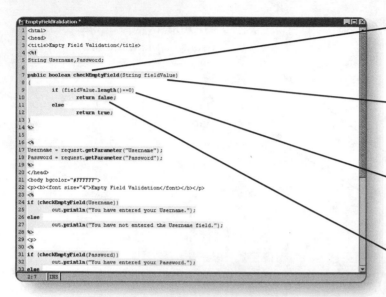

1. Create the checkEmptyField method to determine whether a form field is blank.

2. The checkEmptyField method takes the retrieved form data as a parameter.

3. If the retrieved value has a length of zero, then the field has been left blank.

4. A false value is returned if the field is blank.

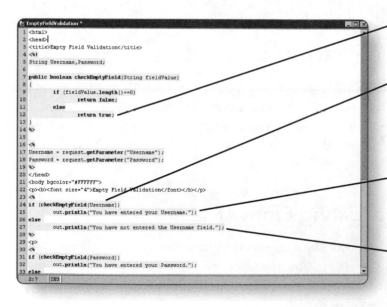

5. A true value is returned if the field contains information.

6. Pass the retrieved form data to the checkEmptyField method. Either a true or false value will be returned.

7. If true is returned, the field is not blank. Print an appropriate message.

8. If false is returned, the field is blank. Inform the user that the field must be completed.

NOTE

The checkEmptyField method can be reused to test other fields as well.

Validating E-Mail Addresses

Collecting the e-mail addresses of your visitors is very important. You will then be able to contact them later and promote your new products and services. E-mail addresses follow a specific pattern, but they can be very easy for users to accidentally mistype.

1. Create the checkEmail method to ensure that a field contains a valid e-mail address.

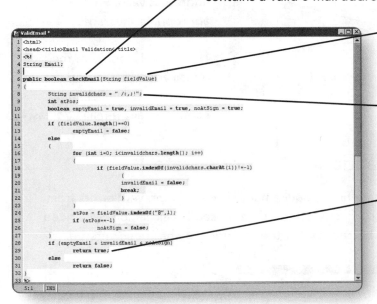

2. The checkEmail method takes the retrieved form data as a parameter.

3. The checkEmail method tests the data for the existence of only one @ symbol and no invalid characters (/ : ; ' " !).

4. If the e-mail address passes all tests and is not empty, a true value is returned.

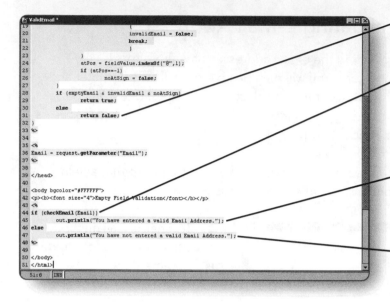

5. If the e-mail address fails all tests, a false value is returned.

6. Pass the retrieved form data to the checkEmail method. Either a true or false value will be returned.

7. If true is returned, the e-mail address is valid. Print an appropriate message.

8. If false is returned, the e-mail address is invalid. Inform the user that the field must contain a valid e-mail address.

Validating Numeric Data

Some fields require numeric data. To prevent errors from occurring when this data is used in calculations, you need to be certain that the numeric data has been entered.

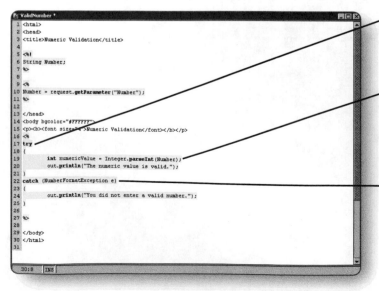

1. Use the try-catch error-handling mechanism to detect a non-numeric value.

2. Pass the retrieved value to the parseInt method. If the value is not a number, an exception will be thrown.

3. If the NumberFormatException is caught, inform the user that a number must be entered.

11

Sending E-Mail Messages

E-mail is certainly an important communication tool. Visitors to your Web site will use it to provide feedback and inquiries. You might also need to send e-mail messages from a Web site to acknowledge user registration, reissue lost passwords, promote new products, and confirm orders. JavaMail is a simple yet powerful API (*Application Programming Interface*) used to implement messaging functionality in a JSP page. In this chapter, you'll learn how to:

- Use the JavaMail API
- Send a simple e-mail message
- Send blind and carbon copies of an e-mail message
- Create and process an e-mail form
- Send HTML-formatted e-mail messages

Using the JavaMail API

The JavaMail API is a powerful cross-platform framework for implementing messaging in Java applications. It is portable, robust, protocol-independent, and easy to use. The API includes classes to handle mail-related protocols such as POP (*Post Office Protocol*) and SMTP (*Simple Mail Transport Protocol*). The JavaMail API requires the JAF (*Java Activation Framework*) to attach files of various MIME (*Multipurpose Internet Mail Extensions*) types to an e-mail message. MIME provides a common way for image, audio, and video files to be represented and attached to an e-mail message.

NOTE

SMTP is used to send e-mail over the Internet, while POP retrieves e-mail messages.

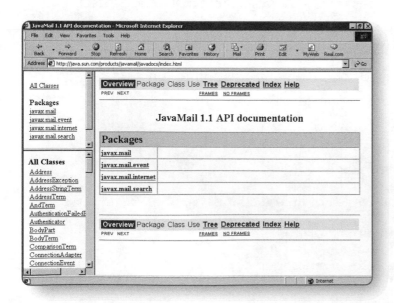

Table 11.1 describes some core JavaMail classes.

Table 11.1 JavaMail Classes

Core JavaMail Classes	Description
javax.mail.Session	The Session class stores the properties associated with the current mail session, including the host name, user name, and password.
javax.mail.internet.InternetAddress	The InternetAddress class is used to set the To, From, CC, and BCC e-mail addresses.
javax.mail.Message	The Message class constructs the actual e-mail message by setting the recipient, sender, subject, message, and MIME body parts.
javax.mail.internet.MimeMessage	The MimeMessage class is used by the Message class to implement messages that include attachments of different MIME types.
javax.mail.Transport	The Transport class sends a message over SMTP or retrieves a message using the POP3 protocol.

> **NOTE**
>
> You must download and install both the JavaMail API and the Java Activation Framework. JavaMail can be downloaded from http://java.sun.com/products/javamail. JAF can be downloaded from http://java.sun.com/beans/glasgow/jaf.html. If your JSP applications are hosted externally, you'll need to make sure that the server has the required classes installed.

Sending E-Mail

It is very easy to send an e-mail message with the JavaMail API. Put simply, all you need to do is start an e-mail session, specify the SMTP host, specify the To and From e-mail addresses, create an e-mail message and add the subject and message content, and then send the e-mail message. You can also easily send blind and carbon copies of e-mail messages to other recipients.

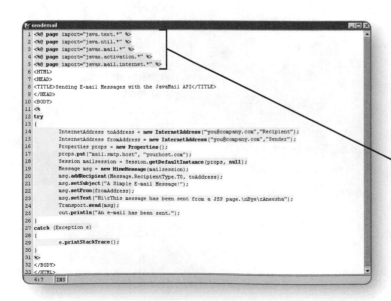

Sending a Simple E-Mail Message

Follow these steps to learn how to send a simple e-mail message using the JavaMail API.

1. Use the import directive to include the required JavaMail API and JAF classes. The javax.mail.*, javax.activation.*, and javax.mail.internet.* packages are all required to send e-mail from a JSP page.

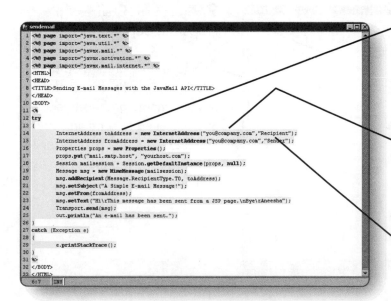

```
1  <%@ page import="java.text.*" %>
2  <%@ page import="java.util.*" %>
3  <%@ page import="javax.mail.*" %>
4  <%@ page import="javax.activation.*" %>
5  <%@ page import="javax.mail.internet.*" %>
6  <HTML>
7  <HEAD>
8  <TITLE>Sending E-mail Messages with the JavaMail API</TITLE>
9  </HEAD>
10 <BODY>
11 <%
12 try
13 {
14     InternetAddress toAddress = new InternetAddress("you@company.com","Recipient");
15     InternetAddress fromAddress = new InternetAddress("you@company.com","Sender");
16     Properties props = new Properties();
17     props.put("mail.smtp.host", "yourhost.com");
18     Session mailsession = Session.getDefaultInstance(props, null);
19     Message msg = new MimeMessage(mailsession);
20     msg.addRecipient(Message.RecipientType.TO, toAddress);
21     msg.setSubject("A Simple E-mail Message!");
22     msg.setFrom(fromAddress);
23     msg.setText("Hi!\rThis message has been sent from a JSP page.\nBye\rAneesha");
24     Transport.send(msg);
25     out.println("An e-mail has been sent.");
26 }
27 catch (Exception e)
28 {
29     e.printStackTrace();
30 }
31 %>
32 </BODY>
33 </HTML>
```

2. Use the try-catch exception-handling mechanism to deal with any unexpected conditions that might occur. It is very important that exceptions are handled in an elegant manner. Refer to Chapter 8, "Handling Exceptions," for more information about handling exceptions.

TIP

This JSP script is very easy to customize. You only need to change the e-mail addresses and SMTP server details.

3. Create an InternetAddress object to store the recipient's e-mail address. Use the InternetAddress constructor to create a new e-mail address.

4. Pass the recipient's e-mail address as the first parameter to the InternetAddress constructor.

5. Pass the name of the recipient as the second parameter to the InternetAddress constructor. This is an optional parameter.

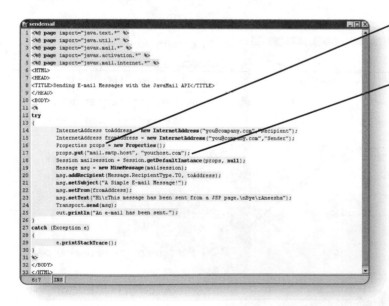

```
1  <%@ page import="java.text.*" %>
2  <%@ page import="java.util.*" %>
3  <%@ page import="javax.mail.*" %>
4  <%@ page import="javax.activation.*" %>
5  <%@ page import="javax.mail.internet.*" %>
6  <HTML>
7  <HEAD>
8  <TITLE>Sending E-mail Messages with the JavaMail API</TITLE>
9  </HEAD>
10 <BODY>
11 <%
12 try
13 {
14     InternetAddress toAddress = new InternetAddress("you@company.com","Recipient");
15     InternetAddress fromAddress = new InternetAddress("you@company.com","Sender");
16     Properties props = new Properties();
17     props.put("mail.smtp.host", "yourhost.com");
18     Session mailsession = Session.getDefaultInstance(props, null);
19     Message msg = new MimeMessage(mailsession);
20     msg.addRecipient(Message.RecipientType.TO, toAddress);
21     msg.setSubject("A Simple E-mail Message!");
22     msg.setFrom(fromAddress);
23     msg.setText("Hi\rThis message has been sent from a JSP page.\nBye\rAneesha");
24     Transport.send(msg);
25     out.println("An e-mail has been sent.");
26 }
27 catch (Exception e)
28 {
29     e.printStackTrace();
30 }
31 %>
32 </BODY>
33 </HTML>
    6:7    INS
```

6. Create an InternetAddress object to store the sender's e-mail address. Use the InternetAddress constructor to create a new e-mail address.

7. Pass the sender's e-mail address as the first parameter to the InternetAddress constructor.

8. Pass the name of the sender as the second parameter to the InternetAddress constructor. This is an optional parameter.

```
1  <%@ page import="java.text.*" %>
2  <%@ page import="java.util.*" %>
3  <%@ page import="javax.mail.*" %>
4  <%@ page import="javax.activation.*" %>
5  <%@ page import="javax.mail.internet.*" %>
6  <HTML>
7  <HEAD>
8  <TITLE>Sending E-mail Messages with the JavaMail API</TITLE>
9  </HEAD>
10 <BODY>
11 <%
12 try
13 {
14     InternetAddress toAddress = new InternetAddress("you@company.com","Recipient");
15     InternetAddress fromAddress = new InternetAddress("you@company.com","Sender");
16     Properties props = new Properties();
17     props.put("mail.smtp.host", "yourhost.com");
18     Session mailsession = Session.getDefaultInstance(props, null);
19     Message msg = new MimeMessage(mailsession);
20     msg.addRecipient(Message.RecipientType.TO, toAddress);
21     msg.setSubject("A Simple E-mail Message!");
22     msg.setFrom(fromAddress);
23     msg.setText("Hi\rThis message has been sent from a JSP page.\nBye\rAneesha");
24     Transport.send(msg);
25     out.println("An e-mail has been sent.");
26 }
27 catch (Exception e)
28 {
29     e.printStackTrace();
30 }
31 %>
32 </BODY>
33 </HTML>
    6:7    INS
```

9. Create an instance of the Properties object.

10. Use the put method to specify the mail protocol and the host name of the server. SMTP is used to send an e-mail message. The first parameter passed to the put method must be mail.smtp.host.

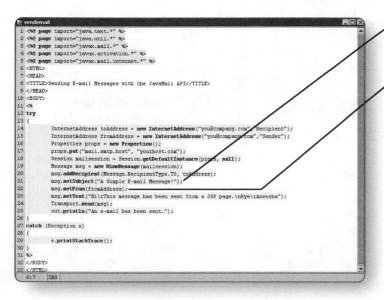

```
sendemail
1  <%@ page import="java.text.*" %>
2  <%@ page import="java.util.*" %>
3  <%@ page import="javax.mail.*" %>
4  <%@ page import="javax.activation.*" %>
5  <%@ page import="javax.mail.internet.*" %>
6  <HTML>
7  <HEAD>
8  <TITLE>Sending E-mail Messages with the JavaMail API</TITLE>
9  </HEAD>
10 <BODY>
11 <%
12 try
13 {
14         InternetAddress toAddress = new InternetAddress("you@company.com","Recipient");
15         InternetAddress fromAddress = new InternetAddress("you@company.com","Sender");
16         Properties props = new Properties();
17         props.put("mail.smtp.host", "yourhost.com");
18         Session mailsession = Session.getDefaultInstance(props, null);
19         Message msg = new MimeMessage(mailsession);
20         msg.addRecipient(Message.RecipientType.TO, toAddress);
21         msg.setSubject("A Simple E-mail Message!");
22         msg.setFrom(fromAddress);
23         msg.setText("Hi!\rThis message has been sent from a JSP page.\nBye\rAneesha");
24         Transport.send(msg);
25         out.println("An e-mail has been sent.");
26 }
27 catch (Exception e)
28 {
29         e.printStackTrace();
30 }
31 %>
32 </BODY>
33 </HTML>
6:7      INS
```

11. Create an instance of the Session object with the current mail server properties.

12. Create a new e-mail message by calling the MimeMessage constructor.

13. Use the addRecipient method to assign the recipient's e-mail address to the Message.RecipientType.TO property.

```
sendemail
1  <%@ page import="java.text.*" %>
2  <%@ page import="java.util.*" %>
3  <%@ page import="javax.mail.*" %>
4  <%@ page import="javax.activation.*" %>
5  <%@ page import="javax.mail.internet.*" %>
6  <HTML>
7  <HEAD>
8  <TITLE>Sending E-mail Messages with the JavaMail API</TITLE>
9  </HEAD>
10 <BODY>
11 <%
12 try
13 {
14         InternetAddress toAddress = new InternetAddress("you@company.com","Recipient");
15         InternetAddress fromAddress = new InternetAddress("you@company.com","Sender");
16         Properties props = new Properties();
17         props.put("mail.smtp.host", "yourhost.com");
18         Session mailsession = Session.getDefaultInstance(props, null);
19         Message msg = new MimeMessage(mailsession);
20         msg.addRecipient(Message.RecipientType.TO, toAddress);
21         msg.setSubject("A Simple E-mail Message!");
22         msg.setFrom(fromAddress);
23         msg.setText("Hi!\rThis message has been sent from a JSP page.\nBye\rAneesha");
24         Transport.send(msg);
25         out.println("An e-mail has been sent.");
26 }
27 catch (Exception e)
28 {
29         e.printStackTrace();
30 }
31 %>
32 </BODY>
33 </HTML>
6:7      INS
```

14. Use the setSubject method to set the message subject.

15. Use the setFrom method to set the sender's e-mail address.

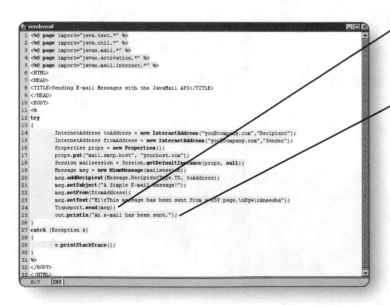

```
1  <%@ page import="java.text.*" %>
2  <%@ page import="java.util.*" %>
3  <%@ page import="javax.mail.*" %>
4  <%@ page import="javax.activation.*" %>
5  <%@ page import="javax.mail.internet.*" %>
6  <HTML>
7  <HEAD>
8  <TITLE>Sending E-mail Messages with the JavaMail API</TITLE>
9  </HEAD>
10 <BODY>
11 <%
12 try
13 {
14      InternetAddress toAddress = new InternetAddress("you@company.com","Recipient");
15      InternetAddress fromAddress = new InternetAddress("you@company.com","Sender");
16      Properties props = new Properties();
17      props.put("mail.smtp.host", "yourhost.com");
18      Session mailsession = Session.getDefaultInstance(props, null);
19      Message msg = new MimeMessage(mailsession);
20      msg.addRecipient(Message.RecipientType.TO, toAddress);
21      msg.setSubject("A Simple E-mail Message!");
22      msg.setFrom(fromAddress);
23      msg.setText("Hi\rThis message has been sent from a JSP page.\nBye\rAneesha");
24      Transport.send(msg);
25      out.println("An e-mail has been sent.");
26 }
27 catch (Exception e)
28 {
29      e.printStackTrace();
30 }
31 %>
32 </BODY>
33 </HTML>
```

16. Use the setText method to set the body of the e-mail message.

> ### NOTE
>
> A line break can be inserted by typing **\n** in the message body. A paragraph break can be inserted by typing **\r** in the message body.

```
1  <%@ page import="java.text.*" %>
2  <%@ page import="java.util.*" %>
3  <%@ page import="javax.mail.*" %>
4  <%@ page import="javax.activation.*" %>
5  <%@ page import="javax.mail.internet.*" %>
6  <HTML>
7  <HEAD>
8  <TITLE>Sending E-mail Messages with the JavaMail API</TITLE>
9  </HEAD>
10 <BODY>
11 <%
12 try
13 {
14      InternetAddress toAddress = new InternetAddress("you@company.com","Recipient");
15      InternetAddress fromAddress = new InternetAddress("you@company.com","Sender");
16      Properties props = new Properties();
17      props.put("mail.smtp.host", "yourhost.com");
18      Session mailsession = Session.getDefaultInstance(props, null);
19      Message msg = new MimeMessage(mailsession);
20      msg.addRecipient(Message.RecipientType.TO, toAddress);
21      msg.setSubject("A Simple E-mail Message!");
22      msg.setFrom(fromAddress);
23      msg.setText("Hi\rThis message has been sent from a JSP page.\nBye\rAneesha");
24      Transport.send(msg);
25      out.println("An e-mail has been sent.");
26 }
27 catch (Exception e)
28 {
29      e.printStackTrace();
30 }
31 %>
32 </BODY>
33 </HTML>
```

17. Send the message by calling the Transport.send method.

18. Print an appropriate message to the JSP page. This message will usually acknowledge that the e-mail has been sent successfully.

Sending Blind and Carbon Copies of an E-Mail Message

Sending a carbon copy of an e-mail message allows you to send a copy of the message to another person. When the message is opened, all recipient e-mail addresses can readily be viewed. Sending a blind carbon copy, on the other hand, hides the recipient addresses.

```
1  <%@ page import="java.text.*" %>
2  <%@ page import="java.util.*" %>
3  <%@ page import="javax.mail.*" %>
4  <%@ page import="javax.activation.*" %>
5  <%@ page import="javax.mail.internet.*" %>
6  <HTML>
7  <HEAD>
8  <TITLE>Sending CC and BCC E-mail Messages</TITLE>
9  </HEAD>
10 <BODY>
11 <%
12 try
13 {
14      InternetAddress toAddress = new InternetAddress ("you@company.com","Recipient");
15      InternetAddress ccAddress = new InternetAddress ("person1@company.com","CCRecipient");
16      InternetAddress bccAddress = new InternetAddress ("person2@company.com","BCCRecipient");
17      InternetAddress fromAddress = new InternetAddress ("person3@company.com","Sender");
18      Properties props = new Properties();
19      props.put("mail.smtp.host", "company.com");
20      Session mailsession = Session.getDefaultInstance(props, null);
21      Message msg = new MimeMessage(mailsession);
22      msg.addRecipient(Message.RecipientType.TO, toAddress);
23      msg.addRecipient(Message.RecipientType.CC, ccAddress);
24      msg.addRecipient(Message.RecipientType.BCC, bccAddress);
25      msg.setSubject("A Simple E-mail Message!");
26      msg.setFrom(fromAddress);
27      msg.setText("Hi\rThis message has been sent from a JSP page.\nBye\rAneesha");
28      Transport.send(msg);
29      out.println("An e-mail has been sent.");
30 }
31 catch (Exception e)
32 {
33      e.printStackTrace();
```

1. Use the import directive to include the required JavaMail API and JAF classes.

2. Use the try-catch exception-handling mechanism to deal with any unexpected conditions that might occur.

```
6  <HTML>
7  <HEAD>
8  <TITLE>Sending CC and BCC E-mail Messages</TITLE>
9  </HEAD>
10 <BODY>
11 <%
12 try
13 {
14      InternetAddress toAddress = new InternetAddress ("you@company.com","Recipient");
15      InternetAddress ccAddress = new InternetAddress ("person1@company.com","CCRecipient");
16      InternetAddress bccAddress = new InternetAddress ("person2@company.com","BCCRecipient");
17      InternetAddress fromAddress = new InternetAddress ("person3@company.com","Sender");
18      Properties props = new Properties();
19      props.put("mail.smtp.host", "company.com");
20      Session mailsession = Session.getDefaultInstance(props, null);
21      Message msg = new MimeMessage(mailsession);
22      msg.addRecipient(Message.RecipientType.TO, toAddress);
23      msg.addRecipient(Message.RecipientType.CC, ccAddress);
24      msg.addRecipient(Message.RecipientType.BCC, bccAddress);
25      msg.setSubject("A Simple E-mail Message!");
26      msg.setFrom(fromAddress);
27      msg.setText("Hi\rThis message has been sent from a JSP page.\nBye\rAneesha");
28      Transport.send(msg);
29      out.println("An e-mail has been sent.");
30 }
31 catch (Exception e)
32 {
33      e.printStackTrace();
34 }
35 %>
36 </BODY>
37 </HTML>
38
```

3. Create InternetAddress objects to store the To, From, CC, and BCC e-mail addresses.

4. Create an instance of the Properties object.

5. Use the put method to specify the mail protocol and the host name of the server. E-mail is sent over SMTP; the first parameter passed to the put method must be mail.smtp.host.

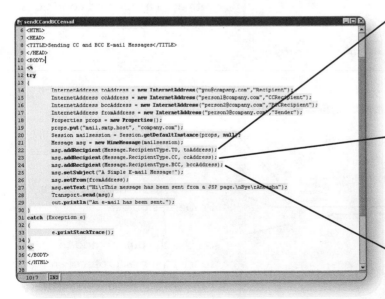

```
 6 <HTML>
 7 <HEAD>
 8 <TITLE>Sending CC and BCC E-mail Messages</TITLE>
 9 </HEAD>
10 <BODY>
11 <%
12 try
13 {
14         InternetAddress toAddress = new InternetAddress("you@company.com","Recipient");
15         InternetAddress ccAddress = new InternetAddress("person1@company.com","CCRecipient");
16         InternetAddress bccAddress = new InternetAddress("person2@company.com","BCCRecipient");
17         InternetAddress fromAddress = new InternetAddress("person3@company.com","Sender");
18         Properties props = new Properties();
19         props.put("mail.smtp.host", "company.com");
20         Session mailsession = Session.getDefaultInstance(props, null);
21         Message msg = new MimeMessage(mailsession);
22         msg.addRecipient(Message.RecipientType.TO, toAddress);
23         msg.addRecipient(Message.RecipientType.CC, ccAddress);
24         msg.addRecipient(Message.RecipientType.BCC, bccAddress);
25         msg.setSubject("A Simple E-mail Message!");
26         msg.setFrom(fromAddress);
27         msg.setText("Hi\rThis message has been sent from a JSP page.\nBye\rAneesha");
28         Transport.send(msg);
29         out.println("An e-mail has been sent.");
30 }
31 catch (Exception e)
32 {
33         e.printStackTrace();
34 }
35 %>
36 </BODY>
37 </HTML>
38
```

6. Create an instance of the Session object with the current mail server properties.

7. Create a new e-mail message by calling the MimeMessage constructor.

```
 6 <HTML>
 7 <HEAD>
 8 <TITLE>Sending CC and BCC E-mail Messages</TITLE>
 9 </HEAD>
10 <BODY>
11 <%
12 try
13 {
14         InternetAddress toAddress = new InternetAddress("you@company.com","Recipient");
15         InternetAddress ccAddress = new InternetAddress("person1@company.com","CCRecipient");
16         InternetAddress bccAddress = new InternetAddress("person2@company.com","BCCRecipient");
17         InternetAddress fromAddress = new InternetAddress("person3@company.com","Sender");
18         Properties props = new Properties();
19         props.put("mail.smtp.host", "company.com");
20         Session mailsession = Session.getDefaultInstance(props, null);
21         Message msg = new MimeMessage(mailsession);
22         msg.addRecipient(Message.RecipientType.TO, toAddress);
23         msg.addRecipient(Message.RecipientType.CC, ccAddress);
24         msg.addRecipient(Message.RecipientType.BCC, bccAddress);
25         msg.setSubject("A Simple E-mail Message!");
26         msg.setFrom(fromAddress);
27         msg.setText("Hi\rThis message has been sent from a JSP page.\nBye\rAneesha");
28         Transport.send(msg);
29         out.println("An e-mail has been sent.");
30 }
31 catch (Exception e)
32 {
33         e.printStackTrace();
34 }
35 %>
36 </BODY>
37 </HTML>
38
```

8. Use the addRecipient method to assign the recipient's e-mail address to the Message.RecipientType.TO property.

9. Use the addRecipient method to assign the recipient's e-mail address to the Message.RecipientType.CC property.

10. Use the addRecipient method to assign the recipient's e-mail address to the Message.RecipientType.BCC property.

```
sendCCandBCCemail                                                    _ _ X
 6  <HTML>
 7  <HEAD>
 8  <TITLE>Sending CC and BCC E-mail Messages</TITLE>
 9  </HEAD>
10  <BODY>
11  <%
12  try
13  {
14          InternetAddress toAddress = new InternetAddress("you@company.com","Recipient");
15          InternetAddress ccAddress = new InternetAddress("person1@company.com","CCRecipient");
16          InternetAddress bccAddress = new InternetAddress("person2@company.com","BCCRecipient");
17          InternetAddress fromAddress = new InternetAddress("person3@company.com","Sender");
18          Properties props = new Properties();
19          props.put("mail.smtp.host", "company.com");
20          Session mailsession = Session.getDefaultInstance(props, null);
21          Message msg = new MimeMessage(mailsession);
22          msg.addRecipient(Message.RecipientType.TO, toAddress);
23          msg.addRecipient(Message.RecipientType.CC, ccAddress);
24          msg.addRecipient(Message.RecipientType.BCC, bccAddress);
25          msg.setSubject("A Simple E-mail Message!");
26          msg.setFrom(fromAddress);
27          msg.setText("Hi\rThis message has been sent from a JSP page.\nBye\rAneesha");
28          Transport.send(msg);
29          out.println("An e-mail has been sent.");
30  }
31  catch (Exception e)
32  {
33          e.printStackTrace();
34  }
35  %>
36  </BODY>
37  </HTML>
38
10:7     INS
```

11. Use the setFrom method to set the sender's e-mail address.

12. Use the setSubject method to set the message subject.

13. Use the setText method to set the body of the e-mail message.

```
sendCCandBCCemail                                                    _ _ X
 6  <HTML>
 7  <HEAD>
 8  <TITLE>Sending CC and BCC E-mail Messages</TITLE>
 9  </HEAD>
10  <BODY>
11  <%
12  try
13  {
14          InternetAddress toAddress = new InternetAddress("you@company.com","Recipient");
15          InternetAddress ccAddress = new InternetAddress("person1@company.com","CCRecipient");
16          InternetAddress bccAddress = new InternetAddress("person2@company.com","BCCRecipient");
17          InternetAddress fromAddress = new InternetAddress("person3@company.com","Sender");
18          Properties props = new Properties();
19          props.put("mail.smtp.host", "company.com");
20          Session mailsession = Session.getDefaultInstance(props, null);
21          Message msg = new MimeMessage(mailsession);
22          msg.addRecipient(Message.RecipientType.TO, toAddress);
23          msg.addRecipient(Message.RecipientType.CC, ccAddress);
24          msg.addRecipient(Message.RecipientType.BCC, bccAddress);
25          msg.setSubject("A Simple E-mail Message!");
26          msg.setFrom(fromAddress);
27          msg.setText("Hi\rThis message has been sent from a JSP page.\nBye\rAneesha");
28          Transport.send(msg);
29          out.println("An e-mail has been sent.");
30  }
31  catch (Exception e)
32  {
33          e.printStackTrace();
34  }
35  %>
36  </BODY>
37  </HTML>
36
11:3     INS
```

14. Send the message by calling the Transport.send method.

15. Print an appropriate message to the JSP page to acknowledge that the e-mail has been sent.

Working with E-Mail Forms

An HTML form is used to gather information from a user and send an e-mail message. Most Web sites include this feature so that users can send feedback or make inquiries.

Implementing form to e-mail functionality within a JSP page is quite reliable because all processing occurs on the server. This means that you don't need to worry about invalid Internet e-mail addresses and server details.

Creating an E-Mail Form

To create an e-mail form, simply follow these steps.

1. Create a form. You will need to insert opening and closing <form> tags.

2. Set the method attribute of the form tag to post.

3. Set the action attribute to the file name of the page that will process the e-mail form.

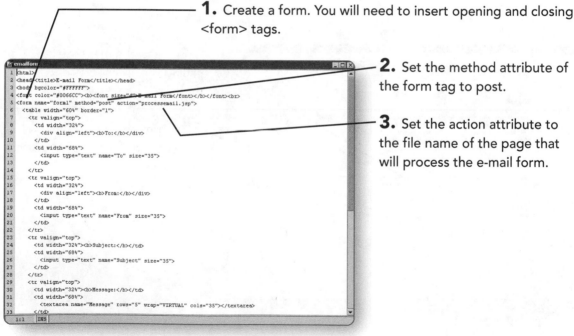

```
 1  <html>
 2  <head><title>E-mail Form</title></head>
 3  <body bgcolor="#FFFFFF">
 4  <font color="#0066CC"><b><font size="4">E-mail Form</font></b></font><br>
 5  <form name="form1" method="post" action="processemail.jsp">
 6    <table width="60%" border="1">
 7      <tr valign="top">
 8        <td width="32%">
 9          <div align="left"><b>To:</b></div>
10        </td>
11        <td width="68%">
12          <input type="text" name="To" size="35">
13        </td>
14      </tr>
15      <tr valign="top">
16        <td width="32%">
17          <div align="left"><b>From:</b></div>
18        </td>
19        <td width="68%">
20          <input type="text" name="From" size="35">
21        </td>
22      </tr>
23      <tr valign="top">
24        <td width="32%"><b>Subject:</b></td>
25        <td width="68%">
26          <input type="text" name="Subject" size="35">
27        </td>
28      </tr>
29      <tr valign="top">
30        <td width="32%"><b>Message:</b></td>
31        <td width="68%">
32          <textarea name="Message" rows="5" wrap="VIRTUAL" cols="35"></textarea>
33        </td>
```

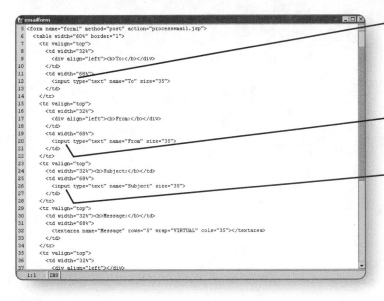

```
emailform                                                          _ □ X
5  <form name="form1" method="post" action="processemail.jsp">
6    <table width="60%" border="1">
7      <tr valign="top">
8        <td width="32%">
9          <div align="left"><b>To:</b></div>
10       </td>
11       <td width="68%">
12         <input type="text" name="To" size="35">
13       </td>
14     </tr>
15     <tr valign="top">
16       <td width="32%">
17         <div align="left"><b>From:</b></div>
18       </td>
19       <td width="68%">
20         <input type="text" name="From" size="35">
21       </td>
22     </tr>
23     <tr valign="top">
24       <td width="32%"><b>Subject:</b></td>
25       <td width="68%">
26         <input type="text" name="Subject" size="35">
27       </td>
28     </tr>
29     <tr valign="top">
30       <td width="32%"><b>Message:</b></td>
31       <td width="68%">
32         <textarea name="Message" rows="5" wrap="VIRTUAL" cols="35"></textarea>
33       </td>
34     </tr>
35     <tr valign="top">
36       <td width="32%">
37         <div align="left"></div>
1:1   INS
```

4. Type a text input field by setting the type attribute of the input tag to text. This input field will contain the To address.

5. Type a text input field to store the From address.

6. Type a text input field to store the Subject.

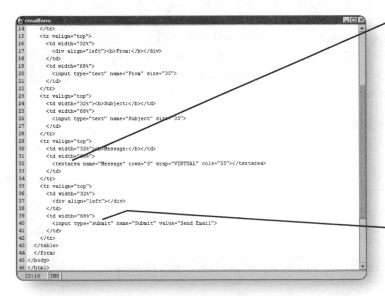

```
emailform                                                          _ □ X
14     </tr>
15     <tr valign="top">
16       <td width="32%">
17         <div align="left"><b>From:</b></div>
18       </td>
19       <td width="68%">
20         <input type="text" name="From" size="35">
21       </td>
22     </tr>
23     <tr valign="top">
24       <td width="32%"><b>Subject:</b></td>
25       <td width="68%">
26         <input type="text" name="Subject" size="35">
27       </td>
28     </tr>
29     <tr valign="top">
30       <td width="32%"><b>Message:</b></td>
31       <td width="68%">
32         <textarea name="Message" rows="5" wrap="VIRTUAL" cols="35"></textarea>
33       </td>
34     </tr>
35     <tr valign="top">
36       <td width="32%">
37         <div align="left"></div>
38       </td>
39       <td width="68%">
40         <input type="submit" name="Submit" value="Send Email">
41       </td>
42     </tr>
43   </table>
44   </form>
45 </body>
46 </html>
22:10   INS
```

7. Type a textarea input field in which users can type their e-mail messages.

NOTE
A textarea field is used because it allows users to enter many lines of text.

8. Insert a submit button. When clicked, the page specified in the forms action attribute will open and the e-mail message will be sent.

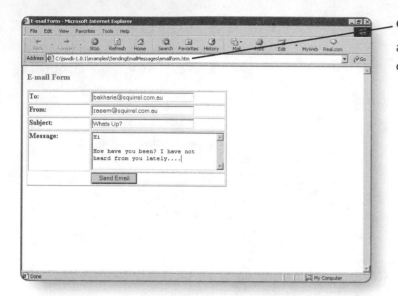

9. Preview the Web page in a browser. The form will be displayed.

Processing an E-Mail Form

The request.getParameter method can be used to retrieve the To, From, Subject, and Message details from the posted form. These values are then modeled into an e-mail message and sent via SMTP.

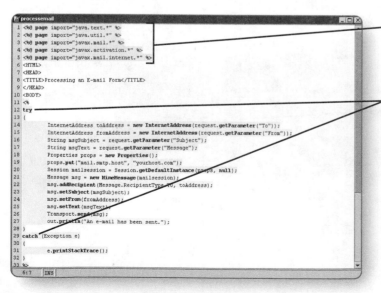

1. Use the import directive to include the required JavaMail API and JAF classes.

2. Use the try-catch exception-handling mechanism to deal with any unexpected conditions that might occur.

3. Retrieve the contents of the To text field with the request.getParameter method and store the result in an InternetAddress object.

4. Retrieve the contents of the From text field with the request.getParameter method and store the result in an InternetAddress object.

5. Retrieve the contents of the Subject text field with the request.getParameter method and store the result as a string variable.

6. Retrieve the contents of the Message text field with the request.getParameter method and store the result as a string variable.

7. Create an instance of the Properties object.

8. Use the put method to specify the mail protocol and the host name of the server.

```
processemail *                                                    _ □ X
 6 <HTML>
 7 <HEAD>
 8 <TITLE>Processing an E-mail Form</TITLE>
 9 </HEAD>
10 <BODY>
11 <%
12 try
13 {
14       InternetAddress toAddress = new InternetAddress(request.getParameter("To"));
15       InternetAddress fromAddress = new InternetAddress(request.getParameter("From"));
16       String msgSubject = request.getParameter("Subject");
17       String msgText = request.getParameter("Message");
18       Properties props = new Properties();
19       props.put("mail.smtp.host", "yourhost.com");
20       Session mailsession = Session.getDefaultInstance(props, null);
21       Message msg = new MimeMessage(mailsession);
22       msg.addRecipient(Message.RecipientType.TO, toAddress);
23       msg.setSubject(msgSubject);
24       msg.setFrom(fromAddress);
25       msg.setText(msgText);
26       Transport.send(msg);
27       out.println("An e-mail has been sent.");
28 }
29 catch (Exception e)
30 {
31       e.printStackTrace();
32 }
33 %>
34 </BODY>
35 </HTML>

10:7    INS
```

```
processemail *                                                    _ □ X
 6 <HTML>
 7 <HEAD>
 8 <TITLE>Processing an E-mail Form</TITLE>
 9 </HEAD>
10 <BODY>
11 <%
12 try
13 {
14       InternetAddress toAddress = new InternetAddress(request.getParameter("To"));
15       InternetAddress fromAddress = new InternetAddress(request.getParameter("From"));
16       String msgSubject = request.getParameter("Subject");
17       String msgText = request.getParameter("Message");
18       Properties props = new Properties();
19       props.put("mail.smtp.host", "yourhost.com");
20       Session mailsession = Session.getDefaultInstance(props, null);
21       Message msg = new MimeMessage(mailsession);
22       msg.addRecipient(Message.RecipientType.TO, toAddress);
23       msg.setSubject(msgSubject);
24       msg.setFrom(fromAddress);
25       msg.setText(msgText);
26       Transport.send(msg);
27       out.println("An e-mail has been sent.");
28 }
29 catch (Exception e)
30 {
31       e.printStackTrace();
32 }
33 %>
34 </BODY>
35 </HTML>

10:7    INS
```

```
processemail *                                              _□×
6  <HTML>
7  <HEAD>
8  <TITLE>Processing an E-mail Form</TITLE>
9  </HEAD>
10 <BODY>|
11 <%
12 try
13 {
14      InternetAddress toAddress = new InternetAddress(request.getParameter("To"));
15      InternetAddress fromAddress = new InternetAddress(request.getParameter("From"));
16      String msgSubject = request.getParameter("Subject");
17      String msgText = request.getParameter("Message");
18      Properties props = new Properties();
19      props.put("mail.smtp.host", "yourhost.com");
20      Session mailsession = Session.getDefaultInstance(props, null);
21      Message msg = new MimeMessage(mailsession);
22      msg.addRecipient(Message.RecipientType.TO, toAddress);
23      msg.setSubject(msgSubject);
24      msg.setFrom(fromAddress);
25      msg.setText(msgText);
26      Transport.send(msg);
27      out.println("An e-mail has been sent.");
28 }
29 catch (Exception e)
30 {
31      e.printStackTrace();
32 }
33 %>
34 </BODY>
35 </HTML>

10:7    INS
```

9. Create an instance of the Session object with the current mail server properties.

10. Create a new e-mail message by calling the MimeMessage constructor.

11. Use the addRecipient method to assign the To e-mail address to the Message.RecipientType.TO property.

```
processemail *                                              _□×
6  <HTML>
7  <HEAD>
8  <TITLE>Processing an E-mail Form</TITLE>
9  </HEAD>
10 <BODY>|
11 <%
12 try
13 {
14      InternetAddress toAddress = new InternetAddress(request.getParameter("To"));
15      InternetAddress fromAddress = new InternetAddress(request.getParameter("From"));
16      String msgSubject = request.getParameter("Subject");
17      String msgText = request.getParameter("Message");
18      Properties props = new Properties();
19      props.put("mail.smtp.host", "yourhost.com");
20      Session mailsession = Session.getDefaultInstance(props, null);
21      Message msg = new MimeMessage(mailsession);
22      msg.addRecipient(Message.RecipientType.TO, toAddress);
23      msg.setSubject(msgSubject);
24      msg.setFrom(fromAddress);
25      msg.setText(msgText);
26      Transport.send(msg);
27      out.println("An e-mail has been sent.");
28 }
29 catch (Exception e)
30 {
31      e.printStackTrace();
32 }
33 %>
34 </BODY>
35 </HTML>

10:7    INS
```

12. Use the setSubject method to set the message subject.

13. Use the setFrom method to set the From e-mail address.

14. Use the setText method to set the body of the e-mail message.

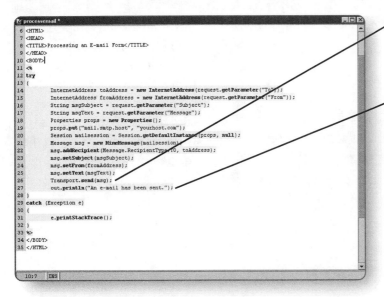

```
6  <HTML>
7  <HEAD>
8  <TITLE>Processing an E-mail Form</TITLE>
9  </HEAD>
10 <BODY>
11 <%
12 try
13 {
14      InternetAddress toAddress = new InternetAddress(request.getParameter("To"));
15      InternetAddress fromAddress = new InternetAddress(request.getParameter("From"));
16      String msgSubject = request.getParameter("Subject");
17      String msgText = request.getParameter("Message");
18      Properties props = new Properties();
19      props.put("mail.smtp.host", "yourhost.com");
20      Session mailsession = Session.getDefaultInstance(props, null);
21      Message msg = new MimeMessage(mailsession);
22      msg.addRecipient(Message.RecipientType.TO, toAddress);
23      msg.setSubject(msgSubject);
24      msg.setFrom(fromAddress);
25      msg.setText(msgText);
26      Transport.send(msg);
27      out.println("An e-mail has been sent.");
28 }
29 catch (Exception e)
30 {
31      e.printStackTrace();
32 }
33 %>
34 </BODY>
35 </HTML>
```

15. Send the message by calling the Transport.send method.

16. Print an appropriate message to the JSP page to acknowledge that the e-mail message has been sent.

Sending HTML-Formatted E-Mail Messages

E-mail messages, by default, are sent in a plain text format. This provides you with almost no flexibility when designing the layout of your message. Many popular e-mail clients such as Netscape Messenger and Microsoft Outlook are already capable of displaying HTML-formatted e-mail messages. HTML messages can be sent with JavaMail, but you need to explicitly set the content type. You can

```
1  <%@ page import="java.text.*" %>
2  <%@ page import="java.util.*" %>
3  <%@ page import="javax.mail.*" %>
4  <%@ page import="javax.activation.*" %>
5  <%@ page import="javax.mail.internet.*" %>
6  <HTML>
7  <HEAD><TITLE>Sending HTML E-mail Messages with the JavaMail API</TITLE></HEAD>
8  <BODY>
9  <%
10 try
11 {
12      InternetAddress toAddress = new InternetAddress("bakharia@squirrel.com.au","Aneesha");
13      InternetAddress fromAddress = new InternetAddress("bakharia@squirrel.com.au","Aneesha");
14      String msgSubject  = "HTML Formatted Email";
15
16      String msgText  = "<HTML><HEAD></HEAD>";
17      msgText  = msgText + "<BODY>";
18      msgText  = msgText + "<HR><DIV ALIGN='CENTER'><B><FONT COLOR='#330099' SIZE='5'>";
19      msgText  = msgText + "Newsletter Title";
20      msgText  = msgText + "<BR></FONT></B></DIV>";
21      msgText  = msgText + "<HR><BR>";
22      msgText  = msgText + "A basic table:";
23      msgText  = msgText + "<TABLE WIDTH='50%' BORDER='1' CELLSPACING='3' CELLPADDING='3'>";
24      msgText  = msgText + "<TR><TD>Text in a table cell</TD><TD> </TD></TR>";
25      msgText  = msgText + "<TR><TD> </TD><TD> </TD></TR>";
26      msgText  = msgText + "</TABLE><BR>";
27      msgText  = msgText + "A link:<BR>";
28      msgText  = msgText + "<A HREF='http://www.prima-tech.com/'>http://www.prima-tech.com/</A><BR>";
29      msgText  = msgText + "An image:<BR>";
30      msgText  = msgText + "<IMG SRC='http://netessentials.squirrel.com.au/sample.gif'";
31      msgText  = msgText + "WIDTH='195' HEIGHT='101'>";
32      msgText  = msgText + "</BODY></HTML>";
```

- Format text with the font, size, and color of your choice.

- Use tables to create complex layouts.

- Include links.

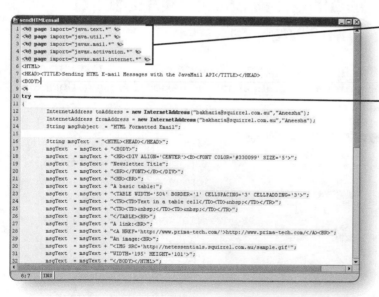

```
1  <%@ page import="java.text.*" %>
2  <%@ page import="java.util.*" %>
3  <%@ page import="javax.mail.*" %>
4  <%@ page import="javax.activation.*" %>
5  <%@ page import="javax.mail.internet.*" %>
6  <HTML>
7  <HEAD><TITLE>Sending HTML E-mail Messages with the JavaMail API</TITLE></HEAD>
8  <BODY>
9  <%
10 try
11 {
12     InternetAddress toAddress = new InternetAddress ("bakharia@squirrel.com.au","Aneesha");
13     InternetAddress fromAddress = new InternetAddress ("bakharia@squirrel.com.au","Aneesha");
14     String msgSubject = "HTML Formatted Email";
15
16     String msgText = "<HTML><HEAD></HEAD>";
17     msgText = msgText + "<BODY>";
18     msgText = msgText + "<HR><DIV ALIGN='CENTER'><B><FONT COLOR='#330099' SIZE='5'>";
19     msgText = msgText + "Newsletter Title";
20     msgText = msgText + "<BR></FONT></B></DIV>";
21     msgText = msgText + "<HR><BR>";
22     msgText = msgText + "A basic table:";
23     msgText = msgText + "<TABLE WIDTH='50%' BORDER='1' CELLSPACING='3' CELLPADDING='3'>";
24     msgText = msgText + "<TR><TD>Text in a table cell</TD><TD> </TD></TR>";
25     msgText = msgText + "<TR><TD> </TD><TD> </TD></TR>";
26     msgText = msgText + "</TABLE><BR>";
27     msgText = msgText + "A link:<BR>";
28     msgText = msgText + "<A HREF='http://www.prima-tech.com/'>http://www.prima-tech.com/</A><BR>";
29     msgText = msgText + "An image:<BR>";
30     msgText = msgText + "<IMG SRC='http://netessentials.squirrel.com.au/sample.gif'";
31     msgText = msgText + "WIDTH='195' HEIGHT='101'>";
32     msgText = msgText + "</BODY></HTML>";
```

● Insert images in either GIF or JPEG format. You will not be able to use other image formats because they can't be displayed in HTML. Be sure to use absolute URLs when referencing images that reside on a Web server.

```
1  <%@ page import="java.text.*" %>
2  <%@ page import="java.util.*" %>
3  <%@ page import="javax.mail.*" %>
4  <%@ page import="javax.activation.*" %>
5  <%@ page import="javax.mail.internet.*" %>
6  <HTML>
7  <HEAD><TITLE>Sending HTML E-mail Messages with the JavaMail API</TITLE></HEAD>
8  <BODY>
9  <%
10 try
11 {
12     InternetAddress toAddress = new InternetAddress ("bakharia@squirrel.com.au","Aneesha");
13     InternetAddress fromAddress = new InternetAddress ("bakharia@squirrel.com.au","Aneesha");
14     String msgSubject = "HTML Formatted Email";
15
16     String msgText = "<HTML><HEAD></HEAD>";
17     msgText = msgText + "<BODY>";
18     msgText = msgText + "<HR><DIV ALIGN='CENTER'><B><FONT COLOR='#330099' SIZE='5'>";
19     msgText = msgText + "Newsletter Title";
20     msgText = msgText + "<BR></FONT></B></DIV>";
21     msgText = msgText + "<HR><BR>";
22     msgText = msgText + "A basic table:";
23     msgText = msgText + "<TABLE WIDTH='50%' BORDER='1' CELLSPACING='3' CELLPADDING='3'>";
24     msgText = msgText + "<TR><TD>Text in a table cell</TD><TD> </TD></TR>";
25     msgText = msgText + "<TR><TD> </TD><TD> </TD></TR>";
26     msgText = msgText + "</TABLE><BR>";
27     msgText = msgText + "A link:<BR>";
28     msgText = msgText + "<A HREF='http://www.prima-tech.com/'>http://www.prima-tech.com/</A><BR>";
29     msgText = msgText + "An image:<BR>";
30     msgText = msgText + "<IMG SRC='http://netessentials.squirrel.com.au/sample.gif'";
31     msgText = msgText + "WIDTH='195' HEIGHT='101'>";
32     msgText = msgText + "</BODY></HTML>";
```

1. Use the import directive to include the required JavaMail API and JAF classes.

2. Use the try-catch exception-handling mechanism to deal with any unexpected conditions that might occur.

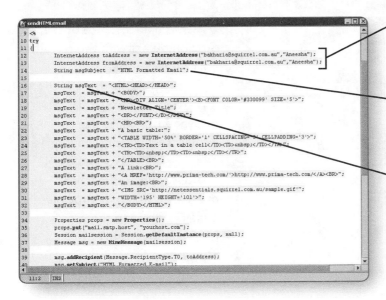

3. Create an InternetAddress object to store the To and From e-mail addresses.

4. Declare a variable as a string and use it to store the subject of the e-mail message.

5. Declare a variable as a string and use it to store the HTML-formatted e-mail message.

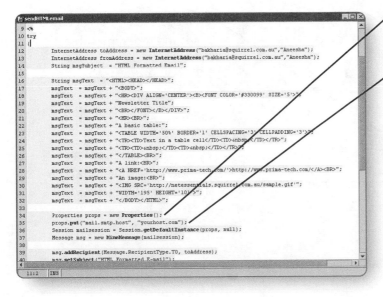

6. Create an instance of the Properties object.

7. Use the put method to specify the mail protocol and the host name of the server. E-mail is sent over SMTP, so the first parameter passed to the put method must be mail.smtp.host.

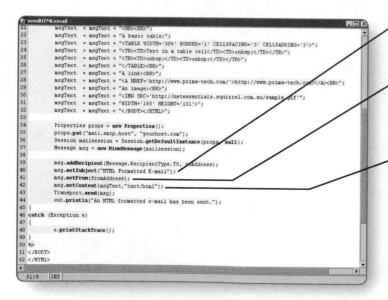

```
21      msgText = msgText + "<HR><BR>";
22      msgText = msgText + "A basic table:";
23      msgText = msgText + "<TABLE WIDTH='50%' BORDER='1' CELLSPACING='3' CELLPADDING='3'>";
24      msgText = msgText + "<TR><TD>Text in a table cell</TD><TD> </TD></TR>";
25      msgText = msgText + "<TR><TD> </TD><TD> </TD></TR>";
26      msgText = msgText + "</TABLE><BR>";
27      msgText = msgText + "A link:<BR>";
28      msgText = msgText + "<A HREF='http://www.prima-tech.com/'>http://www.prima-tech.com/</A><BR>";
29      msgText = msgText + "An image:<BR>";
30      msgText = msgText + "<IMG SRC='http://netessentials.squirrel.com.au/sample.gif'";
31      msgText = msgText + "WIDTH='195' HEIGHT='101'>";
32      msgText = msgText + "</BODY></HTML>";
33
34      Properties props = new Properties();
35      props.put("mail.smtp.host", "yourhost.com");
36      Session mailsession = Session.getDefaultInstance(props, null);
37      Message msg = new MimeMessage(mailsession);
38
39      msg.addRecipient(Message.RecipientType.TO, toAddress);
40      msg.setSubject("HTML Formatted E-mail");
41      msg.setFrom(fromAddress);
42      msg.setContent(msgText,"text/html");
43      Transport.send(msg);
44      out.println("An HTML formatted e-mail has been sent.");
45 }
46 catch (Exception e)
47 {
48      e.printStackTrace();
49 }
50 %>
51 </BODY>
52 </HTML>
```

8. Create an instance of the Session object with the current mail server properties.

9. Create a new e-mail message by calling the MimeMessage constructor.

10. Use the addRecipient method to assign the recipient's e-mail address to the Message.RecipientType.TO property.

11. Use the setSubject method to set the message subject.

12. Use the setFrom method to set the sender's e-mail address.

13. Use the setContent method to set the MIME type of the message to text/html.

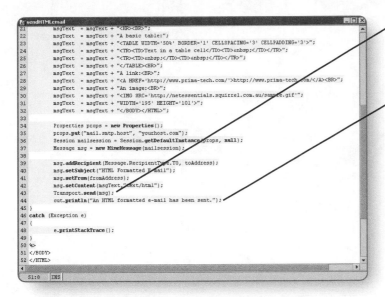

```
21       msgText = msgText + "<HR><BR>";
22       msgText = msgText + "A basic table:";
23       msgText = msgText + "<TABLE WIDTH='50%' BORDER='1' CELLSPACING='3' CELLPADDING='3'>";
24       msgText = msgText + "<TR><TD>Text in a table cell</TD><TD> </TD></TR>";
25       msgText = msgText + "<TR><TD> </TD><TD> </TD></TR>";
26       msgText = msgText + "</TABLE><BR>";
27       msgText = msgText + "A link:<BR>";
28       msgText = msgText + "<A HREF='http://www.prima-tech.com/'>http://www.prima-tech.com/</A><BR>";
29       msgText = msgText + "An image:<BR>";
30       msgText = msgText + "<IMG SRC='http://netessentials.squirrel.com.au/sample.gif'";
31       msgText = msgText + "WIDTH='195' HEIGHT='101'>";
32       msgText = msgText + "</BODY></HTML>";
33
34       Properties props = new Properties();
35       props.put("mail.smtp.host", "yourhost.com");
36       Session mailsession = Session.getDefaultInstance(props, null);
37       Message msg = new MimeMessage(mailsession);
38
39       msg.addRecipient(Message.RecipientType.TO, toAddress);
40       msg.setSubject("HTML Formatted E-mail");
41       msg.setFrom(fromAddress);
42       msg.setContent(msgText,"text/html");
43       Transport.send(msg);
44       out.println("An HTML formatted e-mail has been sent.");
45 }
46 catch (Exception e)
47 {
48       e.printStackTrace();
49 }
50 %>
51 </BODY>
52 </HTML>
```

14. Send the message by calling the Transport.send method.

15. Print an appropriate message to the JSP page to acknowledge that the e-mail message has been sent.

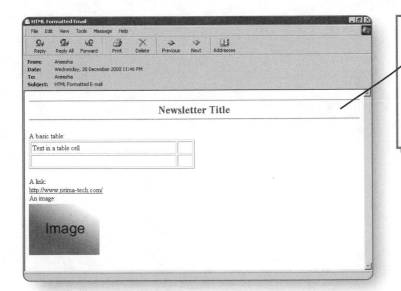

NOTE

This is what the message will look like when viewed in an e-mail client such as Microsoft Outlook Express.

12

Working with Files and Folders

The java.io package contains an assortment of methods for the manipulation of files and directories. You can display file and directory properties, as well as retrieve and store data in a file. Storing data in a file is sometimes a viable alternative to using a database, particularly if you only have a small amount of data that will not be searched or edited regularly. In this chapter, you'll learn how to:

- Display file attributes
- List all files in a directory
- Read a file
- Write to a file
- Append data to a file
- Create a guestbook for your Web site

Displaying File Attributes

The File class is used to create objects that represent files and directories. It contains a comprehensive set of methods for manipulating and inspecting file attributes. In particular, the File class contains methods to determine whether a file exists, is readable, is hidden, or can be written to. You can also create new files and rename and delete existing ones. Table 12.1 lists the methods and properties in the File class.

Table 12.1 Methods and Properties in the File Class

Method	Purpose
String getName()	Returns the name of a file
String getAbsolutePath()	Returns the drive and directory path in which the file is located
boolean isFile()	Returns true if the file is not a directory
boolean isDirectory()	Returns true if the file is a directory
boolean canRead()	Returns true if the file is readable
boolean canWrite()	Returns true if data can be written to the file
boolean isHidden()	Returns true if the file is hidden
boolean exists()	Returns true if the file exists
String lastModified()	Returns the date of the last file edit
Long length()	Returns the size of a file in bytes
boolean createNewFile()	Creates an empty, new file if the specified file does not exist
boolean setReadOnly()	Changes the attributes of a file so that it can't be written to
boolean delete()	Deletes a specified file or directory
boolean mkdir()	Creates a new directory
boolean rename()	Changes the name of an existing file

This example determines whether a file exists before displaying its properties on a Web page.

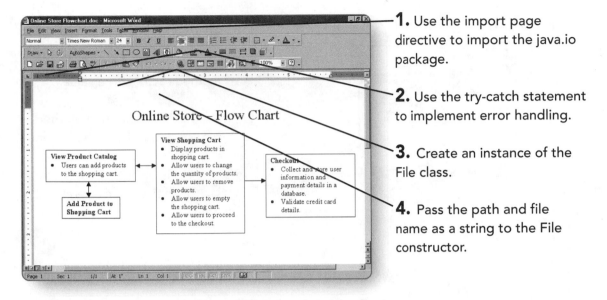

1. Use the import page directive to import the java.io package.

2. Use the try-catch statement to implement error handling.

3. Create an instance of the File class.

4. Pass the path and file name as a string to the File constructor.

NOTE

The "/" symbol is used as a path separator on a Unix system. The "\" symbol is used as the path separator on a Windows system. The Windows path separator is also the escape character in Java. You must, therefore, include the escape symbol(\) before the Windows path separator symbol (\) when specifying the path.

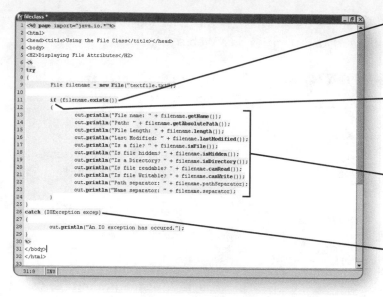

```
1  <%@ page import="java.io.*"%>
2  <html>
3  <head><title>Using the File Class</title></head>
4  <body>
5  <H2>Displaying File Attributes</H2>
6  <%
7  try
8  {
9         File filename = new File("textfile.txt");
10
11        if (filename.exists())
12        {
13               out.println("File name: " + filename.getName());
14               out.println("Path: " + filename.getAbsolutePath());
15               out.println("File Length: " + filename.length());
16               out.println("Last Modified: " + filename.lastModified());
17               out.println("Is a file? " + filename.isFile());
18               out.println("Is file hidden? " + filename.isHidden());
19               out.println("Is a Directory? " + filename.isDirectory());
20               out.println("Is file readable? " + filename.canRead());
21               out.println("Is file Writable? " + filename.canWrite());
22               out.println("Path separator: " + filename.pathSeparator);
23               out.println("Name separator: " + filename.separator);
24        }
25 )
26 catch (IOException excep)
27 {
28        out.println("An IO exception has occured.");
29 }
30 %>
31 </body>
32 </html>
33
```

5. Use the exists method to check whether the specified file exists.

6. Use an if statement to list the file properties, should the exists method return a true value.

7. Use the out.println method to display the file attributes on the Web page.

8. Catch the IOException and print a suitable error message.

Listing the Contents of a Directory

The list method of the File class returns a string array of all the files and subdirectories within a specified directory. Displaying a list of files in a directory dynamically is handy when the content of the directory constantly changes. This allows you to provide links for users to either view or download files.

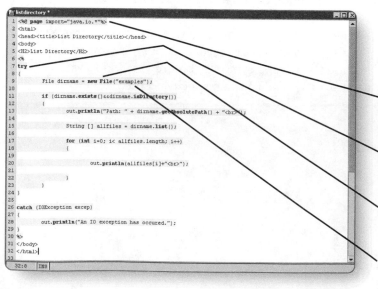

```
1  <%@ page import="java.io.*"%>
2  <html>
3  <head><title>List Directory</title></head>
4  <body>
5  <H2>List Directory</H2>
6  <%
7  try
8  {
9         File dirname = new File("examples");
10
11        if (dirname.exists()&&dirname.isDirectory())
12        {
13               out.println("Path: " + dirname.getAbsolutePath() + "<br>");
14
15               String [] allfiles = dirname.list();
16
17               for (int i=0; i< allfiles.length; i++)
18               {
19
20                      out.println(allfiles[i]+"<br>");
21
22               }
23        }
24 }
25
26 catch (IOException excep)
27 {
28        out.println("An IO exception has occured.");
29 }
30 %>
31 </body>
32 </html>
33
```

1. Use the import page directive to import the java.io package.

2. Use the try-catch statement to implement error handling.

3. Create an instance of the File class.

4. Pass the directory as a string to the File constructor.

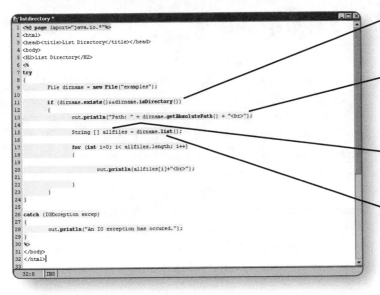

5. Test whether the directory actually exists and is not a file.

6. Print the full directory path by calling the getAbsolutePath method. This step is optional.

7. Declare an array to store the list of files in a directory.

8. Call the list method and assign the result to the array.

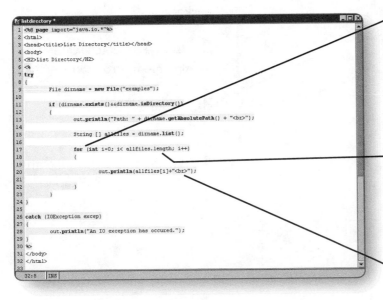

9. Use a for loop to iterate through the array and print the file name of each element in the array.

NOTE

The length property is used to determine the number of files in the directory.

---

10. Use the println method to display, on the Web page, the file name stored at the current array index.

Reading a File

The File class does not include any methods for reading from or writing to a file. You must first create a file input stream before data can be retrieved from a file. You need to create an instance of the FileReader class and pass the object to the BufferedReader constructor. The BufferedReader class contains the readLine method, which allows data to be read one line at a time from a file.

Implementing error handling is necessary because both the FileReader and BufferedReader constructor might throw File Not Found or I/O exceptions. In the following example, a text file is opened and read, and the data is displayed one line at a time.

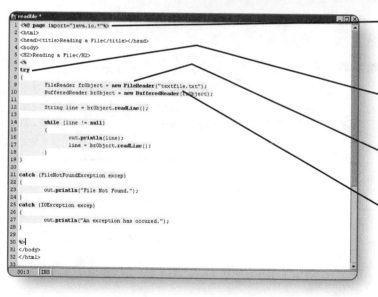

1. Use the import page directive to import the java.io package.

2. Use the try-catch statement to implement error handling.

3. Create an instance of the FileReader class.

4. Pass the file name and path as a string to the FileReader constructor.

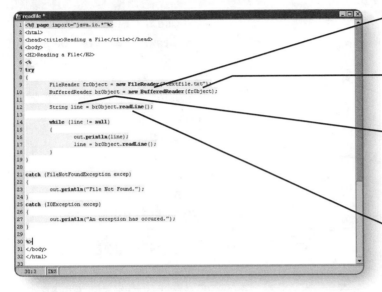

```
readfile *                                                          _ □ x
1  <%@ page import="java.io.*"%>
2  <html>
3  <head><title>Reading a File</title></head>
4  <body>
5  <H2>Reading a File</H2>
6  <%
7  try
8  {
9        FileReader frObject = new FileReader("textfile.txt");
10       BufferedReader brObject = new BufferedReader(frObject);
11
12       String line = brObject.readLine();
13
14       while (line != null)
15       {
16             out.println(line);
17             line = brObject.readLine();
18       }
19 }
20
21 catch (FileNotFoundException excep)
22 {
23       out.println("File Not Found.");
24 }
25 catch (IOException excep)
26 {
27       out.println("An exception has occured.");
28 }
29
30 %>
31 </body>
32 </html>
33
   30:3    INS
```

5. Create an instance of the BufferedReader class.

6. Pass the FileReader object to the BufferedReader contructor.

7. Declare a string variable. This variable will be used to store a line of text that is retrieved from a file.

8. Call the readLine method to retrieve the first line of text from the file and store the result in a variable.

```
readfile *                                                          _ □ x
1  <%@ page import="java.io.*"%>
2  <html>
3  <head><title>Reading a File</title></head>
4  <body>
5  <H2>Reading a File</H2>
6  <%
7  try
8  {
9        FileReader frObject = new FileReader("textfile.txt");
10       BufferedReader brObject = new BufferedReader(frObject);
11
12       String line = brObject.readLine();
13
14       while (line != null)
15       {
16             out.println(line);
17             line = brObject.readLine();
18       }
19 }
20
21 catch (FileNotFoundException excep)
22 {
23       out.println("File Not Found.");
24 }
25 catch (IOException excep)
26 {
27       out.println("An exception has occured.");
28 }
29
30 %>
31 </body>
32 </html>
33
   30:3    INS
```

9. Use a while loop to repeatedly retrieve a line of text from the file until the end of file is reached.

NOTE

The variable will be NULL when the end of the file is reached. Steps 10 and 11 will be executed only if the end of the file is not reached.

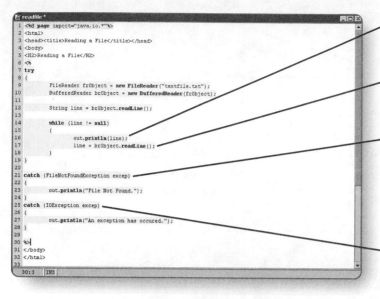

10. Use the println method to output text to the Web page.

11. Call the readLine method to retrieve the next line of text.

12. Catch the FileNotFoundException, which might be thrown if the file does not exist. Then, print an appropriate error message.

13. Catch the IOException, which might be thrown if the file is not readable or can't be opened.

Writing a File

You must create a file output stream before you can write data to a file. You must also create an instance of the PrintWriter class. This will allow you to use the print and println methods to output data one line at a time to a file.

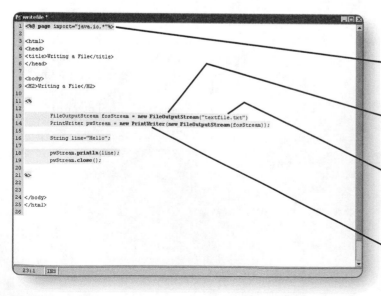

1. Use the import page directive to import the java.io package.

2. Create an instance of the FileOutputStream class.

3. Pass the file name and path to the FileOutputStream constructor.

4. Create an instance of the PrintWriter class.

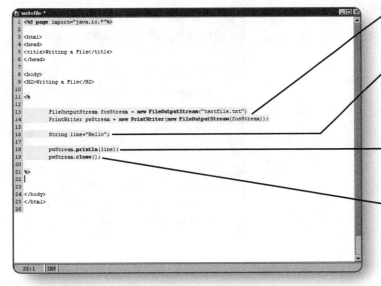

5. Pass the stream object to the PrintWriter constructor.

6. Declare a string variable to store the text to be written to the output file.

7. Use the println method to save the text to the output file.

8. Call the close method. This will close the output stream.

NOTE

The PrintWriter constructor does not throw any exceptions, so there is no need to use a try-catch statement.

Appending Data to a File

The RandomAccessFile class allows you to insert or retrieve data anywhere within a file. This provides you with greater flexibility. The RandomAccessFile class has a pointer that can be moved to any location in the file. This example uses the RandomAccessFile class to append data to a file.

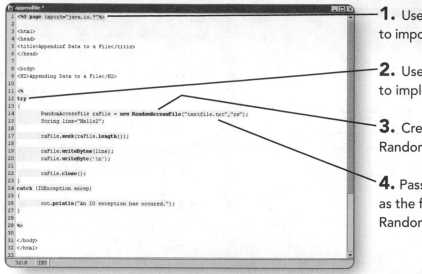

1. Use the import page directive to import the java.io package.

2. Use the try-catch statement to implement error handling.

3. Create an instance of the RandomAccessFile class.

4. Pass the file name and path as the first parameter to the RandomAccessFile constructor.

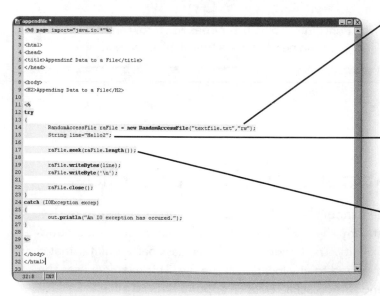

5. Pass rw as the second parameter to the RandomAccessFile constructor. This will open the file in read/write mode.

6. Store the data to be appended to the file in a string variable.

7. Use the seek method to find the end of the file and reposition the file pointer. The length method is used to determine the end of the file.

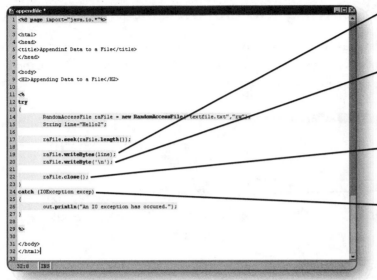

```
1 <%@ page import="java.io.*"%>
2
3 <html>
4 <head>
5 <title>Appendinf Data to a File</title>
6 </head>
7
8 <body>
9 <H2>Appending Data to a File</H2>
10
11 <%
12 try
13 {
14        RandomAccessFile raFile = new RandomAccessFile("textfile.txt","rw");
15        String line="Hello2";
16
17        raFile.seek(raFile.length());
18
19        raFile.writeBytes(line);
20        raFile.writeByte('\n');
21
22        raFile.close();
23 }
24 catch (IOException excep)
25 {
26        out.println("An IO exception has occured.");
27 }
28
29 %>
30
31 </body>
32 </html>
33
```

8. Use the writeBytes method to append the data to the file.

9. Use the writeByte method to insert a new line character after the data.

10. Call the close method. This will close the file.

11. Catch the IOException, which might be thrown if the file can't be opened.

Creating a Guestbook

A guestbook is a simple Web application that relies on storing and retrieving information in a file. A guestbook allows Web site visitors to make comments and suggestions about your Web site. The guestbook requires the following functionality:

- The ability to retrieve previous Guestbook entries from a text file (Guestbook.jsp)

- A form on which the user can enter comments (Guestbook.jsp)

- The ability to retrieve the comments entered by a user, add HTML formatting, and append the data to a text file (AddToGuestBook.jsp)

Displaying the Guestbook

The Guestbook.jsp Web page will display all of the guestbook entries stored in a text file and will include a form for the user to add new entries.

```
 1  <html>
 2  <head>
 3  <title>Displaying the Guestbook</title>
 4  <meta http-equiv="Content-Type" content="text/html; charset=iso-8859-1">
 5  </head>
 6
 7  <body bgcolor="#FFFFFF">
 8
 9  <H2>Guestbook</H1>
10
11  <jsp:include page="Guestbook.txt" flush="true"/>
12
13  <form method="post" action="AddToGuestbook.jsp" name="GuestBook">
14
15     <p>Add an Entry</p>
16     <p>
17        Name: <input type="text" name="Name"><br>
18        E-mail: <input type="text" name="Email"><br>
19        Comments: <br>
20        <textarea name="Entry" cols="80" rows="6" wrap="VIRTUAL"></textarea>
21     </p>
22     <p>
23        <input type="submit" name="Submit" value="Submit">
24     </p>
25  </form>
26  </body>
27  </html>
28
```

1. Create the Guestbook Web page. The page must have a .jsp extension.

2. Use the include tag to insert the text file that stores the guestbook entries.

NOTE

There is no need to read the text file line by line unless you want to process the data (for example, to remove unwanted phrases). In this case, the data is merely inserted into a Web page, so the include tag offers the simplest solution.

```
 1  <html>
 2  <head>
 3  <title>Displaying the Guestbook</title>
 4  <meta http-equiv="Content-Type" content="text/html; charset=iso-8859-1">
 5  </head>
 6
 7  <body bgcolor="#FFFFFF">
 8
 9  <H2>Guestbook</H1>
10
11  <jsp:include page="Guestbook.txt" flush="true"/>
12
13  <form method="post" action="AddToGuestbook.jsp" name="GuestBook">
14
15     <p>Add an Entry</p>
16     <p>
17        Name: <input type="text" name="Name"><br>
18        E-mail: <input type="text" name="Email"><br>
19        Comments: <br>
20        <textarea name="Entry" cols="80" rows="6" wrap="VIRTUAL"></textarea>
21     </p>
22     <p>
23        <input type="submit" name="Submit" value="Submit">
24     </p>
25  </form>
26  </body>
27  </html>
28
```

3. Use the <form> tag to create a form.

4. Set the action attribute of the form to the AddToGuestbook.jsp page. This JSP page will process the form data.

5. Insert a text input field for the user to enter his name.

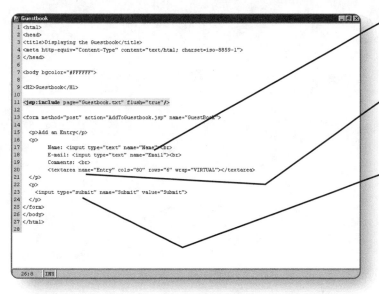

6. Insert a text input field for the user to enter an e-mail address.

7. Insert a multi-line text entry field (in other words, a textarea) for the user to enter comments.

8. Use a submit button to send the data to the server.

Appending the Guestbook Entry to a File

The AddToGuestbook.jsp page retrieves the data entered by the user, applies HTML formatting, and appends the entry to the Guestbook.txt file.

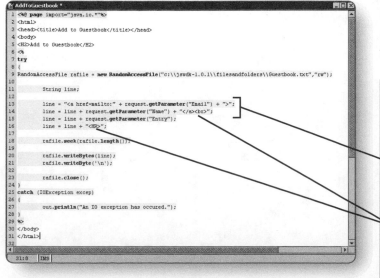

Use the JSP code that you developed earlier in the chapter to append data to a file.

NOTE

The following changes have been made:

- The data appended to the file is retrieved from the posted form.

- HTML formatting is included before the data is appended to the file.

13

Creating Interactive Web Pages

A successful Web site provides the user with an interesting, intuitive, and interactive experience. JSP provides all the tools you need to personalize your Web site. The best way to keep visitors returning is to offer compelling and up-to-date content. This chapter presents simple JSP techniques that produce dynamic content. In this chapter, you'll learn how to:

- Greet your visitors
- Display random content
- Use the include directive
- Redirect visitors
- Generate Microsoft Word and Excel documents
- Create dynamic images

Greeting Your Visitors

Many Web sites display a friendly greeting when a user visits a site. Using the techniques you learned in Chapter 4, "Performing Calculations," you can determine the current time and display an appropriate greeting.

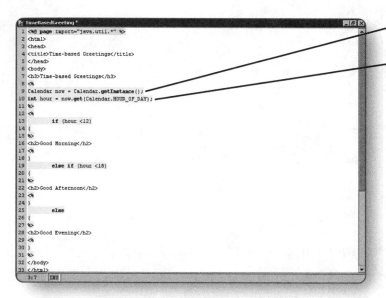

1. Create a Calendar object.

2. Use the get method to retrieve the current hour. The hour will be returned in 24-hour time.

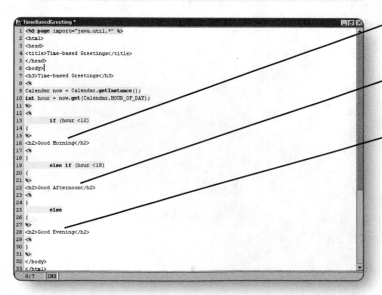

3. If the current hour is <12, display "Good Morning."

4. If the current hour is <18, display "Good Afternoon."

5. If the current hour is >18, display "Good Evening."

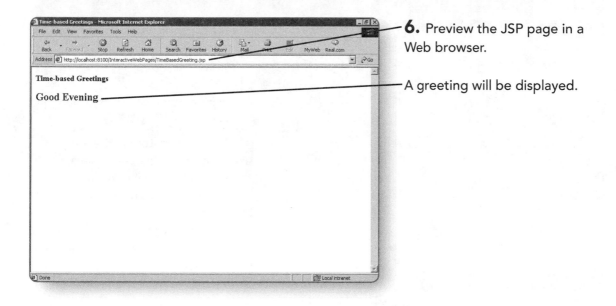

6. Preview the JSP page in a Web browser.

A greeting will be displayed.

Displaying Random Text

There is no need to display the same content each time a page is requested. You can store an array of tips, news-related items, or messages, and then make a random selection. You might have noticed that many Web sites already have a tip of the day archive. These steps show you how you can create something similar.

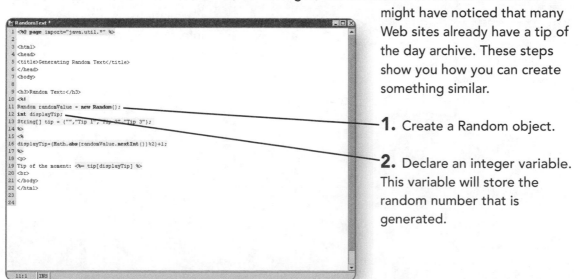

1. Create a Random object.

2. Declare an integer variable. This variable will store the random number that is generated.

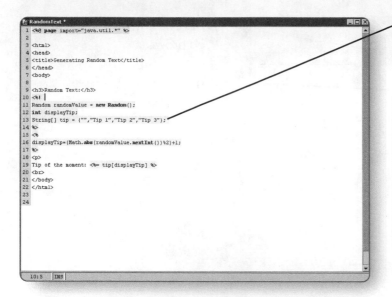

3. Declare and initialize an array with tips, news-related items, or messages.

NOTE

The first item in the array must be left blank because a random number that equals zero (the first item index of the array) will not be generated.

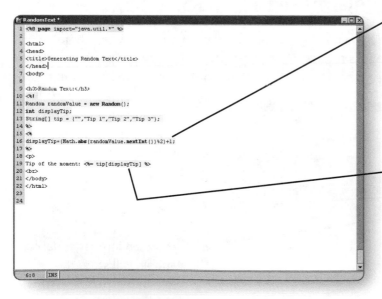

4. Generate a random number between 1 and 3 (because only three items exist in the array). Refer to Chapter 4, "Performing Calculations," for more information on generating random numbers.

5. Use the Expression tag to display the randomly selected text.

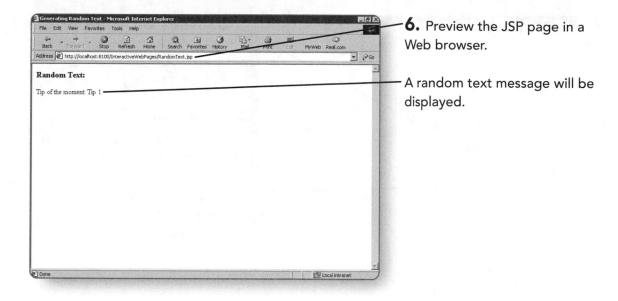

6. Preview the JSP page in a Web browser.

A random text message will be displayed.

Generating Random Images

If you want to use many images but your Web site design allows you to display only one, why not consider displaying a randomly selected image each time the page is requested? This will certainly add an element of unpredictability to your Web site, and will keep visitors returning.

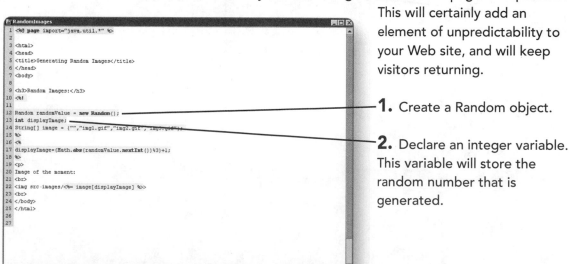

1. Create a Random object.

2. Declare an integer variable. This variable will store the random number that is generated.

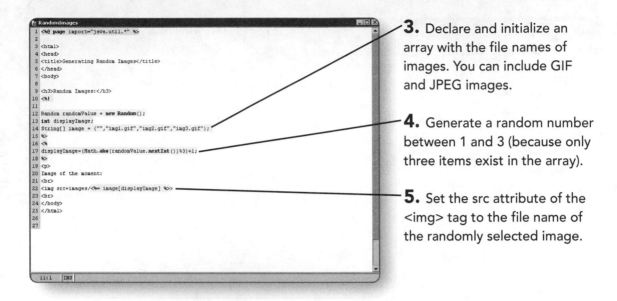

3. Declare and initialize an array with the file names of images. You can include GIF and JPEG images.

4. Generate a random number between 1 and 3 (because only three items exist in the array).

5. Set the src attribute of the <img> tag to the file name of the randomly selected image.

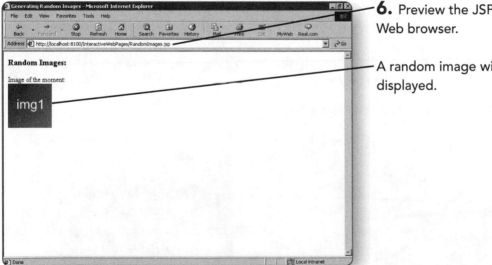

6. Preview the JSP page in a Web browser.

A random image will be displayed.

Using the Include Directive

Pages in your Web site will all have common elements such as the page header and footer. You could manually insert the HTML code for these elements in every page, but that is not practical. You need to store the common HTML elements in separate files so they can easily be updated in a central location. You can then use the include directive to insert the common elements in multiple JSP pages.

First, you should create an include file. Here is an example of a page header used as an include file.

```
Header                                          _ □ X
1  <HR>
2  <center>
3  <H1>HEADER</H1>
4  </center>
5  <HR>
6

1:1   INS
```

NOTE

The include file must only contain the HTML code for the common element. The include file can't contain any opening and closing <HTML>, <HEAD>, or <BODY> tags.

```
UsingIncludes                                   _ □ X
1  <html>
2  <head>
3  <title>Including Files</title>
4  </head>
5  <body>
6
7  <h3>Including Files</h3>
8  <%@ include file="Header.htm" %>
9  <p>
10 Document Text goes here.
11 <p>
12 <%@ include file="Footer.htm" %>
13 </body>
14 </html>
15
16
17

17:1   INS
```

The include directive can now be used to import the contents of an include file.

1. Insert the include directive.

2. Specify the name of the file that contains the common HTML element.

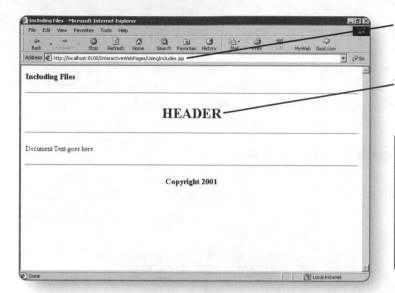

3. Preview the JSP page in a browser.

The header will be inserted into the page.

> **TIP**
>
> JSP code can also be inserted into an include file. You can then utilize methods and variables across multiple JSP pages.

Forwarding Requests

The structure of your Web site will change as new content is addressed. Both the folder structure and the names of individual pages will change. The problem is that users like to bookmark pages that they regularly visit. To prevent a File Not Found error from being displayed, you should remove the content stored in the file and insert a JSP forward action tag. When a user requests an out-of-date page, they will automatically be redirected to the new page.

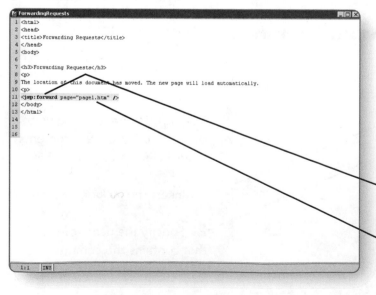

1. Insert the forward JSP action tag.

2. Specify the path of the page to which the users must be forwarded.

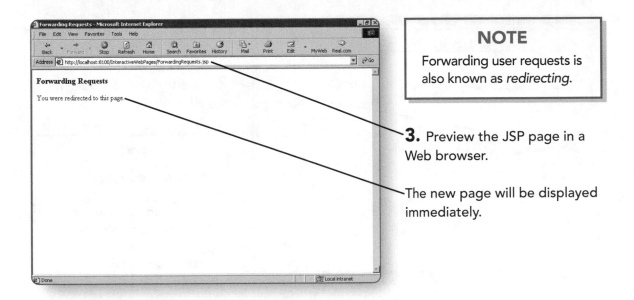

NOTE

Forwarding user requests is also known as *redirecting*.

3. Preview the JSP page in a Web browser.

The new page will be displayed immediately.

Generating Microsoft Word Documents

HTML is used to format text and images so that they can be displayed in a Web browser. There will be times, however, when you will need to generate content that can easily be edited by Web site visitors. It is unlikely that they'll know HTML, but they might be comfortable using Microsoft Word. By changing the content type of an HTML-formatted page to application/msword, you can trick the browser into thinking that the Web page is, in fact, a Word document. The user can then view and edit the document in Microsoft Word.

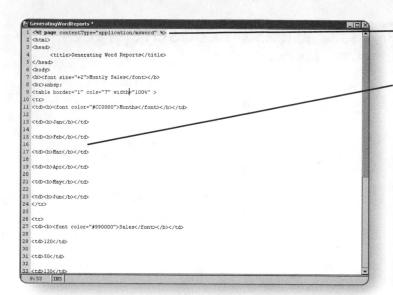

1. Set the content type of the JSP page to "application/msword".

2. Insert the HTML code after the page directive.

NOTE

Word will recognize HTML fonts and tables. You can specify the font, font size, and color. You can also use tables to display tabular data.

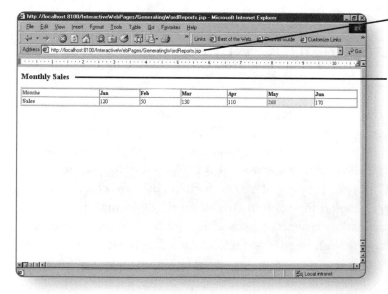

3. Preview the JSP page in a Web browser.

Internet Explorer will load Word in the browser window and display the document. Netscape, however, will ask users whether they want to open or save the Word document.

Generating Microsoft Excel Spreadsheets

Excel spreadsheets can also be generated using the same technique outlined in the previous section. The content type needs to be set to "application/vnd.ms-excel" for the browser to identify the file as a Microsoft Excel spreadsheet.

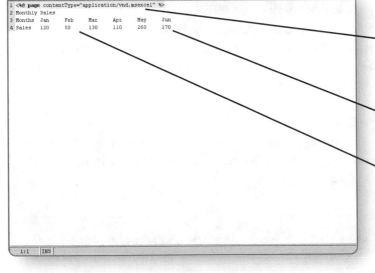

1. Set the content type of the JSP page to "application/vnd.ms-excel".

2. Use a separate line for each row of data.

3. Separate individual columns with a tab.

4. Preview the JSP page in a Web browser.

Internet Explorer will load Excel in the browser window and display the document. Netscape will ask users whether they want to open or save the spreadsheet.

Creating Dynamic Images

Thus far, you have only displayed images that were created using image manipulation and editing software such as Adobe Photoshop, Macromedia Fireworks, and JASC Paint Shop Pro. These were static images that you embedded in your Web site. Generating custom images not only makes your site more interesting, but it also allows you to express dynamic information in a visual manner. With the aid of JSP, you can graph data, manipulate images, and generate custom maps. You can even blur, emboss, and fade existing images. Generating graphics in JSP is made possible by the Graphics class.

The Graphics class implements numerous methods for drawing lines, ovals, and rectangles, and even rendering text as an image. Table 13.1 lists the essential methods found in the Graphics class.

Table 13.1 Common Methods in the Graphics Class	
To	**Use**
Draw a line	drawLine(int startx, int starty, int endx, int endy)
Draw a rectangle	drawRect(int startx, int starty, int width, int height)
Draw a filled rectangle	fillRect(int startx, int starty, int width, int height)
Draw an oval	drawOval(int startx, int starty, int width, int height)
Draw a filled oval	fillOval(int startx, int starty, int width, int height)
Insert text	drawString(String string, int startx, int starty)

Java uses a different coordinate system. You just need to remember that:

- The origin (0,0) of the drawing area begins in the upper-left corner.
- The positive x-axis extends to the right.
- The positive y-axis extends downward.

You can also select the color that is used when drawing shapes in an image. The Color class includes constants that define popular colors. You can use these or define your own colors using the Color constructor. You need to pass to the Color constructor the red, green, and blue color intensities that comprise the color, for example: Color newColor = new Color(150, 40, 76). Here are some common color constants.

- Color.black
- Color.gray
- Color.red
- Color.pink
- Color.blue
- Color.green
- Color.white
- Color.yellow
- Color.orange

Drawing a Line

Before generating an image using JSP, you need to change the content type to image/jpeg and reset the output stream. Use the BufferedImage class to create an image that is stored in memory. You can draw shapes and render text to the image stored in memory and then, when you are done, use the JPEGImageEncoder class to convert the image to the JPEG format and send it the browser. In this example, only JPEG images will be created because all browers support them and the JPEGImageEncoder is already installed on your computer. You can also download other image encoders.

The drawLine method is used to draw a line. You need to specify the x and y coordinates at the start and end of the line.

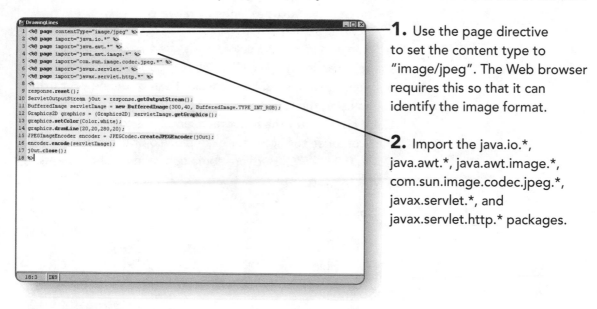

1. Use the page directive to set the content type to "image/jpeg". The Web browser requires this so that it can identify the image format.

2. Import the java.io.*, java.awt.*, java.awt.image.*, com.sun.image.codec.jpeg.*, javax.servlet.*, and javax.servlet.http.* packages.

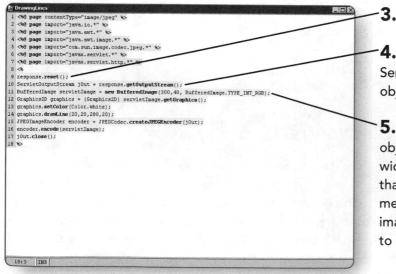

3. Reset the response object.

4. Create a ServletOutputStream object.

5. Create a BufferedImage object. You need to specify the width, height, and type of image that you will be storing in memory. You must set the image type to TYPE_INT_RGB to create an RGB image.

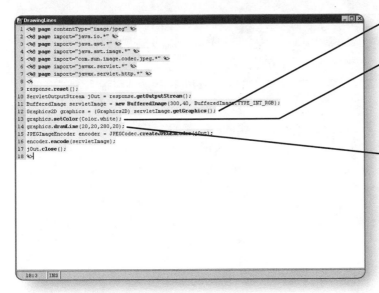

```
DrawingLines
1  <%@ page contentType="image/jpeg" %>
2  <%@ page import="java.io.*" %>
3  <%@ page import="java.awt.*" %>
4  <%@ page import="java.awt.image.*" %>
5  <%@ page import="com.sun.image.codec.jpeg.*" %>
6  <%@ page import="javax.servlet.*" %>
7  <%@ page import="javax.servlet.http.*" %>
8  <%
9  response.reset();
10 ServletOutputStream jOut = response.getOutputStream();
11 BufferedImage servletImage = new BufferedImage(300,40, BufferedImage.TYPE_INT_RGB);
12 Graphics2D graphics = (Graphics2D) servletImage.getGraphics();
13 graphics.setColor(Color.white);
14 graphics.drawLine(20,20,280,20);
15 JPEGImageEncoder encoder = JPEGCodec.createJPEGEncoder(jOut);
16 encoder.encode(servletImage);
17 jOut.close();
18 %>

18:3   INS
```

6. Create a Graphics2D object.

7. Use the setColor method to change the color. You will need to pass a color constant to the setColor method.

8. Use the drawLine method to draw a line from the start to the end coordinates that you supply.

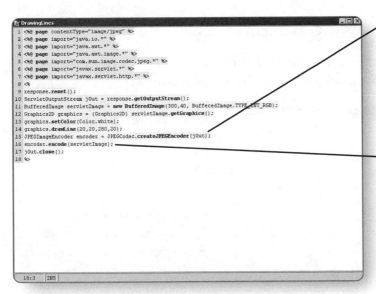

```
DrawingLines
1  <%@ page contentType="image/jpeg" %>
2  <%@ page import="java.io.*" %>
3  <%@ page import="java.awt.*" %>
4  <%@ page import="java.awt.image.*" %>
5  <%@ page import="com.sun.image.codec.jpeg.*" %>
6  <%@ page import="javax.servlet.*" %>
7  <%@ page import="javax.servlet.http.*" %>
8  <%
9  response.reset();
10 ServletOutputStream jOut = response.getOutputStream();
11 BufferedImage servletImage = new BufferedImage(300,40, BufferedImage.TYPE_INT_RGB);
12 Graphics2D graphics = (Graphics2D) servletImage.getGraphics();
13 graphics.setColor(Color.white);
14 graphics.drawLine(20,20,280,20);
15 JPEGImageEncoder encoder = JPEGCodec.createJPEGEncoder(jOut);
16 encoder.encode(servletImage);
17 jOut.close();
18 %>

18:3   INS
```

9. Create an image encoder to convert the image stored in memory into JPEG format and to send the image to the browser using the servlet's output stream.

10. Convert the image stored in memory into a JPEG image.

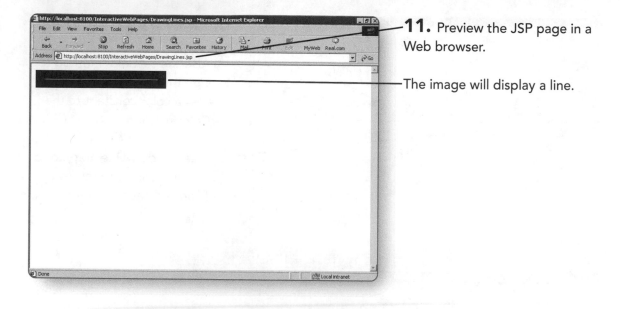

11. Preview the JSP page in a Web browser.

The image will display a line.

Drawing Rectangles

The drawRect method draws the outline of a rectangle. You must specify the origin, width, and height of the rectangle. If the width and height are equal, you will draw a square on the image. You can also use the fillRect method to draw a filled rectangle.

1. Use the page directive to set the content type to "image/jpeg". The Web browser requires this so that it can identify the image format.

2. Import the java.io.*, java.awt.*, java.awt.image.*, com.sun.image.codec.jpeg.*, javax.servlet.*, and javax.servlet.http.* packages.

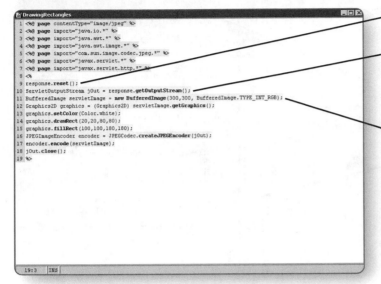

```
DrawingRectangles
 1  <%@ page contentType="image/jpeg" %>
 2  <%@ page import="java.io.*" %>
 3  <%@ page import="java.awt.*" %>
 4  <%@ page import="java.awt.image.*" %>
 5  <%@ page import="com.sun.image.codec.jpeg.*" %>
 6  <%@ page import="javax.servlet.*" %>
 7  <%@ page import="javax.servlet.http.*" %>
 8  <%
 9  response.reset();
10  ServletOutputStream jOut = response.getOutputStream();
11  BufferedImage servletImage = new BufferedImage(300,300, BufferedImage.TYPE_INT_RGB);
12  Graphics2D graphics = (Graphics2D) servletImage.getGraphics();
13  graphics.setColor(Color.white);
14  graphics.drawRect(20,20,80,80);
15  graphics.fillRect(100,100,180,180);
16  JPEGImageEncoder encoder = JPEGCodec.createJPEGEncoder(jOut);
17  encoder.encode(servletImage);
18  jOut.close();
19  %>

19:3    INS
```

3. Reset the response object.

4. Create a ServletOutputStream object.

5. Create a BufferedImage object. You need to specify the width, height, and type of image that you will be storing in memory. You must set the image type to TYPE_INT_RGB to create an RGB image.

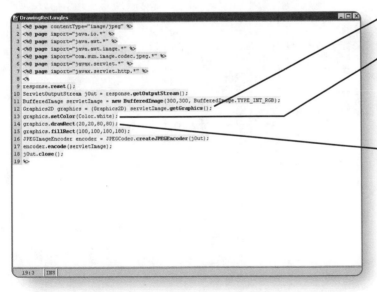

```
DrawingRectangles
 1  <%@ page contentType="image/jpeg" %>
 2  <%@ page import="java.io.*" %>
 3  <%@ page import="java.awt.*" %>
 4  <%@ page import="java.awt.image.*" %>
 5  <%@ page import="com.sun.image.codec.jpeg.*" %>
 6  <%@ page import="javax.servlet.*" %>
 7  <%@ page import="javax.servlet.http.*" %>
 8  <%
 9  response.reset();
10  ServletOutputStream jOut = response.getOutputStream();
11  BufferedImage servletImage = new BufferedImage(300,300, BufferedImage.TYPE_INT_RGB);
12  Graphics2D graphics = (Graphics2D) servletImage.getGraphics();
13  graphics.setColor(Color.white);
14  graphics.drawRect(20,20,80,80);
15  graphics.fillRect(100,100,180,180);
16  JPEGImageEncoder encoder = JPEGCodec.createJPEGEncoder(jOut);
17  encoder.encode(servletImage);
18  jOut.close();
19  %>

19:3    INS
```

6. Create a Graphics2D object.

7. Use the setColor method to change the color. You will need to pass a color constant to the setColor method.

8. Use the drawRect method to draw a rectangle.

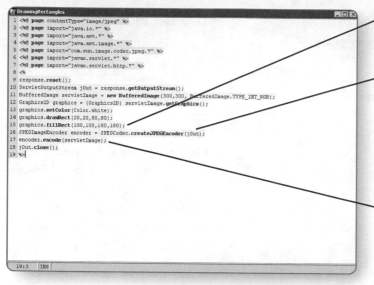

```
1 <%@ page contentType="image/jpeg" %>
2 <%@ page import="java.io.*" %>
3 <%@ page import="java.awt.*" %>
4 <%@ page import="java.awt.image.*" %>
5 <%@ page import="com.sun.image.codec.jpeg.*" %>
6 <%@ page import="javax.servlet.*" %>
7 <%@ page import="javax.servlet.http.*" %>
8 <%
9 response.reset();
10 ServletOutputStream jOut = response.getOutputStream();
11 BufferedImage servletImage = new BufferedImage(300,300, BufferedImage.TYPE_INT_RGB);
12 Graphics2D graphics = (Graphics2D) servletImage.getGraphics();
13 graphics.setColor(Color.white);
14 graphics.drawRect(20,20,80,80);
15 graphics.fillRect(100,100,180,180);
16 JPEGImageEncoder encoder = JPEGCodec.createJPEGEncoder(jOut);
17 encoder.encode(servletImage);
18 jOut.close();
19 %>
```

9. Use the fillRect method to draw a filled rectangle.

10. Create an image encoder to convert the image stored in memory into JPEG format and to send the image to the browser using the servlet's output stream.

11. Convert the image stored in memory into a JPEG image.

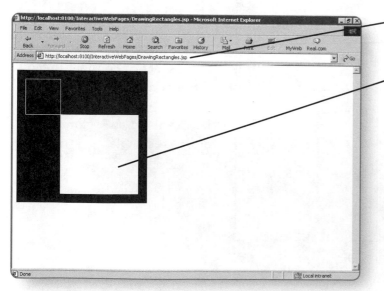

12. Preview the JSP page in a Web browser.

The image will display an outline of a rectangle and a filled rectangle.

Drawing Ovals

The drawOval method draws the outline of an oval. You can draw a circle using the drawOval method if the width and height are equal. The fillOval method simply draws a filled oval on the image.

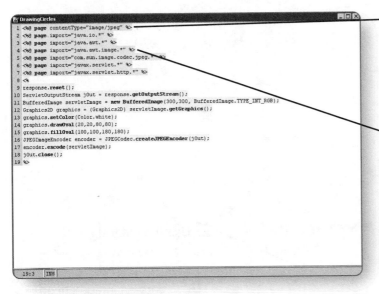

1. Use the page directive to set the content type to "image/jpeg". The Web browser requires this so that it can identify the image format.

2. Import the java.io.*, java.awt.*, java.awt.image.*, com.sun.image.codec.jpeg.*, javax.servlet.*, and javax.servlet.http.* packages.

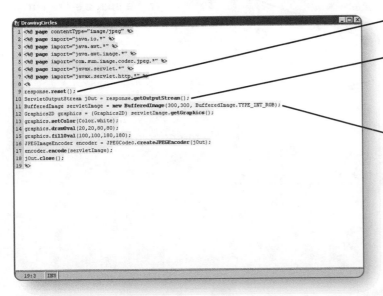

3. Reset the response object.

4. Create a ServletOutputStream object.

5. Create a BufferedImage object. You need to specify the width, height, and type of image that you will be storing in memory. You must set the image type to TYPE_INT_RGB to create an RGB image.

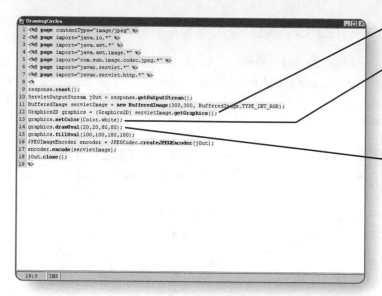

6. Create a Graphics2D object.

7. Use the setColor method to change the color. You will need to pass a color constant to the setColor method.

8. Use the drawOval method to draw an oval.

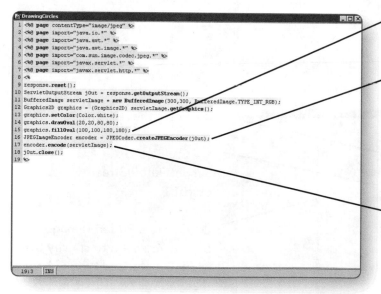

9. Use the fillOval method to draw a filled oval.

10. Create an image encoder to convert the image stored in memory into JPEG format and to send the image to the browser using the servlet's output stream.

11. Convert the image stored in memory into a JPEG image.

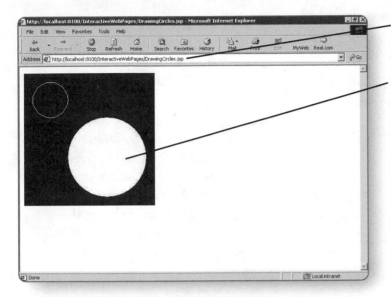

12. Preview the JSP page in a Web browser.

The image will display the outline of an oval and a filled oval.

Rendering Text

You can display text by using the drawString method of the Graphics class. You need to specify the position in the image where the text must be drawn. The text will be drawn using the default system font and size.

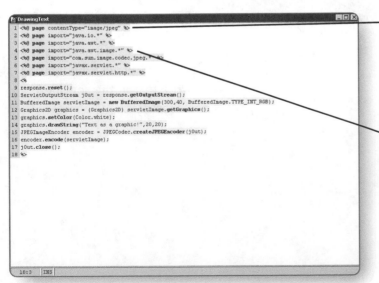

1. Use the page directive to set the content type to "image/jpeg". The Web browser requires this so that it can identify the image format.

2. Import the java.io.*, java.awt.*, java.awt.image.*, com.sun.image.codec.jpeg.*, javax.servlet.*, and javax.servlet.http.* packages.

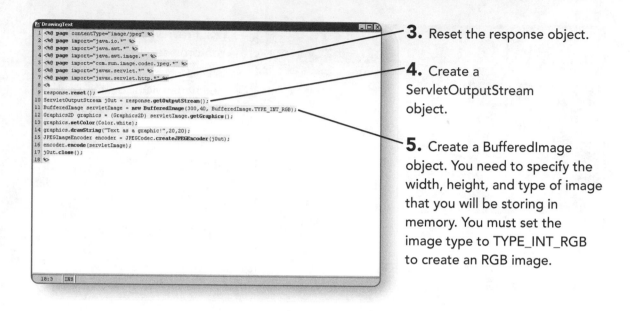

3. Reset the response object.

4. Create a ServletOutputStream object.

5. Create a BufferedImage object. You need to specify the width, height, and type of image that you will be storing in memory. You must set the image type to TYPE_INT_RGB to create an RGB image.

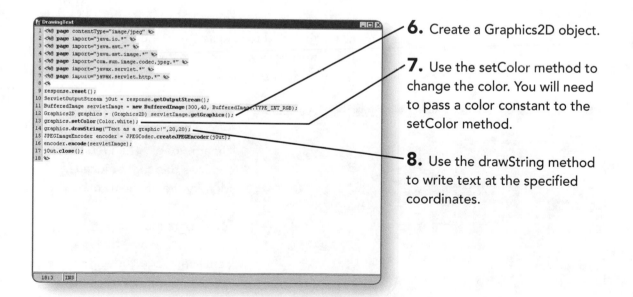

6. Create a Graphics2D object.

7. Use the setColor method to change the color. You will need to pass a color constant to the setColor method.

8. Use the drawString method to write text at the specified coordinates.

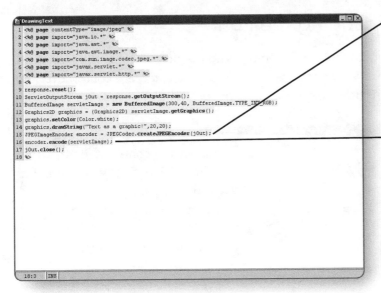

```
DrawingText
 1  <%@ page contentType="image/jpeg" %>
 2  <%@ page import="java.io.*" %>
 3  <%@ page import="java.awt.*" %>
 4  <%@ page import="java.awt.image.*" %>
 5  <%@ page import="com.sun.image.codec.jpeg.*" %>
 6  <%@ page import="javax.servlet.*" %>
 7  <%@ page import="javax.servlet.http.*" %>
 8  <%
 9  response.reset();
10  ServletOutputStream jOut = response.getOutputStream();
11  BufferedImage servletImage = new BufferedImage(300,40, BufferedImage.TYPE_INT_RGB);
12  Graphics2D graphics = (Graphics2D) servletImage.getGraphics();
13  graphics.setColor(Color.white);
14  graphics.drawString("Text as a graphic!",20,20);
15  JPEGImageEncoder encoder = JPEGCodec.createJPEGEncoder(jOut);
16  encoder.encode(servletImage);
17  jOut.close();
18  %>
```

9. Create an image encoder to convert the image stored in memory into JPEG format and to send the image to the browser using the servlet's output stream.

10. Convert the image stored in memory into a JPEG image.

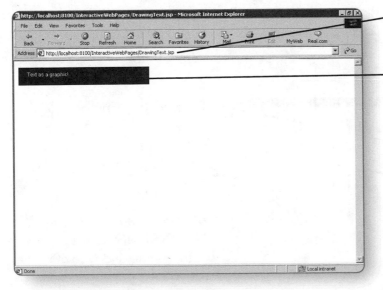

11. Preview the JSP page in a Web browser.

The image will display the text in the default font and size.

Changing the Font

You are not restricted to using the default font. The Font class has methods that allow you to have complete control over the font, font size, and font style (plain, bold, or italic).

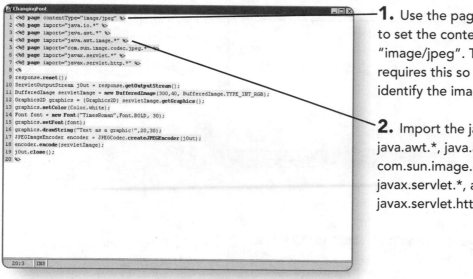

1. Use the page directive to set the content type to "image/jpeg". The Web browser requires this so that it can identify the image format.

2. Import the java.io.*, java.awt.*, java.awt.image.*, com.sun.image.codec.jpeg.*, javax.servlet.*, and javax.servlet.http.* packages.

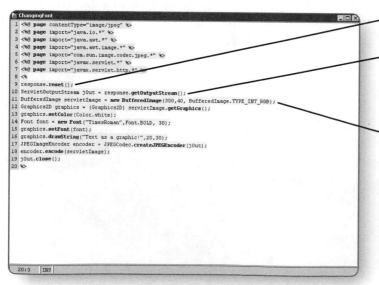

3. Reset the response object.

4. Create a ServletOutputStream object.

5. Create a BufferedImage object. You need to specify the width, height, and type of image that you will store in memory. You must set the image type to TYPE_INT_RGB to create an RGB image.

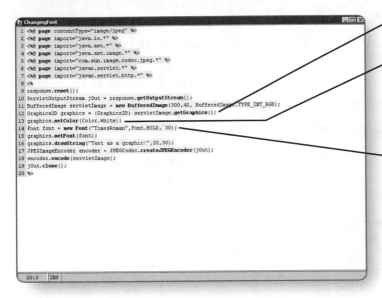

6. Create a Graphics2D object.

7. Use the setColor method to change the color. You will need to pass a color constant to the setColor method.

8. Create a new Font object. Specify the font, style, and size of the font.

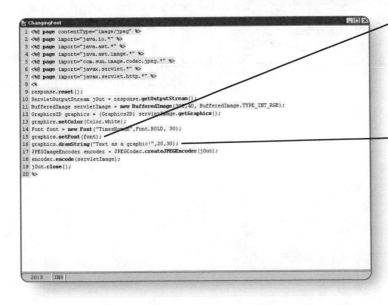

9. Pass the Font object to the setFont method. After calling the setFont method, the text will be displayed in the new font.

10. Use the drawString method to write the text at the specified coordinates.

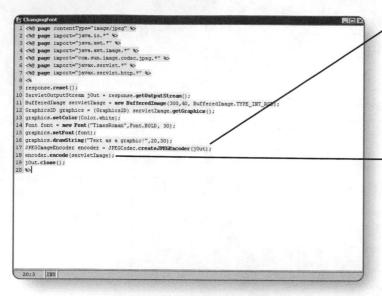

```
ChangingFont
1  <%@ page contentType="image/jpeg" %>
2  <%@ page import="java.io.*" %>
3  <%@ page import="java.awt.*" %>
4  <%@ page import="java.awt.image.*" %>
5  <%@ page import="com.sun.image.codec.jpeg.*" %>
6  <%@ page import="javax.servlet.*" %>
7  <%@ page import="javax.servlet.http.*" %>
8  <%
9  response.reset();
10 ServletOutputStream jOut = response.getOutputStream();
11 BufferedImage servletImage = new BufferedImage(300,40, BufferedImage.TYPE_INT_RGB);
12 Graphics2D graphics = (Graphics2D) servletImage.getGraphics();
13 graphics.setColor(Color.white);
14 Font font = new Font("TimesRoman",Font.BOLD, 30);
15 graphics.setFont(font);
16 graphics.drawString("Text as a graphic!",20,30);
17 JPEGImageEncoder encoder = JPEGCodec.createJPEGEncoder(jOut);
18 encoder.encode(servletImage);
19 jOut.close();
20 %>

20:3   INS
```

11. Create an image encoder to convert the image stored in memory into JPEG format and to send the image to the browser using the servlet's output stream.

12. Convert the image stored in memory into a JPEG image.

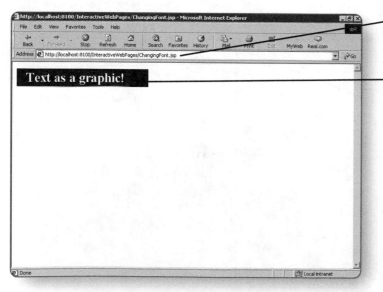

13. Preview the JSP page in a Web browser.

The image will display the text in the specified font and size.

Generating Dynamic Image Banners

It is time to use the Graphics class to generate dynamic images. The example in this section develops a JSP page that retrieves text from the query string and generates an image banner that displays the text is a visually attractive manner. The image banner will render the text with a drop-shadow.

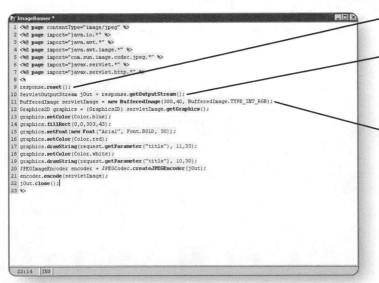

```
1  <%@ page contentType="image/jpeg" %>
2  <%@ page import="java.io.*" %>
3  <%@ page import="java.awt.*" %>
4  <%@ page import="java.awt.image.*" %>
5  <%@ page import="com.sun.image.codec.jpeg.*" %>
6  <%@ page import="javax.servlet.*" %>
7  <%@ page import="javax.servlet.http.*" %>
8  <%
9  response.reset();
10 ServletOutputStream jOut = response.getOutputStream();
11 BufferedImage servletImage = new BufferedImage(300,40, BufferedImage.TYPE_INT_RGB);
12 Graphics2D graphics = (Graphics2D) servletImage.getGraphics();
13 graphics.setColor(Color.blue);
14 graphics.fillRect(0,0,303,43);
15 graphics.setFont(new Font("Arial", Font.BOLD, 30));
16 graphics.setColor(Color.red);
17 graphics.drawString(request.getParameter("title"), 11,33);
18 graphics.setColor(Color.white);
19 graphics.drawString(request.getParameter("title"), 10,30);
20 JPEGImageEncoder encoder = JPEGCodec.createJPEGEncoder(jOut);
21 encoder.encode(servletImage);
22 jOut.close();
23 %>
```

1. Use the page directive to set the content type to "image/jpeg". The Web browser requires this so that it can identify the image format.

2. Import the java.io.*, java.awt.*, java.awt.image.*, com.sun.image.codec.jpeg.*, javax.servlet.*, and javax.servlet.http.* packages.

3. Reset the response object.

4. Create a ServletOutputStream object.

5. Create a BufferedImage object. The image banner is 300 pixels wide and 40 pixels high.

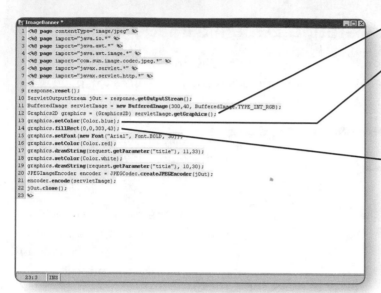

6. Create a Graphics2D object.

7. Use the setColor method to set the color to blue. This will be the background color of the image banner.

8. Use the fillRect method to create the background of the image banner.

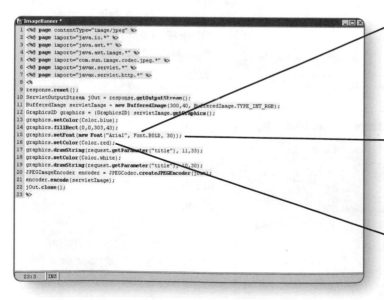

9. Create a new Font object. The text on the banner uses an Arial font and a boldface attribute, and has a size of 30 points.

10. Pass the Font object to the setFont method. After calling the setFont method, all text will be displayed in the new font.

11. Use the setColor method to change the color to red. The drop-shadow text will be in red.

12. Use the drawString method to insert the drop-shadow text at the specified coordinates. The text is retrieved from the query string using the getParameter method.

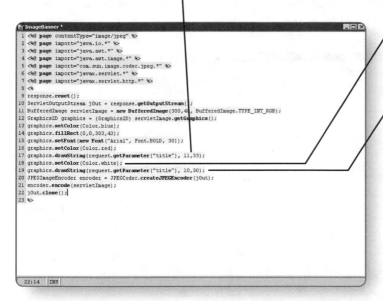

13. Use the setColor method to change the color to white. The banner title text must be in white.

14. Use the drawString method to write the banner title at the specified coordinates. The banner title text is retrieved from the query string using the getParameter method.

NOTE

The banner title text is placed 2 pixels above and 3 pixels to the left of the drop-shadow text. This will give the banner title a three-dimensional effect.

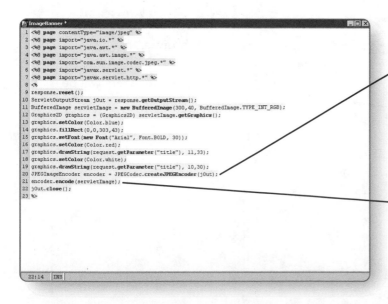

15. Create an image encoder to convert the image stored in memory into JPEG format and to send the image to the browser using the servlet's output stream.

16. Convert the image stored in memory into a JPEG image.

Displaying the Image Banner

This section demonstrates how to display a banner on a Web page. You can use the <img> tag to insert the dynamically generated banner.

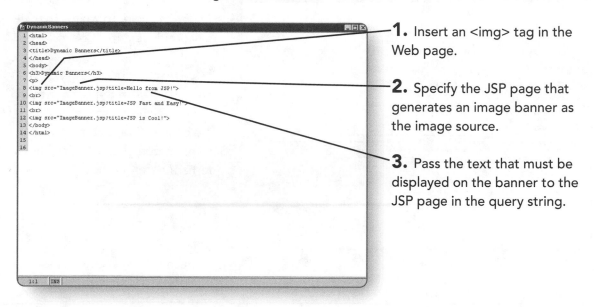

1. Insert an <img> tag in the Web page.

2. Specify the JSP page that generates an image banner as the image source.

3. Pass the text that must be displayed on the banner to the JSP page in the query string.

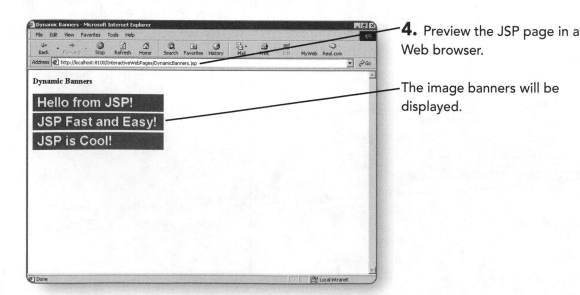

4. Preview the JSP page in a Web browser.

The image banners will be displayed.

Drawing Bar Charts

A bar chart is quite simple to generate if it is broken up into separate components. It is really only made up of rectangles (the bars), lines (the axes), and text (the labels for the axes). This chapter has presented all the theory you need to generate a bar chart.

```
8  <%
9  String[] Quarters = {"1st","2nd","3rd","4th"};
10 int[] Sales = {120,130,110,260};
11 int x = 50, y = 300, width = 20, gap = 5;
12 response.reset();
13 ServletOutputStream jOut = response.getOutputStream();
14 BufferedImage servletImage = new BufferedImage(170,350, BufferedImage.TYPE_INT_RGB);
15 Graphics2D graphics = (Graphics2D) servletImage.getGraphics();
16 graphics.setColor(Color.white);
17 graphics.fill3DRect(0,0,172,352,true);
18 graphics.setColor(Color.blue);
19 graphics.drawLine(x,y,x+12*(width+gap),y);
20 graphics.drawLine(x,y,x,30);
21 for (int m=0;m<Sales.length;m++)
22 {
23         graphics.drawString(Quarters[m],m*(width+gap)+gap+x,y+20);
24 }
25 for (int i=0;i<y;i+=100)
26 {
27         graphics.drawString(String.valueOf(i),20,y-i);
28 }
29 for (int month=0;month<Quarters.length;month++)
30 {
31         graphics.fillRect(month*(width+gap)+gap+x,y-Sales[month],width,Sales[month]);
32 }
33 graphics.setColor(Color.blue);
34 JPEGImageEncoder encoder = JPEGCodec.createJPEGEncoder(jOut);
35 encoder.encode(servletImage);
36 jOut.close();
37 %>
```

Here is some sample code that displays quarterly sales in a bar chart.

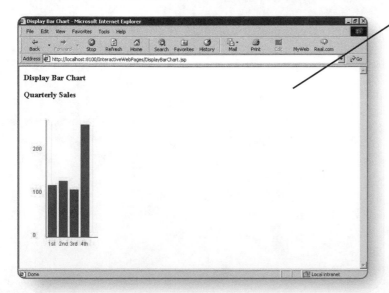

This is what the generated chart looks like when previewed in a browser.

14

Persisting User Information

HTTP (*Hypertext Transfer Protocol*) is a stateless protocol because it does not store any information about the requested Web page or the data that is sent to the Web browser. In fact, each time a page is retrieved, a separate connection to the Web server is opened. This certainly poses numerous challenges in the development of Web applications that rely on state maintenance. Cookies and sessions provide the only practical solution. Cookies enable you to store data, which can be retrieved when the user returns to your Web site, over long periods of time. Sessions, however, allow data to be shared across multiple pages in your Web site. In this chapter, you'll learn how to:

- Store and retrieve cookies
- Use cookies to remember user login details
- Create and store session variables
- Use session variables to password-protect a Web site

Using Cookies

Cookies provide a simple solution to state management. A cookie is a piece of information that is stored in a text file on a user's computer. The information stored within a cookie can be retrieved immediately or when the user returns to the Web site. You are responsible for determining when a cookie will expire. Cookies can only be accessed by Web pages that reside within the same domain, so you don't need to worry about other Web sites retrieving your cookies. This is an excellent security feature.

The fact that a cookie is stored on the user's computer is a big disadvantage. This means that the user must always visit your Web site from the same computer using the same Web browser. Most popular Web browsers allow cookies to be disabled. It is, therefore, not wise to build a Web application that is totally reliant upon cookies.

Creating a Cookie

Calling the Cookie constructor creates a cookie. The Cookie constructor takes as parameters the name and value of the cookie to be created. Each cookie that you store must be given a unique name. You will also need to specify an expiration date. The expiration date you specify will determine whether the cookie will expire after the user leaves the site or at a later date.

1. Create a new cookie by calling the Cookie constructor.

2. Type the name of the cookie as the first parameter passed to the Cookie constructor.

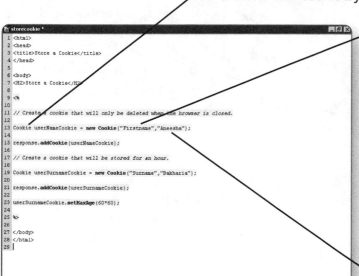

CAUTION
The cookie name should not contain any blank spaces or any of these characters: [ ] ( ) = , " / ? @ : ;

3. Type the value of the cookie as the second parameter passed to the Cookie constructor.

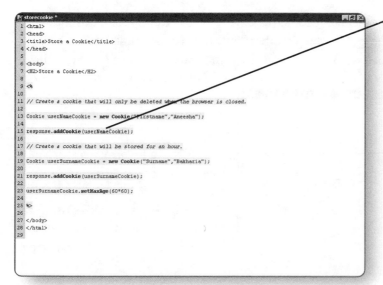

4. Pass the name of the cookie instance to the response.addCookie method. This inserts the cookie into the response header of the Web page.

NOTE
If no expiration date is set, the cookie will be deleted when the browser is closed.

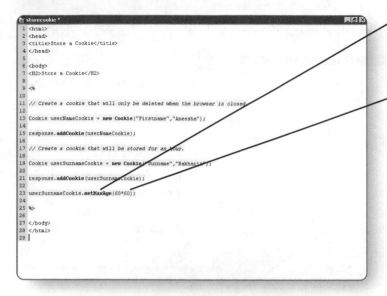

```
storecookie *                                              _ 日 X
1  <html>
2  <head>
3  <title>Store a Cookie</title>
4  </head>
5
6  <body>
7  <H2>Store a Cookie</H2>
8
9  <%
10
11 // Create a cookie that will only be deleted when the browser is closed.
12
13 Cookie userNameCookie = new Cookie("Firstname","Aneesha");
14
15 response.addCookie(userNameCookie);
16
17 // Create a cookie that will be stored for an hour.
18
19 Cookie userSurnameCookie = new Cookie("Surname","Bakharia");
20
21 response.addCookie(userSurnameCookie);
22
23 userSurnameCookie.setMaxAge(60*60);
24
25 %>
26
27 </body>
28 </html>
29 |
```

5. Call the setMaxAge method to specify the amount of time to store the cookie.

6. Pass the time (in seconds) to the setMaxAge method.

> **NOTE**
>
> Passing a value of -1 to the setMaxAge method will cause the cookie to be deleted when a browser is closed. Passing a value of 0 to the setMaxAge method will delete the cookie immediately.

Reading a Cookie

To retrieve a cookie you need to call the getCookies method. The getCookies method returns an array of all available cookies. You will need to loop though the array and use the getName and getValue methods to retrieve the name and value of a cookie.

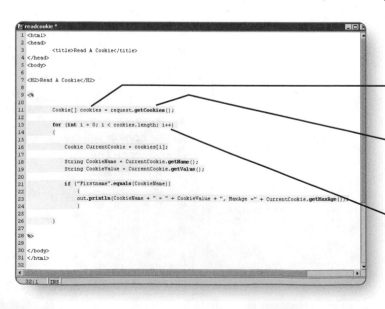

```
readcookie *                                               _ 日 X
1  <html>
2  <head>
3         <title>Read A Cookie</title>
4  </head>
5  <body>
6
7  <H2>Read A Cookie</H2>
8
9  <%
10
11       Cookie[] cookies = request.getCookies();
12
13       for (int i = 0; i < cookies.length; i++)
14       {
15
16           Cookie CurrentCookie = cookies[i];
17
18           String CookieName = CurrentCookie.getName();
19           String CookieValue = CurrentCookie.getValue();
20
21           if ("Firstname".equals(CookieName))
22           {
23               out.println(CookieName + " = " + CookieValue + ", MaxAge =" + CurrentCookie.getMaxAge());
24           }
25
26       }
27
28 %>
29
30 </body>
31 </html>
32
32:1    INS
```

1. Create an array to store all available cookie objects.

2. Retrieve all cookies using the request.getCookies method and store the result in the array.

3. Loop through all of the retrieved cookie objects using a for loop.

NOTE

You can calculate the number of available cookies by determining the length of the cookies array. When the value is reached, the code within the loop will not be executed again.

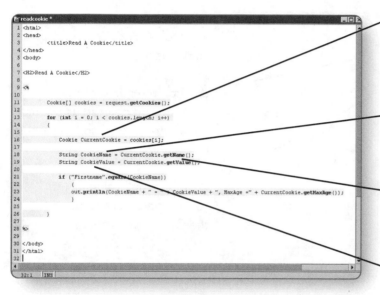

```
1  <html>
2  <head>
3          <title>Read A Cookie</title>
4  </head>
5  <body>
6
7  <H2>Read A Cookie</H2>
8
9  <%
10
11         Cookie[] cookies = request.getCookies();
12
13         for (int i = 0; i < cookies.length; i++)
14         {
15
16             Cookie CurrentCookie = cookies[i];
17
18             String CookieName = CurrentCookie.getName();
19             String CookieValue = CurrentCookie.getValue();
20
21             if ("Firstname".equals(CookieName))
22             {
23                 out.println(CookieName + " = " + CookieValue + ", MaxAge =" + CurrentCookie.getMaxAge());
24             }
25
26         }
27
28  %>
29
30  </body>
31  </html>
32
```

4. Create a cookie object to store the cookie that is currently being retrieved from the array of cookie objects.

5. Declare a variable as a string. The variable will store the name of the current cookie.

6. Use the getName method to retrieve the cookie name and assign the result to the variable.

7. Declare a variable as a string. The variable will store the value of the current cookie.

8. Use the getValue method to retrieve the value of the cookie and assign the result to the variable.

9. Use an if statement to test whether the name of the cookie matches the name of the cookie you wish to retrieve. Step 10 will only execute if this is true.

10. Print the cookie name, value, and expiration date to the Web page using the out.println method.

Deleting a Cookie

A cookie can be deleted at any time by setting the expiration date to zero. The setMaxAge method is used to set the expiration date.

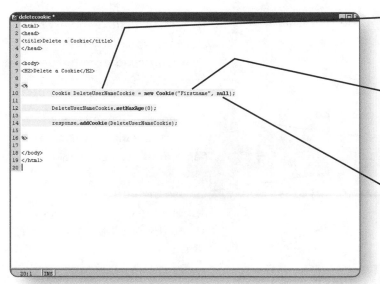

1. Create a new instance of the cookie by calling the Cookie constructor.

2. Type the name of the cookie to be deleted as the first parameter passed to the Cookie constructor.

3. Type a null value as the second parameter passed to the Cookie constructor.

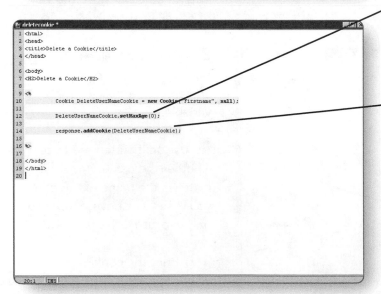

4. Pass 0 to the setMaxAge method. A cookie with an expiration date of 0 is deleted immediately.

5. Pass the name of the cookie instance to the response.addCookie method. The response header of the Web page will direct the browser to delete the cookie.

NOTE

A cookie should be deleted when the data that it stores is no longer valid.

Using Cookies to Remember Login Details

Many Web sites require you to register before you can access certain password-protected areas. It is certainly difficult for a user to remember the separate login details for each regularly visited Web site. Cookies can provide you with a handy solution if security is not a major concern. A cookie can be used to store user name and password login details. When users return to the login Web page, all of their details can then be retrieved from the cookie.

Creating a Login Page

The login Web page needs to:

- Retrieve the user name and password if they were previously stored

- Allow users to enter their user names and passwords

- Allow users to decide whether they want to store personal details in a cookie

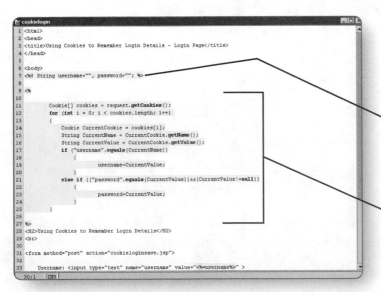

- Display the retrieved user name and password in the form fields so that users aren't required to re-enter their details

1. Declare two variables as strings. These variables will store the user name and password that are retrieved from a cookie.

2. Retrieve the cookies that store the user name and password. The JSP code discussed earlier in this chapter is used to retrieve the cookie.

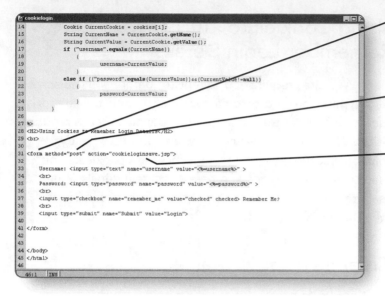

3. Create a form. You will need to insert opening and closing <form> tags.

4. Set the method attribute of the form tag to Post.

5. Set the action attribute to the file name of the page that will process the login details.

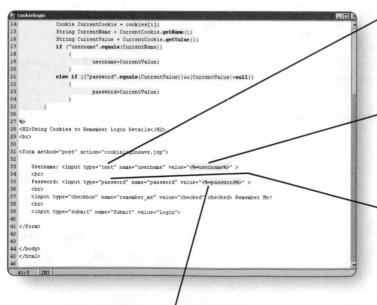

6. Create a text input field by setting the type attribute of the input tag to text. A user name will be typed into this field.

7. Use the Expression delimiters (<%= and %>) to display the user name that was retrieved from the cookie.

8. Create a password input field by setting the type attribute of the input tag to password. This input field will contain the password.

9. Use the Expression delimiters (<%= and %>) to display the password retrieved from the cookie.

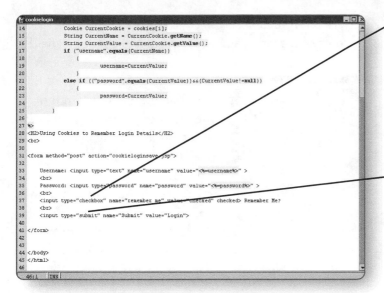

```
14          Cookie CurrentCookie = cookies[i];
15          String CurrentName = CurrentCookie.getName();
16          String CurrentValue = CurrentCookie.getValue();
17          if ("username".equals(CurrentName))
18              {
19                  username=CurrentValue;
20              }
21          else if (("password".equals(CurrentValue))&&(CurrentValue!=null))
22              {
23                  password=CurrentValue;
24              }
25      }
26
27  %>
28  <H2>Using Cookies to Remember Login Details</H2>
29  <br>
30
31  <form method="post" action="cookieloginsave.jsp">
32
33      Username: <input type="text" name="username" value="<%=username%>" >
34      <br>
35      Password: <input type="password" name="password" value="<%=password%>" >
36      <br>
37      <input type="checkbox" name="remember me" value="checked" checked> Remember Me?
38      <br>
39      <input type="submit" name="Submit" value="Login">
40
41  </form>
42
43
44  </body>
45  </html>
46
```

10. Create a check box by setting the type attribute of the input tag to checkbox. The check box will be selected by default. If users deselect the check box, their details will not be stored in a cookie.

11. Insert a submit button. When the Submit button is clicked, the login details will be submitted to the server for processing. The page that you specified in the action attribute of the form will be loaded.

Processing the Login Details

The login processing Web page must:

- Retrieve the user name and password entered by the user

- Retrieve the value stored in the Remember Me check box and determine whether the login details should be stored in a cookie

- Determine whether the user wishes to store their details

- If required, store the user name and password in a cookie

> ### NOTE
> Usually, you will need to check the user name and password against details stored in a registration database. This information has not been included, so you can concentrate on concepts related to cookies. In Chapter 15, "Working with Databases," you will learn how to query a database.

1. Declare three variables as strings. These variables will store the contents of the user name, password, and check box fields.

2. Retrieve the contents of the user name text field with the request.getParameter method and store the result in the username variable.

3. Retrieve the contents of the password text field with the request.getParameter method and store the result in the password variable.

4. Retrieve the contents of the check box field with the request.getParameter method and store the result in a variable.

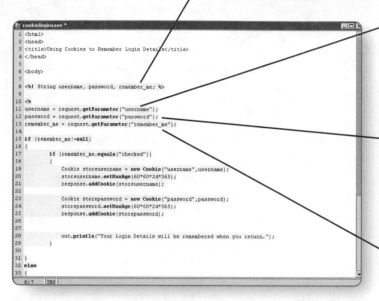

5. Use an if statement to detect whether the Remember Me check box is selected. The variable that stores the value of the check box will be null if it has been deselected. If the variable is not null, the login details can be stored in a cookie.

6. Store the user name and password in appropriately named cookies. You will use the code developed earlier to do this.

7. If the check box has been deselected, inform the user that he will need to enter his personal login details each time he visits the Web site. This is done by printing an appropriate message.

Using Sessions

A session begins when a user enters your Web site and ends when a user leaves. Sessions can only be used to store information while a user is visiting your Web site. (In other words, sessions retain data between each request to the server.) Sessions are much simpler than cookies to use because an expiration date isn't required. Sessions rely on cookies, but the JSP engine takes care of all the hard work. When a session begins, only a unique session identifier is stored as a cookie. All session variables are actually stored on the Web server. This is much more secure because no personal data entered by the user is stored as a cookie. Session variables are specific to a particular user.

Creating a Session Variable

Calling the getSession method of HttpServletRequest creates a session. The putValue method is used to create and assign values to session variables.

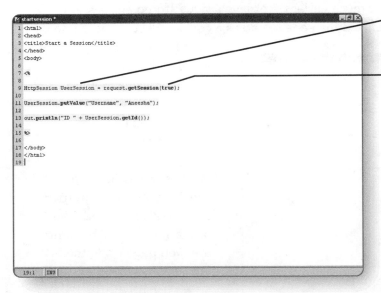

1. Create an instance of the HttpSession object.

2. Create a new session by calling the request.getSession method.

NOTE

The getSession method will return a null value if the user is not currently engaged in a session. Passing true to the getSession method will automatically create a new session.

3. Call the putValue method to store a session variable.

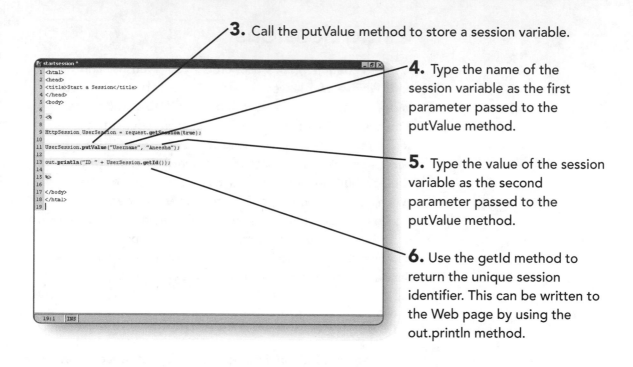

```
startsession
1  <html>
2  <head>
3  <title>Start a Session</title>
4  </head>
5  <body>
6
7  <%
8
9  HttpSession UserSession = request.getSession(true);
10
11 UserSession.putValue("Username", "Aneesha");
12
13 out.println("ID " + UserSession.getId());
14
15 %>
16
17 </body>
18 </html>
19

19:1    INS
```

4. Type the name of the session variable as the first parameter passed to the putValue method.

5. Type the value of the session variable as the second parameter passed to the putValue method.

6. Use the getId method to return the unique session identifier. This can be written to the Web page by using the out.println method.

Reading a Session Variable

It is much easier to retrieve a value stored in a session variable than one stored as a cookie. All you have to do is pass the name of the session variable that you want to read to the getValue method.

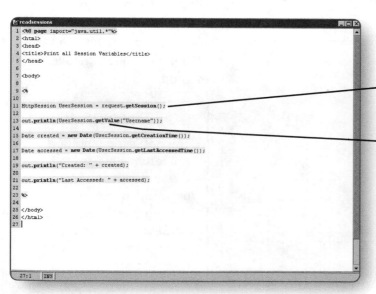

```
readsessions
1  <%@ page import="java.util.*"%>
2  <html>
3  <head>
4  <title>Print all Session Variables</title>
5  </head>
6
7  <body>
8
9  <%
10
11 HttpSession UserSession = request.getSession();
12
13 out.println(UserSession.getValue("Username"));
14
15 Date created = new Date(UserSession.getCreationTime());
16
17 Date accessed = new Date(UserSession.getLastAccessedTime());
18
19 out.println("Created: " + created);
20
21 out.println("Last Accessed: " + accessed);
22
23 %>
24
25 </body>
26 </html>
27

27:1    INS
```

1. Create an instance of the HttpSession object.

2. Pass the name of the session variable you want to retrieve to the getValue method. The value of the variable will be printed to the Web page using the out.println method.

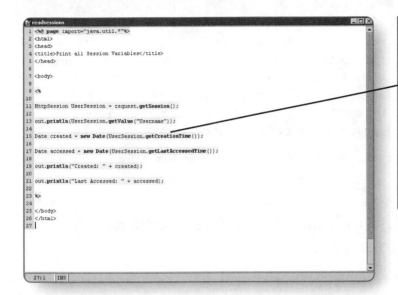

NOTE

You can also use the:

- getCreationTime method to retrieve the time the session began.

- getCreationDate method to retrieve the date the session was created.

Deleting a Session

You can use the invalidate method to delete a session and all of its associated variables. Sessions will automatically be terminated when the limit defined by the setMaxInactiveInterval is reached. The getMaxInactiveInterval method returns the timeout limit.

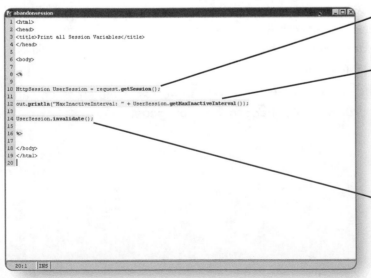

1. Create an instance of the HttpSession object.

2. Call the getMaxInactiveInterval method to return the amount of time that a session can remain inactive before it becomes invalid.

3. Call the invalidate method to end a session and delete all associated session variables.

NOTE

If the getMaxInactiveInterval method returns a negative value, the session will never time out. You can set the amount of time before a session becomes inactive with the setMaxInactiveInterval method, such as in the example: UserSession.setMaxInactiveInterval(60*60).

Using Sessions to Password-Protect Your Web Site

This section implements a practical password-protection system that utilizes sessions.

First, you must create these Web pages:

- A login page where the user enters a password.

- A password-processing page that determines whether the password is correct and displays links to Web pages that the user can access. A session variable will be used as a flag to indicate that a user has logged in.

- A password-protected Web page, which users can only access after they have logged in. If the session variable has not been flagged, an Access Denied error message will be displayed.

- An error page that displays an Access Denied message and provides a link back to the Login page.

```
login
1  <html>
2  <head>
3  <title>Password Protection - Login Page</title>
4  </head>
5
6  <body>
7
8  <H2>Password Protection - Login Page</H2>
9
10 <br>
11
12 <form method="post" action="checkpassword.jsp">
13
14 Enter the Secret Password: <input type="password" name="password" value="abc123" >
15
16 <br>
17
18 <input type="submit" name="Submit" value="Login">
19
20 </form>
21
22 </body>
23
24 </html>
25

25:1   INS
```

Creating the Login Page

The Login page contains a form with a password input field and a submit button. The action attribute of the <form> tag must contain the name of the Web page that will process the login details. The page that processes the login details needs to determine whether the password is correct and set the session variable accordingly.

Creating the Password-Processing Web Page

The password must be retrieved from the form and verified for correctness, and then a session variable must be set. The session variable will be used as a flag to indicate that the user has access to any Web pages that are password-protected. If the password is correct, links to all restricted Web pages will be displayed.

```
checkpassword *
1  <html>
2  <head><title>Password Protection - Check Password</title></head>
3  <body>
4  <%! String password; %>
5
6  <%
7
8  password = request.getParameter("password");
9
10 if ((password!=null)&&(password.length()>0))
11 {
12
13          if (password.equals("abc123"))
14          {
15
16                  HttpSession ViewProtectedPage = request.getSession(true)
17
18                  ViewProtectedPage.putValue("password","correct");
19
20                  out.println("You may View the <a href=passwordprotectedpage.jsp>secret page</a>.");
21          }
22          else
23          {
24              out.println("Your password is incorrect.");
25          }
26
27 }
28
29 %>
30 </body>
31 </html>
32

31:8   INS
```

1. Declare a variable as a string. This variable stores the password that the user has entered.

2. Store the user's password in the variable.

```
checkpassword *                                                    _ □ X
 1  <html>
 2  <head><title>Password Protection - Check Password</title></head>
 3  <body>
 4  <%! String password; %>
 5
 6  <%
 7
 8  password = request.getParameter("password");
 9
10  if ((password!=null)&&(password.length()>0))
11  {
12
13          if (password.equals("abc123"))
14          {
15
16                  HttpSession ViewProtectedPage = request.getSession(true);
17
18                  ViewProtectedPage.putValue("password","correct");
19
20                  out.println("You may View the <a href=passwordprotectedpage.jsp>secret page</a>.");
21          }
22          else
23          {
24              out.println("Your password is incorrect.");
25          }
26
27  }
28
29  %>
30  </body>
31  </html>
32
31:8    INS
```

3. Use an if statement to test whether a password has been entered. A password has been entered if the variable is not null and has a length greater than zero.

4. Use an if statement to determine whether the password is correct. Steps 5 and 6 will only execute if the password is correct.

```
checkpassword *                                                    _ □ X
 1  <html>
 2  <head><title>Password Protection - Check Password</title></head>
 3  <body>
 4  <%! String password; %>
 5
 6  <%
 7
 8  password = request.getParameter("password");
 9
10  if ((password!=null)&&(password.length()>0))
11  {
12
13          if (password.equals("abc123"))
14          {
15
16                  HttpSession ViewProtectedPage = request.getSession(true);
17
18                  ViewProtectedPage.putValue("password","correct");
19
20                  out.println("You may View the <a href=passwordprotectedpage.jsp>secret page</a>.");
21          }
22          else
23          {
24              out.println("Your password is incorrect.");
25          }
26
27  }
28
29  %>
30  </body>
31  </html>
32
31:8    INS
```

5. Use the putValue method to create a new session variable. This variable will be used as a flag to indicate that the user has entered the correct password. You can use the code developed earlier in this chapter to do this.

6. Display the list of Web pages accessible by the user.

7. Use the out.println method to display an error message if the password is incorrect.

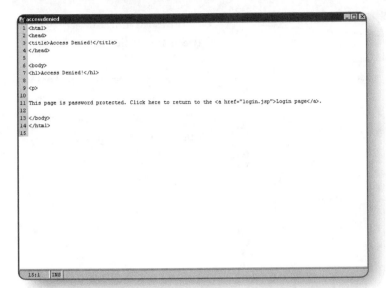

Creating the Access Denied Error Page

This page is very simple—it contains no JSP code at all. It merely displays the error message and a link back to the login page.

Creating a Password-Protected Web Page

You will be quite surprised at the simplicity of this process. All you need to do is retrieve the session variable and check it to determine whether it has the correct value. If it does not exist or has an incorrect value, you simply redirect the user to the page that displays the Access Denied error message.

NOTE

All pages that include this password-protection code must have a .jsp extension. The JSP code to password-protect your Web page must be inserted before any HTML is sent to the Web browser.

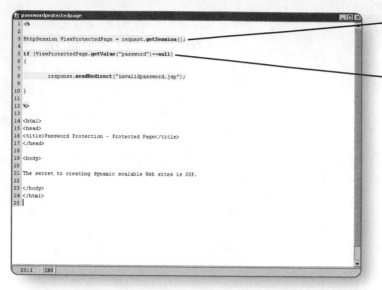

1. Create an instance of the HttpSession object.

2. Use an if statement to test whether the password session variable is null. It will be null if the user has not logged in.

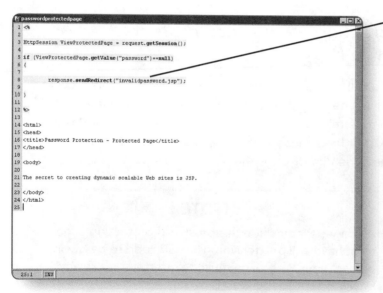

3. Pass the name of the page that will display the Access Denied error message to the sendRedirect method. If the user has not logged in or has entered an incorrect password, an Access Denied error message will be displayed.

NOTE

Insert this code at the beginning of all pages you want to password-protect. This code will still work if the Web page contains JSP tags and code.

15

Working with Databases

A database is essential in the development of dynamic Web sites. Databases are used to store large amounts of data in a manner conducive to data manipulation. They are designed to allow new data to be added, as well as enabling existing data to be easily searched, updated, and deleted. JDBC (*Java Database Connectivity*) will be used to database-enable a JSP page. In this chapter, you'll learn how to:

- Use JDBC to connect to a Microsoft Access database
- Use SQL (*Structured Query Language*) to query a database
- Display records in a table with alternate row colors
- Display summary search results and link to full records
- Insert new records into a database
- Update existing records in a database
- Delete records from a database
- Create paged search results

What is JDBC?

The JDBC API provides a standard library for accessing relational databases. With JDBC, you can use identical syntax to access databases built by different vendors. In other words, the Java code to retrieve data from a small desktop database (such as Microsoft Access) is the same as the code to retrieve data from an industrial strength client-server database (such as Oracle). The JDBC API classes and interfaces are included in the java.sql and javax.sql packages.

JDBC provides an interface between JSP and a database. It provides a number of objects that will allow you to fulfill all of your database maintenance needs. In particular, the Connection object allows you to connect to a database, and the ResultSet object stores the set of records returned in a query. The ResultSet object allows you to access the individual table fields returned. The fact that JDBC is easy to use, fast, and not memory-intensive makes it ideal for Web development.

A JDBC driver is required before JDBC can communicate with a database. A JDBC driver is a class, provided by Sun or a database vendor, that is required to interface JDBC with a database. A comprehensive list of JDBC drivers is available at Sun's Web site, at http://industry.java.sun.com/products/jdbc/drivers. The following four types of drivers are available.

- **Type 1: JDBC-ODBC Bridge**. The JDBC-ODBC Bridge allows you to access any database that has an ODBC driver. ODBC is Microsoft's equivalent of JDBC. This driver will be used throughout this chapter to connect to a Microsoft Access database. The JDBC-ODBC Bridge is installed with the JDK.

- **Type 2: Native API Driver**. Native API Drivers convert JDBC requests to vendor-specific instructions. This is similar to a JDBC-ODBC Bridge. This solution is not portable.

- **Type 3: JDBC-Net Pure Java Driver**. JDBC requests are translated to a database-independent network protocol. This is then converted to the native database instructions and sent to the database.

- **Type 4: Native-Protocol Pure Driver**. Type 4 drivers are pure Java drivers that send JDBC requests directly to the database. They are written specifically for the database. Type 4 drivers provide the best performance.

Setting up a System DSN for an Access Database

A DSN (*Data Source Name*) is a shortcut that stores the location of your ODBC-compliant database. You will need to specify the DSN when using the JDBC-ODBC Bridge driver. The Access database used throughout this chapter (Employee.mdb) is provided on the CD-ROM included with this book. The structure of the database is very simple. The Employee database only contains two tables.

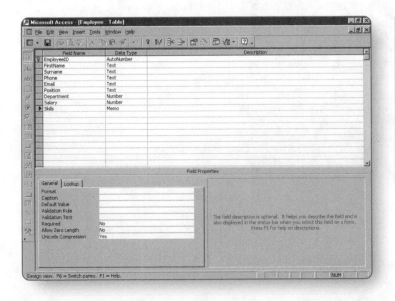

NOTE

The Employee table contains fields to store the first name, surname, phone number, e-mail address, salary, position, department, and skills of an employee.

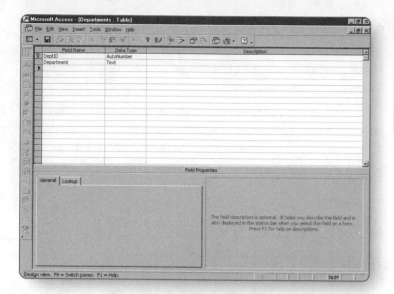

NOTE

The Departments table stores the different departments to which an employee can belong.

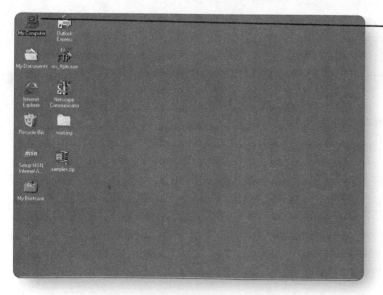

1. Double-click on the My Computer icon on your desktop. Your My Computer window will open.

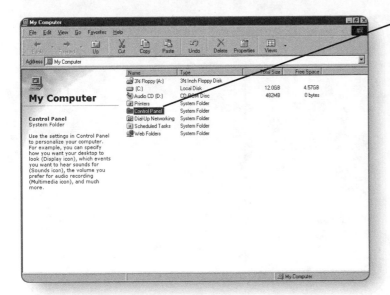

2. Double-click on the Control Panel folder or icon. The Control Panel will open.

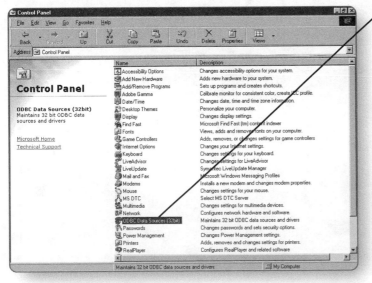

3. Double-click on ODBC Data Sources (32bit). The ODBC Data Source Administrator dialog box will open.

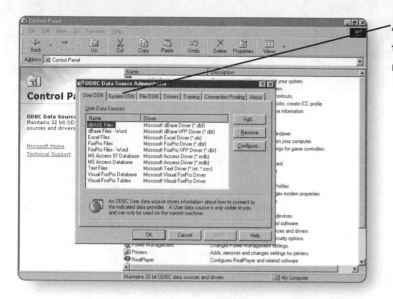

4. Click on the System DSN tab. The System DSN page will move to the front.

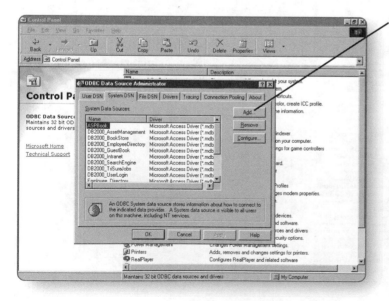

5. Click on Add. The Create New Data Source dialog box will open.

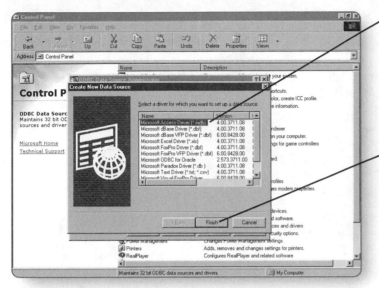

6. Click on the driver that matches your database. If you created an Access database, then click on Microsoft Access Driver (*.mdb). The option will be selected.

7. Click on Finish. The ODBC Microsoft Access Setup dialog box will open.

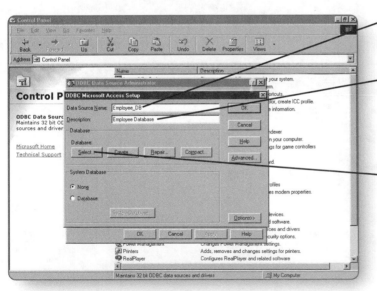

8. Type the DSN name into the Data Source Name field.

9. Type a description for the DSN in the Description field. This should be a description of what the database stores.

10. Click on Select. The Select Database dialog box will open.

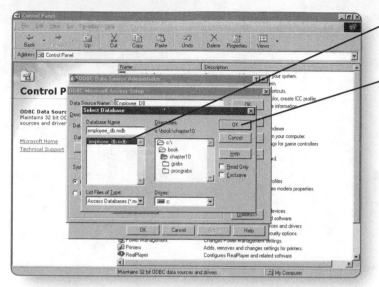

11. Click on the database file. The file name will be highlighted.

12. Click on OK. The Select Database dialog box will close.

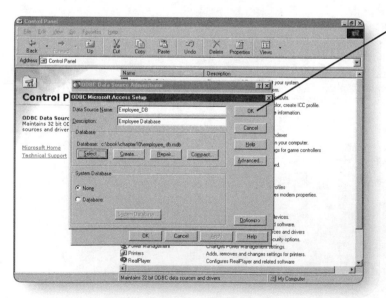

13. Click on OK to close the ODBC Microsoft Access Setup dialog box.

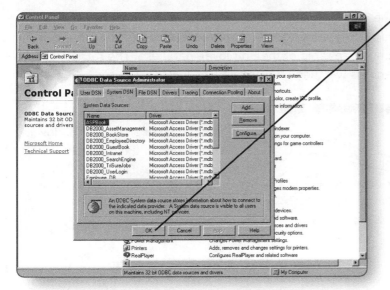

14. Click on OK to close the ODBC Data Source Administrator dialog box.

Connecting to a Database

The JDBC-ODBC Bridge will now be used to Web-enable a Microsoft Access database. The JDBC-ODBC Bridge translates JDBC to ODBC. Web-enabling a database with JDBC involves only seven steps.

1. Load the JDBC driver.

2. Specify the location of the database.

3. Establish a connection.

4. Create a statement object.

5. Execute an SQL query.

6. Display/process the records returned in the ResultSet.

7. Close the database connection.

The code to perform these steps will be inserted into a JSP page. The JSP page will retrieve all records stored in the Employee table of the Employee database. The retrieved records will then be displayed in an HTML table.

```
DisplayRecords
1  <html>
2  <head>
3  <title>Displaying Records</title>
4  </head>
5  <body>
6  <h3>Displaying Records</h3>
7  <P>
8  <%
9  Class.forName("sun.jdbc.odbc.JdbcOdbcDriver");
10 java.sql.Connection connection = java.sql.DriverManager.getConnection("jdbc:odbc:Employee","","");
11 java.sql.Statement statement = connection.createStatement();
12 java.sql.ResultSet RS = statement.executeQuery("SELECT * FROM EMPLOYEE");
13 %>
14 <table BORDER WIDTH="100%" >
15 <tr>
16         <td><b>ID</b></td>
17         <td><b>First Name</b></td>
18         <td><b>Surname</b></td>
19         <td><b>Position</b></td>
20         <td><b>Phone</b></td>
21         <td><b>Email</b></td>
22 </tr>
23
24 <%
25 while(RS.next())
26         {
27 %>
28
29 <tr>
30         <td><%=RS.getString("EmployeeID") %></td>
31         <td><%=RS.getString("FirstName") %></td>
32         <td><%=RS.getString("Surname") %></td>
33         <td><%=RS.getString("Position") %></td>
8:3    INS
```

1. Use the Class.forName method to load the JDBC driver. The name of the class that contains the JDBC-ODBC Bridge is sun.jdbc.odbc.JdbcOdbcDriver.

2. Create a connection object.

3. Pass the location of the database to the getConnection method of the DriverManager class.

> **NOTE**
>
> The location of the database is specified with a connection URL that has this syntax: jdbc:driver name:*database name or DSN name.*

```
DisplayRecords
1  <html>
2  <head>
3  <title>Displaying Records</title>
4  </head>
5  <body>
6  <h3>Displaying Records</h3>
7  <P>
8  <%
9  Class.forName("sun.jdbc.odbc.JdbcOdbcDriver");
10 java.sql.Connection connection = java.sql.DriverManager.getConnection("jdbc:odbc:Employee","","");
11 java.sql.Statement statement = connection.createStatement();
12 java.sql.ResultSet RS = statement.executeQuery("SELECT * FROM EMPLOYEE");
13 %>
14 <table BORDER WIDTH="100%" >
15 <tr>
16         <td><b>ID</b></td>
17         <td><b>First Name</b></td>
18         <td><b>Surname</b></td>
19         <td><b>Position</b></td>
20         <td><b>Phone</b></td>
21         <td><b>Email</b></td>
22 </tr>
23
24 <%
25 while(RS.next())
26         {
27 %>
28
29 <tr>
30         <td><%=RS.getString("EmployeeID") %></td>
31         <td><%=RS.getString("FirstName") %></td>
32         <td><%=RS.getString("Surname") %></td>
33         <td><%=RS.getString("Position") %></td>
8:3    INS
```

4. Create a statement object by calling the createStatement method. A statement object is used to send queries to a database.

5. Call the executeQuery method of the statement object.

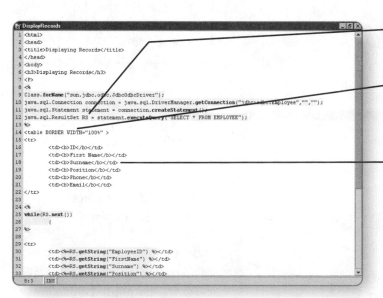

```
DisplayRecords
1  <html>
2  <head>
3  <title>Displaying Records</title>
4  </head>
5  <body>
6  <h3>Displaying Records</h3>
7  <P>
8  <%
9  Class.forName("sun.jdbc.odbc.JdbcOdbcDriver");
10 java.sql.Connection connection = java.sql.DriverManager.getConnection("jdbc:odbc:Employee","","");
11 java.sql.Statement statement = connection.createStatement();
12 java.sql.ResultSet RS = statement.executeQuery("SELECT * FROM EMPLOYEE");
13 %>
14 <table BORDER WIDTH="100%" >
15 <tr>
16     <td><b>ID</b></td>
17     <td><b>First Name</b></td>
18     <td><b>Surname</b></td>
19     <td><b>Position</b></td>
20     <td><b>Phone</b></td>
21     <td><b>Email</b></td>
22 </tr>
23
24 <%
25 while(RS.next())
26     {
27 %>
28
29 <tr>
30     <td><%=RS.getString("EmployeeID") %></td>
31     <td><%=RS.getString("FirstName") %></td>
32     <td><%=RS.getString("Surname") %></td>
33     <td><%=RS.getString("Position") %></td>
8:3   INS
```

6. Pass the SQL query to the executeQuery method. The "SELECT * FROM EMPLOYEE" query simply returns all records stored in the Employee table.

NOTE

Don't worry if you're not familiar with SQL. The next section, "Using SQL to Query a Database," will help you get up to speed quickly.

```
DisplayRecords
1  <html>
2  <head>
3  <title>Displaying Records</title>
4  </head>
5  <body>
6  <h3>Displaying Records</h3>
7  <P>
8  <%
9  Class.forName("sun.jdbc.odbc.JdbcOdbcDriver");
10 java.sql.Connection connection = java.sql.DriverManager.getConnection("jdbc:odbc:Employee","","");
11 java.sql.Statement statement = connection.createStatement();
12 java.sql.ResultSet RS = statement.executeQuery("SELECT * FROM EMPLOYEE");
13 %>
14 <table BORDER WIDTH="100%" >
15 <tr>
16     <td><b>ID</b></td>
17     <td><b>First Name</b></td>
18     <td><b>Surname</b></td>
19     <td><b>Position</b></td>
20     <td><b>Phone</b></td>
21     <td><b>Email</b></td>
22 </tr>
23
24 <%
25 while(RS.next())
26     {
27 %>
28
29 <tr>
30     <td><%=RS.getString("EmployeeID") %></td>
31     <td><%=RS.getString("FirstName") %></td>
32     <td><%=RS.getString("Surname") %></td>
33     <td><%=RS.getString("Position") %></td>
8:3   INS
```

7. Store the returned records in a ResultSet object.

8. Insert a table in the JSP page. The retrieved records will be displayed in a table.

9. Include table column headings for each field that will be displayed in the table.

10. Use a while loop to iterate through all records returned. The next method of the ResultSet object will return false when there are no more records in the ResultSet object. This will end the loop.

11. Pass the database field name to the getString method of the ResultSet object. This will return the data stored in the field as a string.

12. Use the Expression tag to print the data returned with the getString method to a table cell.

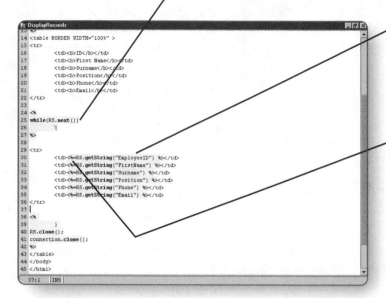

```
DisplayRecords                                              _ □ ×
14 <table BORDER WIDTH="100%" >
15 <tr>
16          <td><b>ID</b></td>
17          <td><b>First Name</b></td>
18          <td><b>Surname</b></td>
19          <td><b>Position</b></td>
20          <td><b>Phone</b></td>
21          <td><b>Email</b></td>
22 </tr>
23
24 <%
25 while(RS.next())
26          {
27 %>
28
29 <tr>
30          <td><%=RS.getString("EmployeeID") %></td>
31          <td><%=RS.getString("FirstName") %></td>
32          <td><%=RS.getString("Surname") %></td>
33          <td><%=RS.getString("Position") %></td>
34          <td><%=RS.getString("Phone") %></td>
35          <td><%=RS.getString("Email") %></td>
36 </tr>
37 |
38 <%
39          }
40 RS.close();
41 connection.close();
42 %>
43 </table>
44 </body>
45 </html>
37:1    INS
```

NOTE

You can also use the getInt method to return integer data.

---

13. Repeat steps 11 and 12 for each field that must be retrieved.

14. Call the close method of the ResultSet object.

15. Call the close method of the Connection object. This will close the database connection.

```
DisplayRecords                                              _ □ ×
14 <table BORDER WIDTH="100%" >
15 <tr>
16          <td><b>ID</b></td>
17          <td><b>First Name</b></td>
18          <td><b>Surname</b></td>
19          <td><b>Position</b></td>
20          <td><b>Phone</b></td>
21          <td><b>Email</b></td>
22 </tr>
23
24 <%
25 while(RS.next())
26          {
27 %>
28
29 <tr>
30          <td><%=RS.getString("EmployeeID") %></td>
31          <td><%=RS.getString("FirstName") %></td>
32          <td><%=RS.getString("Surname") %></td>
33          <td><%=RS.getString("Position") %></td>
34          <td><%=RS.getString("Phone") %></td>
35          <td><%=RS.getString("Email") %></td>
36 </tr>
37
38 <%
39          }
40 RS.close();
41 connection.close();
42 %>
43 </table>
44 </body>
45 </html>
37:1    INS
```

Using SQL to Query a Database

SQL is used to query and manage data stored in a relational database. You can use SQL to select, insert, update, and delete data stored in a database. This section will cover querying a database in some depth, because it is very important. Without some knowledge of SQL, you will not be able to effectively search a database for the data that you require.

NOTE

After reading this section, you can visit http://www.sqlcourse.com to get more experience with SQL.

A SQL query returns a result set. A result set is really just a subset of data stored in your database. It contains a row for each record returned, as well as columns for each field that makes up the record.

The SELECT statement is used to retrieve data from a database. In a SELECT statement you need to specify

- The fields that must be returned
- The table that stores the data
- The criteria that the returned records must match
- The sort order of the records

The basic syntax of a SELECT statement is

```
SELECT field1, field2, ..., fieldN FROM table1,
➡ table2, ..., tableN WHERE criterion is matched
➡ ORDER BY field1, field2, ..., fieldN
```

Specifying the Fields Returned in a Query

Always specify the exact fields (in other words, table column names) that must be returned in a query. This reduces the amount of data returned to the ResultSet object. As a general rule, you should only retrieve fields that will be displayed.

NOTE

In the following examples, the Java code used to connect and retrieve data from a database will not be explained again, so that you can concentrate on the SQL queries.

```
SelectingColumns *
1  <html>
2  <head>
3  <title>Selecting Columns</title>
4  </head>
5  <body>
6
7  <h3>Selecting Columns</h3>
8  <P>
9  <%
10 Class.forName("sun.jdbc.odbc.JdbcOdbcDriver");
11 java.sql.Connection connection = java.sql.DriverManager.getConnection("jdbc:odbc:Employee","","");
12 java.sql.Statement statement = connection.createStatement();
13 java.sql.ResultSet RS =
14 statement.executeQuery("SELECT EmployeeID,FirstName,Surname,Position,Phone,Email FROM EMPLOYEE");
15 %>
16 <table BORDER WIDTH="100%" >
17 <tr>
18        <td><b>ID</b></td>
19        <td><b>First Name</b></td>
20        <td><b>Surname</b></td>
21        <td><b>Position</b></td>
22        <td><b>Phone</b></td>
23        <td><b>Email</b></td>
24 </tr>
25
26 <%
27 while(RS.next())
28        {
29 %>
30
31 <tr>
32        <td><%=RS.getString("EmployeeID") %></td>

15:3    INS
```

This query retrieves the EmployeeID, FirstName, Surname, Position, Phone, and Email fields for each record stored in the Employee table.

Defining Search Criteria

The SELECT statement can include a WHERE clause that is used to specify the criteria that returned records must match. You must use comparison operators to define search criteria. Table 15.1 lists the SQL comparison operators.

Table 15.1 SQL Comparison Operators

Operator	Comparison
<	Less than
<=	Less than or equal to
=	Equal to (case sensitive)
LIKE	Equal to (case insensitive)
>	Greater than
>=	Greater than or equal to
<>	Not equal to

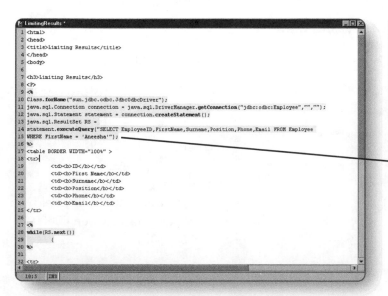

```
LimitingResults *
1  <html>
2  <head>
3  <title>Limiting Results</title>
4  </head>
5  <body>
6
7  <h3>Limiting Results</h3>
8  <P>
9  <%
10 Class.forName("sun.jdbc.odbc.JdbcOdbcDriver");
11 java.sql.Connection connection = java.sql.DriverManager.getConnection("jdbc:odbc:Employee","","");
12 java.sql.Statement statement = connection.createStatement();
13 java.sql.ResultSet RS =
14 statement.executeQuery("SELECT EmployeeID,FirstName,Surname,Position,Phone,Email FROM Employee
15 WHERE FirstName = 'Aneesha'");
16 %>
17 <table BORDER WIDTH="100%" >
18 <tr>
19        <td><b>ID</b></td>
20        <td><b>First Name</b></td>
21        <td><b>Surname</b></td>
22        <td><b>Position</b></td>
23        <td><b>Phone</b></td>
24        <td><b>Email</b></td>
25 </tr>
26
27 <%
28 while(RS.next())
29        {
30 %>
31
32 <tr>
18:5    INS
```

NOTE

SQL uses <> to designate not equal to, instead of the Java != sign.

This query returns all records where the FirstName field is equal to Aneesha.

Using Boolean Search Criteria

You can use the AND and OR Boolean operators to specify multiple search criteria. The AND operator will make sure that each criterion is met. The OR operator will return records that meet any of the criteria.

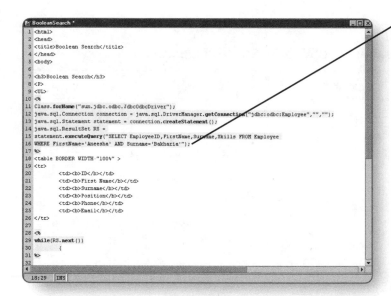

In this example, only records where the FirstName equals Aneesha and the Surname equals Bakharia will be returned.

Searching for a Range of Values

The BETWEEN keyword is used to define the range of values that must be used as the search criteria.

This query will only return records where the Salary field stores a value between 40000 and 50000.

Wildcard Searching

The % operator is used to represent a placeholder for 0 or more characters when searching for text in a database. You must use the LIKE comparison operator when a wildcard operator is used.

This query will retrieve all employee records that have ASP listed as a skill. The ASP string can be located at the beginning, end, or anywhere within the Skills field.

Retrieving Distinct Records

Occasionally, you might want to display all the distinct values that exist in a particular database field. This is easily achieved by placing the DISTINCT keyword after the SELECT statement.

This query retrieves the distinct positions stored in the Position field of the Employee table.

Using the Column Aggregate Functions

SQL provides functions that return the count of records, and the minimum, the maximum, the average, and the sum of all fields in a table column. Table 15.2 lists the SQL aggregate functions.

Table 15.2 SQL Aggregate Functions

Function	Purpose
count(column name)	Counts the number of records returned
max(column name)	Returns the maximum value stored in a table column
min(column name)	Returns the minimum value stored in a table column
avg(column name)	Returns the average value stored in a table column
sum(column name)	Returns the sum of all values stored in a table column

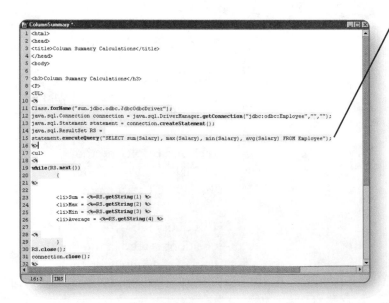

This query returns the maximum, minimum, and average salary of an employee. The total salary expenditure is also displayed.

```
1  <html>
2  <head>
3  <title>Column Summary Calculations</title>
4  </head>
5  <body>
6
7  <h3>Column Summary Calculations</h3>
8  <P>
9  <UL>
10 <%
11 Class.forName("sun.jdbc.odbc.JdbcOdbcDriver");
12 java.sql.Connection connection = java.sql.DriverManager.getConnection("jdbc:odbc:Employee","","");
13 java.sql.Statement statement = connection.createStatement();
14 java.sql.ResultSet RS =
15 statement.executeQuery("SELECT sum(Salary), max(Salary), min(Salary), avg(Salary) FROM Employee");
16 %>
17 <ul>
18 <%
19 while(RS.next())
20       {
21 %>
22
23       <li>Sum = <%=RS.getString(1) %>
24       <li>Max = <%=RS.getString(2) %>
25       <li>Min = <%=RS.getString(3) %>
26       <li>Average = <%=RS.getString(4) %>
27
28 <%
29       }
30 RS.close();
31 connection.close();
32 %>
```

Sorting Records

A query returns records in an arbitrary manner. You can use the ORDER BY clause to return records in ascending order. You will need to specify the field that will be used to sort the records. By default, records are returned in ascending order; however, if the DESC keyword is used, records will be returned in descending order. The ORDER BY clause can be used with fields that contain both text and numeric data. Fields that store text will be arranged in alphabetical order.

```
SortingRecords                                                    _ □ ×
1  <html>
2  <head>
3  <title>Sorting Records</title>
4  </head>
5  <body>
6
7  <h3>Sorting Records</h3>
8  <P>
9  <%
10 Class.forName("sun.jdbc.odbc.JdbcOdbcDriver");
11 java.sql.Connection connection = java.sql.DriverManager.getConnection("jdbc:odbc:Employee","","");
12 java.sql.Statement statement = connection.createStatement();
13 java.sql.ResultSet RS = statement.executeQuery("SELECT * FROM Employee ORDER BY Surname");
14 %>
15 <table BORDER WIDTH="100%" >
16 <tr>
17     <td><b>ID</b></td>
18     <td><b>First Name</b></td>
19     <td><b>Surname</b></td>
20     <td><b>Position</b></td>
21     <td><b>Phone</b></td>
22     <td><b>Email</b></td>
23 </tr>
24
25 <%
26 while(RS.next())
27     {
28 %>
29
30 <tr>
31     <td><%=RS.getString("EmployeeID") %></td>
32     <td><%=RS.getString("FirstName") %></td>
33     <td><%=RS.getString("Surname") %></td>
14:3    INS
```

This query uses the Surname field to order records.

Performing Multi-Table Queries

Each of the examples thus far has only queried a single table. In reality, a relational database can contain many linked tables. When querying linked tables you need to

- Use the field table name as a prefix when specifying the fields. This helps avoid ambiguity and clearly identifies the table that stores the field.

- Specify all the tables that are included in the query.

- Define the criteria that link the tables in the WHERE clause.

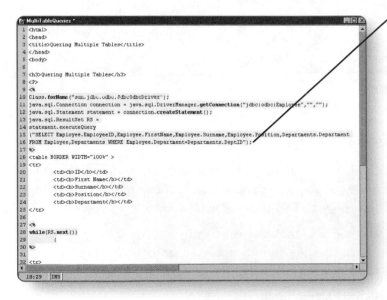

The Employee Microsoft Access database has a relationship between the DeptID field in the Departments table and the Department field in the Employee table. This is a numeric link. When a query is performed on the Employee table, the ID number of the department to which the employee belongs is returned. You need to construct a query that will return the name of the department.

In this query, the name of the department is retrieved from the record in the Departments table that matches the ID stored in the Department field of the Employee table.

Displaying Records in a Table with Alternate Row Colors

It is sometimes difficult to read rows and rows of data. Alternating the background colors used in table rows is a simple, effective way to enhance the readability and visual appeal of tabular data. This is achieved by inserting Java code to determine whether the row is even or odd and then applying the appropriate background color to the table row.

1. Use the Class.forName method to load the JDBC driver. The name of the class that contains the JDBC-ODBC Bridge is sun.jdbc.odbc.JdbcOdbcDriver.

2. Create a connection object.

3. Pass the location of the database to the getConnection method of the DriverManager class.

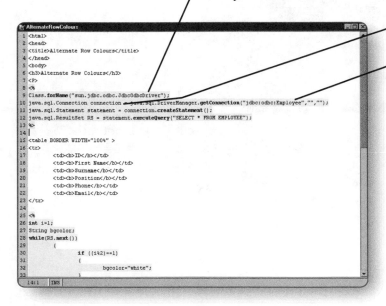

```
AlternateRowColours
1  <html>
2  <head>
3  <title>Alternate Row Colours</title>
4  </head>
5  <body>
6  <h3>Alternate Row Colours</h3>
7  <P>
8  <%
9  Class.forName("sun.jdbc.odbc.JdbcOdbcDriver");
10 java.sql.Connection connection = java.sql.DriverManager.getConnection("jdbc:odbc:Employee","","");
11 java.sql.Statement statement = connection.createStatement();
12 java.sql.ResultSet RS = statement.executeQuery("SELECT * FROM EMPLOYEE");
13 %>
14
15 <table BORDER WIDTH="100%" >
16 <tr>
17         <td><b>ID</b></td>
18         <td><b>First Name</b></td>
19         <td><b>Surname</b></td>
20         <td><b>Position</b></td>
21         <td><b>Phone</b></td>
22         <td><b>Email</b></td>
23 </tr>
24
25 <%
26 int i=1;
27 String bgcolor;
28 while(RS.next())
29         {
30                 if ((i%2)==1)
31                 {
32                         bgcolor="white";
33                 }
14:1    INS
```

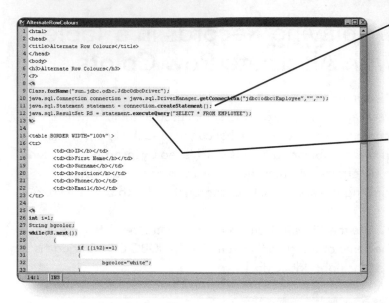

4. Create a statement object by calling the createStatement method. A statement object is used to send queries to a database.

5. Call the executeQuery method of the statement object.

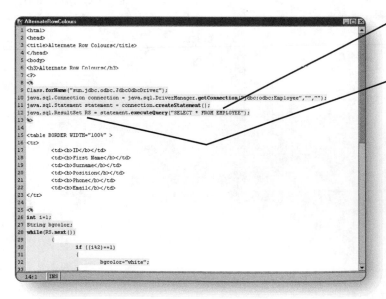

6. Pass the SQL query to the executeQuery method.

7. Store the returned records in a ResultSet object.

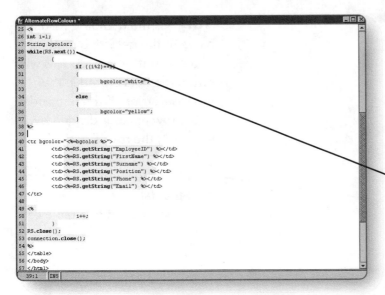

```
25 <%
26 int i=1;
27 String bgcolor;
28 while(RS.next())
29          {
30                  if ((i%2)==1)
31                  {
32                          bgcolor="white";
33                  }
34                  else
35                  {
36                          bgcolor="yellow";
37                  }
38 %>
39 |
40 <tr bgcolor="<%=bgcolor %>">
41          <td><%=RS.getString("EmployeeID") %></td>
42          <td><%=RS.getString("FirstName") %></td>
43          <td><%=RS.getString("Surname") %></td>
44          <td><%=RS.getString("Position") %></td>
45          <td><%=RS.getString("Phone") %></td>
46          <td><%=RS.getString("Email") %></td>
47 </tr>
48
49 <%
50                  i++;
51          }
52 RS.close();
53 connection.close();
54 %>
55 </table>
56 </body>
57 </html>
39:1    INS
```

8. Insert a table in the JSP page. The retrieved records will be displayed in a table.

9. Include table column headings for each field that will be displayed in the table.

10. Use a while loop to iterate through all records returned. The next method of the ResultSet object will return false when there are no more records in the ResultSet object. This will end the loop.

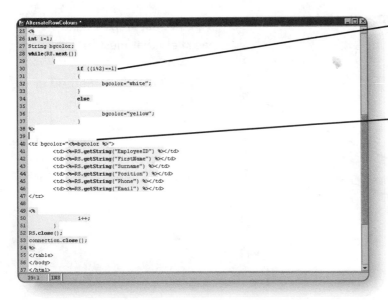

```
25 <%
26 int i=1;
27 String bgcolor;
28 while(RS.next())
29          {
30                  if ((i%2)==1)
31                  {
32                          bgcolor="white";
33                  }
34                  else
35                  {
36                          bgcolor="yellow";
37                  }
38 %>
39 |
40 <tr bgcolor="<%=bgcolor %>">
41          <td><%=RS.getString("EmployeeID") %></td>
42          <td><%=RS.getString("FirstName") %></td>
43          <td><%=RS.getString("Surname") %></td>
44          <td><%=RS.getString("Position") %></td>
45          <td><%=RS.getString("Phone") %></td>
46          <td><%=RS.getString("Email") %></td>
47 </tr>
48
49 <%
50                  i++;
51          }
52 RS.close();
53 connection.close();
54 %>
55 </table>
56 </body>
57 </html>
39:1    INS
```

11. Use an if-else statement to determine whether the current row is odd or even and set the appropriate background color.

12. Use the Expression tag to set the bgcolor attribute of the table row. You can specify colors by their hex values or use the color constants for the eight basic colors.

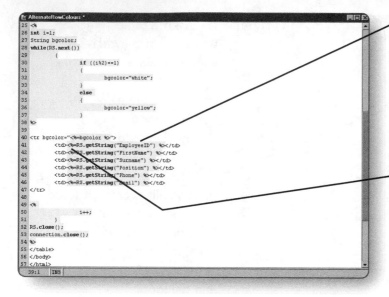

13. Pass the database field name to the getString method of the ResultSet object. This will return the data stored in the field as a string. If the remainder of the row number divided by 2 returns 1, the row is odd.

14. Use the Expression tag to print the data returned with the getString method to a table cell.

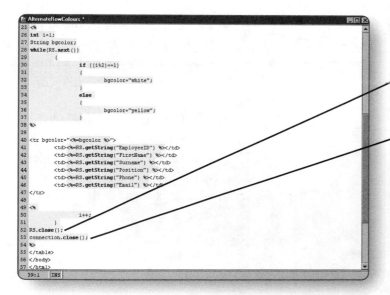

15. Repeat steps 13 and 14 for each field that must be retrieved.

16. Call the close method of the ResultSet object.

17. Call the close method of the connection object. This will close the database connection.

Working with Prepared Statements

The queries used in Web applications will be executed repeatedly. Even if the parameters passed to a query change, the structure of many queries will remain the same. A prepared statement is a parameterized query that is sent to the database for compilation before the query is run. Instead of hard coding variables in a query, question marks are used to indicate the position where a value must be substituted. Prepared statements significantly improve performance. They also simplify the syntax of constructing complex queries.

1. Use the Class.forName method to load the JDBC driver. The name of the class that contains the JDBC-ODBC Bridge is sun.jdbc.odbc.JdbcOdbcDriver.

2. Create a connection object.

3. Pass the location of the database to the getConnection method of the DriverManager class.

```
PreparedStatements
 1 <html>
 2 <head>
 3 <title>Displaying Records</title>
 4 </head>
 5 <body>
 6 <h3>Displaying Records</h3>
 7 <P>
 8 <%
 9 Class.forName("sun.jdbc.odbc.JdbcOdbcDriver");
10 java.sql.Connection connection = java.sql.DriverManager.getConnection("jdbc:odbc:Employee","","");
11 String query = "SELECT * FROM Employee WHERE Surname = ?";
12 java.sql.PreparedStatement statement = connection.prepareStatement(query);
13 statement.setString(1,"Bakharia");
14 java.sql.ResultSet RS = statement.executeQuery();
15 %>
16 <table BORDER WIDTH="100%" >
17 <tr>
18      <td><b>-</b></td>
19      <td><b>First Name</b></td>
20      <td><b>Surname</b></td>
21      <td><b>Position</b></td>
22      <td><b>Phone</b></td>
23      <td><b>Email</b></td>
24 </tr>
25 |
26 <%
27 while(RS.next())
28      {
29 %>
30
31 <tr>
32      <td><%=RS.getString("EmployeeID") %></td>
33      <td><%=RS.getString("FirstName") %></td>
```
25:1   INS

4. Store the SQL query in a string variable.

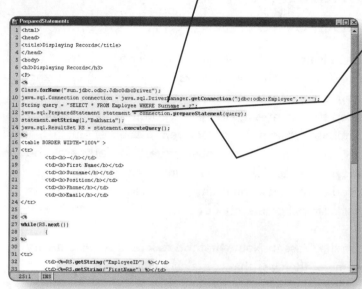

5. Create a PreparedStatement object by calling the prepareStatement method.

6. Pass the query to the prepareStatement method.

```
PreparedStatements
1  <html>
2  <head>
3  <title>Displaying Records</title>
4  </head>
5  <body>
6  <h3>Displaying Records</h3>
7  <P>
8  <%
9  Class.forName("sun.jdbc.odbc.JdbcOdbcDriver");
10 java.sql.Connection connection = java.sql.DriverManager.getConnection("jdbc:odbc:Employee","","");
11 String query = "SELECT * FROM Employee WHERE Surname = ?";
12 java.sql.PreparedStatement statement = connection.prepareStatement(query);
13 statement.setString(1,"Bakharia");
14 java.sql.ResultSet RS = statement.executeQuery();
15 %>
16 <table BORDER WIDTH="100%" >
17 <tr>
18         <td><b>-</b></td>
19         <td><b>First Name</b></td>
20         <td><b>Surname</b></td>
21         <td><b>Position</b></td>
22         <td><b>Phone</b></td>
23         <td><b>Email</b></td>
24 </tr>
25
26 <%
27 while(RS.next())
28         {
29 %>
30
31 <tr>
32         <td><%=RS.getString("EmployeeID") %></td>
33         <td><%=RS.getString("FirstName") %></td>
25:1   INS
```

7. Use the setString method of the PreparedStatement object to replace each question mark in the query with a value. The index for referencing question mark parameters is 1.

> **NOTE**
>
> You can also use the setInt method to insert integer values.

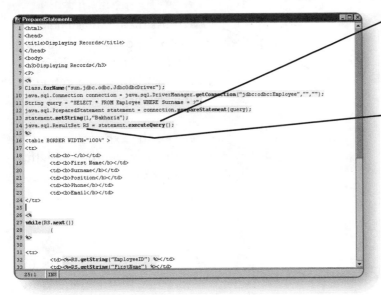

8. Call the executeQuery method of the PreparedStatement object.

9. Store the returned records in a ResultSet object.

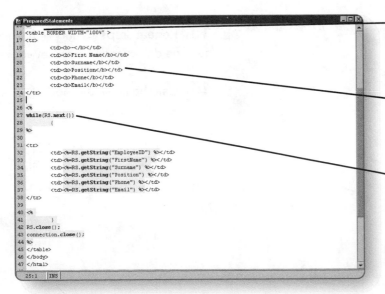

10. Insert a table in the JSP page. The retrieved records will be displayed in a table.

11. Include table column headings for each field that will be displayed in the table.

12. Use a while loop to iterate through all records returned. The next method of the ResultSet object will return false when there are no more records in the ResultSet object. This will end the loop.

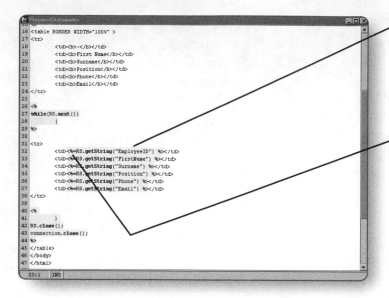

13. Pass the database field name to the getString method of the ResultSet object. This will return the data stored in the field as a string.

14. Use the Expression tag to print the data returned with the getString method to a table cell.

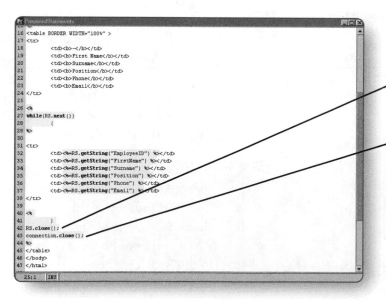

15. Repeat steps 13 and 14 for each field that must be retrieved.

16. Call the close method of the ResultSet object.

17. Call the close method of the connection object. This will close the database connection.

Displaying Summary Search Results and Linking to Full Records

It is simply not practical to display all database fields in a table. A record might consist of many fields, which can't all be displayed on the same screen. You should always display the fields that describe the essence of a record and include a link, on which the user can click to view the full record if they wish. This section shows you how to append the unique record ID to the query string so that the record selected by the user will be retrieved and displayed in full.

Linking to a Full Record

The following steps show you how to link to a full record.

1. Use the Class.forName method to load the JDBC driver. The name of the class that contains the JDBC-ODBC Bridge is sun.jdbc.odbc.JdbcOdbcDriver.

2. Create a connection object.

3. Pass the location of the database to the getConnection method of the DriverManager class.

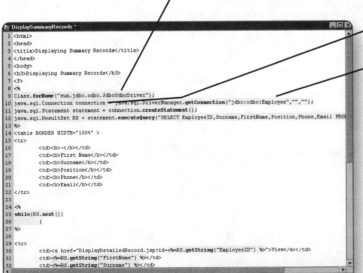

```
DisplaySummaryRecords *
 1 <html>
 2 <head>
 3 <title>Displaying Summary Records</title>
 4 </head>
 5 <body>
 6 <h3>Displaying Summary Records</h3>
 7 <P>
 8 <%
 9 Class.forName("sun.jdbc.odbc.JdbcOdbcDriver");
10 java.sql.Connection connection = java.sql.DriverManager.getConnection("jdbc:odbc:Employee","","");
11 java.sql.Statement statement = connection.createStatement();
12 java.sql.ResultSet RS = statement.executeQuery("SELECT EmployeeID,Surname,FirstName,Position,Phone,Email FRO
13 %>
14 <table BORDER WIDTH="100%" >
15 <tr>
16        <td><b>-</b></td>
17        <td><b>First Name</b></td>
18        <td><b>Surname</b></td>
19        <td><b>Position</b></td>
20        <td><b>Phone</b></td>
21        <td><b>Email</b></td>
22 </tr>
23
24 <%
25 while(RS.next())
26        {
27 %>
28
29 <tr>
30        <td><a href="DisplayDetailedRecord.jsp?id=<%=RS.getString("EmployeeID") %>">View</a></td>
31        <td><%=RS.getString("FirstName") %></td>
32        <td><%=RS.getString("Surname") %></td>

28:1    INS
```

4. Create a statement object by calling the createStatement method. A statement object is used to send queries to a database.

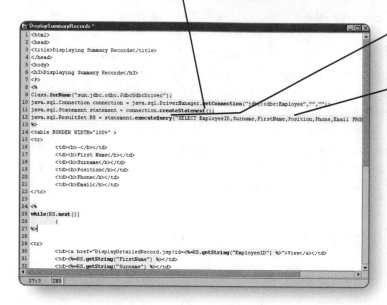

5. Call the executeQuery method of the statement object.

6. Pass the SQL query to the executeQuery method.

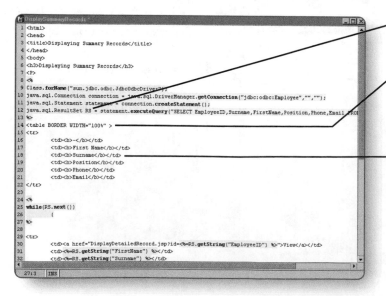

7. Store the returned records in a ResultSet object.

8. Insert a table in the JSP page. The retrieved records will be displayed in a table.

9. Include table column headings for each field that will be displayed in the table.

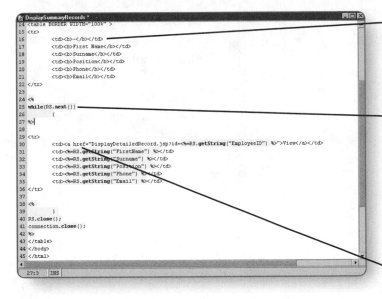

10. Include an extra column for displaying a link on which the user can click to display the full record.

11. Use a while loop to iterate through all records returned. The next method of the ResultSet object will return false when there are no more records in the ResultSet object. This will end the loop.

12. Insert a link to the JSP page that displays the full record.

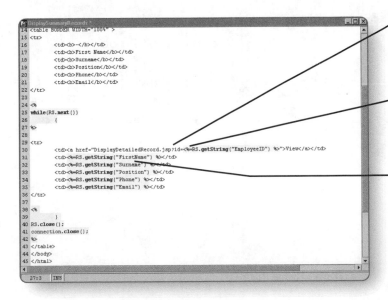

13. Pass the unique ID field name to the getString method of the ResultSet object.

14. Use the Expression tag to add the record's unique ID to the query string.

15. Pass the database field name to the getString method of the ResultSet object. This will return the data stored in the field as a string.

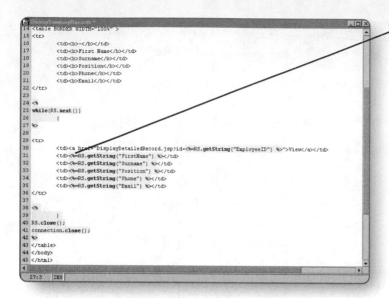

16. Use the Expression tag to print the data returned with the getString method to a table cell.

17. Repeat steps 15 and 16 for each field that must be retrieved.

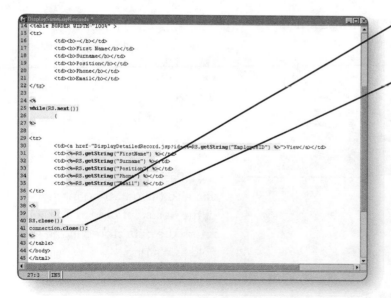

18. Call the close method of the ResultSet object.

19. Call the close method of the connection object. This will close the database connection.

Displaying a Full Record

This page needs to retrieve the record's unique ID from the query string and insert it into the SQL query. The record ID will be the only change to the query. This is the ideal situation in which to use a PreparedStatement.

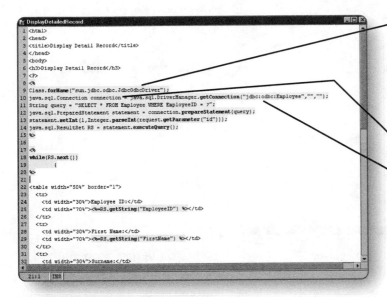

1. Use the Class.forName method to load the JDBC driver. The name of the class that contains the JDBC-ODBC Bridge is sun.jdbc.odbc.JdbcOdbcDriver.

2. Create a connection object.

3. Pass the location of the database to the getConnection method of the DriverManager class.

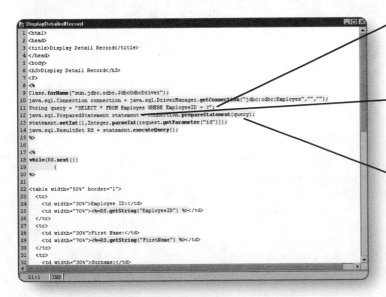

4. Store the SQL query in a string variable. Insert a question mark for the record's ID number.

5. Create a PreparedStatement object by calling the prepareStatement method.

6. Pass the query to the prepareStatement method.

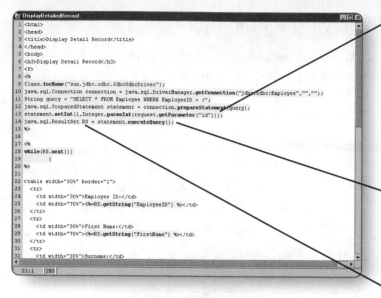

```
DisplayDetailedRecord                                        _ □ X
1  <html>
2  <head>
3  <title>Display Detail Record</title>
4  </head>
5  <body>
6  <h3>Display Detail Record</h3>
7  <P>
8  <%
9  Class.forName("sun.jdbc.odbc.JdbcOdbcDriver");
10 java.sql.Connection connection = java.sql.DriverManager.getConnection("jdbc:odbc:Employee","","");
11 String query = "SELECT * FROM Employee WHERE EmployeeID = ?";
12 java.sql.PreparedStatement statement = connection.prepareStatement(query);
13 statement.setInt(1,Integer.parseInt(request.getParameter("id")));
14 java.sql.ResultSet RS = statement.executeQuery();
15 %>
16
17 <%
18 while(RS.next())
19       {
20 %>
21
22 <table width="50%" border="1">
23   <tr>
24     <td width="30%">Employee ID:</td>
25     <td width="70%"><%=RS.getString("EmployeeID") %></td>
26   </tr>
27   <tr>
28     <td width="30%">First Name:</td>
29     <td width="70%"><%=RS.getString("FirstName") %></td>
30   </tr>
31   <tr>
32     <td width="30%">Surname:</td>

21:1    INS
```

7. Use the setInt method of the PreparedStatement object to replace each question mark in the query with the ID retrieved from the query string. The getParameter method is used to retrieve the ID field from the query string.

8. Call the executeQuery method of the PreparedStatement object.

9. Store the returned records in a ResultSet object.

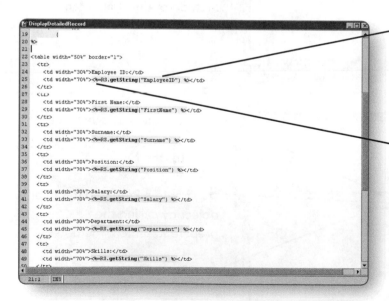

```
DisplayDetailedRecord                                        _ □ X
19       {
20 %>
21 |
22 <table width="50%" border="1">
23   <tr>
24     <td width="30%">Employee ID:</td>
25     <td width="70%"><%=RS.getString("EmployeeID") %></td>
26   </tr>
27   <tr>
28     <td width="30%">First Name:</td>
29     <td width="70%"><%=RS.getString("FirstName") %></td>
30   </tr>
31   <tr>
32     <td width="30%">Surname:</td>
33     <td width="70%"><%=RS.getString("Surname") %></td>
34   </tr>
35   <tr>
36     <td width="30%">Position:</td>
37     <td width="70%"><%=RS.getString("Position") %></td>
38   </tr>
39   <tr>
40     <td width="30%">Salary:</td>
41     <td width="70%"><%=RS.getString("Salary") %></td>
42   </tr>
43   <tr>
44     <td width="30%">Department:</td>
45     <td width="70%"><%=RS.getString("Department") %></td>
46   </tr>
47   <tr>
48     <td width="30%">Skills:</td>
49     <td width="70%"><%=RS.getString("Skills") %></td>
50   </tr>

21:1    INS
```

10. Pass the database field name to the getString method of the ResultSet object. This will return the data stored in the field as a string.

11. Use the Expression tag to print the data returned with the getString method to the JSP page.

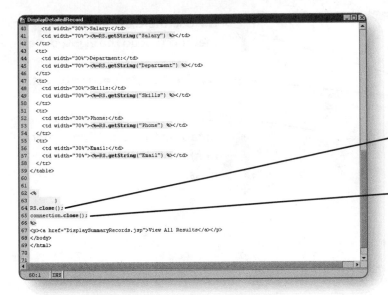

12. Repeat steps 10 and 11 for each field that must be retrieved. Remember that this page should display the entire record.

13. Call the close method of the ResultSet object.

14. Call the close method of the connection object. This will close the database connection.

Inserting Records

You also need the ability to add new records to a Web-enabled database. Information entered by a user into a form can be retrieved on the server and stored in a database. You can insert new records into a database table by writing an appropriate SQL query. The SQL statement to insert a new record is simple. You just need to specify the table and the data to be inserted. The SQL statement to insert a new record in a table must follow this syntax:

```
INSERT INTO tablename(column_name,...,column_name)
VALUES (value1,...,value2)
```

You must specify values in the same order as the table column names.

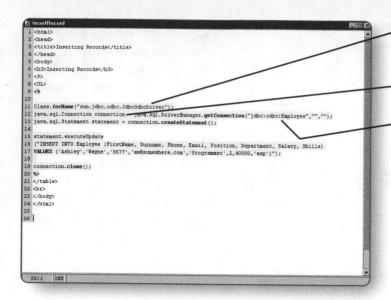

1. Use the Class.forName method to load the JDBC driver.

2. Create a connection object.

3. Pass the location of the database to the getConnection method of the DriverManager class.

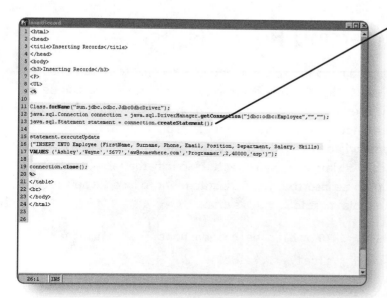

4. Create a statement object by calling the createStatement method. A statement object is used to send queries to a database.

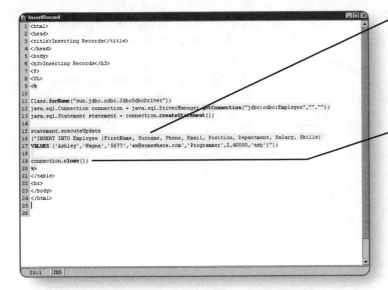

5. Pass the INSERT SQL query to the executeUpdate method. The record will be inserted. The executeUpdate method does not return a ResultSet.

6. Call the close method of the connection object. This will close the database connection.

Updating Records

Millions of people can access a dynamic database-driven Web site. It is important that the data stored in the database is kept up to date. You will need to provide a Web interface that allows users to edit data. The UPDATE SQL statement will allow you to update existing records. All you need to do is specify the table that contains the record to be updated, the new values to be stored in the record, and the record that needs to be updated. The SQL statement to update an existing record in a table must follow this syntax:

```
UPDATE tablename
SET (column_name=value1,...,column_name=value2)
WHERE column_name = value
```

You must specify values in the same order as the table column names.

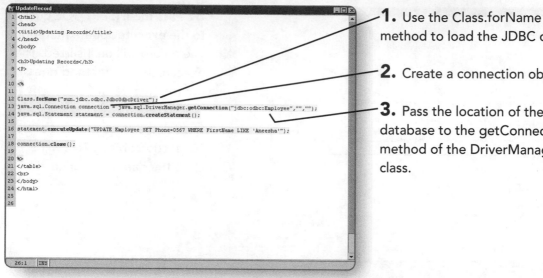

1. Use the Class.forName method to load the JDBC driver.

2. Create a connection object.

3. Pass the location of the database to the getConnection method of the DriverManager class.

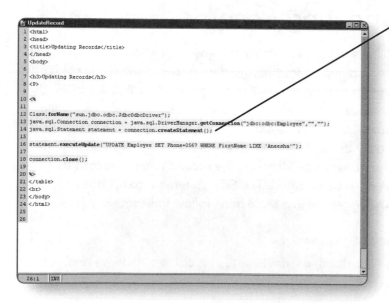

4. Create a statement object by calling the createStatement method. A statement object is used to send queries to a database.

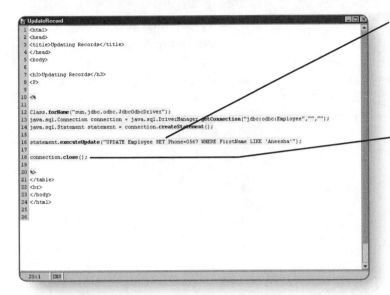

```
UpdateRecord                                                      _ □ ×
 1  <html>
 2  <head>
 3  <title>Updating Records</title>
 4  </head>
 5  <body>
 6
 7  <h3>Updating Records</h3>
 8  <P>
 9
10  <%
11
12  Class.forName("sun.jdbc.odbc.JdbcOdbcDriver");
13  java.sql.Connection connection = java.sql.DriverManager.getConnection("jdbc:odbc:Employee","","");
14  java.sql.Statement statement = connection.createStatement();
15
16  statement.executeUpdate("UPDATE Employee SET Phone=0567 WHERE FirstName LIKE 'Aneesha'");
17
18  connection.close();
19
20  %>
21  </table>
22  <br>
23  </body>
24  </html>
25
26

25:1    INS
```

5. Pass the UPDATE SQL query to the executeUpdate method. The record will be updated. The executeUpdate method does not return a ResultSet.

6. Call the close method of the connection object. This will close the database connection.

Deleting Records

Records that are no longer valid should be deleted. This frees up valuable space and increases the speed at which a database searches. The DELETE SQL statement is extremely simple. (Perhaps it's too simple for a command that has the potential to be quite dangerous if placed in the wrong hands. You need to be careful when using it.) You only need to specify the table that contains the data to be deleted and define the criteria for deleting records. If the criteria you specify is broad, you risk the possibility of deleting all the records in a table. The criteria you specify must be as specific as possible. The SQL statement to delete an existing record from a table must follow this syntax:

```
DELETE FROM tablename
WHERE column_name = value
```

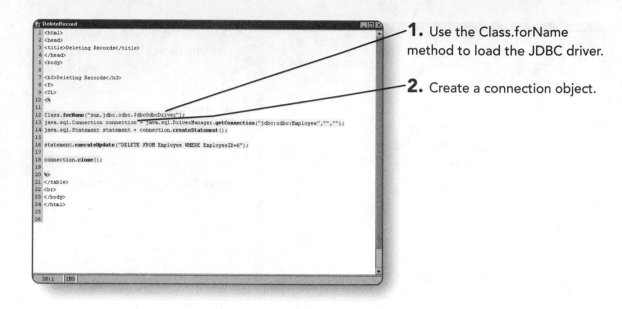

1. Use the Class.forName method to load the JDBC driver.

2. Create a connection object.

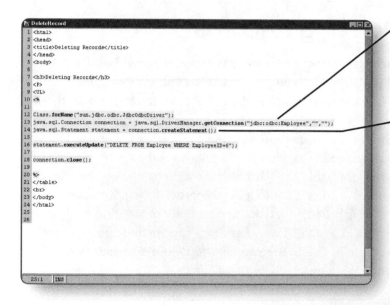

3. Pass the location of the database to the getConnection method of the DriverManager class.

4. Create a statement object by calling the createStatement method. A statement object is used to send queries to a database.

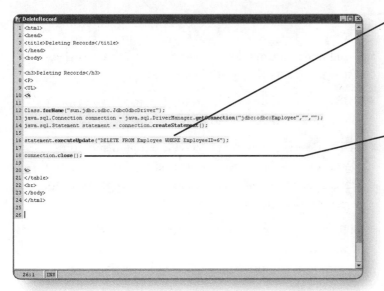

```
DeleteRecord
 1 <html>
 2 <head>
 3 <title>Deleting Records</title>
 4 </head>
 5 <body>
 6
 7 <h3>Deleting Records</h3>
 8 <P>
 9 <UL>
10 <%
11
12 Class.forName("sun.jdbc.odbc.JdbcOdbcDriver");
13 java.sql.Connection connection = java.sql.DriverManager.getConnection("jdbc:odbc:Employee","","");
14 java.sql.Statement statement = connection.createStatement();
15
16 statement.executeUpdate("DELETE FROM Employee WHERE EmployeeID=6");
17
18 connection.close();
19
20 %>
21 </table>
22 <br>
23 </body>
24 </html>
25
26 |

26:1    INS
```

5. Pass the DELETE SQL query to the executeUpdate method. The record will be deleted. The executeUpdate method does not return a ResultSet.

6. Call the close method of the connection object. This will close the database connection.

Creating Paged Search Results

A database search can return thousands of records, even if the search criteria is very specific. It is not practical to display all of these records on a single page because it would take too long for the entire page to download. Search results should be displayed in a user-friendly and intuitive manner. You should never overload the user with information. The solution is to send only a few records to the browser at a time. Search results can be split over multiple pages and the user can then navigate through the pages. Major Internet search engines employ this technique.

The following JSP script uses the CachedRowSet JavaBean to limit the number of records displayed on a page and allow the user to navigate between pages. The current location in the set of pages is also displayed. The script is quite complex, but it has been written so that you can easily configure it to your needs.

NOTE

You will need to download these extensions before you can use the CachedRowSet JavaBean:

- JDBC 2.0 Optional Package from http://java.sun.com/products/jdbc/download.html.

- JDBC RowSet from http://developer.java.sun.com/developer/earlyAccess/crs. This is currently on Early Release, so you will have to sign up to register before it can be downloaded.

- JNDI (*Java Naming and Directory Interface*) from http://java.sun.com/products/jndi/index.html. Remember to update your CLASSPATH variable accordingly.

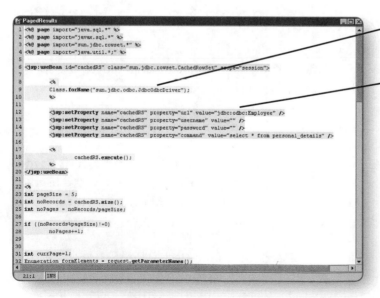

1. Specify a JDBC driver for your database.

2. Specify the connection URL for your database. This defines the location of your database.

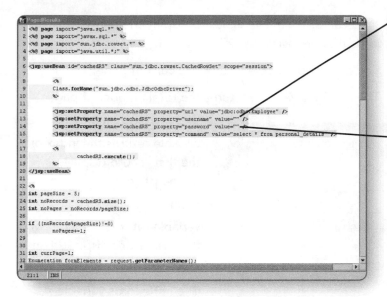

3. Enter the user name required to access the database. Leave this blank if your database is not password-protected.

4. Enter the password to access the database. Leave this blank if your database is not password-protected.

5. Specify the SQL query that defines the search criteria.

6. Set the maximum number of records to be displayed per page.

NOTE

The JSP code will automatically determine the number of pages required.

7. You can use some variables to display the page and records that are currently being viewed.

● The currPage variable returns the current page.

● The noPages variable returns the total number of pages.

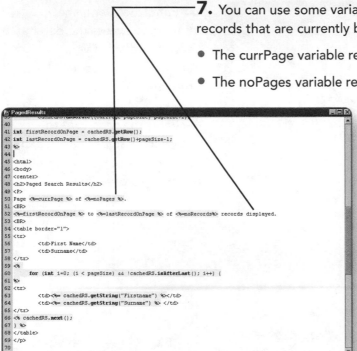

● The firstRecordOnPage variable returns the index of the first record displayed on the page.

● The lastRecordOnPage variable returns the index of the last record displayed on the page.

● The noRecords variable returns the total number of records returned.

You can use the Expression tag to print these variables to the screen and display a record or page status bar.

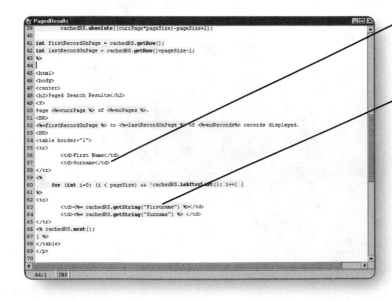

8. Insert table column names for the database fields that will be displayed in the table.

9. Use the getString method to retrieve the fields for each record.

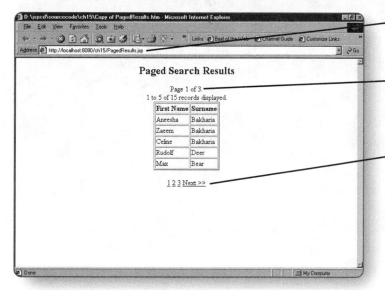

10. Preview the JSP page in a Web browser.

The status bar will display the current location in the paged results.

The navigation bar can be used to navigate through the pages. The user can use the Next link to move forward to the next page or the Previous link to return to the previous page. Links to individual pages are also displayed. The Previous link is not displayed on the first page, and the Next link is not displayed on the last page.

16

XML and JSP

Over the past few years, there has been a lot of publicity surrounding XML (*Extensible Markup Language*). XML is a markup language similar to HTML that is used to describe data and not format it. This chapter will provide you with a broad understanding of this exciting technology and how you can use it and JSP to enhance your Web site. In this chapter, you'll learn how to:

- Create an XML document
- Use JSP to generate XML from a database
- Use XSL to format XML
- Use JSP and Xalan to perform XSL transformations

What is XML?

XML is a markup language that is used to describe data. While XML and HTML might share similar tag-based syntax, they perform very different roles. HTML tags are used to apply formatting before a Web page is rendered in a browser. XML, on the other hand, allows you to define tags that best describe your data.

Before XML came along, data had to be stored in a proprietary format that could not easily be understood. This presented a number of problems when you had to electronically provide information to companies that used a different database, platform, and server. XML solved this problem by providing a common format for data storage and transfer. XML is predominantly used to integrate disparate data sources. It has had, thus far, the biggest impact on e-commerce applications.

Creating an XML Document

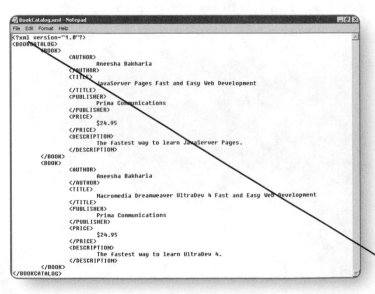

In this section, you will create a simple XML document that describes a catalog of books published by Prima Tech. For each book, the catalog must include the author, title, publisher, price, and a brief description.

1. Create a new text file and save the file with an .xml extension.

2. Use the <?xml ?> tag to define the XML document.

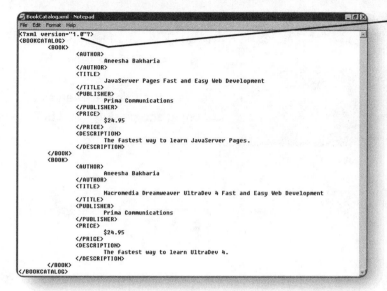

3. Set the version attribute of the <?xml ?> tag to 1.0. This tells the parser that the document is compliant with version 1.0 of the XML standard.

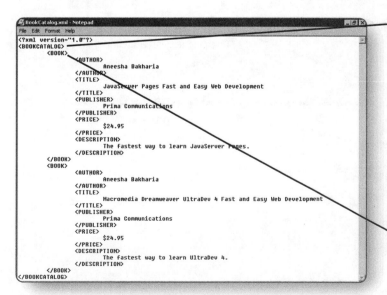

4. Insert an opening tag for the root element (BOOKCATALOG, in this example).

NOTE
All XML documents must have a root node to be valid.

5. Insert an opening tag for the child node (BOOK, in this example).

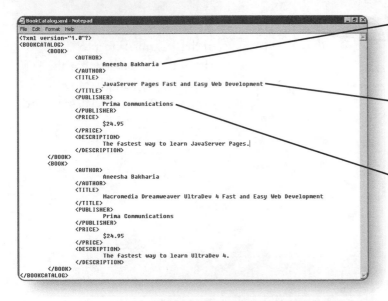

6. Type the name of the author between the opening and closing <AUTHOR> tags.

7. Type the title between the opening and closing <TITLE> tags.

8. Type the name of the publisher between the opening and closing <PUBLISHER> tags.

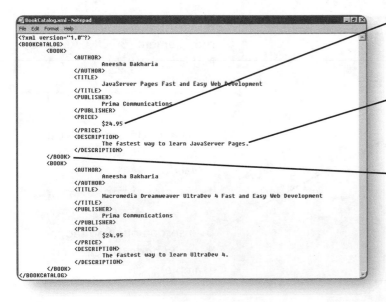

9. Type the price between the opening and closing <PRICE> tags.

10. Type the description between the opening and closing <DESCRIPTION> tags.

11. Insert a closing tag for the BOOK child tag.

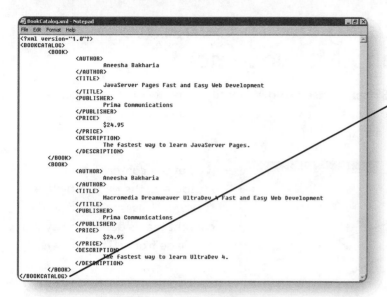

12. Repeat steps 5 through 11 for each book you want to include.

13. Insert a closing tag for the BOOKCATALOG root node.

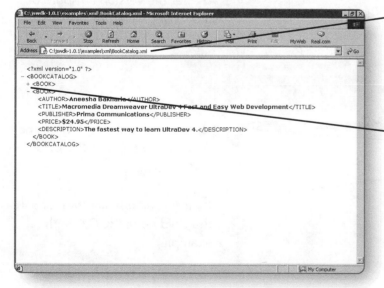

14. Preview the XML document in Microsoft Internet Explorer. The XML document will be represented by a tree structure.

15. You can click on the + sign next to a child node to expand the node. Or, you can click on the – sign next to a child node to collapse the node.

Using JSP to Generate an XML Document

JSP can be used to dynamically generate an XML document. You will need to set the content type of the document to "text/xml".

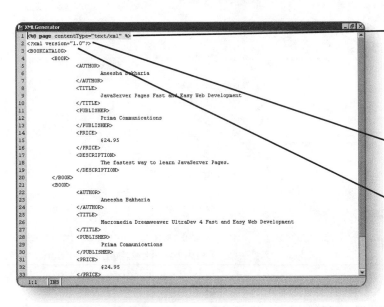

1. Set the contentType attribute of the page directive to "text/xml". This will change the content that is generated by the JSP page from HTML to XML.

2. Use the <?xml ?> tag to define the XML document.

3. Set the version attribute of the <?xml ?> tag to 1.0.

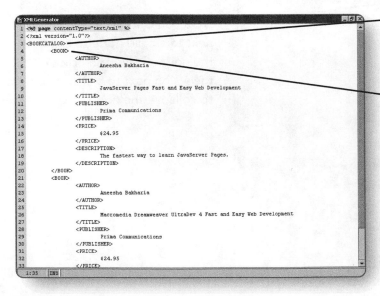

4. Insert an opening tag for the root element (BOOKCATALOG, in this example).

5. Insert an opening tag for the child node (BOOK, in this example).

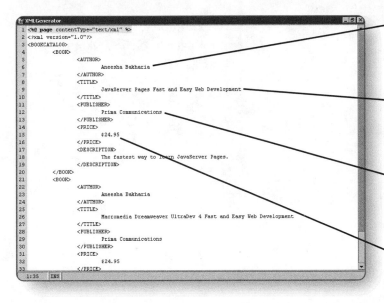

```
1 <%@ page contentType="text/xml" %>
2 <?xml version="1.0"?>
3 <BOOKCATALOG>
4     <BOOK>
5         <AUTHOR>
6             Aneesha Bakharia
7         </AUTHOR>
8         <TITLE>
9             JavaServer Pages Fast and Easy Web Development
10        </TITLE>
11        <PUBLISHER>
12            Prima Communications
13        </PUBLISHER>
14        <PRICE>
15            $24.95
16        </PRICE>
17        <DESCRIPTION>
18            The fastest way to learn JavaServer Pages.
19        </DESCRIPTION>
20    </BOOK>
21    <BOOK>
22        <AUTHOR>
23            Aneesha Bakharia
24        </AUTHOR>
25        <TITLE>
26            Macromedia Dreamweaver UltraDev 4 Fast and Easy Web Development
27        </TITLE>
28        <PUBLISHER>
29            Prima Communications
30        </PUBLISHER>
31        <PRICE>
32            $24.95
33        </PRICE>
```

6. Type the name of the author between the opening and closing <AUTHOR> tags.

7. Type the title between the opening and closing <TITLE> tags.

8. Type the name of the publisher between the opening and closing <PUBLISHER> tags.

9. Type the price between the opening and closing <PRICE> tags.

10. Type the description between the opening and closing <DESCRIPTION> tags.

11. Insert a closing tag for the BOOK child tag.

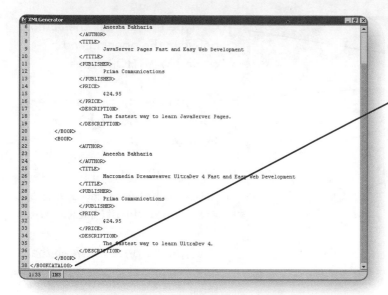

12. Repeat steps 5 through 11 for each book you want to include.

13. Insert a closing tag for the BOOKCATALOG root node.

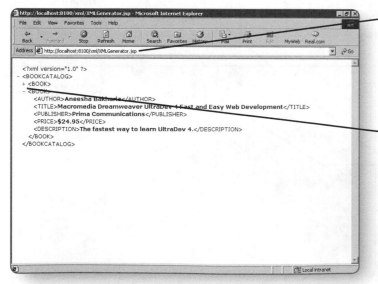

14. Preview the JSP-generated XML document in Microsoft Internet Explorer. The XML document will be represented by a tree structure.

15. You can click on a + sign next to a child node to expand the node. Or, you can click on a – sign next to a child node to collapse the node.

Generating XML from a Database

With the aid of JSP and JDBC, you can convert records stored in a database to XML. This will allow other Web applications to retrieve and process the data without any knowledge of the database structure or format.

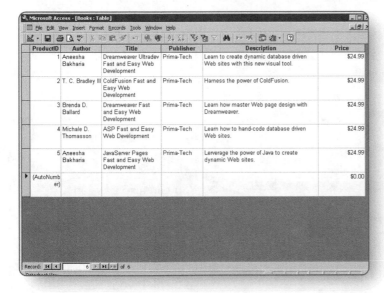

On the included CD-ROM, you will find the Books.mdb Microsoft Access 2000 database. This database contains a single table, Books, which contains a record for each book in the catalog. The table has fields that store the author, title, publisher, price, and book description.

In the example that follows, each record will be retrieved from a database and exported as an XML document. This common scenario faces many Web developers when working with data stored in a database.

1. Set the contentType attribute of the page directive to "text/xml". This will change the content generated by the JSP page from HTML to XML.

2. Load the JDBC-ODBC Bridge driver. The class name for the driver is sun.jdbc.odbc.JdbcOdbcDriver.

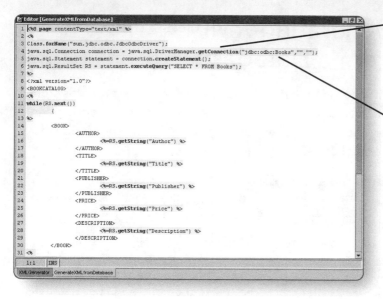

3. Call the DriverManager.getConnection method to connect to the database.

4. Pass the URL for the database as the first parameter to the getConnection method.

```
Editor [GenerateXMLfromDatabase]
1  <%@ page contentType="text/xml" %>
2  <%
3  Class.forName ("sun.jdbc.odbc.JdbcOdbcDriver");
4  java.sql.Connection connection = java.sql.DriverManager.getConnection("jdbc:odbc:Books","","");
5  java.sql.Statement statement = connection.createStatement();
6  java.sql.ResultSet RS = statement.executeQuery("SELECT * FROM Books");
7  %>
8  <?xml version="1.0"?>
9  <BOOKCATALOG>
10 <%
11 while(RS.next())
12      {
13 %>
14     <BOOK>
15         <AUTHOR>
16             <%=RS.getString("Author") %>
17         </AUTHOR>
18         <TITLE>
19             <%=RS.getString("Title") %>
20         </TITLE>
21         <PUBLISHER>
22             <%=RS.getString("Publisher") %>
23         </PUBLISHER>
24         <PRICE>
25             <%=RS.getString("Price") %>
26         </PRICE>
27         <DESCRIPTION>
28             <%=RS.getString("Description") %>
29         </DESCRIPTION>
30     </BOOK>
31 <%
1:1   INS
XML Generator   GenerateXMLfromDatabase
```

5. You can also pass an optional user name and password as the second and third parameters to the getConnection method. Leave these blank if your database does not have a password set.

```
Editor [GenerateXMLfromDatabase]
1  <%@ page contentType="text/xml" %>
2  <%
3  Class.forName ("sun.jdbc.odbc.JdbcOdbcDriver");
4  java.sql.Connection connection = java.sql.DriverManager.getConnection("jdbc:odbc:Books","","");
5  java.sql.Statement statement = connection.createStatement();
6  java.sql.ResultSet RS = statement.executeQuery("SELECT * FROM Books");
7  %>
8  <?xml version="1.0"?>
9  <BOOKCATALOG>
10 <%
11 while(RS.next())
12      {
13 %>
14     <BOOK>
15         <AUTHOR>
16             <%=RS.getString("Author") %>
17         </AUTHOR>
18         <TITLE>
19             <%=RS.getString("Title") %>
20         </TITLE>
21         <PUBLISHER>
22             <%=RS.getString("Publisher") %>
23         </PUBLISHER>
24         <PRICE>
25             <%=RS.getString("Price") %>
26         </PRICE>
27         <DESCRIPTION>
28             <%=RS.getString("Description") %>
29         </DESCRIPTION>
30     </BOOK>
31 <%
1:1   INS
XML Generator   GenerateXMLfromDatabase
```

```
Editor [GenerateXMLfromDatabase]
1  <%@ page contentType="text/xml" %>
2  <%
3  Class.forName("sun.jdbc.odbc.JdbcOdbcDriver");
4  java.sql.Connection connection = java.sql.DriverManager.getConnection("jdbc:odbc:Books","","");
5  java.sql.Statement statement = connection.createStatement();
6  java.sql.ResultSet RS = statement.executeQuery("SELECT * FROM Books");
7  %>
8  <?xml version="1.0"?>
9  <BOOKCATALOG>
10 <%
11 while(RS.next())
12     {
13 %>
14     <BOOK>
15         <AUTHOR>
16             <%=RS.getString("Author") %>
17         </AUTHOR>
18         <TITLE>
19             <%=RS.getString("Title") %>
20         </TITLE>
21         <PUBLISHER>
22             <%=RS.getString("Publisher") %>
23         </PUBLISHER>
24         <PRICE>
25             <%=RS.getString("Price") %>
26         </PRICE>
27         <DESCRIPTION>
28             <%=RS.getString("Description") %>
29         </DESCRIPTION>
30     </BOOK>
31 <%
1:1   INS
XMLGenerator   GenerateXMLfromDatabase
```

6. Create a statement object.

7. Pass the SQL query to the executeQuery method and store the records that are retrieved in a ResultSet object.

NOTE

The "SELECT * FROM Books" query will retrieve all records in the Books table.

```
Editor [GenerateXMLfromDatabase]
1  <%@ page contentType="text/xml" %>
2  <%
3  Class.forName("sun.jdbc.odbc.JdbcOdbcDriver");
4  java.sql.Connection connection = java.sql.DriverManager.getConnection("jdbc:odbc:Books","","");
5  java.sql.Statement statement = connection.createStatement();
6  java.sql.ResultSet RS = document.executeQuery("SELECT * FROM Books");
7  %>
8  <?xml version="1.0"?>
9  <BOOKCATALOG>
10 <%
11 while(RS.next())
12     {
13 %>
14     <BOOK>
15         <AUTHOR>
16             <%=RS.getString("Author") %>
17         </AUTHOR>
18         <TITLE>
19             <%=RS.getString("Title") %>
20         </TITLE>
21         <PUBLISHER>
22             <%=RS.getString("Publisher") %>
23         </PUBLISHER>
24         <PRICE>
25             <%=RS.getString("Price") %>
26         </PRICE>
27         <DESCRIPTION>
28             <%=RS.getString("Description") %>
29         </DESCRIPTION>
30     </BOOK>
31 <%
1:1   INS
XMLGenerator   GenerateXMLfromDatabase
```

8. Use the <?xml ?> tag to define the XML document.

9. Set the version attribute of the <?xml ?> tag to 1.0.

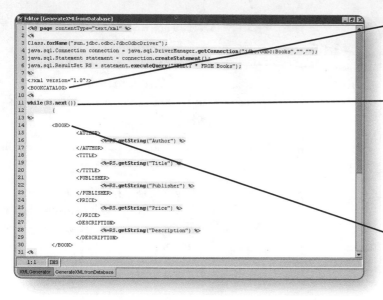

10. Insert the <BOOKCATALOG> opening tag.

11. Use a while loop to iterate through the returned records. The next method will return false when there are no more records. This will stop the execution of the loop.

12. Insert an opening <BOOK> tag.

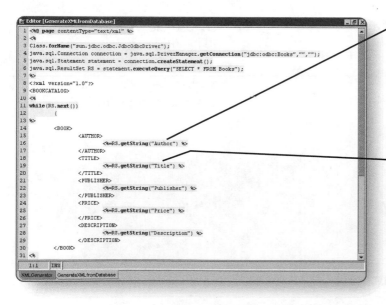

13. Use the getString method of the ResultSet object to retrieve the data stored in the Author field, and insert it between the opening and closing <AUTHOR> tags.

14. Use the getString method to retrieve the data stored in the Title field, and insert it between the opening and closing <TITLE> tags.

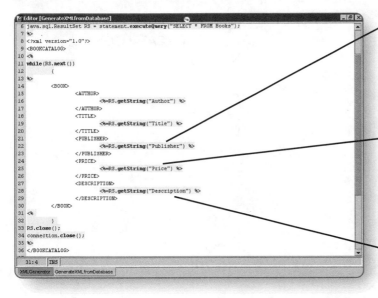

15. Use the getString method to retrieve the data stored in the Publisher field, and insert it between the opening and closing <PUBLISHER> tags.

16. Use the getString method to retrieve the data stored in the Price field, and insert it between the opening and closing <PRICE> tags.

17. Use the getString method to retrieve the data stored in the Description field, and insert it between the opening and closing <DESCRIPTION> tags.

18. Insert a closing <BOOK> tag.

19. Use the close method to close the ResultSet.

20. Use the close method to close the database connection.

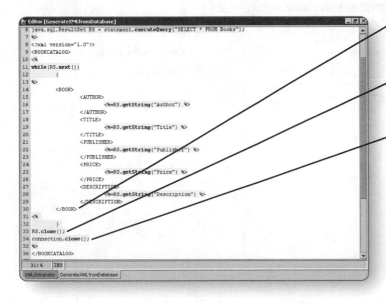

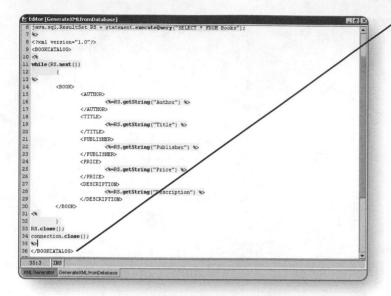

21. Insert a closing <BOOKCATALOG> tag.

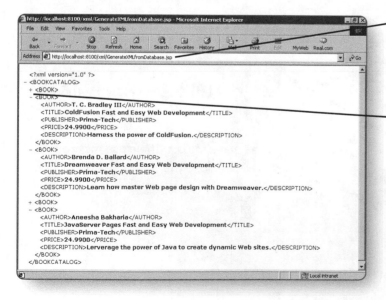

22. Preview the JSP page in Internet Explorer. The XML document will be represented by a tree structure.

23. You can click on a + sign next to a child node to expand the node. Or, you can click on a – sign next to a child node to collapse the node.

Using XSL to Format an XML Document

An HTML file stores both information and formatting instructions as to how a Web page must be displayed in a browser. This presents a problem when you need to display the document in a different format or target other Internet-ready devices such as WAP- (Wireless Application Protocol) enabled mobile phones.

XML, with the aid of XSL (*Extensible Style Language*), provides a practical solution. An XSL file is an external template used to define the formatting of an XML document. XSL can transform XML into HTML or WML, which is supported by WAP-enabled mobile phones.

Creating an XSL Style Sheet

XSL has a rich set of processing directives that allow for filtering, manipulation, and sorting of data stored in an XML document. Explaining XSL is beyond the scope of this book; however, an example of an XSL Style Sheet is presented here that will display the XML data in an HTML table.

NOTE
You'll find an excellent tutorial on using XSL at http://www.w3schools.com/xsl.

```
BookCatalog.xsl - Notepad
File  Edit  Search  Help
<?xml version="1.0"?>
<xsl:stylesheet xmlns:xsl="http://www.w3.org/TR/WD-xsl">
<xsl:template match="/">
  <html>
  <body>
    <table border="1">
      <tr>
        <td><b>Author</b></td>
        <td><b>Title</b></td>
        <td><b>Description</b></td>
        <td><b>Publisher</b></td>
        <td><b>Price</b></td>
      </tr>
      <xsl:for-each select="BOOKCATALOG/BOOK">
      <tr>
        <td><xsl:value-of select="AUTHOR" /></td>
        <td><xsl:value-of select="TITLE" /></td>
        <td><xsl:value-of select="DESCRIPTION" /></td>
        <td><xsl:value-of select="PUBLISHER" /></td>
        <td><xsl:value-of select="PRICE" /></td>
      </tr>
      </xsl:for-each>
    </table>
  </body>
  </html>
</xsl:template>
</xsl:stylesheet>
```

1. Create a new text file and save the file with an .xsl extension.

2. Use the <?xml ?> tag to define the XML document.

3. Set the version attribute of the <?xml ?> tag to 1.0. This tells the parser that the document is compliant with version 1.0 of the XML standard.

```
BookCatalog.xsl - Notepad
File  Edit  Search  Help
<?xml version="1.0"?>
<xsl:stylesheet xmlns:xsl="http://www.w3.org/TR/WD-xsl">
<xsl:template match="/">
  <html>
  <body>
    <table border="1">
      <tr>
        <td><b>Author</b></td>
        <td><b>Title</b></td>
        <td><b>Description</b></td>
        <td><b>Publisher</b></td>
        <td><b>Price</b></td>
      </tr>
      <xsl:for-each select="BOOKCATALOG/BOOK">
      <tr>
        <td><xsl:value-of select="AUTHOR" /></td>
        <td><xsl:value-of select="TITLE" /></td>
        <td><xsl:value-of select="DESCRIPTION" /></td>
        <td><xsl:value-of select="PUBLISHER" /></td>
        <td><xsl:value-of select="PRICE" /></td>
      </tr>
      </xsl:for-each>
    </table>
  </body>
  </html>
</xsl:template>
</xsl:stylesheet>
```

4. Insert an opening <xsl:stylesheet> tag.

5. Set the xmlns:xsl tag attribute to http://www.w3.org/TR/WD-xsl.

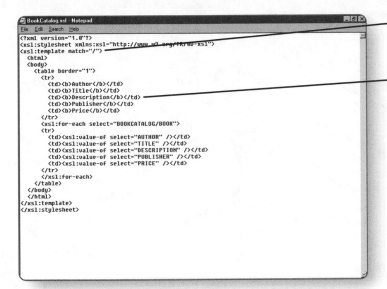

6. Insert an opening <xsl:template> tag.

7. Set the match attribute to /. This matches the template to the root of the XML documents.

8. Insert the HTML code. Opening HTML tags, as well as headings for the table columns, will be inserted.

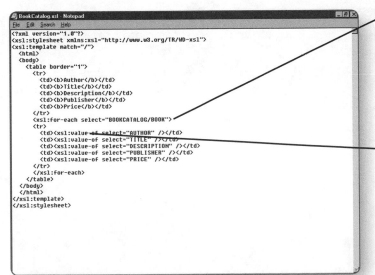

9. Insert the <xsl:for-each> tag to loop through all the BOOK child nodes that are found in the XML document. The select attribute must be set to BOOKCATALOG/BOOK.

10. Insert the <xsl:value-of> tag to retrieve the tagged data from the XML document. The select attribute must specify the tag name.

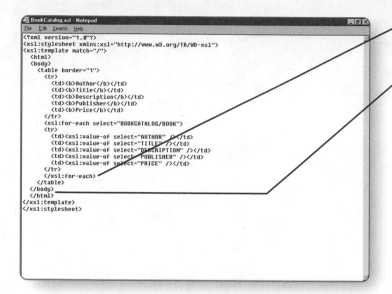

11. Insert a closing <xsl:for-each> tag.

12. Insert the closing HTML tags.

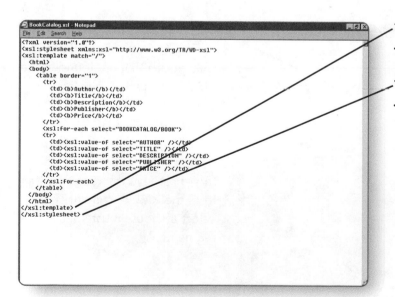

13. Insert a closing <xsl:template> tag.

14. Insert a closing <xsl:stylesheet> tag.

Specifying an XSL Style Sheet

The XSL file must be specified in the XML document. When the XML document is viewed in an XSL-compliant browser such as Internet Explorer, it will be rendered according to the XSL style sheet.

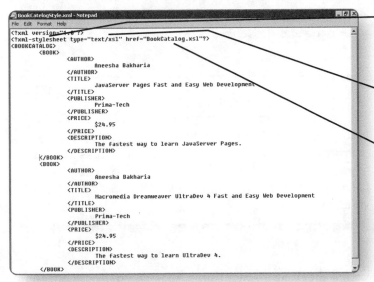

1. Insert the <?xml-stylesheet ?> tag after the <?xml ?> tag.

2. Set the type attribute to "text/xsl".

3. Use the href attribute to specify the XSL stylesheet. The XSL stylesheet must have an .xsl extension.

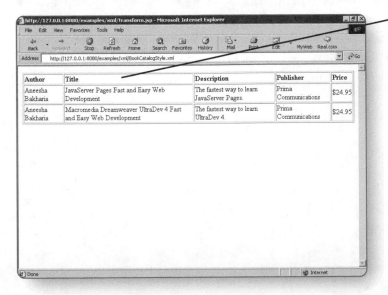

4. Preview the XML document in Microsoft Internet Explorer. The XML data will be displayed in an HTML table.

Using JSP and Xalan to Perform XSL Transformations

In the previous section, you relied upon the Web browser to apply the XSL style sheet. However, not all browsers are able to use XSL to transform XSM into HTML. With the aid of Xalan, an XSL processor, you are able to perform the transformation in a JSP page and deliver the HTML output to the browser.

NOTE

You can download Xalan at http://xml.apache.org/xalan/index.html. You will need to follow the installation instructions and include the xalan.jar and xerces.jar files in your CLASSPATH. See Chapter 2, "Getting Started," for more information on setting your CLASSPATH variable.

The code that follows might seem a bit complex and difficult to understand at first glance, but you can easily modify it to transform your XML document. I suggest that you use the code as a template and only modify the names of the XML and XSL files.

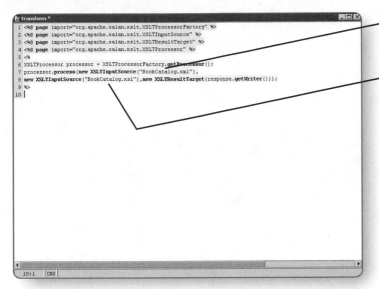

1. Specify the name of your XML document.

2. Specify the name of the XSL style sheet.

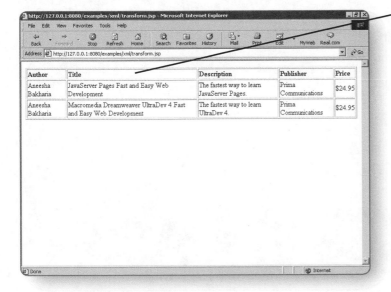

3. Preview the JSP page in any Web browser. The XML data will be displayed in an HTML table.

17

Working with Servlets

A servlet is a Java class that is designed to receive and respond to HTTP requests made by a Web browser. In terms of functionality, servlets are very similar to JSP and are equally capable of delivering complex Web solutions. Servlets are not template-based, and they use print statements to write each line of HTML to a browser. Servlets are better suited to processing data and making decisions than presenting the front-end of a Web application. Servlets and JSP are not competing technologies and should be used to complement each other. In this chapter, you'll learn how to:

- Create and compile a basic servlet
- Use a servlet to process forms
- Generate images
- Integrate servlets and JSP

Creating a Basic Servlet

Servlets are Sun's answer to CGI (*Common Gateway Interface*) scripts. CGI, which was programmed using Perl, C, or Visual Basic, was initially used to produce dynamic Web content. A CGI script was executed as an external program each time a request was made by a Web browser. This was very processor-intensive and consumed a considerable amount of memory. A Web server, as a result, could only handle a limited amount of simultaneous requests. If a CGI application crashed, it usually brought down the Web server as well.

The languages used to build CGI scripts were also not suited to Web development. They offered very little built-in support for processing forms, connecting to a database, and tracking user sessions (in other words, maintaining state).

Servlets address all of these issues. They are small Java programs that stay resident in memory and start a lightweight thread each time a request is made. A servlet is loaded into memory the first time that a Web browser makes a request. A method within the servlet class is invoked each time an additional request is made. Servlets are much more efficient than CGI programs.

Servlets are pure Java classes and have access to an extensive list of APIs for network support and database access. Java, as an object-oriented language, supports error handling and minimizes memory leaks through garbage collection. Sun has also developed the Servlet API, which incorporates standard functionality required to develop Web applications. You can easily retrieve user input, send a response to the browser, and generate a unique ID to track users using the Servlet API.

A servlet is created by either implementing the servlet interface or subclassing from a class that already implements the servlet interface. The next steps create a simple servlet that generates HTML code by subclassing GenericServlet.

```
SimpleServlet
1  import javax.servlet.*;
2  import java.io.*;
3
4  public class SimpleServlet extends GenericServlet
5  {
6          public void service(ServletRequest request,ServletResponse response) throws IOException
7          {
8                  response.setContentType("text/html");
9
10                 PrintWriter out = response.getWriter();
11
12                 out.println("<HTML>");
13                 out.println("<HEAD>");
14                 out.println("<TITLE>Output of Simple Servlet</TITLE>");
15                 out.println("</HEAD>");
16                 out.println("<BODY>");
17                 out.println("<H2>HTML - Generated by a servlet.</H1>");
18                 out.println("</BODY>");
19                 out.println("<HTML>");
20         }
21
22 }

21:1   INS
```

1. Create a new file with a .java file extension. The file name must match the class name of the servlet that you are about to create. You need to save the servlet file to the servlets directory for your servlet engine.

NOTE

In this example, SimpleServlet is the name of the class and SimpleServlet.java is the name of the file.

```
SimpleServlet
1  import javax.servlet.*;
2  import java.io.*;
3
4  public class SimpleServlet extends GenericServlet
5  {
6          public void service(ServletRequest request,ServletResponse response) throws IOException
7          {
8                  response.setContentType("text/html");
9
10                 PrintWriter out = response.getWriter();
11
12                 out.println("<HTML>");
13                 out.println("<HEAD>");
14                 out.println("<TITLE>Output of Simple Servlet</TITLE>");
15                 out.println("</HEAD>");
16                 out.println("<BODY>");
17                 out.println("<H2>HTML - Generated by a servlet.</H1>");
18                 out.println("</BODY>");
19                 out.println("<HTML>");
20         }
21  |
22 }

21:1   INS
```

2. Import the javax.servlet and java.io packages. Both of these packages are required to create a servlet class that is capable of generating HTML. The javax.servlet package contains classes that can be implemented and extended by all servlets.

3. Subclass GenericServlet to create a new servlet class.

4. You must include a service method in the class.

NOTE

The service method is invoked each time a request is made for the servlet. The service method takes two arguments: an object containing request information and an object containing the response sent back to the browser. The service method can throw an IOException.

5. Specify the type of content that is being generated. In this case, HTML code is being created. You need to pass "text/html" as a parameter to the setContentType method of the response object. This actually sets the content type in the HTTP response header.

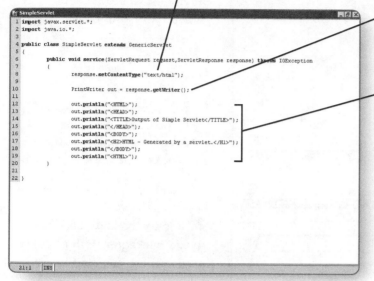

```
SimpleServlet
1  import javax.servlet.*;
2  import java.io.*;
3
4  public class SimpleServlet extends GenericServlet
5  {
6          public void service(ServletRequest request,ServletResponse response) throws IOException
7          {
8                  response.setContentType("text/html");
9
10                 PrintWriter out = response.getWriter();
11
12                 out.println("<HTML>");
13                 out.println("<HEAD>");
14                 out.println("<TITLE>Output of Simple Servlet</TITLE>");
15                 out.println("</HEAD>");
16                 out.println("<BODY>");
17                 out.println("<H2>HTML - Generated by a servlet.</H1>");
18                 out.println("</BODY>");
19                 out.println("<HTML>");
20         }
21
22 }

21:1     INS
```

6. Create a new PrintWriter object. This is required to output HTML code to the browser.

7. Use the println method to print the HTML page out line by line. The HTML code must be passed to the println method as a string.

NOTE

The HTML code that you output to a browser must be valid. You must include opening and closing <HTML>, <HEAD>, and <BODY> tags.

CAUTION

As you can see, HTML code is actually embedded in Java code. This makes it hard to edit and maintain complex HTML pages. Once the HTML code is placed in a servlet, you can't use a visual HTML editor (such as Macromedia Dreamweaver or Microsoft FrontPage) to make minor modifications.

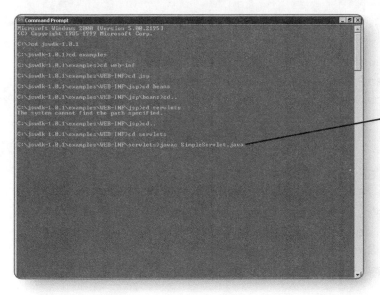

8. Save the servlet class file. The file must be saved in the servlets folder on your Web server.

9. Type **javac** followed by the servlet file name at the command prompt. The javac compiler will create a .class file. (Compiled servlets are represented as a .class file.) Refer to Chapter 2, "Getting Started," for details on setting the CLASSPATH variable.

TIP

You might receive a Class Not Found error. This occurs because the compiler can't locate the javax.servlet class, and is easily fixed. You need to include the path to the servlet.jar file in the CLASSPATH variable.

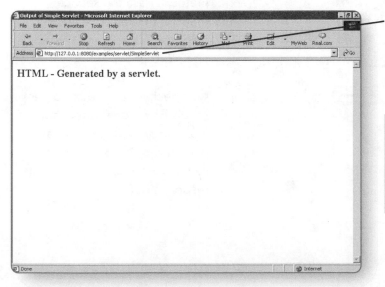

10. The servlet can be accessed via a URL from a Web browser. The servlet name is referenced in the URL.

NOTE

The servlets directory is usually aliased to /servlet in the URL.

Processing Forms

The previous servlet only generated a simple Web page. Servlets can also retrieve and process posted form data. The HttpServlet must be subclassed because it handles Get and Post requests received from a browser. HttpServlet is extended from GenericServlet.

In Chapter 10, "Retrieving Information from a User," you learned how to retrieve the values stored in specific form fields. As you recall, the name of the form field had to be passed to the getParameter method of the request object. The servlet that is outlined in the next steps lists the contents of all form fields.

1. Import the javax.servlet, java.io, and java.util packages. These packages are required to create a servlet class that is capable of retrieving and processing form data.

```
FormServlet *
1  import javax.servlet.*;
2  import javax.servlet.http.*;
3  import java.io.*;
4  import java.util.*;
5  public class FormServlet extends HttpServlet
6  {
7      public void service(HttpServletRequest request,HttpServletResponse response) throws IOException
8      {
9          response.setContentType("text/html");
10         PrintWriter out = response.getWriter();
11         out.println("<HTML>");
12         out.println("<HEAD>");
13         out.println("<TITLE>Servlet - Retrieve Form Data</TITLE>");
14         out.println("</HEAD>");
15         out.println("<BODY>");
16         out.println("<H2>Form Elements</H1>");
17         out.println("<P>");
18
19         Enumeration formElements = request.getParameterNames();
20
21         while ( formElements.hasMoreElements())
22         {
23             String formElementName = (String) formElements.nextElement();
24             String formElementvalue = request.getParameter(formElementName);
25
26             out.println("<B>" + formElementName + ":</B> " + formElementvalue);
27             out.println("<BR>");
28         }
29         out.println("</BODY>");
30         out.println("</HTML>");
31     }
32 }
18:1   INS
```

2. Subclass HttpServlet to create a new servlet class.

3. Implement the service method. Pass the service method to the request and response objects and throw an IOException.

4. Specify the type of content that is being generated. You must pass "text/html" as a parameter to the setContentType method of the response object.

5. Create a new PrintWriter object. This is required to output HTML code to the browser.

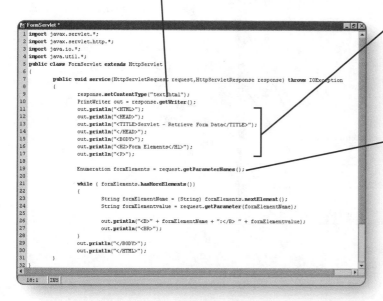

6. Use the println method to print the HTML page out line by line. The HTML code must be passed to the println method as a string.

7. Use the getParameterNames method of the request object to retrieve all of the form fields that were sent to the server, and to store the result in an enumeration object.

NOTE

An enumeration object is required because it's necessary to store the name of the form field and its associated value.

---

8. Use a while loop to iterate through the items stored in the enumeration object. Use the hasMoreElements method to end the loop. It will return false when no elements are left.

9. Use the nextElement method to retrieve the name of the current form field. You will need to cast the data type to a string.

```
1  import javax.servlet.*;
2  import javax.servlet.http.*;
3  import java.io.*;
4  import java.util.*;
5  public class FormServlet extends HttpServlet
6  {
7        public void service(HttpServletRequest request,HttpServletResponse response) throws IOException
8        {
9              response.setContentType("text/html");
10             PrintWriter out = response.getWriter();
11             out.println("<HTML>");
12             out.println("<HEAD>");
13             out.println("<TITLE>Servlet - Retrieve Form Data</TITLE>");
14             out.println("</HEAD>");
15             out.println("<BODY>");
16             out.println("<H2>Form Elements</H1>");
17             out.println("<P>");
18
19             Enumeration formElements = request.getParameterNames();
20
21             while ( formElements.hasMoreElements())
22             {
23                   String formElementName = (String) formElements.nextElement();
24                   String formElementvalue = request.getParameter(formElementName);
25
26                   out.println("<B>" + formElementName + ":</B> " + formElementvalue);
27                   out.println("<BR>");
28             }
29             out.println("</BODY>");
30             out.println("</HTML>");
31       }
32 }
```

10. Pass the form field name to the getParameter method and store the result in a variable.

11. Print the form field name and value to the Web page.

12. Write closing </BODY> and </HTML> tags to the Web page.

Generating Images

Servlets are not restricted to generating HTML content. By setting the appropriate content type, you can dynamically create images, XML, Excel spreadsheets (.csv files), Word documents, and plain text. Table 17.1 lists the generated content for some MIME types.

Table 17.1 MIME Types

Generated Content	MIME Types
Plain text	text/plain
HTML	text/html
GIF image	image/gif
JPEG image	image/jpeg
Word document	application/msword
Excel spreadsheet	application/vnd.ms-excel

```
ImageServlet
1  import javax.servlet.*;
2  import java.io.*;
3  import java.awt.*;
4  import java.awt.image.*;
5  import com.sun.image.codec.jpeg.*;
6
7  public class ImageServlet extends GenericServlet
8  {
9        public void service(ServletRequest request,ServletResponse response) throws IOException
10       {
11
12              BufferedImage servletImage = new BufferedImage(300,40, BufferedImage.TYPE_INT_RGB);
13              Graphics2D graphics = (Graphics2D) servletImage.getGraphics();
14
15              graphics.setColor(Color.blue);
16              graphics.fill3DRect(0,0,600,40,true);
17
18              graphics.setFont(new Font("Arial", Font.BOLD, 30));
19              graphics.setColor(Color.red);
20              graphics.drawString("JavaServer Pages", 11,33);
21              graphics.setColor(Color.white);
22              graphics.drawString("JavaServer Pages", 10,30);
23
24
25              response.setContentType("image/jpeg");
26
27              JPEGImageEncoder encoder = JPEGCodec.createJPEGEncoder(response.getOutputStream());
28              encoder.encode(servletImage);
29       }
30
31 }

6:1    INS
```

This example servlet creates a JPEG image. In Chapter 13, "Creating Interactive Web Pages," the code was developed, but it was embedded within a JSP page. A servlet is more appropriate for generating non-HTML content.

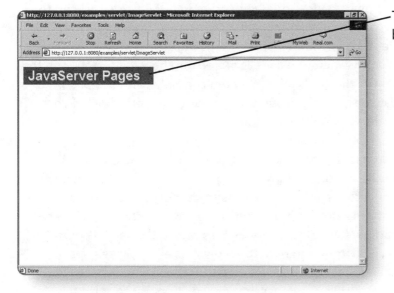

This is what the resulting image banner looks like.

Servlets versus JSP

The three practical servlet examples presented in this chapter should provide you with an overview of servlet technology and how to generate dynamic content. Servlets and JSP can achieve similar functionality. In some respects, JSP and servlets can be seen as competing technologies, but they can also be used together. While both are fully capable of creating complex Web applications, they each have their own strengths and weaknesses.

JSP is a presentation technology. It allows you to embed Java code in an HTML Web page that can still be edited in a visual HTML editor. This template-based approach simplifies the development of Web interfaces. It also means that the layout of a Web page can be updated without affecting the Java code. However, a problem occurs when a JSP page contains too much code. Code embedded in a JSP page is forced to be predominantly procedural in nature. It is also very hard to debug complex JSP applications because it is difficult to identify where the code is stored and how it interacts with the rest of the application. You can certainly place the code in a JavaBean, but you might not want to implement all of your code as a reusable component.

Servlets, on the other hand, are pure Java classes and, as a result, are great at processing data and making decisions. Servlets use print statements to output HTML code to a browser. However, generating a complex Web page is very cumbersome with a servlet. This makes the servlet source code lengthy and hard to follow. It is also very tedious to change the layout of a Web page when using servlets. Sun created JSP as template-based solution just to solve this problem. A JSP page is actually translated to a servlet before it is compiled.

```
ExpressionTag *
 1 <html>
 2 <head>
 3 <title>Using the Expression Tag</title>
 4 </head>
 5 <body>
 6
 7 <h3>Using the Expression tag to display the result of an expression:</h3>
 8 <p>
 9
10 <ul>
11 <li>2*6= <%=2*6 %></li>
12
13 <li>sqrt(8)= <%=Math.sqrt(8) %></li>
14
15 <li>The current date and time - <%=new java.util.Date() %></li>
16
17 </ul>
18
19 </body>
20 </html>
21
22
```

This is an example of a simple JSP page that displays the current date and performs simple calculations...

```
ExpressionTag *
 1 package C_0003a.jswdk_0002d_00031_0005f_00030_0005f_00031.examples.jspbasics;
 2
 3 import javax.servlet.*;
 4 import javax.servlet.http.*;
 5 import javax.servlet.jsp.*;
 6 import java.io.PrintWriter;
 7 import java.io.IOException;
 8 import java.io.FileInputStream;
 9 import java.io.ObjectInputStream;
10 import java.util.Vector;
11 import com.sun.jsp.runtime.*;
12 import java.beans.*;
13 import com.sun.jsp.JspException;
14
15 public class jspbasics_0005cExpressionTag_0002ejspExpressionTag_jsp_1 extends HttpJspBase {
16
17     static char[][] _jspx_html_data = null;
18
19     public jspbasics_0005cExpressionTag_0002ejspExpressionTag_jsp_1( ) {
20     }
21
22     private static boolean _jspx_inited = false;
23
24     public final void _jspx_init() throws JspException {
25         ObjectInputStream oin = null;
26         int numStrings = 0;
27         try {
28             FileInputStream fin = new FileInputStream("work\\%3A8080%2Fexamples\\C_0003a.jswdk_0002d_00031_00
29             oin = new ObjectInputStream(fin);
30             _jspx_html_data = (char[][]) oin.readObject();
31         } catch (Exception ex) {
32             throw new JspException("Unable to open data file");
```

...and this is the resulting servlet after the translation process.

As you can see, both servlets and JSP have their advantages. Rather than using them separately, your application can benefit from both. You can use servlets to implement business logic and JSP to format the HTML output. This is all possible because servlets can request and pass data to a JSP page.

Integrating Servlets and JSP

A servlet can process a user request and determine the appropriate JSP page to display. This can be more useful than you realize. In some Web applications, the interface that is displayed depends upon the type of user. For example, the Web site's administrator would have more privileges than would a visitor. A single JSP page could present different views, but the page would be full of conditional statements. The solution is to use a servlet to identify access privileges and display the JSP that incorporates the required functionality.

The next steps implement a much simpler example. A servlet will be used to randomly select and display one of three JSP pages.

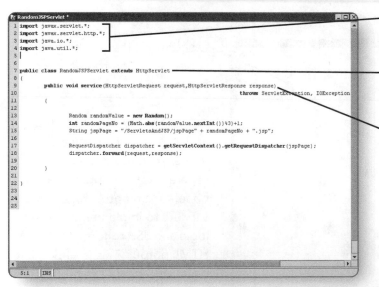

1. Import the javax.servlet and java.io packages.

2. Subclass HttpServlet to create a new servlet class.

3. Implement the service method. Pass the service method and the request and response objects, and throw an IOException and a ServletException.

```
RandomJSPServlet *
 1 import javax.servlet.*;
 2 import javax.servlet.http.*;
 3 import java.io.*;
 4 import java.util.*;
 5
 6
 7 public class RandomJSPServlet extends HttpServlet
 8 {
 9         public void service(HttpServletRequest request,HttpServletResponse response)
10                                                     throws ServletException, IOException
11         {
12
13             Random randomValue = new Random();
14             int randomPageNo = (Math.abs(randomValue.nextInt())%3)+1;
15             String jspPage = "/ServletsAndJSP/jspPage" + randomPageNo + ".jsp";
16
17             RequestDispatcher dispatcher = getServletContext().getRequestDispatcher(jspPage);
18             dispatcher.forward(request,response);
19
20         }
21
22 }
23
24
25
5:1    INS
```

4. Create an object to store random numbers.

5. Generate a random number between 1 and 3.

NOTE

If you require more information on using the Random class and generating random numbers, refer to Chapter 4, "Performing Calculations."

```
RandomJSPServlet *
 1 import javax.servlet.*;
 2 import javax.servlet.http.*;
 3 import java.io.*;
 4 import java.util.*;
 5
 6
 7 public class RandomJSPServlet extends HttpServlet
 8 {
 9         public void service(HttpServletRequest request,HttpServletResponse response)
10                                                     throws ServletException, IOException
11         {
12
13             Random randomValue = new Random();
14             int randomPageNo = (Math.abs(randomValue.nextInt())%3)+1;
15             String jspPage = "/ServletsAndJSP/jspPage" + randomPageNo + ".jsp";
16
17             RequestDispatcher dispatcher = getServletContext().getRequestDispatcher(jspPage);
18             dispatcher.forward(request,response);
19
20         }
21
22 }
23
24
25
5:1    INS
```

6. Store the file name of the JSP page to be selected in a variable. The file name is dynamically created by concatenating the file name prefix with the random number. The three possible files that could be displayed are jspPage1.jsp, jspPage2.jsp, and jspPage3.jsp.

NOTE

The URL must be relative to the server root.

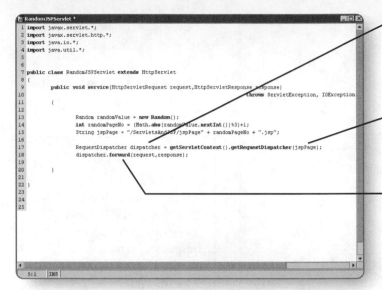

```
Random.JSPServlet *
 1  import javax.servlet.*;
 2  import javax.servlet.http.*;
 3  import java.io.*;
 4  import java.util.*;
 5
 6
 7  public class RandomJSPServlet extends HttpServlet
 8  {
 9          public void service(HttpServletRequest request,HttpServletResponse response)
10                                                      throws ServletException, IOException
11      {
12
13              Random randomValue = new Random();
14              int randomPageNo = (Math.abs(randomValue.nextInt())%3)+1;
15              String jspPage = "/ServletsAndJSP/jspPage" + randomPageNo + ".jsp";
16
17              RequestDispatcher dispatcher = getServletContext().getRequestDispatcher(jspPage);
18              dispatcher.forward(request,response);
19
20          }
21
22  }
23
24
25

5:1     INS
```

7. Create a RequestDispatcher object by calling the getRequestDispatcher method of ServletContext.

8. Pass the URL that was randomly generated to the getRequestDispatcher method.

9. Use the forward method to retrieve the JSP page. The forward method must be passed to the request and response objects.

NOTE

You can also use the query string to pass data to the JSP page, for example: /ServletsAndJSP/jsppage1.jsp?name=Aneesha&access=1.

18

Creating Custom Tags

Tag libraries present yet another way for you to extend JSP. You can create tags that can be reused to perform common tasks. Tag libraries are very similar to JavaBeans, but have distinct advantages. Tags are very easy to use—anybody with a limited knowledge of HTML can use a tag library and implement complex functionality. You can also use tags to manipulate the content on a Web page. Creating a tag library is more involved than modeling a JavaBean. The aim of this chapter is to outline the process involved in a simple and intuitive manner. In this chapter, you'll learn how to:

- Create a tag to display the current date
- Create a tag that accepts attributes
- Create tags to format and manipulate the body of a tag
- Utilize existing tag libraries
- Use JRun's custom tag libraries

What Is a Tag Library?

HTML is a markup language that uses tags to format Web pages. HTML is ideal for static content. When you create a dynamic Web application, you need to embed Java code within the HTML. This code gets processed on the server. A tag library allows you to define new tags that can be inserted in a JSP page. These tags look like normal HTML tags but instead of formatting the page, they can insert dynamic content. Any task that you can perform on a JSP page can be implemented as a reusable tag.

You can also think of a tag library as a component. It is true that tag libraries are very similar to JavaBeans. They both encapsulate complex functionality, but tag libraries are simpler to use and give you the ability to manipulate and format HTML.

You need to create the following three files to define and use a tag library:

- **A tag handler class**. You must create a class that implements the tag functionality. The tag handler class must be saved in the WEB-INF/classes folder. If the classes are contained in a jar file, the jar file must be saved in the WEB-INF/lib folder.

- **A tag library descriptor (TLD) file**. This is an XML file that describes the tags included in the library. You must save the tag handler class in the WEB-INF folder.

- **A JSP page that uses the tag library**.

CAUTION

JSWDK does not support tag libraries. JRun and Tomcat, however, are ideal to get you started.

Creating a Simple Tag Library

There is no better way to start than to create a tag that simply inserts some text into a Web page. The following three files are required:

- The tag handler class (SimpleTag.class)
- The tag library descriptor file (SimpleTag.tld)
- The JSP page that uses the tag (SimpleTag.jsp)

Creating the Tag Handler Class

The tag handler class file models the tag functionality. In this section, you will create a very simple tag that inserts some text into the JSP page. The class must implement the javax.servlet.jsp.tagext.Tag interface and extend the TagSupport class. You can also extend the BodyTagSupport class, but you only need to do this if your tag needs to process the tag body. You should use the Tag Support class if your class has no body or needs to ignore the body. Your class requires a doStartTag, which is called when the tag is first encountered. The doStartTag needs to obtain the JspWriter from pageContext so that it can print text to the JSP page. The doStartTag method must return the SKIP_BODY constant if the body of the text is ignored.

```
1  import javax.servlet.jsp.*;
2  import javax.servlet.jsp.tagext.*;
3  import java.io.*;
4
5  public class SimpleTag extends TagSupport
6  {
7        public int doStartTag()
8        {
9              try
10             {
11                   JspWriter out = pageContext.getOut();
12                   out.print("SimpleTag says Hello!");
13             }
14             catch(IOException err)
15             {
16                   System.out.println("Error in SimpleTag: " + err);
17             }
18
19             return(SKIP_BODY);
20       }
21 }
22
23
```

1. Import the javax.servlet.jsp.*, javax.servlet.jsp.tagext.*, and the java.io.* packages.

2. Declare a public class.

```
SimpleTag                                                      _ □ ×
1  import javax.servlet.jsp.*;
2  import javax.servlet.jsp.tagext.*;
3  import java.io.*;
4
5  public class SimpleTag extends TagSupport
6  {
7       public int doStartTag()
8       {
9            try
10           {
11                JspWriter out = pageContext.getOut();
12                out.print("SimpleTag says Hello!");
13           }
14           catch(IOException err)
15           {
16                System.out.println("Error in SimpleTag: " + err);
17           }
18
19           return(SKIP_BODY);
20      }
21 }
22
23
21:2    INS
```

3. Declare a public doStartTag method that returns an integer. The doStartTag is invoked when the opening tag is found.

4. Place your code within a try block.

```
SimpleTag                                                      _ □ ×
1  import javax.servlet.jsp.*;
2  import javax.servlet.jsp.tagext.*;
3  import java.io.*;
4
5  public class SimpleTag extends TagSupport
6  {
7       public int doStartTag()
8       {
9            try
10           {
11                JspWriter out = pageContext.getOut();
12                out.print("SimpleTag says Hello!");
13           }
14           catch(IOException err)
15           {
16                System.out.println("Error in SimpleTag: " + err);
17           }
18
19           return(SKIP_BODY);
20      }
21 }
22
23
21:2    INS
```

5. Use the getOut method of the pageContext object to obtain a JspWriter.

6. Use the print method to insert text into the JSP page.

7. Catch the IOException that is thrown by the print method.

```
SimpleTag                                                          _ 8 X
1  import javax.servlet.jsp.*;
2  import javax.servlet.jsp.tagext.*;
3  import java.io.*;
4
5  public class SimpleTag extends TagSupport
6  {
7          public int doStartTag()
8          {
9              try
10             {
11                 JspWriter out = pageContext.getOut();
12                 out.print("SimpleTag says Hello!");
13             }
14             catch(IOException err)
15             {
16                 System.out.println("Error in SimpleTag: " + err);
17             }
18
19             return(SKIP_BODY);
20         }
21  }
22
23
21:2    INS
```

8. Print an appropriate error message.

9. The doStartTag must return the SKIP_BODY constant because the tag body is not processed.

Creating the Tag Library Descriptor File (TLD)

The tag library descriptor file is an XML file that stores the name, tag handler class, and description of the tag library. It must follow valid XML syntax. You should use the following TLD file as a template. You need only to update the data within the tags.

```
simpletaglib                                                       _ □ X
1  <?xml version="1.0"?>
2  <taglib>
3  <tlibversion>1.0</tlibversion>
4  <jspversion>1.1</jspversion>
5  <shortname>simpletaglib</shortname>
6  <info>My First Tag Library</info>
7  <tag>
8      <name>tag</name>
9      <tagclass>SimpleTag</tagclass>
10     <bodycontent>empty</bodycontent>
11  </tag>
12  </taglib>
13
14
15
16
14:1    INS
```

1. Insert the <?xml ?> tag as the first line in the TLD file.

2. Specify 1.0 as the version.

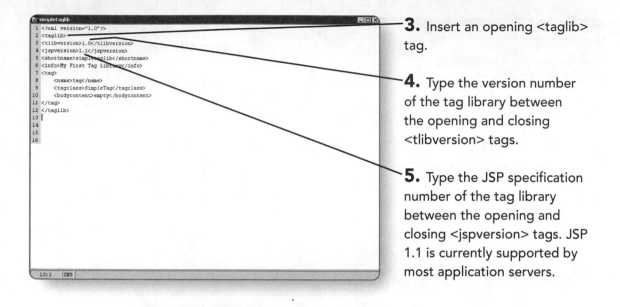

3. Insert an opening <taglib> tag.

4. Type the version number of the tag library between the opening and closing <tlibversion> tags.

5. Type the JSP specification number of the tag library between the opening and closing <jspversion> tags. JSP 1.1 is currently supported by most application servers.

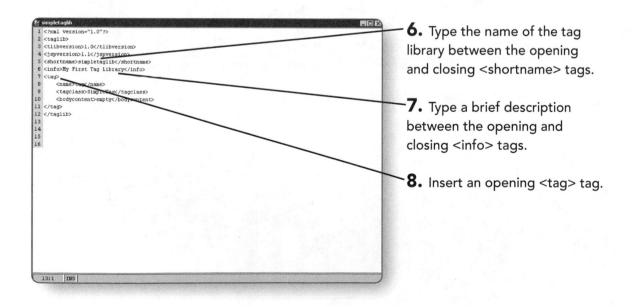

6. Type the name of the tag library between the opening and closing <shortname> tags.

7. Type a brief description between the opening and closing <info> tags.

8. Insert an opening <tag> tag.

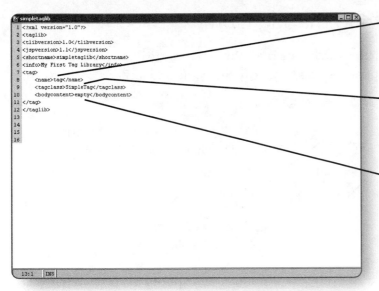

9. Type the name of the tag library between the opening and closing <name> tags.

10. Type the tag handler class file name between the opening and closing <tagclass> tags.

11. Type **empty** between the opening and closing <bodycontent> tags. You must specify empty when the tag body is not required.

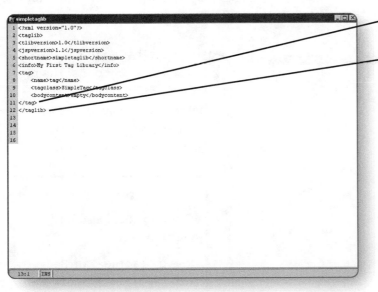

12. Insert a closing <tag> tag.

13. Insert a closing <taglib> tag.

Using the Tag Library

Using a tag library is an absolute breeze. You need to use the taglib directive to specify the name and location of the TLD file before you insert a tag into a JSP page. A date can now be inserted without any prior knowledge of Java. Tags are great for content developers and graphic designers.

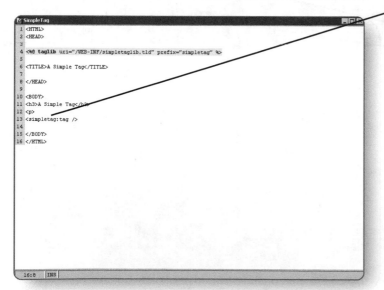

1. Insert the taglib directive in the JSP page.

2. Specify the path to the TLD file.

3. Specify a prefix for the tag library.

4. Insert the tag that you want to use in the JSP page. The tag library prefix must be placed before the tagname. A colon must also separate the tag library prefix and tag name.

NOTE

The tag could also be written as:

```
<simple:tag>Tag Body
➥ Text</simple:tag>
```

This example does not process the tag body, so it can be reduced to:

```
<simple:tag />
```

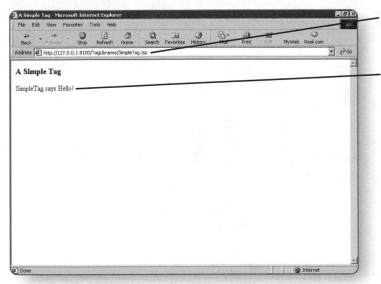

5. Preview the JSP page in a Web browser.

6. The output of the tag will be displayed.

Creating a Tag to Display the Date

In this section, you will create a tag that is more useful, in that it inserts the current date into a JSP page. The following three files are required:

- The tag handler class (DateTag.class)

- The tag library descriptor file (DateTag.tld)

- The JSP page that uses the tag (DateTag.jsp)

Creating the Tag Handler Class

First, you need to create a date object that stores the current date and time. The doStartTag method must then use the print method of the JspWriter object to output the date to the JSP page.

```
DateTag                                                            _ □ X
1  import javax.servlet.jsp.*;
2  import javax.servlet.jsp.tagext.*;
3  import java.io.*;
4  import java.util.*;
5
6  public class DateTag extends TagSupport
7  {
8         Date today = new Date();
9
10        public int doStartTag()
11        {
12              try
13                  {
14                        JspWriter out = pageContext.getOut();
15                        out.print(today);
16                  }
17              catch(IOException err)
18                  {
19                        System.out.println("Error in DateTag: " + err);
20                  }
21
22              return(SKIP_BODY);
23        }
24  }
25
26

25:1    INS
```

1. Import the javax.servlet.jsp.*, javax.servlet.jsp.tagext.*, and the java.io.* packages.

2. Declare a public class.

3. Create a date object that stores the current date.

```
DateTag                                                            _ □ X
1  import javax.servlet.jsp.*;
2  import javax.servlet.jsp.tagext.*;
3  import java.io.*;
4  import java.util.*;
5
6  public class DateTag extends TagSupport
7  {
8         Date today = new Date();
9
10        public int doStartTag()
11        {
12              try
13                  {
14                        JspWriter out = pageContext.getOut();
15                        out.print(today);
16                  }
17              catch(IOException err)
18                  {
19                        System.out.println("Error in DateTag: " + err);
20                  }
21
22              return(SKIP_BODY);
23        }
24  }
25
26

25:1    INS
```

4. Declare a public doStartTag method that returns an integer. The doStartTag is invoked when the opening tag is found.

5. Place your code within a try block.

```
DateTag                                                                    _□X
 1 import javax.servlet.jsp.*;
 2 import javax.servlet.jsp.tagext.*;
 3 import java.io.*;
 4 import java.util.*;
 5
 6 public class DateTag extends TagSupport
 7 {
 8         Date today = new Date();
 9
10         public int doStartTag()
11         {
12                 try
13                 {
14                         JspWriter out = pageContext.getOut();
15                         out.print(today);
16                 }
17                 catch(IOException err)
18                 {
19                         System.out.println("Error in DateTag: " + err);
20                 }
21
22                 return(SKIP_BODY);
23         }
24 }
25
26
```
```
25;1    INS
```

6. Use the getOut method of the pageContext object to obtain a JspWriter.

7. Use the print method to insert the current date and time into the JSP page.

8. Catch the IOException that is thrown by the print method.

```
DateTag                                                                    _□X
 1 import javax.servlet.jsp.*;
 2 import javax.servlet.jsp.tagext.*;
 3 import java.io.*;
 4 import java.util.*;
 5
 6 public class DateTag extends TagSupport
 7 {
 8         Date today = new Date();
 9
10         public int doStartTag()
11         {
12                 try
13                 {
14                         JspWriter out = pageContext.getOut();
15                         out.print(today);
16                 }
17                 catch(IOException err)
18                 {
19                         System.out.println("Error in DateTag: " + err);
20                 }
21
22                 return(SKIP_BODY);
23         }
24 }
25
26 |
```
```
26;1    INS
```

9. Print an appropriate error message.

10. The doStartTag must return the SKIP_BODY constant because the tag body is not processed.

Creating the Tag Library Descriptor File

Now, you need to update the TLD file and the details for the Date tag that was just created.

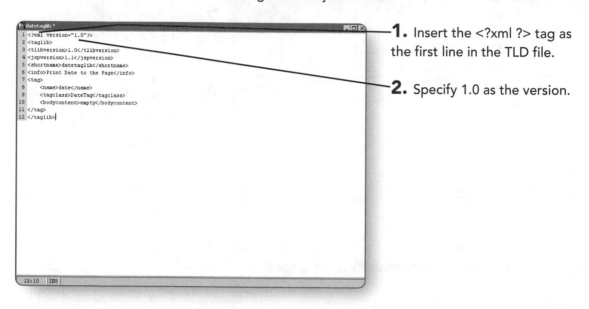

1. Insert the <?xml ?> tag as the first line in the TLD file.

2. Specify 1.0 as the version.

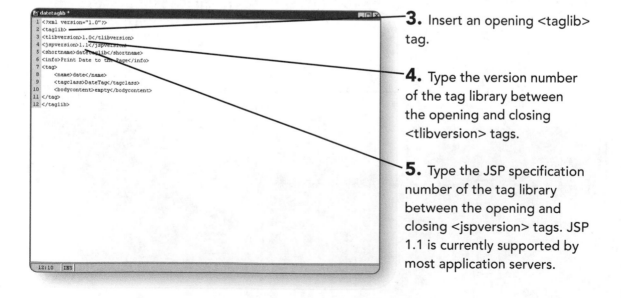

3. Insert an opening <taglib> tag.

4. Type the version number of the tag library between the opening and closing <tlibversion> tags.

5. Type the JSP specification number of the tag library between the opening and closing <jspversion> tags. JSP 1.1 is currently supported by most application servers.

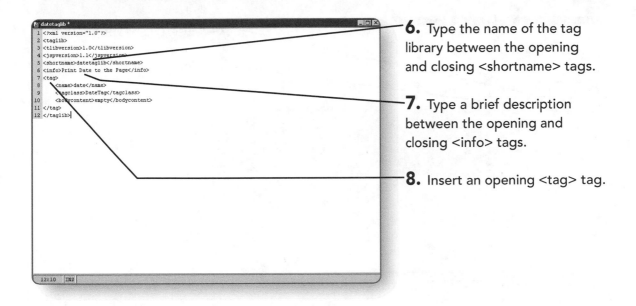

6. Type the name of the tag library between the opening and closing <shortname> tags.

7. Type a brief description between the opening and closing <info> tags.

8. Insert an opening <tag> tag.

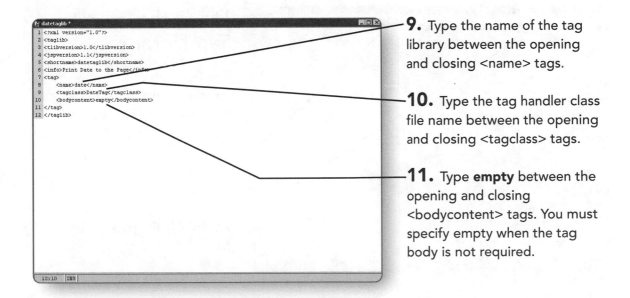

9. Type the name of the tag library between the opening and closing <name> tags.

10. Type the tag handler class file name between the opening and closing <tagclass> tags.

11. Type **empty** between the opening and closing <bodycontent> tags. You must specify empty when the tag body is not required.

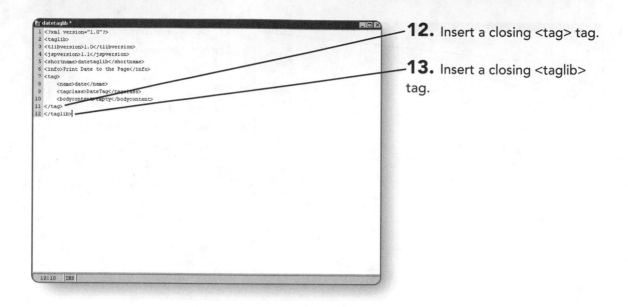

12. Insert a closing <tag> tag.

13. Insert a closing <taglib> tag.

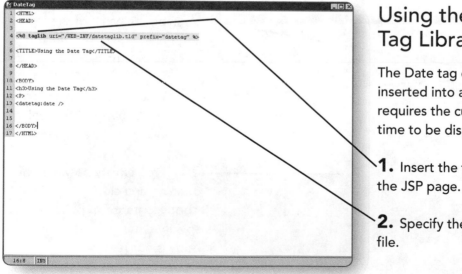

Using the Tag Library

The Date tag can now be inserted into any JSP page that requires the current date and time to be displayed.

1. Insert the taglib directive in the JSP page.

2. Specify the path to the TLD file.

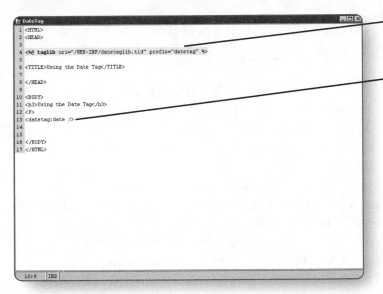

```
DateTag                                                              _ □ X
 1  <HTML>
 2  <HEAD>
 3
 4  <%@ taglib uri="/WEB-INF/datetaglib.tld" prefix="datetag" %>
 5
 6  <TITLE>Using the Date Tag</TITLE>
 7
 8  </HEAD>
 9
10  <BODY>
11  <h3>Using the Date Tag</h3>
12  <P>
13  <datetag:date />
14
15
16  </BODY>
17  </HTML>

16:8    INS
```

3. Specify a prefix for the tag library.

4. Insert the tag that you would like to use in the JSP page. The tag library prefix must be placed before the tag name.

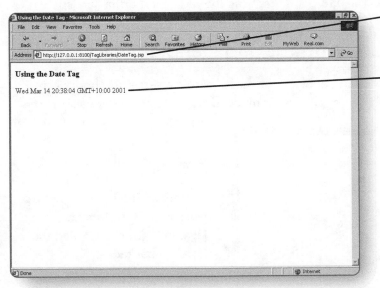

```
Using the Date Tag - Microsoft Internet Explorer                    _ 8 X
File  Edit  View  Favorites  Tools  Help

Back  Forward  Stop  Refresh  Home   Search  Favorites  History   Mail  Print  Edit  MyWeb  Real.com
Address  http://127.0.0.1:8100/TagLibraries/DateTag.jsp                     ▼  Go

Using the Date Tag

Wed Mar 14 20:38:04 GMT+10:00 2001

Done                                                    Internet
```

5. Preview the JSP page in a Web browser.

■ The current date and time will be displayed.

Creating a Tag that Accepts Attributes

The Date tag that you just created is not very flexible—it can't be formatted to appear the way a date is typically displayed. However, it is certainly possible to change the format of the date before it is displayed. In Chapter 4, "Performing Calculations," you learned to use the DateFormat class. As you might recall, a date could be formatted to a short, medium, long, or full format. This new tag needs to allow the user to specify which format to apply when the date is displayed. Including a dateformat attribute will allow this functionality. The following three files are required:

- The tag handler class (DateFormatTag.class)
- The tag library descriptor file (DateFormatTag.tld)
- The JSP page that uses the tag (DateFormatTag.jsp)

Creating the Tag Handler Class

The tag handler class must contain a setter method for the attribute. The setter method needs to store the value of the attribute in an instance variable that can be used by the doStartTag method.

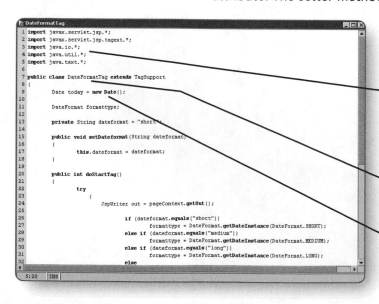

1. Import the javax.servlet.jsp.*, javax.servlet.jsp.tagext.*, java.util.*, java.text.*, and the java.io.* packages.

2. Declare a public class that extends the TagSupport class.

3. Create a Date object.

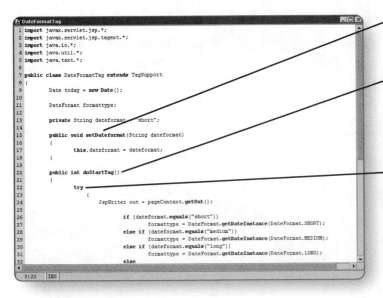

```
DateFormatTag
1 import javax.servlet.jsp.*;
2 import javax.servlet.jsp.tagext.*;
3 import java.io.*;
4 import java.util.*;
5 import java.text.*;
6
7 public class DateFormatTag extends TagSupport
8 {
9         Date today = new Date();
10
11        DateFormat formattype;
12
13        private String dateformat = "short";
14
15        public void setDateformat(String dateformat)
16        {
17                this.dateformat = dateformat;
18        }
19
20        public int doStartTag()
21        {
22                try
23                {
24                        JspWriter out = pageContext.getOut();
25
26                                if (dateformat.equals("short"))
27                                        formattype = DateFormat.getDateInstance(DateFormat.SHORT);
28                                else if (dateformat.equals("medium"))
29                                        formattype = DateFormat.getDateInstance(DateFormat.MEDIUM);
30                                else if (dateformat.equals("long"))
31                                        formattype = DateFormat.getDateInstance(DateFormat.LONG);
32                                else
5:20    INS
```

4. Create a DateFormat object.

5. Declare a private instance variable to store the attribute value. The name of this variable must match the tag attribute name. Assign a default value to the attribute. This will be used if the attribute is left blank.

6. Declare a setter method for the attribute instance variable.

7. Declare a public doStartTag method that returns an integer. The doStartTag is invoked when the opening tag is found.

8. Place your code within a try block.

```
DateFormatTag                                                    _ □ X
15        public void setDateformat(String dateformat)
16        {
17                this.dateformat = dateformat;
18        }
19 |
20        public int doStartTag()
21        {
22                try
23                {
24                        JspWriter out = pageContext.getOut();
25
26                        if (dateformat.equals("short"))
27                                formattype = DateFormat.getDateInstance(DateFormat.SHORT);
28                        else if (dateformat.equals("medium"))
29                                formattype = DateFormat.getDateInstance(DateFormat.MEDIUM);
30                        else if (dateformat.equals("long"))
31                                formattype = DateFormat.getDateInstance(DateFormat.LONG);
32                        else
33                                formattype = DateFormat.getDateInstance(DateFormat.FULL);
34
35                        out.print(formattype.format(today));
36                }
37                catch(IOException err)
38                {
39                        System.out.println("Error in DateTag: " + err);
40                }
41
42                return(SKIP_BODY);
43        }
44 }
45
46
19:1    INS
```

9. Use the getOut method of the pageContext object to obtain a JspWriter.

10. Use an if, else if branch to determine the value of the attribute. Apply the required formatting using the getDateInstance method.

```
DateFormatTag                                                    _ □ X
15        public void setDateformat(String dateformat)
16        {
17                this.dateformat = dateformat;
18        }
19
20        public int doStartTag()
21        {
22                try
23                {
24                        JspWriter out = pageContext.getOut();
25
26                        if (dateformat.equals("short"))
27                                formattype = DateFormat.getDateInstance(DateFormat.SHORT);
28                        else if (dateformat.equals("medium"))
29                                formattype = DateFormat.getDateInstance(DateFormat.MEDIUM);
30                        else if (dateformat.equals("long"))
31                                formattype = DateFormat.getDateInstance(DateFormat.LONG);
32                        else
33                                formattype = DateFormat.getDateInstance(DateFormat.FULL);
34
35                        out.print(formattype.format(today));
36                }
37                catch(IOException err)
38                {
39                        System.out.println("Error in DateTag: " + err);
40                }
41
42                return(SKIP_BODY);
43        }
44 }
45
46
19:1    INS
```

11. Use the print method to insert the formatted date into the JSP page.

12. Catch the IOException that is thrown by the print method.

```
15          public void setDateformat(String dateformat)
16          {
17                  this.dateformat = dateformat;
18          }
19
20          public int doStartTag()
21          {
22                  try
23                  {
24                          JspWriter out = pageContext.getOut();
25
26                          if (dateformat.equals("short"))
27                                  formattype = DateFormat.getDateInstance(DateFormat.SHORT);
28                          else if (dateformat.equals("medium"))
29                                  formattype = DateFormat.getDateInstance(DateFormat.MEDIUM);
30                          else if (dateformat.equals("long"))
31                                  formattype = DateFormat.getDateInstance(DateFormat.LONG);
32                          else
33                                  formattype = DateFormat.getDateInstance(DateFormat.FULL);
34
35                          out.print(formattype.format(today));
36                  }
37                  catch(IOException err)
38                  {
39                          System.out.println("Error in DateTag: " + err);
40                  }
41
42                  return(SKIP_BODY);
43          }
44  }
45
```

13. Print an appropriate error message.

14. The doStartTag must return the SKIP_BODY constant because the tag body is not processed.

Creating the Tag Library Descriptor File

The TLD file needs to describe the tag library, the tags within the library, and the tag attributes. You will need to specify whether the attribute is required and whether it can contain JSP code.

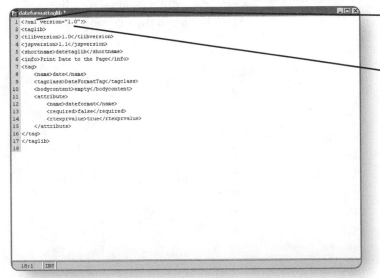

```
1  <?xml version="1.0"?>
2  <taglib>
3  <tlibversion>1.0</tlibversion>
4  <jspversion>1.1</jspversion>
5  <shortname>datetaglib</shortname>
6  <info>Print Date to the Page</info>
7  <tag>
8      <name>date</name>
9      <tagclass>DateFormatTag</tagclass>
10     <bodycontent>empty</bodycontent>
11     <attribute>
12         <name>dateformat</name>
13         <required>false</required>
14         <rtexprvalue>true</rtexprvalue>
15     </attribute>
16 </tag>
17 </taglib>
18
```

1. Insert the <?xml ?> tag as the first line in the TLD file.

2. Specify 1.0 as the version.

3. Insert an opening <taglib> tag.

4. Type the version number of the tag library between the opening and closing <tlibversion> tags.

5. Type the JSP specification number of the tag library between the opening and closing <jspversion> tags. JSP 1.1 is currently supported by most application servers.

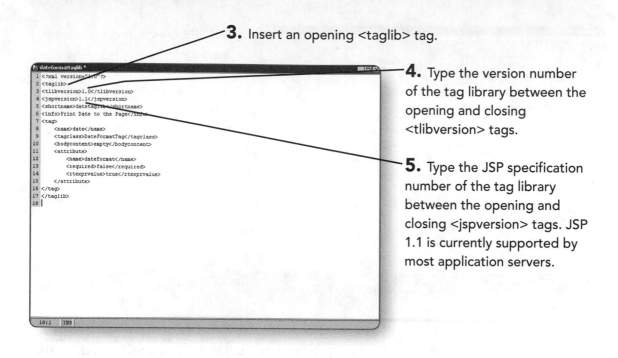

6. Type the name of the tag library between the opening and closing <shortname> tags.

7. Type a brief description between the opening and closing <info> tags.

8. Insert an opening <tag> tag.

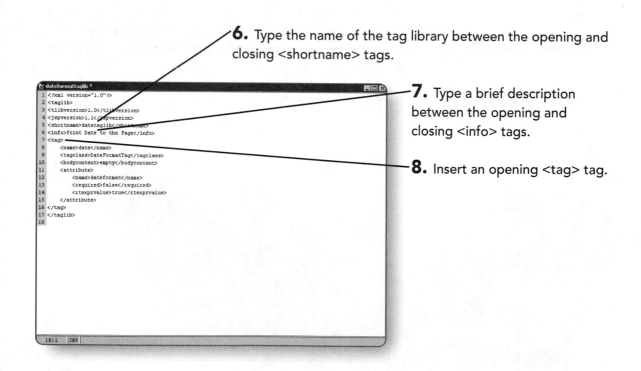

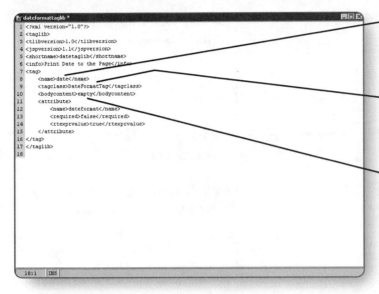

9. Type the name of the tag library between the opening and closing <name> tags.

10. Type the tag handler class file name between the opening and closing <tagclass> tags.

11. Type **empty** between the opening and closing <bodycontent> tags. You must specify empty when the tag body is not required.

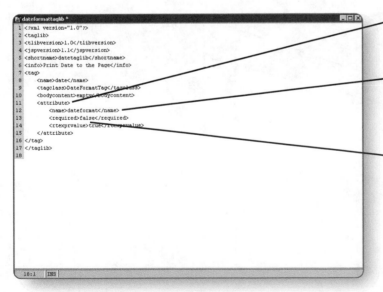

12. Insert an opening <attribute> tag.

13. Type the attribute name between the opening and closing <name> tags.

14. Type **false** between the opening and closing <required> tags if the attribute could be left blank. Type **true** if the attribute must contain a value.

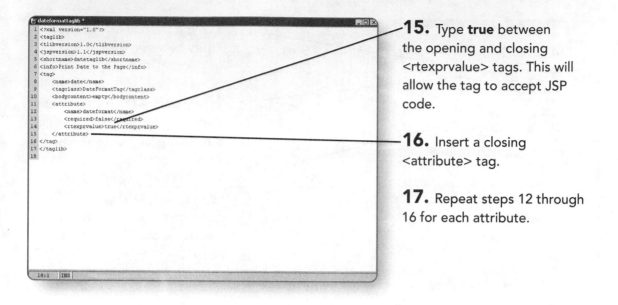

15. Type **true** between the opening and closing <rtexprvalue> tags. This will allow the tag to accept JSP code.

16. Insert a closing <attribute> tag.

17. Repeat steps 12 through 16 for each attribute.

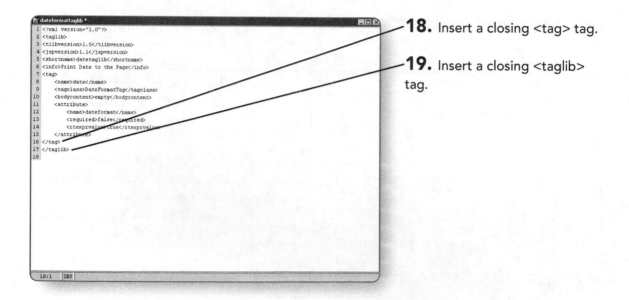

18. Insert a closing <tag> tag.

19. Insert a closing <taglib> tag.

Using the Tag Library

You have now developed a tag that will insert the current date according to the specified format. The dateformat attribute must be assigned one of the following values: full, long, short, or medium.

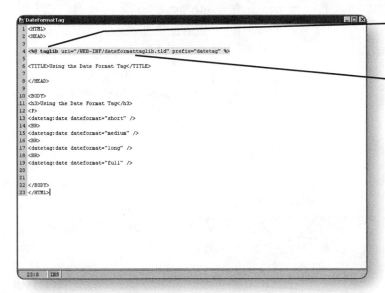

1. Insert the taglib directive in the JSP page.

2. Specify the path to the TLD file.

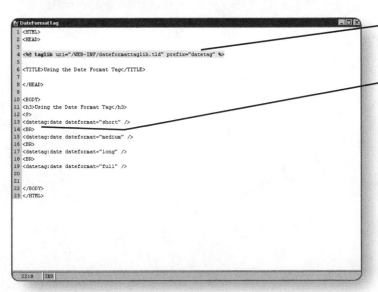

3. Specify a prefix for the tag library.

4. Insert the tag that you want to use in the JSP page. The tag library prefix must be placed before the tag name.

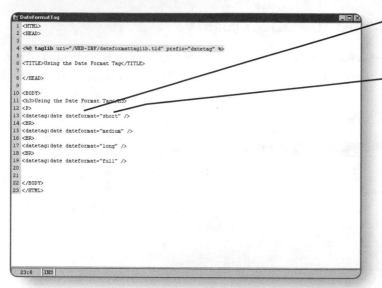

5. Insert the name of the tag attribute within the tag.

6. Specify the value of the attribute. The value must be enclosed in single or double quotes.

NOTE

In this example, all of the attribute values will be tested.

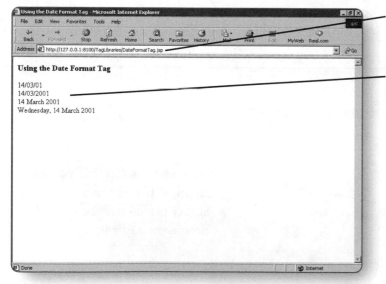

7. Preview the JSP page in a Web browser.

The current date will be displayed in the four different formats.

Formatting the Body of a Tag

A JSP tag can process the HTML tags contained within its body. You can easily format the body of a tag by placing HTML tags before and after the body text. In this section, you will create a tag to format headings that are inserted into a Web page. This will allow you to update the font, color, and size of the heading at any time without editing individual pages. The following three files are required:

- The tag handler class (HeaderTag.class)

- The tag library descriptor file (BodyTag.tld)

- The JSP page that uses the tag (BodyTag.jsp)

Creating the Tag Handler Class

The doStartTag method needs to return EVAL_BODY_INCLUDE instead of SKIP_BODY. This will print the body of the tag back to the JSP page. This is necessary in order to place HTML tags before and after the body content. The tag handler class will also need to include the doEndTag method. The doEndTag method is called when the closing tag is encountered. The doEndTag method needs to print the closing HTML tags to the JSP page and return EVAL_PAGE so that the rest of the page is evaluated.

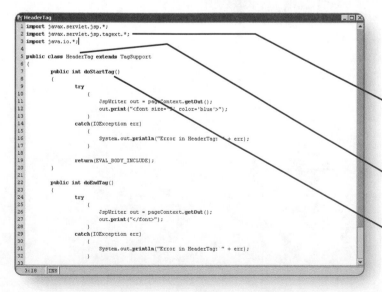

```
1  import javax.servlet.jsp.*;
2  import javax.servlet.jsp.tagext.*;
3  import java.io.*;
4
5  public class HeaderTag extends TagSupport
6  {
7      public int doStartTag()
8      {
9          try
10         {
11             JspWriter out = pageContext.getOut();
12             out.print("<font size='5' color='blue'>");
13         }
14         catch(IOException err)
15         {
16             System.out.println("Error in HeaderTag: " + err);
17         }
18
19         return(EVAL_BODY_INCLUDE);
20     }
21
22     public int doEndTag()
23     {
24         try
25         {
26             JspWriter out = pageContext.getOut();
27             out.print("</font>");
28         }
29         catch(IOException err)
30         {
31             System.out.println("Error in HeaderTag: " + err);
32         }
33
```

1. Import the javax.servlet.jsp.*, javax.servlet.jsp.tagext.*, and java.io.* packages.

2. Declare a public class that extends the TagSupport class.

3. Declare a public doStartTag method that returns an integer. The doStartTag is invoked when the opening tag is found.

```
HeaderTag                                                           _ □ X
 1 import javax.servlet.jsp.*;
 2 import javax.servlet.jsp.tagext.*;
 3 import java.io.*;
 4
 5 public class HeaderTag extends TagSupport
 6 {
 7        public int doStartTag()
 8        {
 9              try
10              {
11                    JspWriter out = pageContext.getOut();
12                    out.print("<font size='5' color='blue'>");
13              }
14              catch(IOException err)
15              {
16                    System.out.println("Error in HeaderTag: " + err);
17              }
18
19              return(EVAL_BODY_INCLUDE);
20        }
21
22        public int doEndTag()
23        {
24              try
25              {
26                    JspWriter out = pageContext.getOut();
27                    out.print("</font>");
28              }
29              catch(IOException err)
30              {
31                    System.out.println("Error in HeaderTag: " + err);
32              }
33
3:18    INS
```

4. Place your code within a try block.

5. Use the getOut method of the pageContext object to obtain a JspWriter.

6. Use the print method to insert the opening HTML tags into the JSP page.

```
HeaderTag                                                           _ □ X
 1 import javax.servlet.jsp.*;
 2 import javax.servlet.jsp.tagext.*;
 3 import java.io.*;
 4
 5 public class HeaderTag extends TagSupport
 6 {
 7        public int doStartTag()
 8        {
 9              try
10              {
11                    JspWriter out = pageContext.getOut();
12                    out.print("<font size='5' color='blue'>");
13              }
14              catch(IOException err)
15              {
16                    System.out.println("Error in HeaderTag: " + err);
17              }
18
19              return(EVAL_BODY_INCLUDE);
20        }
21
22        public int doEndTag()
23        {
24              try
25              {
26                    JspWriter out = pageContext.getOut();
27                    out.print("</font>");
28              }
29              catch(IOException err)
30              {
31                    System.out.println("Error in HeaderTag: " + err);
32              }
33
3:18    INS
```

7. Catch the IOException that is thrown by the print method.

8. Print an appropriate error message.

```
HeaderTag
4
5  public class HeaderTag extends TagSupport
6  {
7        public int doStartTag()
8        {
9              try
10             {
11                   JspWriter out = pageContext.getOut();
12                   out.print("<font size='5' color='blue'>");
13             }
14             catch(IOException err)
15             {
16                   System.out.println("Error in HeaderTag: " + err);
17             }
18
19             return(EVAL_BODY_INCLUDE);
20       }
21
22       public int doEndTag()
23       {
24             try
25             {
26                   JspWriter out = pageContext.getOut();
27                   out.print("</font>");
28             }
29             catch(IOException err)
30             {
31                   System.out.println("Error in HeaderTag: " + err);
32             }
33
34             return(EVAL_PAGE);
35       }
36 }
5:43   INS
```

9. The doStartTag must return the EVAL_BODY_INCLUDE constant, because the tag body needs to be written to the JSP page.

10. Declare a public doEndTag method that returns an integer. The doEndTag is invoked when the closing tag is found.

```
HeaderTag
4
5  public class HeaderTag extends TagSupport
6  {
7        public int doStartTag()
8        {
9              try
10             {
11                   JspWriter out = pageContext.getOut();
12                   out.print("<font size='5' color='blue'>");
13             }
14             catch(IOException err)
15             {
16                   System.out.println("Error in HeaderTag: " + err);
17             }
18
19             return(EVAL_BODY_INCLUDE);
20       }
21
22       public int doEndTag()
23       {
24             try
25             {
26                   JspWriter out = pageContext.getOut();
27                   out.print("</font>");
28             }
29             catch(IOException err)
30             {
31                   System.out.println("Error in HeaderTag: " + err);
32             }
33
34             return(EVAL_PAGE);
35       }
36 }
5:43   INS
```

11. Place your code within a try block.

12. Use the getOut method of the pageContext object to obtain a JspWriter.

13. Use the print method to insert the closing HTML tags into the JSP page.

```
HeaderTag
4
5   public class HeaderTag extends TagSupport
6   {
7           public int doStartTag()
8           {
9                   try
10                  {
11                          JspWriter out = pageContext.getOut();
12                          out.print("<font size='5' color='blue'>");
13                  }
14                  catch(IOException err)
15                  {
16                          System.out.println("Error in HeaderTag: " + err);
17                  }
18
19                  return(EVAL_BODY_INCLUDE);
20          }
21
22          public int doEndTag()
23          {
24                  try
25                  {
26                          JspWriter out = pageContext.getOut();
27                          out.print("</font>");
28                  }
29                  catch(IOException err)
30                  {
31                          System.out.println("Error in HeaderTag: " + err);
32                  }
33
34                  return(EVAL_PAGE);
35          }
36  }

5:43    INS
```

14. Catch the IOException that is thrown by the print method.

15. Print an appropriate error message.

16. The doEndTag must return the EVAL_PAGE constant so that the rest of the page can be processed.

Creating the Tag Library Descriptor File

You need to set the <bodycontent> tag to JSP so that the tag handler can process the tag body. This is the only change necessary to include the tag body.

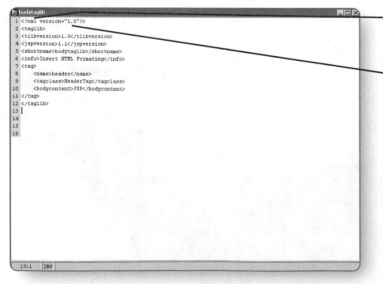

```
bodytaglib
1   <?xml version="1.0"?>
2   <taglib>
3   <tlibversion>1.0</tlibversion>
4   <jspversion>1.1</jspversion>
5   <shortname>bodytaglib</shortname>
6   <info>Insert HTML Formating</info>
7   <tag>
8       <name>header</name>
9       <tagclass>HeaderTag</tagclass>
10      <bodycontent>JSP</bodycontent>
11  </tag>
12  </taglib>
13
14
15
16

13:1    INS
```

1. Insert the <?xml ?> tag as the first line in the TLD file.

2. Specify 1.0 as the version.

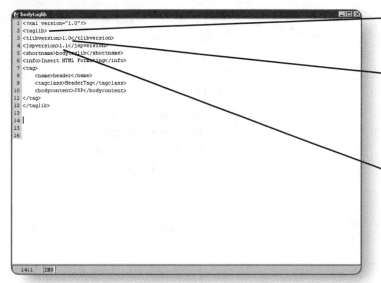

```
bodytaglib                                              _□×
 1 <?xml version="1.0"?>
 2 <taglib>
 3 <tlibversion>1.0</tlibversion>
 4 <jspversion>1.1</jspversion>
 5 <shortname>bodytaglib</shortname>
 6 <info>Insert HTML Formating</info>
 7 <tag>
 8      <name>header</name>
 9      <tagclass>HeaderTag</tagclass>
10      <bodycontent>JSP</bodycontent>
11 </tag>
12 </taglib>
13
14 |
15
16
  14:1    INS
```

3. Insert an opening <taglib> tag.

4. Type the version number of the tag library between the opening and closing <tlibversion> tags.

5. Type the JSP specification number of the tag library between the opening and closing <jspversion> tags. JSP 1.1 is currently supported by most application servers.

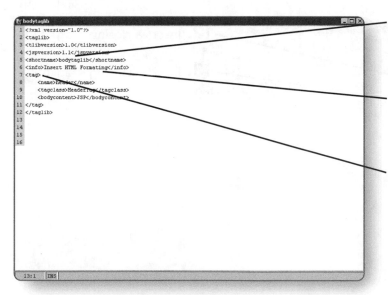

```
bodytaglib                                              _□×
 1 <?xml version="1.0"?>
 2 <taglib>
 3 <tlibversion>1.0</tlibversion>
 4 <jspversion>1.1</jspversion>
 5 <shortname>bodytaglib</shortname>
 6 <info>Insert HTML Formating</info>
 7 <tag>
 8      <name>header</name>
 9      <tagclass>HeaderTag</tagclass>
10      <bodycontent>JSP</bodycontent>
11 </tag>
12 </taglib>
13
14
15
16
  13:1    INS
```

6. Type the name of the tag library between the opening and closing <shortname> tags.

7. Type a brief description between the opening and closing <info> tags.

8. Insert an opening <tag> tag.

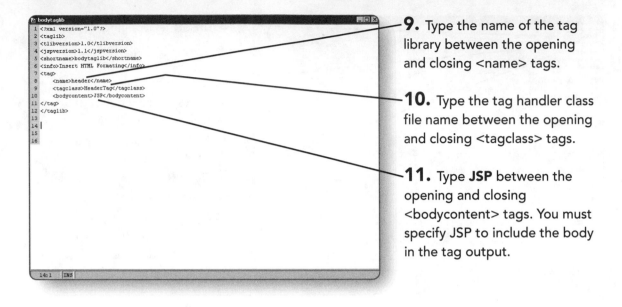

9. Type the name of the tag library between the opening and closing <name> tags.

10. Type the tag handler class file name between the opening and closing <tagclass> tags.

11. Type **JSP** between the opening and closing <bodycontent> tags. You must specify JSP to include the body in the tag output.

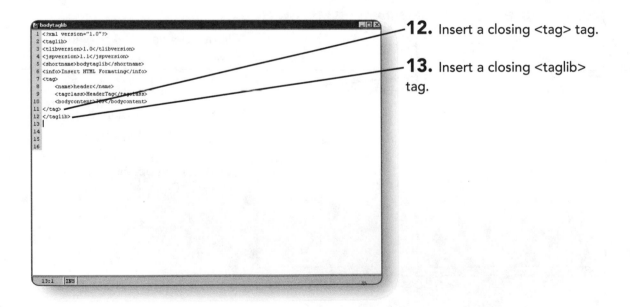

12. Insert a closing <tag> tag.

13. Insert a closing <taglib> tag.

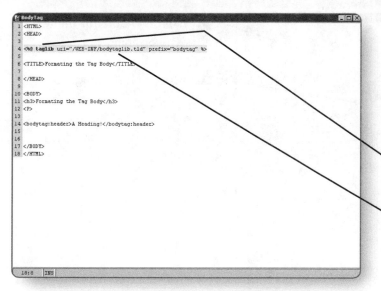

Using the Tag Library

Opening and closing tags are required so that text can be placed in the tag body.

1. Insert the taglib directive in the JSP page.

2. Specify the path to the TLD file.

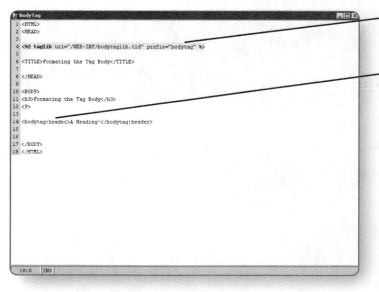

3. Specify a prefix for the tag library.

4. Insert the opening tag for the tag that you want to use in the JSP page. The tag library prefix must be placed before the tag name. A colon must also separate the tag library prefix and tag name.

NOTE

The tag requires a body, so it must be written as:

```
<simple:tag>Tag Body
➡ Text</simple:tag>
```

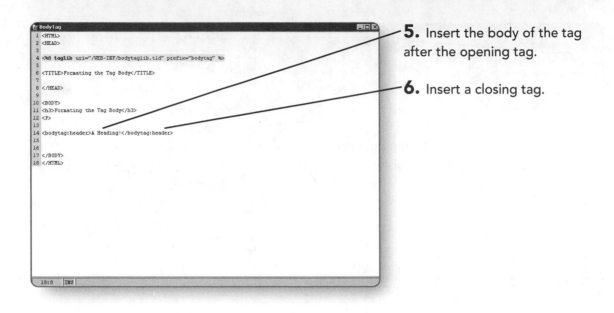

5. Insert the body of the tag after the opening tag.

6. Insert a closing tag.

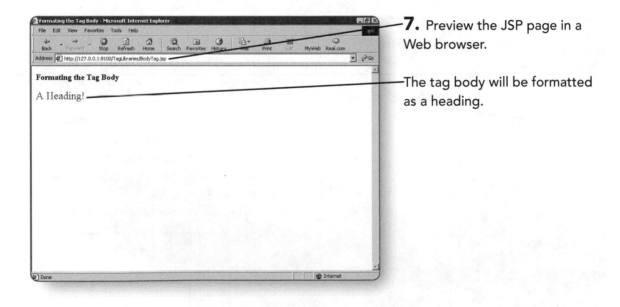

7. Preview the JSP page in a Web browser.

The tag body will be formatted as a heading.

Manipulating the Body of a Tag

In the previous example, only the body text was relayed back to the JSP page. There will be situations when you will need to retrieve the tag body, process it, and then write the output to the JSP page. The steps to create a tag that converts the tag body to uppercase are included in this section. The following three files are required:

- The tag handler class (UppercaseTag.class)
- The tag library descriptor file (UppercaseTag.tld)
- The JSP page that uses the tag (UppercaseTag.jsp)

Creating the Tag Handler Class

The tag handler class needs to extend the BodyTagSupport class instead of the TagSupport class. The tag handler only needs to implement the doAfterBody method. The doAfterTag method must return the SKIP_BODY constant because the tag body must not be sent back to the JSP page in its current form—it must first be processed. To retrieve the tag body, you need to create a BodyContent object and call the getString method.

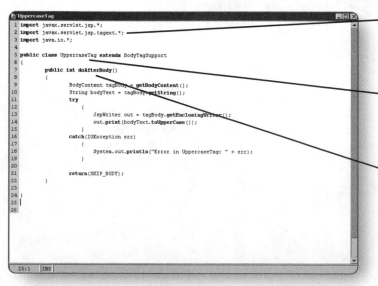

```
1  import javax.servlet.jsp.*;
2  import javax.servlet.jsp.tagext.*;
3  import java.io.*;
4
5  public class UppercaseTag extends BodyTagSupport
6  {
7      public int doAfterBody()
8      {
9          BodyContent tagBody = getBodyContent();
10         String bodyText = tagBody.getString();
11         try
12         {
13             JspWriter out = tagBody.getEnclosingWriter();
14             out.print(bodyText.toUpperCase());
15         }
16         catch(IOException err)
17         {
18             System.out.println("Error in UppercaseTag: " + err);
19         }
20
21         return(SKIP_BODY);
22     }
23
24 }
25
26
```

1. Import the javax.servlet.jsp.*, javax.servlet.jsp.tagext.*, and java.io.* packages.

2. Declare a public class that extends the BodyTagSupport class.

3. Declare a public doAfterBody method that returns an integer. The doAfterBody is invoked after the tag body is retrieved.

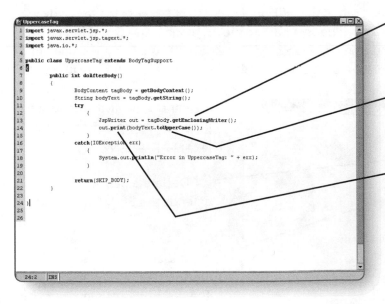

```
1  import javax.servlet.jsp.*;
2  import javax.servlet.jsp.tagext.*;
3  import java.io.*;
4
5  public class UppercaseTag extends BodyTagSupport
6  {
7      public int doAfterBody()
8      {
9          BodyContent tagBody = getBodyContent();
10         String bodyText = tagBody.getString();
11         try
12         {
13             JspWriter out = tagBody.getEnclosingWriter();
14             out.print(bodyText.toUpperCase());
15         }
16         catch(IOException err)
17         {
18             System.out.println("Error in UppercaseTag: " + err);
19         }
20
21         return(SKIP_BODY);
22     }
23
24 }
25
26
```

4. Create a BodyContent object by calling the getBodyContent method.

5. Use the getString method to retrieve the tag body as a string.

6. Place your code within a try block.

```
1  import javax.servlet.jsp.*;
2  import javax.servlet.jsp.tagext.*;
3  import java.io.*;
4
5  public class UppercaseTag extends BodyTagSupport
6  {
7      public int doAfterBody()
8      {
9          BodyContent tagBody = getBodyContent();
10         String bodyText = tagBody.getString();
11         try
12         {
13             JspWriter out = tagBody.getEnclosingWriter();
14             out.print(bodyText.toUpperCase());
15         }
16         catch(IOException err)
17         {
18             System.out.println("Error in UppercaseTag: " + err);
19         }
20
21         return(SKIP_BODY);
22     }
23
24 )
25
26
```

7. Use the getEnclosingWriter method of the BodyContent object.

8. Use the toUpperCase method to convert the tag body to uppercase.

9. Use the print method to print the processed tag body to the JSP page.

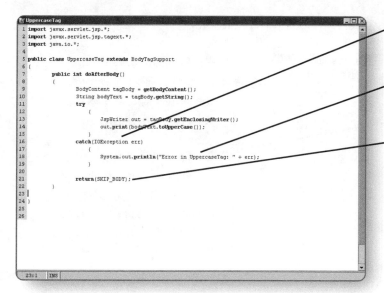

```
UppercaseTag
1  import javax.servlet.jsp.*;
2  import javax.servlet.jsp.tagext.*;
3  import java.io.*;
4
5  public class UppercaseTag extends BodyTagSupport
6  {
7        public int doAfterBody()
8        {
9                BodyContent tagBody = getBodyContent();
10               String bodyText = tagBody.getString();
11               try
12               {
13                       JspWriter out = tagBody.getEnclosingWriter();
14                       out.print(bodyText.toUpperCase());
15               }
16               catch(IOException err)
17               {
18                       System.out.println("Error in UppercaseTag: " + err);
19               }
20
21               return(SKIP_BODY);
22        }
23
24  }
25
26
```

10. Catch the IOException that is thrown by the print method.

11. Print an appropriate error message.

12. The doAfterBody must return the SKIP_BODY constant because the tag body is not processed.

Creating the Tag Library Descriptor File

The <bodycontent> tag needs to be set to JSP. This indicates that the tag requires a body and that the body will be processed.

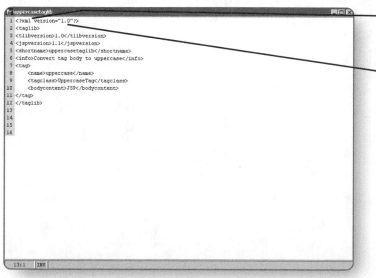

```
uppercasetaglib
1  <?xml version="1.0"?>
2  <taglib>
3  <tlibversion>1.0</tlibversion>
4  <jspversion>1.1</jspversion>
5  <shortname>uppercasetaglib</shortname>
6  <info>Convert tag body to uppercase</info>
7  <tag>
8      <name>uppercase</name>
9      <tagclass>UppercaseTag</tagclass>
10     <bodycontent>JSP</bodycontent>
11 </tag>
12 </taglib>
13
14
15
16
```

1. Insert the <?xml ?> tag as the first line in the TLD file.

2. Specify 1.0 as the version.

3. Insert an opening <taglib> tag.

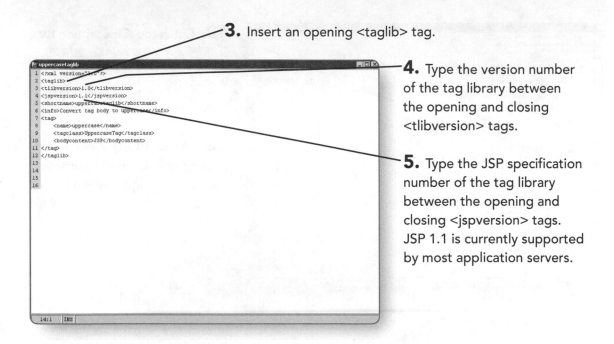

```
1 <?xml version="1.0" ?>
2 <taglib>
3 <tlibversion>1.0</tlibversion>
4 <jspversion>1.1</jspversion>
5 <shortname>uppercasetaglib</shortname>
6 <info>Convert tag body to uppercase</info>
7 <tag>
8     <name>uppercase</name>
9     <tagclass>UppercaseTag</tagclass>
10    <bodycontent>JSP</bodycontent>
11 </tag>
12 </taglib>
13
14
15
16
```

4. Type the version number of the tag library between the opening and closing <tlibversion> tags.

5. Type the JSP specification number of the tag library between the opening and closing <jspversion> tags. JSP 1.1 is currently supported by most application servers.

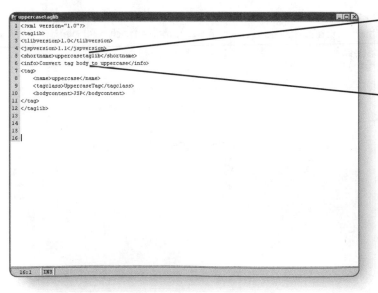

```
1 <?xml version="1.0"?>
2 <taglib>
3 <tlibversion>1.0</tlibversion>
4 <jspversion>1.1</jspversion>
5 <shortname>uppercasetaglib</shortname>
6 <info>Convert tag body to uppercase</info>
7 <tag>
8     <name>uppercase</name>
9     <tagclass>UppercaseTag</tagclass>
10    <bodycontent>JSP</bodycontent>
11 </tag>
12 </taglib>
13
14
15
16
```

6. Type the name of the tag library between the opening and closing <shortname> tags.

7. Type a brief description between the opening and closing <info> tags.

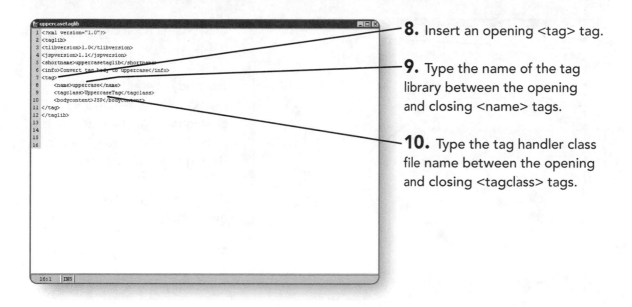

8. Insert an opening <tag> tag.

9. Type the name of the tag library between the opening and closing <name> tags.

10. Type the tag handler class file name between the opening and closing <tagclass> tags.

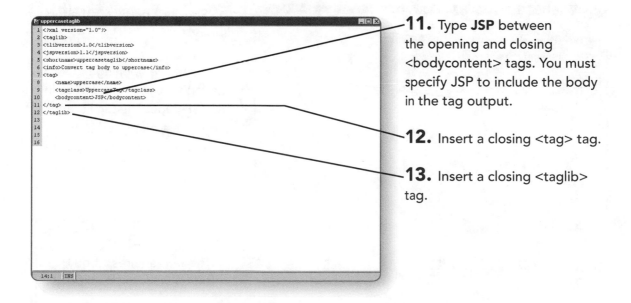

11. Type **JSP** between the opening and closing <bodycontent> tags. You must specify JSP to include the body in the tag output.

12. Insert a closing <tag> tag.

13. Insert a closing <taglib> tag.

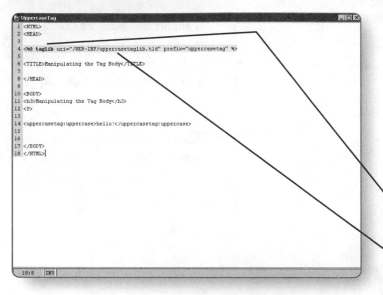

Using the Tag Library

The body content must be placed within opening and closing tags. All the text that is placed within the opening and closing tags will be processed.

1. Insert the taglib directive in the JSP page.

2. Specify the path to the TLD file.

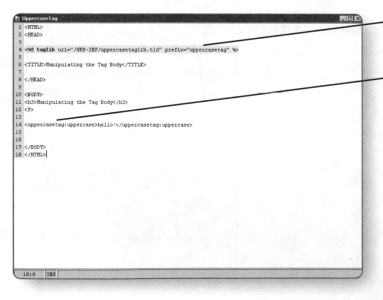

3. Specify a prefix for the tag library.

4. Insert the opening tag for the tag that you want to use in the JSP page. The tag library prefix must be placed before the tag name. A colon must also separate the tag library prefix and tag name.

NOTE

The tag requires a body, so it must be written as:

```
<simple:tag>Tag Body
➥ Text</simple:tag>
```

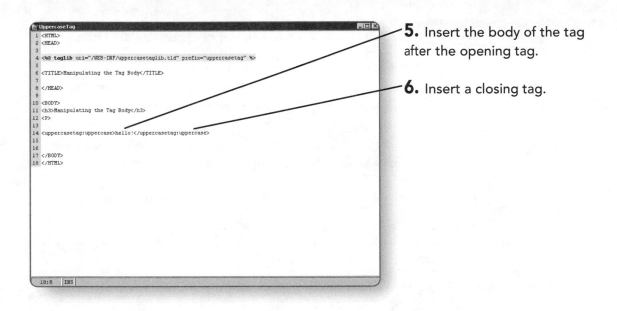

5. Insert the body of the tag after the opening tag.

6. Insert a closing tag.

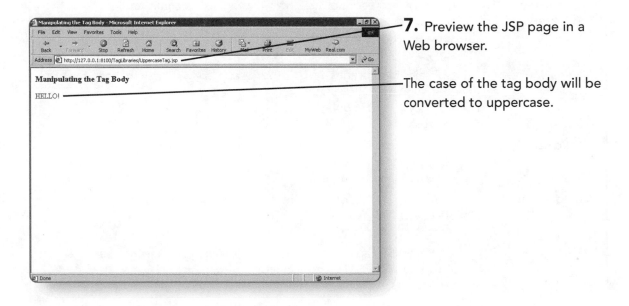

7. Preview the JSP page in a Web browser.

The case of the tag body will be converted to uppercase.

Using Existing Tag Libraries

You don't always need to develop your own tags. You can download many commercial and free offerings from the Web. You will find tags that can greatly improve your productivity. There are tags to send e-mail messages, access databases, perform XSL transformations, and produce 3-D graphs. Table 18.1 lists just a small sample of what is available.

Table 18.1 Tag Libraries

Tag Library	Purpose	URL
IN16 JSP Tag Library	Displays file information, sends e-mail messages, and validates forms.	http://sourceforge.net/projects/jsptags
JRun Custom Tag Library	Contains professional tags to acccess databases, send e-mail messages, use XSL, and validate forms.	http://www.allaire.com/handlers/index.cfm?ID=15990&Method=Full
Jakarta Taglibs	Contains tag libraries that support JDBC, SQL, XSL, JNDI, and regular expressions.	http://jakarta.apache.org/taglibs/index.html
JSPtags.com	Inserts search engine-style results on your database results pages.	http://jsptags.com/tags/navigation/pager
Woolox Chart 1.1	Generates dynamic 3D charts. This is excellent, but not free.	http://www.woolox.com/chart
WMLtags ver. 1.0	Contains JSP tags library for WAP/WML developers.	http://coldjava.hypermart.net/servlets/wmltags.htm

Using the JRun Custom Tag Library

Allaire, the company responsible for the user-friendly JRun application server, also introduced the world to ColdFusion. ColdFusion is a tag-based server-side scripting markup language. ColdFusion tags are very similar to the JSP tags that you have been creating throughout this chapter. ColdFusion has over seventy tags. Allaire has used their experience in developing tags to insert dynamic content to build the most comprehensive tag library available. The great thing is that these tags are installed with JRun, so you can use them immediately. Table 18.2 lists some of the JRun custom tags and their purposes.

Table 18.2 JRun Custom Tags

Tag	Purpose
Sql	Performs JDBC SQL queries.
SendMail	Sends e-mail messages using the JavaMail API.
MailParam	Includes attachments in an e-mail message sent with the SendMail tag.
Query2XML	Converts database records to XML.
XSL	Performs XSL transformations.
Form	Includes JavaScript form validation routines within your JSP page.
Input	Allows you to validate the input form tag. You can ensure that data has been entered and is in the required format.
ForEach	The equivalent of a for loop.
If	An if statement implemented as a tag.

```
1  <HTML>
2  <HEAD>
3
4  <%@ taglib uri="jruntags" prefix="jrun" %>
5
6  <TITLE>Using the JRun SendMail Tag</TITLE>
7
8  </HEAD>
9
10 <BODY>
11 <h3>Using the JRun SendMail Tag</h3>
12 <P>
13 <jrun:sendmail host="www.yourhost.com"
14              sender="you@yourcompany.com"
15              recipient="rec@theircompany.com"
16              subject="Hello from SendMail tag">
17 <jrun:mailparam attachurl="mm.jpg"/>
18 E-mail Message
19 </jrun:sendmail>
20
21
22 </BODY>
23 </HTML>
24 |
```

Using the SendMail Tag

The SendMail tag is exceptionally useful if you want to send e-mail messages without writing any JSP code. You can even include document and image attachments in the message. Sending e-mail messages has never been easier.

Here is an example JSP page that uses the SendMail and MailParam tags.

Performing JavaScript Form Validation

In Chapter 10, "Retrieving Information from a User," you learned how to validate the data entered into form fields on the server using JSP. You can also use JavaScript, a client-side scripting language used to validate the form before it is sent back to the server. JavaScript is a client-side scripting language because it runs within a Web browser. The JRun Form and Input tags insert the JavaScript code required to validate a form. This is great because then you don't need to learn JavaScript as well.

```
7  <h3>Using the JRun Form and Input Tag</h3>
8  <P>
9  <jrun:form name="form1" action="form.jsp">
10 <table width="50%">
11 <tr>
12     <td>Required text field:</td>
13     <td><jrun:input name="text" required="true"/></td>
14 </tr>
15 <tr>
16     <td>Required password field:</td>
17     <td><jrun:input name="password" type="password" required="true"/></td>
18 </tr>
19 <tr>
20     <td>Required checkbox field:</td>
21     <td><jrun:input name="checkbox" type="checkbox" required="true"/>Check!</td>
22 </tr>
23 <tr>
24     <td>Required radio field:</td>
25     <td>
26     <jrun:input name="radiogroup" value="1" type="radio" required="true"/>1st
27     <jrun:input name="radiogroup" value="2" type="radio" required="true"/>2nd
28     </td>
29 </tr>
30
31 <tr>
32     <td> </td>
33     <td><input type="submit" value="Submit"/></td>
34 </tr>
35 </table>
36 </jrun:form>
37
38 </BODY>
39 </HTML>
```

Here is a JSP page that uses the JRun Form and Input tags to validate a text field, a password field, a check box, and a radio button group.

19

Creating an Employee Directory

An employee directory is a simple, database-driven Web application that allows users to view an employee's contact details. I have selected it as a sample Web application because it implements all facets of database integration. The employee directory can be searched and maintained from a Web interface. The administrator has access privileges to insert, update, and delete employee records. The application is suitable for a company intranet as well as the Internet. In this chapter, you'll learn how to build a Web interface that allows users to:

- Search a database
- Insert new records into a database
- Update existing records in a database
- Delete records in a database

Design Requirements

An employee directory should allow users to search for an employee by name, position, or department. The search results must be neatly formatted because they might be printed and forwarded to clients.

The data stored in the database will constantly change. The employee directory, therefore, must provide a Web interface for an administrator to maintain the database. It is essential that the administrator have the ability to delete, update, and add employee records. The administration console must facilitate data entry, be user-friendly, and be intuitive.

Designing the Employee Directory Database

The employee directory is contained in the EmployeeDirectory.mdb Microsoft Access database on the CD-ROM. To keep things simple, the database only contains a single table. The Employee table stores the employee's first name, surname, phone number, e-mail address, position, and department.

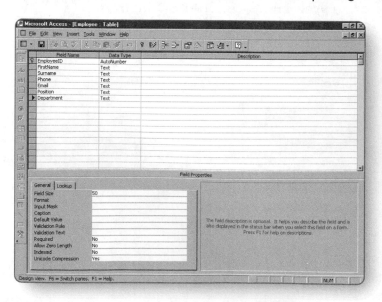

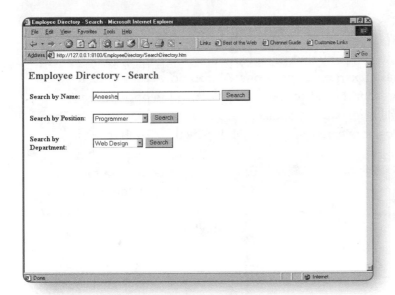

Creating the Search Form

The Search form must allow the user to locate an employee by name, position, or department. To achieve this, you will need to include an HTML form for each search type on the page. Multiple forms can be placed on a Web page as long as each form is placed within opening and closing <form> tags.

Searching by Name

The Search by Name form only requires a single text box in which the user will enter the name of the employee. The form must be submitted to NameSearch.jsp, where the search request will be processed.

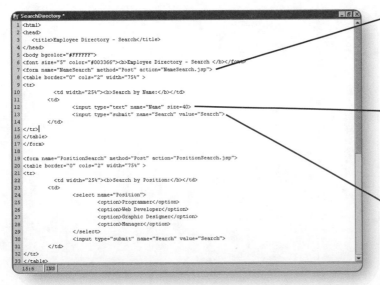

1. Use the <form> tag to insert the NameSearch form. NameSearch.jsp will process the form.

2. Insert the Name input field. The character size of the field must be consistent with the data that is being searched.

3. Insert a submit button. The user will click on the button after entering a search request.

Searching by Position

The company that is implementing the employee directory has a fixed list of positions. A drop-down list will be used to present this list to the user. Selecting the position from a list will eliminate any spelling errors in the search request. The PositionSearch.jsp page will display the search results.

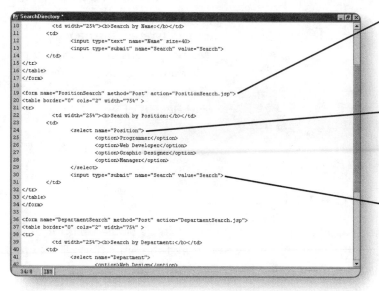

1. Use the <form> tag to insert the PositionSearch form. PositionSearch.jsp will process the form.

2. Insert the Position select field. Use the option tags to specify the positions from which the user can choose.

3. Insert a submit button. The user will click on the button after selecting a position.

Searching by Department

Users require the ability to produce a report from the database that lists the contact details of all employees in a particular department. The Search by Department form needs to display the list of departments and allow the user to select one. The DepartmentSearch.jsp page will process the department list request.

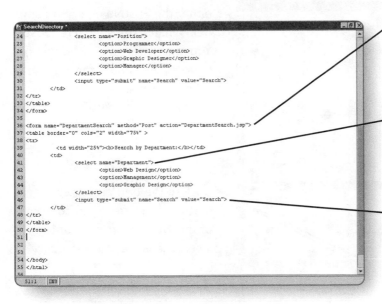

```
24              <select name="Position">
25                  <option>Programmer</option>
26                  <option>Web Developer</option>
27                  <option>Graphic Designer</option>
28                  <option>Manager</option>
29              </select>
30              <input type="submit" name="Search" value="Search">
31          </td>
32  </tr>
33  </table>
34  </form>
35
36  <form name="DepartmentSearch" method="Post" action="DepartmentSearch.jsp">
37  <table border="0" cols="2" width="75%" >
38  <tr>
39          <td width="25%"><b>Search by Department:</b></td>
40          <td>
41              <select name="Department">
42                  <option>Web Design</option>
43                  <option>Management</option>
44                  <option>Graphic Design</option>
45              </select>
46              <input type="submit" name="Search" value="Search">
47          </td>
48  </tr>
49  </table>
50  </form>
51
52
53
54  </body>
55  </html>
56
```

1. Use the <form> tag to insert the DepartmentSearch form. DepartmentSearch.jsp will process the form.

2. Insert the Department select field. Use the option tags to specify the departments within the organization.

3. Insert a submit button. The user will click on the button after selecting a department.

Processing the Search by Name Request

Since a user could search by first name or surname, your query needs to consider this. The query will search both fields and return records where either field matches the search criteria.

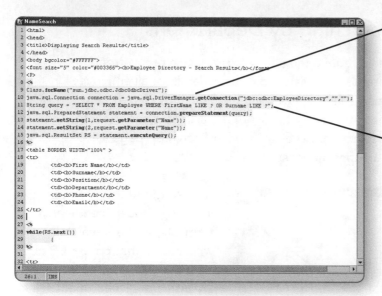

```
NameSearch
1  <html>
2  <head>
3  <title>Displaying Search Results</title>
4  </head>
5  <body bgcolor="#FFFFFF">
6  <font size="5" color="#003366"><b>Employee Directory - Search Results</b></font>
7  <P>
8  <%
9  Class.forName("sun.jdbc.odbc.JdbcOdbcDriver");
10 java.sql.Connection connection = java.sql.DriverManager.getConnection("jdbc:odbc:EmployeeDirectory","","");
11 String query = "SELECT * FROM Employee WHERE FirstName LIKE ? OR Surname LIKE ?";
12 java.sql.PreparedStatement statement = connection.prepareStatement(query);
13 statement.setString(1,request.getParameter("Name"));
14 statement.setString(2,request.getParameter("Name"));
15 java.sql.ResultSet RS = statement.executeQuery();
16 %>
17 <table BORDER WIDTH="100%" >
18 <tr>
19          <td><b>First Name</b></td>
20          <td><b>Surname</b></td>
21          <td><b>Position</b></td>
22          <td><b>Department</b></td>
23          <td><b>Phone</b></td>
24          <td><b>Email</b></td>
25 </tr>
26  |
27 <%
28 while(RS.next())
29          {
30 %>
31
32 <tr>
                                                    26:1   INS
```

1. Create a connection to the EmployeeDirectory.mdb Microsoft Access database. You will first need to set up a DSN for the EmployeeDirectory database.

2. Define a parametized query that will retrieve records where either the FirstName or Surname fields match the search request. You must insert a question mark (?) as a placeholder for the search criteria. A Prepared Statement will be used.

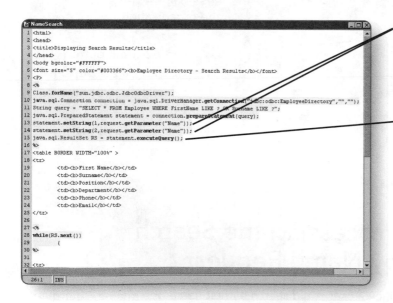

```
NameSearch
1  <html>
2  <head>
3  <title>Displaying Search Results</title>
4  </head>
5  <body bgcolor="#FFFFFF">
6  <font size="5" color="#003366"><b>Employee Directory - Search Results</b></font>
7  <P>
8  <%
9  Class.forName("sun.jdbc.odbc.JdbcOdbcDriver");
10 java.sql.Connection connection = java.sql.DriverManager.getConnection("jdbc:odbc:EmployeeDirectory","","");
11 String query = "SELECT * FROM Employee WHERE FirstName LIKE ? OR Surname LIKE ?";
12 java.sql.PreparedStatement statement = connection.prepareStatement(query);
13 statement.setString(1,request.getParameter("Name"));
14 statement.setString(2,request.getParameter("Name"));
15 java.sql.ResultSet RS = statement.executeQuery();
16 %>
17 <table BORDER WIDTH="100%" >
18 <tr>
19          <td><b>First Name</b></td>
20          <td><b>Surname</b></td>
21          <td><b>Position</b></td>
22          <td><b>Department</b></td>
23          <td><b>Phone</b></td>
24          <td><b>Email</b></td>
25 </tr>
26
27 <%
28 while(RS.next())
29          {
30 %>
31
32 <tr>
                                                    26:1   INS
```

3. Use the getParameter method to retrieve the contents of the Name form field and insert the value into the query.

4. Execute the query and return the ResultSet.

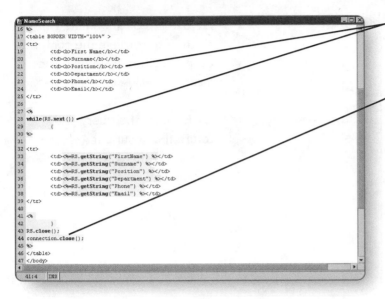

```
16  %>
17  <table BORDER WIDTH="100%" >
18  <tr>
19          <td><b>First Name</b></td>
20          <td><b>Surname</b></td>
21          <td><b>Position</b></td>
22          <td><b>Department</b></td>
23          <td><b>Phone</b></td>
24          <td><b>Email</b></td>
25  </tr>
26
27  <%
28  while(RS.next())
29          {
30  %>
31
32  <tr>
33          <td><%=RS.getString("FirstName") %></td>
34          <td><%=RS.getString("Surname") %></td>
35          <td><%=RS.getString("Position") %></td>
36          <td><%=RS.getString("Department") %></td>
37          <td><%=RS.getString("Phone") %></td>
38          <td><%=RS.getString("Email") %></td>
39  </tr>
40
41  <%
42          }
43  RS.close();
44  connection.close();
45  %>
46  </table>
47  </body>
```
`41:4    INS`

5. Display the results in a table. Use a while loop to display each record in a table row.

6. Close the database connection.

Processing the Search by Position Request

The PositionSearch.jsp page will process the search for employees that share the same position. You must use the getParameter method to retrieve the position that defines the query criteria.

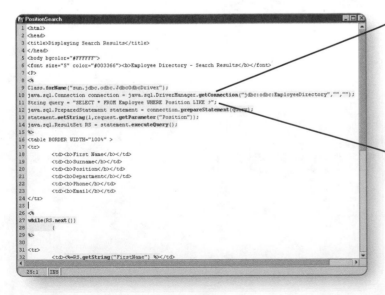

```
1   <html>
2   <head>
3   <title>Displaying Search Results</title>
4   </head>
5   <body bgcolor="#FFFFFF">
6   <font size="5" color="#003366"><b>Employee Directory - Search Results</b></font>
7   <P>
8   <%
9   Class.forName("sun.jdbc.odbc.JdbcOdbcDriver");
10  java.sql.Connection connection = java.sql.DriverManager.getConnection("jdbc:odbc:EmployeeDirectory","","");
11  String query = "SELECT * FROM Employee WHERE Position LIKE ?";
12  java.sql.PreparedStatement statement = connection.prepareStatement(query);
13  statement.setString(1,request.getParameter("Position"));
14  java.sql.ResultSet RS = statement.executeQuery();
15  %>
16  <table BORDER WIDTH="100%" >
17  <tr>
18          <td><b>First Name</b></td>
19          <td><b>Surname</b></td>
20          <td><b>Position</b></td>
21          <td><b>Department</b></td>
22          <td><b>Phone</b></td>
23          <td><b>Email</b></td>
24  </tr>
25  |
26  <%
27  while(RS.next())
28          {
29  %>
30
31  <tr>
32          <td><%=RS.getString("FirstName") %></td>
```
`25:1    INS`

1. Create a connection to the EmployeeDirectory.mdb Microsoft Access database. You will first need to set up a DSN for the EmployeeDirectory database.

2. Define a parametized query that will retrieve records where the Position field matches the search request. Insert a question mark (?) as a placeholder for the search criteria. A Prepared Statement will be used.

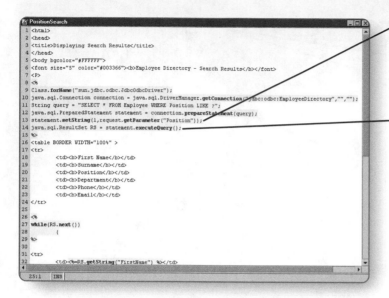

```
1  <html>
2  <head>
3  <title>Displaying Search Results</title>
4  </head>
5  <body bgcolor="#FFFFFF">
6  <font size="5" color="#003366"><b>Employee Directory - Search Results</b></font>
7  <P>
8  <%
9  Class.forName("sun.jdbc.odbc.JdbcOdbcDriver");
10 java.sql.Connection connection = java.sql.DriverManager.getConnection("jdbc:odbc:EmployeeDirectory","","");
11 String query = "SELECT * FROM Employee WHERE Position LIKE ?";
12 java.sql.PreparedStatement statement = connection.prepareStatement(query);
13 statement.setString(1,request.getParameter("Position"));
14 java.sql.ResultSet RS = statement.executeQuery();
15 %>
16 <table BORDER WIDTH="100%" >
17 <tr>
18         <td><b>First Name</b></td>
19         <td><b>Surname</b></td>
20         <td><b>Position</b></td>
21         <td><b>Department</b></td>
22         <td><b>Phone</b></td>
23         <td><b>Email</b></td>
24 </tr>
25
26 <%
27 while(RS.next())
28         {
29 %>
30
31 <tr>
32         <td><%=RS.getString("FirstName") %></td>
```

3. Use the getParameter method to retrieve the contents of the Position form field and insert the value into the query.

4. Execute the query and return the ResultSet.

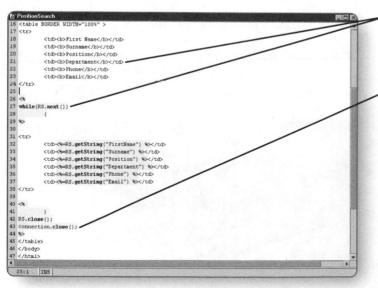

```
16 <table BORDER WIDTH="100%" >
17 <tr>
18         <td><b>First Name</b></td>
19         <td><b>Surname</b></td>
20         <td><b>Position</b></td>
21         <td><b>Department</b></td>
22         <td><b>Phone</b></td>
23         <td><b>Email</b></td>
24 </tr>
25 |
26 <%
27 while(RS.next())
28         {
29 %>
30
31 <tr>
32         <td><%=RS.getString("FirstName") %></td>
33         <td><%=RS.getString("Surname") %></td>
34         <td><%=RS.getString("Position") %></td>
35         <td><%=RS.getString("Department") %></td>
36         <td><%=RS.getString("Phone") %></td>
37         <td><%=RS.getString("Email") %></td>
38 </tr>
39
40 <%
41         }
42 RS.close();
43 connection.close();
44 %>
45 </table>
46 </body>
47 </html>
```

5. Display the results in a table. Use a while loop to display each record in a table row.

6. Close the database connection.

Processing the Search by Department Request

You must retrieve the Department form field using the getParameter method of the request object. The name of the department must be passed to the parametized Prepared Statement. The returned records will be displayed in a table that can easily be printed to produce a departmental contact list.

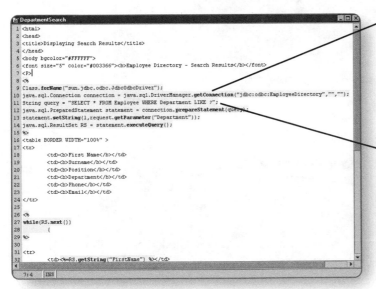

1. Create a connection to the EmployeeDirectory.mdb Microsoft Access database. You will first need to set up a DSN for the EmployeeDirectory database.

2. Define a parametized query that will retrieve all employees who belong to a particular department. Insert a question mark (?) as a placeholder for the search criteria. A Prepared Statement will be used.

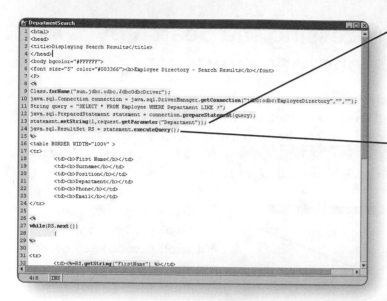

3. Use the getParameter method to retrieve the contents of the Department form field and insert the value into the query.

4. Execute the query and return the ResultSet.

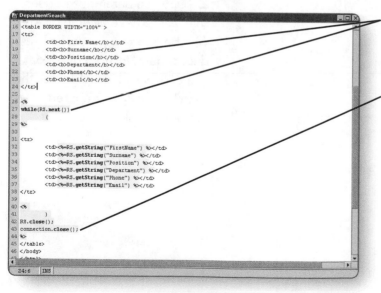

5. Display the results in a table. Use a while loop to display each record in a table row.

6. Close the database connection.

Administering the Employee Directory

The administrator must have a Web interface to insert, update, and delete records. The administration console needs to

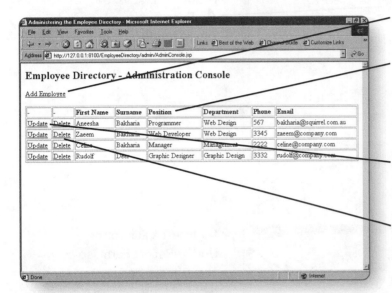

- Include a link to an insert form (InsertForm.htm)

- Allow the administrator to view all records

- Allow the administrator to select a record that needs to be updated

- Allow the administrator to select a record that must be deleted

1. Insert a link to the InsertForm.htm file. This form will be used to insert new records into the database.

2. Create a connection to the EmployeeDirectory.mdb Microsoft Access database.

3. Define a query that will retrieve all employees.

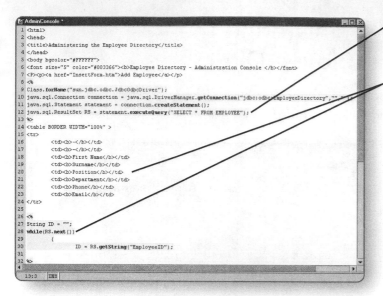

4. Execute the query and return the ResultSet.

5. Display the results in a table. Use a while loop to display each record in a table row.

6. Insert a link to the UpdateRecordForm.jsp page. This link will be inserted for each record in the database because it is within the while loop. The administrator will click on this link to update a record. The record ID needs to be passed in the query string to the UpdateRecordForm.jsp page. The UpdateRecordForm.jsp page will retrieve the record that matches the ID and display the record in a form.

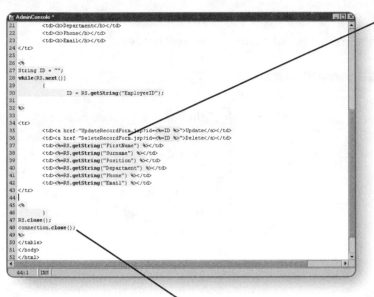

```
AdminConsole *
21          <td><b>Department</b></td>
22          <td><b>Phone</b></td>
23          <td><b>Email</b></td>
24  </tr>
25
26  <%
27  String ID = "";
28  while(RS.next())
29          {
30                  ID = RS.getString("EmployeeID");
31
32  %>
33
34  <tr>
35          <td><a href="UpdateRecordForm.jsp?id=<%=ID %>">Update</a></td>
36          <td><a href="DeleteRecordForm.jsp?id=<%=ID %>">Delete</a></td>
37          <td><%=RS.getString("FirstName") %></td>
38          <td><%=RS.getString("Surname") %></td>
39          <td><%=RS.getString("Position") %></td>
40          <td><%=RS.getString("Department") %></td>
41          <td><%=RS.getString("Phone") %></td>
42          <td><%=RS.getString("Email") %></td>
43  </tr>
44  |
45  <%
46          }
47  RS.close();
48  connection.close();
49  %>
50  </table>
51  </body>
52  </html>

44:1    INS
```

7. Insert a link to the DeleteRecordForm.jsp page. This link will be inserted for each record in the database because it is within the while loop. The administrator will click on this link to delete a record. The record ID needs to be passed in the query string to the DeleteRecordForm.jsp page. The DeleteRecordForm.jsp page will delete the record if the administrator is certain that the record must be deleted.

8. Close the database connection.

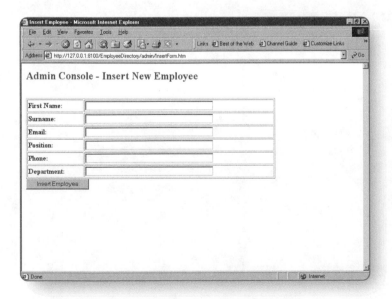

Creating the Insert Form

The Insert form needs to include a form field for each field that makes up a valid record in the database. A form field to insert the record's unique ID is not required. The database will take care of that.

1. Use the <form> tag to create the insert form. The ProcessInsertForm.jsp page will process the form.

```
InsertForm *
1  <html>
2  <head>
3    <title>Insert Employee</title>
4  </head>
5  <body bgcolor="#FFFFFF">
6  <font size="5" color="#003366"><b>Admin Console - Insert New Employee</b></font>
7  <br>
8  <form method="Post" action="ProcessInsertForm.jsp">
9    <table BORDER COLS=2 WIDTH="75%" >
10     <tr>
11       <td><b>First Name:</b></td>
12       <td>
13         <input type="text" name="FirstName" size=40>
14       </td>
15     </tr>
16     <tr>
17       <td><b>Surname:</b></td>
18       <td>
19         <input type="text" name="Surname" size=40>
20       </td>
21     </tr>
22     <tr>
23       <td><b>Email:</b></td>
24       <td>
25         <input type="text" name="Email" size=40>
26       </td>
27     </tr>
28     <tr>
29       <td><b>Position:</b></td>
30       <td>
31         <input type="text" name="Position" size=40>
32       </td>
33     </tr>
8:1    INS
```

2. Insert a form field for each database field that makes up the record. You will need to insert a text input field for the FirstName, Surname, Email, Position, Phone, and Department fields. The names given to form fields should match the table column names in the database. This will make it much easier to insert the data in the corresponding database field.

```
InsertForm *
19         <input type="text" name="Surname" size=40>
20       </td>
21     </tr>
22     <tr>
23       <td><b>Email:</b></td>
24       <td>
25         <input type="text" name="Email" size=40>
26       </td>
27     </tr>
28     <tr>
29       <td><b>Position:</b></td>
30       <td>
31         <input type="text" name="Position" size=40>
32       </td>
33     </tr>
34     <tr>
35       <td><b>Phone:</b></td>
36       <td>
37         <input type="text" name="Phone" size=40>
38       </td>
39     </tr>
40     <tr>
41       <td><b>Department:</b></td>
42       <td>
43         <input type="text" name="Department" size=40>
44       </td>
45     </tr>
46   </table>
47  <input type="submit" name="Insert" value="Insert Employee">
48  </Form>
49  </body>
50  </html>
51
8:1    INS
```

3. Insert a submit button. The administrator will click on the button to insert the record.

Processing the Insert Form

The ProcessInsertForm.jsp page will retrieve the form data and store it as a new record in the database.

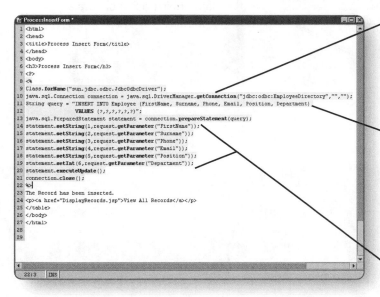

1. Create a connection to the EmployeeDirectory.mdb Microsoft Access database. You will first need to set up a DSN for the EmployeeDirectory database.

2. Define a parametized query that will insert a record into the Employee table. You must insert a question mark (?) as a placeholder for each field in the record. A Prepared Statement will be used.

3. Use the getParameter method to retrieve the contents of the Insert form and pass the values to the Prepared Statement.

4. Execute the query by calling the executeUpdate method. The record will be inserted.

5. Close the database connection.

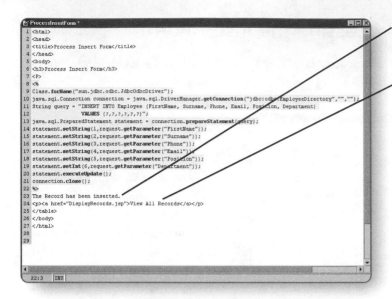

```
ProcessInsertForm *
1  <html>
2  <head>
3  <title>Process Insert Form</title>
4  </head>
5  <body>
6  <h3>Process Insert Form</h3>
7  <P>
8  <%
9  Class.forName("sun.jdbc.odbc.JdbcOdbcDriver");
10 java.sql.Connection connection = java.sql.DriverManager.getConnection("jdbc:odbc:EmployeeDirectory","","");
11 String query = "INSERT INTO Employee (FirstName, Surname, Phone, Email, Position, Department)
12           VALUES (?,?,?,?,?,?)";
13 java.sql.PreparedStatement statement = connection.prepareStatement(query);
14 statement.setString(1,request.getParameter("FirstName"));
15 statement.setString(2,request.getParameter("Surname"));
16 statement.setString(3,request.getParameter("Phone"));
17 statement.setString(4,request.getParameter("Email"));
18 statement.setString(5,request.getParameter("Position"));
19 statement.setInt(6,request.getParameter("Department"));
20 statement.executeUpdate();
21 connection.close();
22 %>
23 The Record has been inserted.
24 <p><a href="DisplayRecords.jsp">View All Records</a></p>
25 </table>
26 </body>
27 </html>
28
29
22:3    INS
```

6. Acknowledge that the record has been inserted.

7. Insert a link back to the administration console.

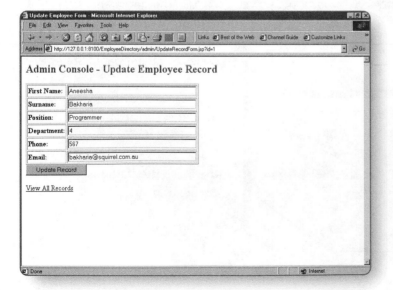

Creating the Update Form

The Update form must display the contents of the selected record in the form. This allows the administrator to edit the existing data and then submit the edited data to the database.

```
UpdateRecordForm
1  <html>
2  <head>
3  <title>Update Employee Form</title>
4  </head>
5  <body bgcolor="#FFFFFF">
6  <font size="5" color="#003366"><b>Admin Console - Update Employee Record</b></font>
7  <P>
8  <%
9  Class.forName("sun.jdbc.odbc.JdbcOdbcDriver");
10 java.sql.Connection connection = java.sql.DriverManager.getConnection("jdbc:odbc:Employee","","");
11 String query = "SELECT * FROM Employee WHERE EmployeeID = ?";
12 java.sql.PreparedStatement statement = connection.prepareStatement(query);
13 statement.setInt(1,Integer.parseInt(request.getParameter("id")));
14 java.sql.ResultSet RS = statement.executeQuery();
15 %>
16
17 <%
18 while(RS.next())
19      {
20 %>
21 <form method="Post" action="ProcessUpdateForm.jsp">
22   <table width="50%" border="1">
23     <input type="hidden" name="EmployeeID" value="<%=RS.getString("EmployeeID") %>">
24     <tr>
25       <td width="30%"><b>First Name:</b></td>
26       <td width="70%">
27         <input type="text" name="FirstName" size=40 value="<%=RS.getString("FirstName") %>">
28       </td>
29     </tr>
30     <tr>
31       <td width="30%"><b>Surname:</b></td>
32       <td width="70%">
33         <input type="text" name="Surname" size=40 value="<%=RS.getString("Surname") %>">
16:1     INS
```

1. Create a connection to the EmployeeDirectory.mdb Microsoft Access database. You will first need to set up a DSN for the EmployeeDirectory database.

2. Define a parametized query that will retrieve the record that matches the ID passed to the page in the query string. You must insert a question mark (?) as a placeholder for the record ID. A Prepared Statement will be used.

```
UpdateRecordForm
1  <html>
2  <head>
3  <title>Update Employee Form</title>
4  </head>
5  <body bgcolor="#FFFFFF">
6  <font size="5" color="#003366"><b>Admin Console - Update Employee Record</b></font>
7  <P>
8  <%
9  Class.forName("sun.jdbc.odbc.JdbcOdbcDriver");
10 java.sql.Connection connection = java.sql.DriverManager.getConnection("jdbc:odbc:Employee","","");
11 String query = "SELECT * FROM Employee WHERE EmployeeID = ?";
12 java.sql.PreparedStatement statement = connection.prepareStatement(query);
13 statement.setInt(1,Integer.parseInt(request.getParameter("id")));
14 java.sql.ResultSet RS = statement.executeQuery();
15 %>
16
17 <%
18 while(RS.next())
19      {
20 %>
21 <form method="Post" action="ProcessUpdateForm.jsp">
22   <table width="50%" border="1">
23     <input type="hidden" name="EmployeeID" value="<%=RS.getString("EmployeeID") %>">
24     <tr>
25       <td width="30%"><b>First Name:</b></td>
26       <td width="70%">
27         <input type="text" name="FirstName" size=40 value="<%=RS.getString("FirstName") %>">
28       </td>
29     </tr>
30     <tr>
31       <td width="30%"><b>Surname:</b></td>
32       <td width="70%">
33         <input type="text" name="Surname" size=40 value="<%=RS.getString("Surname") %>">
16:1     INS
```

3. Use the getParameter method to retrieve the record ID from the query string.

4. Execute the query and return the ResultSet.

5. Use the <form> tag to create the Insert form. The ProcessUpdateForm.jsp page will process the form.

6. Insert a hidden form field to store the record ID. This is required to update the correct record.

7. Insert a form field for each database field that makes up the record. You will need to insert a text input field for the FirstName, Surname, Email, Position, Phone, and Department fields. The names given to form fields should match the table column names in the database. This will make it much easier to update the data in the corresponding database field.

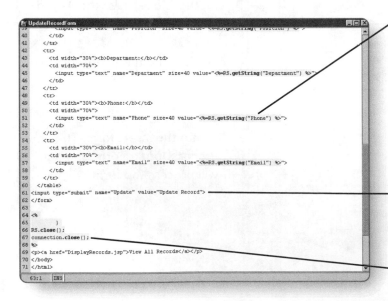

```
17 <%
18 while(RS.next())
19         {
20 %>
21 <form method="Post" action="ProcessUpdateForm.jsp">
22   <table width="50%" border="1">
23     <input type="hidden" name="EmployeeID" value="<%=RS.getString("EmployeeID") %>">
24     <tr>
25       <td width="30%"><b>First Name:</b></td>
26       <td width="70%">
27         <input type="text" name="FirstName" size=40 value="<%=RS.getString("FirstName") %>">
28       </td>
29     </tr>
30     <tr>
31       <td width="30%"><b>Surname:</b></td>
32       <td width="70%">
33         <input type="text" name="Surname" size=40 value="<%=RS.getString("Surname") %>">
34       </td>
35     </tr>
36     <tr>
37       <td width="30%"><b>Position:</b></td>
38       <td width="70%">
39         <input type="text" name="Position" size=40 value="<%=RS.getString("Position") %>">
40       </td>
41     </tr>
42     <tr>
43       <td width="30%"><b>Department:</b></td>
44       <td width="70%">
45         <input type="text" name="Department" size=40 value="<%=RS.getString("Department") %>">
46       </td>
47     </tr>
48     <tr>
49       <td width="30%"><b>Phone:</b></td>
```

8. Retrieve the data from each database field and use the Expression tag to assign it to the value attribute of the corresponding form field. This will display the record in the form so that the administrator can edit the data stored in each field.

```
40       </td>
41     </tr>
42     <tr>
43       <td width="30%"><b>Department:</b></td>
44       <td width="70%">
45         <input type="text" name="Department" size=40 value="<%=RS.getString("Department") %>">
46       </td>
47     </tr>
48     <tr>
49       <td width="30%"><b>Phone:</b></td>
50       <td width="70%">
51         <input type="text" name="Phone" size=40 value="<%=RS.getString("Phone") %>">
52       </td>
53     </tr>
54     <tr>
55       <td width="30%"><b>Email:</b></td>
56       <td width="70%">
57         <input type="text" name="Email" size=40 value="<%=RS.getString("Email") %>">
58       </td>
59     </tr>
60   </table>
61 <input type="submit" name="Update" value="Update Record">
62 </form>
63
64 <%
65         }
66 RS.close();
67 connection.close();
68 %>
69 <p><a href="DisplayRecords.jsp">View All Records</a></p>
70 </body>
71 </html>
```

9. Insert a submit button. The administrator will click on the button to update the record.

10. Close the database connection.

Processing the Update Form

The ProcessUpdateForm.jsp page will retrieve the edited data and use it to replace the existing record. An UPDATE query is used.

```
1  <html>
2  <head>
3  <title>Process Update Form</title>
4  </head>
5  <body bgcolor="#FFFFFF">
6  <font size="5" color="#003366"><b>Admin Console - Updating Record</b></font>
7  <P>
8  <%
9  Class.forName("sun.jdbc.odbc.JdbcOdbcDriver");
10 java.sql.Connection connection = java.sql.DriverManager.getConnection("jdbc:odbc:EmployeeDirectory","","");
11 String query = "UPDATE Employee SET FirstName=?, Surname=?, Phone=?, Email=?, Position=?, Department=?
12 WHERE EmployeeID=?";
13 java.sql.PreparedStatement statement = connection.prepareStatement(query);
14 statement.setString(1,request.getParameter("FirstName"));
15 statement.setString(2,request.getParameter("Surname"));
16 statement.setString(3,request.getParameter("Phone"));
17 statement.setString(4,request.getParameter("Email"));
18 statement.setString(5,request.getParameter("Position"));
19 statement.setInt(6,Integer.parseInt(request.getParameter("Department")));
20 statement.setInt(7,Integer.parseInt(request.getParameter("EmployeeID")));
21 statement.executeUpdate();
22 connection.close();
23 %>
24 The Record has been updated.
25 <p><a href="DisplayRecords.jsp">View All Records</a></p>
26 </body>
27 </html>
28
29
```

1. Create a connection to the EmployeeDirectory.mdb Microsoft Access database. You will first need to set up a DSN for the EmployeeDirectory database.

2. Define a parametized query that will update a record in the Employee table. You must insert a question mark (?) as a placeholder for each field in the record. Add a WHERE clause to update the record that matches the record ID. A Prepared Statement will be used.

```
1  <html>
2  <head>
3  <title>Process Update Form</title>
4  </head>
5  <body bgcolor="#FFFFFF">
6  <font size="5" color="#003366"><b>Admin Console - Updating Record</b></font>
7  <P>
8  <%
9  Class.forName("sun.jdbc.odbc.JdbcOdbcDriver");
10 java.sql.Connection connection = java.sql.DriverManager.getConnection("jdbc:odbc:EmployeeDirectory","","");
11 String query = "UPDATE Employee SET FirstName=?, Surname=?, Phone=?, Email=?, Position=?, Department=?
12 WHERE EmployeeID=?";
13 java.sql.PreparedStatement statement = connection.prepareStatement(query);
14 statement.setString(1,request.getParameter("FirstName"));
15 statement.setString(2,request.getParameter("Surname"));
16 statement.setString(3,request.getParameter("Phone"));
17 statement.setString(4,request.getParameter("Email"));
18 statement.setString(5,request.getParameter("Position"));
19 statement.setInt(6,Integer.parseInt(request.getParameter("Department")));
20 statement.setInt(7,Integer.parseInt(request.getParameter("EmployeeID")));
21 statement.executeUpdate();
22 connection.close();
23 %>
24 The Record has been updated.
25 <p><a href="DisplayRecords.jsp">View All Records</a></p>
26 </body>
27 </html>
28
29
```

3. Use the getParameter method to retrieve the contents of the Update form and pass the values to the Prepared Statement.

4. Execute the query by calling the executeUpdate method. The record will be updated.

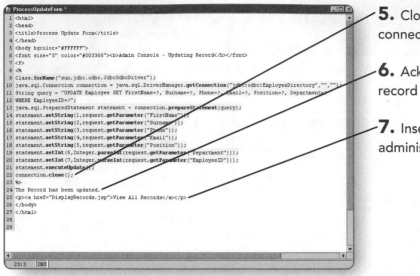

```
ProcessUpdateForm *
 1  <html>
 2  <head>
 3  <title>Process Update Form</title>
 4  </head>
 5  <body bgcolor="#FFFFFF">
 6  <font size="5" color="#003366"><b>Admin Console - Updating Record</b></font>
 7  <P>
 8  <%
 9  Class.forName("sun.jdbc.odbc.JdbcOdbcDriver");
10  java.sql.Connection connection = java.sql.DriverManager.getConnection("jdbc:odbc:EmployeeDirectory","","");
11  String query = "UPDATE Employee SET FirstName=?, Surname=?, Phone=?, Email=?, Position=?, Department
12  WHERE EmployeeID=?";
13  java.sql.PreparedStatement statement = connection.prepareStatement(query);
14  statement.setString(1,request.getParameter("FirstName"));
15  statement.setString(2,request.getParameter("Surname"));
16  statement.setString(3,request.getParameter("Phone"));
17  statement.setString(4,request.getParameter("Email"));
18  statement.setString(5,request.getParameter("Position"));
19  statement.setInt(6,Integer.parseInt(request.getParameter("Department")));
20  statement.setInt(7,Integer.parseInt(request.getParameter("EmployeeID")));
21  statement.executeUpdate();
22  connection.close();
23  %>
24  The Record has been updated.
25  <p><a href="DisplayRecords.jsp">View All Records</a></p>
26  </body>
27  </html>
28
29
```

```
23:3    INS
```

5. Close the database connection.

6. Acknowledge that the record has been updated.

7. Insert a link back to the administration console.

Creating the Delete Form

A Delete form is not really required, because the selected record could just be deleted. It is included here so that you have a method of preventing the accidental deletion of records. The Delete form displays the selected record, and the administrator can then decide whether the record should be deleted.

```
DeleteRecordForm                                                                _ □ ×
1  <html>
2  <head>
3  <title>Delete Employee Record Form</title>
4  </head>
5  <body bgcolor="#FFFFFF">
6  <font size="5" color="#003366"><b>Admin Console - Delete Employee Record</b></font>
7  <P>
8  <%
9  Class.forName("sun.jdbc.odbc.JdbcOdbcDriver");
10 java.sql.Connection connection = java.sql.DriverManager.getConnection("jdbc:odbc:Employee","","");
11 String query = "SELECT * FROM Employee WHERE EmployeeID = ?";
12 java.sql.PreparedStatement statement = connection.prepareStatement(query);
13 statement.setInt(1,Integer.parseInt(request.getParameter("id")));
14 java.sql.ResultSet RS = statement.executeQuery();
15 %>
16
17 <%
18 while(RS.next())
19         {
20 %>
21 <form method="Post" action="ProcessDeleteForm.jsp">
22   <table width="50%" border="1">
23     <input type="hidden" name="EmployeeID" value="<%=RS.getString("EmployeeID") %>">
24     <tr>
25       <td width="30%"><b>First Name:</b></td>
26       <td width="70%"><%=RS.getString("FirstName") %></td>
27     </tr>
28     <tr>
29       <td width="30%"><b>Surname:</b></td>
30       <td width="70%"><%=RS.getString("Surname") %></td>
31     </tr>
32     <tr>
33       <td width="30%"><b>Position:</b></td>
1:1   INS
```

1. Create a connection to the EmployeeDirectory.mdb Microsoft Access database. You will first need to set up a DSN for the EmployeeDirectory database.

2. Define a parametized query that will retrieve the record that matches the ID passed to the page in the query string. You must insert a question mark (?) as a placeholder for the record ID. A Prepared Statement will be used.

```
DeleteRecordForm                                                                _ □ ×
1  <html>
2  <head>
3  <title>Delete Employee Record Form</title>
4  </head>
5  <body bgcolor="#FFFFFF">
6  <font size="5" color="#003366"><b>Admin Console - Delete Employee Record</b></font>
7  <P>
8  <%
9  Class.forName("sun.jdbc.odbc.JdbcOdbcDriver");
10 java.sql.Connection connection = java.sql.DriverManager.getConnection("jdbc:odbc:Employee","","");
11 String query = "SELECT * FROM Employee WHERE EmployeeID = ?";
12 java.sql.PreparedStatement statement = connection.prepareStatement(query);
13 statement.setInt(1,Integer.parseInt(request.getParameter("id")));
14 java.sql.ResultSet RS = statement.executeQuery();
15 %>
16
17 <%
18 while(RS.next())
19         {
20 %>
21 <form method="Post" action="ProcessDeleteForm.jsp">
22   <table width="50%" border="1">
23     <input type="hidden" name="EmployeeID" value="<%=RS.getString("EmployeeID") %>">
24     <tr>
25       <td width="30%"><b>First Name:</b></td>
26       <td width="70%"><%=RS.getString("FirstName") %></td>
27     </tr>
28     <tr>
29       <td width="30%"><b>Surname:</b></td>
30       <td width="70%"><%=RS.getString("Surname") %></td>
31     </tr>
32     <tr>
33       <td width="30%"><b>Position:</b></td>
17:3   INS
```

3. Use the getParameter method to retrieve the record ID from the query string.

4. Execute the query and return the ResultSet.

5. Use the <form> tag to create the Delete form. The ProcessDeleteForm.jsp page will process the form.

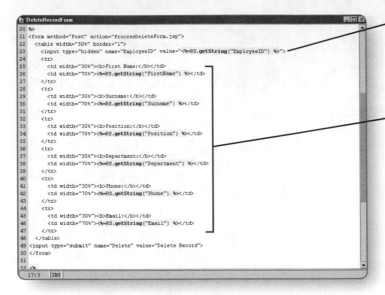

```
20 %>
21 <form method="Post" action="ProcessDeleteForm.jsp">
22   <table width="50%" border="1">
23     <input type="hidden" name="EmployeeID" value="<%=RS.getString("EmployeeID") %>">
24     <tr>
25       <td width="30%"><b>First Name:</b></td>
26       <td width="70%"><%=RS.getString("FirstName") %></td>
27     </tr>
28     <tr>
29       <td width="30%"><b>Surname:</b></td>
30       <td width="70%"><%=RS.getString("Surname") %></td>
31     </tr>
32     <tr>
33       <td width="30%"><b>Position:</b></td>
34       <td width="70%"><%=RS.getString("Position") %></td>
35     </tr>
36     <tr>
37       <td width="30%"><b>Department:</b></td>
38       <td width="70%"><%=RS.getString("Department") %></td>
39     </tr>
40     <tr>
41       <td width="30%"><b>Phone:</b></td>
42       <td width="70%"><%=RS.getString("Phone") %></td>
43     </tr>
44     <tr>
45       <td width="30%"><b>Email:</b></td>
46       <td width="70%"><%=RS.getString("Email") %></td>
47     </tr>
48   </table>
49 <input type="submit" name="Delete" value="Delete Record">
50 </form>
51
52 <%
```

6. Insert a hidden form field to store the record ID. This is required in order to delete the correct record.

7. Display the contents of each field. This is done just to show the administrator the record that will be deleted.

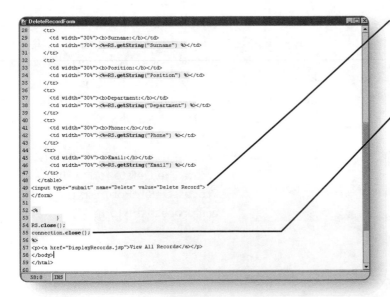

```
28     <tr>
29       <td width="30%"><b>Surname:</b></td>
30       <td width="70%"><%=RS.getString("Surname") %></td>
31     </tr>
32     <tr>
33       <td width="30%"><b>Position:</b></td>
34       <td width="70%"><%=RS.getString("Position") %></td>
35     </tr>
36     <tr>
37       <td width="30%"><b>Department:</b></td>
38       <td width="70%"><%=RS.getString("Department") %></td>
39     </tr>
40     <tr>
41       <td width="30%"><b>Phone:</b></td>
42       <td width="70%"><%=RS.getString("Phone") %></td>
43     </tr>
44     <tr>
45       <td width="30%"><b>Email:</b></td>
46       <td width="70%"><%=RS.getString("Email") %></td>
47     </tr>
48   </table>
49 <input type="submit" name="Delete" value="Delete Record">
50 </form>
51
52 <%
53       }
54 RS.close();
55 connection.close();
56 %>
57 <p><a href="DisplayRecords.jsp">View All Records</a></p>
58 </body>
59 </html>
60
```

8. Insert a submit button. The administrator will review the record and click on this button to confirm the record's deletion.

9. Close the database connection.

Processing the Delete Form

The ProcessDeleteForm.jsp page will delete the selected record. To do this, you must use a DELETE query.

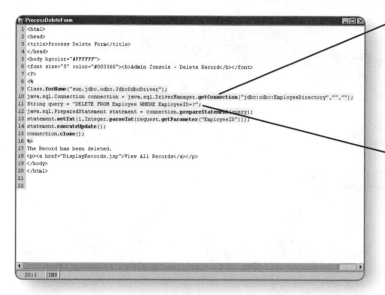

1. Create a connection to the EmployeeDirectory.mdb Microsoft Access database. You will first need to set up a DSN for the EmployeeDirectory database.

2. Define a parametized query that will delete a record in the Employee table that matches the record ID. A Prepared Statement will be used.

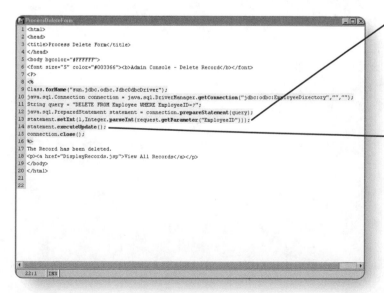

3. Use the getParameter method to retrieve the contents of the Delete form and pass the values to the Prepared Statement.

4. Execute the query by calling the executeUpdate method. The record will be deleted.

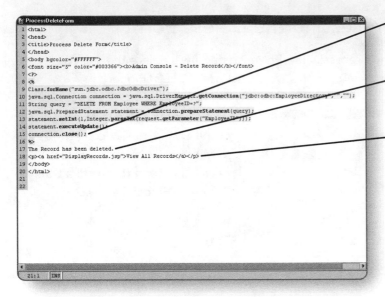

```
1  <html>
2  <head>
3  <title>Process Delete Form</title>
4  </head>
5  <body bgcolor="#FFFFFF">
6  <font size="5" color="#003366"><b>Admin Console - Delete Record</b></font>
7  <P>
8  <%
9  Class.forName("sun.jdbc.odbc.JdbcOdbcDriver");
10 java.sql.Connection connection = java.sql.DriverManager.getConnection("jdbc:odbc:EmployeeDirectory","","");
11 String query = "DELETE FROM Employee WHERE EmployeeID=?";
12 java.sql.PreparedStatement statement = connection.prepareStatement(query);
13 statement.setInt(1,Integer.parseInt(request.getParameter("EmployeeID")));
14 statement.executeUpdate();
15 connection.close();
16 %>
17 The Record has been deleted.
18 <p><a href="DisplayRecords.jsp">View All Records</a></p>
19 </body>
20 </html>
21
22
```

5. Close the database connection.

6. Acknowledge that the record has been deleted.

7. Insert a link back to the administration console.

20

Creating an Online Store

E-commerce-enabled Web applications are becoming exceedingly popular. It is highly likely that, as a Web developer, you will be required to build an online store sometime in the near future. The fundamental functionality that an online store requires is a shopping cart. A shopping cart allows users to browse through a product catalog and select the products that they want to purchase. The shopping cart will be modeled as a JavaBean that you can re-use in your own projects. Developing a shopping cart in JSP is much simpler than doing so using a CGI script. The JSP engine has built-in objects to manage session state. In this chapter, you'll learn how to:

- Design a database for an online store
- Display a product catalog
- Build a shopping cart JavaBean
- Store orders in a database

The Fundamentals of an Online Store

First, it's important that you understand that an online store resembles a traditional store in many respects. In fact, the process in which a product is purchased is almost identical. Table 20.1 lists the differences between taking a trip to a local store and doing a little online shopping.

Table 20.1 A Trip to Your Local Store versus Shopping Online

Shopping at a Store	Shopping Online
Enter the store.	Visit the Web site of an online store.
You will notice that the products are categorized and placed in different locations in the store.	You will be able to view a product listing by selecting an appropriate category. There might also be a search facility that will allow you to locate a product quickly.
You browse the shelves and aisles of the store.	You view the products by category or search for the items that you require.
You add the products that you wish to purchase to your shopping basket.	You click on a button or a link to add the product to a virtual shopping cart.
Before you go to the checkout counter, you can review the contents of your basket to make sure that you have the correct quantity of each item and that you have not exceeded your budget. You can remove and add products to your basket.	You can view the contents of the virtual shopping cart at any time. Each page includes a link to display the shopping cart. You can change the quantity of products, as well as remove them from your cart. The prices of the individual products are also displayed.
When you are done, you proceed to the checkout counter. The price of each item is tallied, and you either pay by cash or credit card.	After you have viewed the contents of your shopping cart, you can continue to shop or proceed to the checkout Web page. There, you will enter your postage and payment details. Your details and the list of products purchased will be stored in a database. Your credit card will either be validated immediately or at a later time.
You take the products home.	The order will be processed and sent to you if your credit card details are valid and you have the money available.

So, apart from physically viewing the products and taking them home with you, there is no real difference between buying goods from a store or over the Internet.

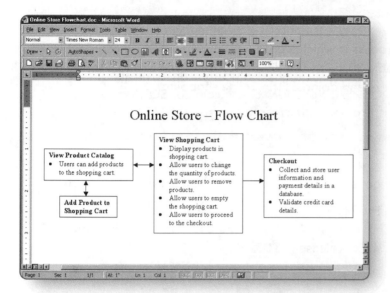

This flow chart details the operation of an online store. By examining the flow chart, you can determine what Web pages are required to build an online store, including

- A page to display the product catalog (Displaycatalog.jsp)

- A page to display the products in the shopping cart (ViewCart.jsp)

- A page to retrieve shipping and payment details (in other words, a checkout page—Checkout.jsp).

- A page to store the shipping, payment, and order details in a database (ProcessCheckout.jsp)

Of course, the best part is that you can use JSP to build all the pages that make up an online store.

Designing a Database for an Online Store

In this chapter, you will be using MySQL instead of Microsoft Access. Access provided you with a good starting point, but it is not capable of handling many simultaneous requests for data. MySQL is a popular open source relational database. It is also suitable for use as a back-end database in Web applications because it is very fast and reliable. It is, however, not as easy to use as Microsoft Access—but that is the price you have to pay for performance improvements. I have also decided to use MySQL in this chapter so that you gain some experience with using JDBC to connect directly to a database. In previous chapters, you used the JDBC-ODBC Bridge driver.

NOTE

You could also use mSQL (http://www.hughes.com.au/products/msql), Oracle (http://www.oracle.com), or SQL Server (http://www.microsoft.com/sql).

To get started with MySQL, you will need to download

- The MySQL binary (http://www.mysql.com/downloads/index.html). As of the writing of this book, the current stable release is 3.23.

- A MySQL JDBC Driver (http://www.mysql.com/downloads/api-jdbc.html). There are a few JDBC drivers that you can choose. This chapter uses the mm JDBC Driver. Don't forget to include the driver in your CLASSPATH.

- MySQLGUI (http://www.mysql.com/downloads/gui-clients.html). This will provide you with a visual interface to create and query databases. I find MySQLGUI much more productive than using the command line.

NOTE

It is beyond the scope of this book to provide you with a step-by step guide to installing MySQL. I would recommend reading the manual that accompanies MySQL. It is a complex installation, but well worth the results.

The back-end database for an online store only requires three simple tables, unless you require additional tables to facilitate internal business processes as well. In this chapter, you will design a database that is easy to modify and apply to your own requirements. You will need to create a database called OnlineStore. On the CD-ROM included with this book, refer to the Chapter 20 folder to find the SQL queries that are required to create and populate the database tables with data. Chapter 15, "Working with Databases," introduced you to SQL from a data manipulation perspective. You will now use SQL queries to actually model the database structure—in other words, to create tables and define the values stored within table columns.

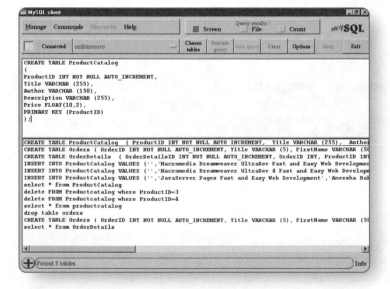

The ProductCatalog table stores the products that the store sells. Each product must have a unique identifier, title, description, and price. The CreateProductCatalog.sql file contains the CREATE TABLE query to construct the table. You can copy the query into MySQLGUI and execute it. This is the only table that you will need to populate with data. The InsertProducts.sql file contains queries to insert products into the table. These are the products that the online store will sell.

The Orders table stores the users' shipping and payment details. Each order must contain a unique ID that can be used to identify the order. The CreateOrders.sql file contains the CREATE TABLE query.

The OrderDetails table will store a record for each item purchased. Each record must contain an order ID that links the purchase back to an entry in the Orders table. A single order, therefore, can have many associated products. Each order must also contain a unique ID of its own, in this case OrderDetailsID. The OrderDetails table needs fields to store the product ID, order ID, and quantity of the product being purchased. The CreateOrderDetails.sql file contains the CREATE TABLE query.

Building the Product Class

The Product class will be used to model the products that will be stored in the shopping cart. Treating each product that is added to the shopping cart as an object simplifies the programming logic and structure of the Shopping Cart JavaBean that you will create in the next section, "Building the Shopping Cart JavaBean."

1. Define a class called Product.

```
 Product
1 public class Product
2 (
3        String id, title;
4        int quantity = 1;
5        double price, total;
6
7        public Product()()
8
9        public Product(String newid, String newtitle, double newprice)
10       (
11              id= newid;
12              title = newtitle;
13              price = newprice;
14       )
15
16       public String getId()
17       (
18              return id;
19       )
20
21       public String getTitle()
22       (
23              return title;
24       )
25
26       public int getQuantity()
27       (
28              return quantity;
29       )
30
31       public double getPrice()
32       (
33              return price;
   2:2   INS
```

2. Declare instance variables to store the product ID, title, quantity, and price of each products. You will also need to declare an instance variable that will store the total cost of the products, which will be determined by multiplying the price of a single item by the quantity being purchased. The price and total instance variable must be declared as double because they will store decimal values. The default quantity is set to 1.

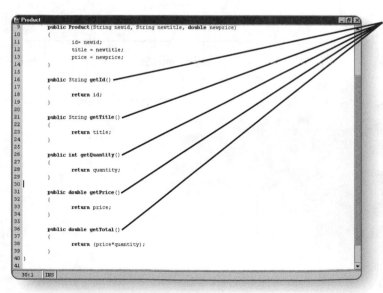

```
Product
1  public class Product
2  {
3        String id, title;
4        int quantity = 1;
5        double price, total;
6
7        public Product(){}
8
9        public Product(String newid, String newtitle, double newprice)
10       {
11             id= newid;
12             title = newtitle;
13             price = newprice;
14       }
15
16       public String getId()
17       {
18             return id;
19       }
20
21       public String getTitle()
22       {
23             return title;
24       }
25
26       public int getQuantity()
27       {
28             return quantity;
29       }
30
31       public double getPrice()
32       {
33             return price;
2:2   INS
```

3. Include a public constructor method that will create a new Product object instance when passed the product ID, title, and price.

NOTE

As you might recall from Chapter 7, "Object-Oriented Programming," the constructor method must have the same name as the class.

```
Product
9         public Product(String newid, String newtitle, double newprice)
10        {
11              id= newid;
12              title = newtitle;
13              price = newprice;
14        }
15
16        public String getId()
17        {
18              return id;
19        }
20
21        public String getTitle()
22        {
23              return title;
24        }
25
26        public int getQuantity()
27        {
28              return quantity;
29        }
30
31        public double getPrice()
32        {
33              return price;
34        }
35
36        public double getTotal()
37        {
38              return (price*quantity);
39        }
40  }
41
30:1   INS
```

4. Include get accessor methods to return the ID, title, quantity, price, and total price of a product.

NOTE

The getTotal method must return the total price by multiplying the price and quantity instance variables of the product object.

Building the Shopping Cart JavaBean

The Shopping Cart JavaBean will encapsulate the entire core shopping cart functionality. The shopping cart uses a vector to store Product objects. A vector is just like an array except that it can be resized as products are added to and removed from the cart. The Shopping Cart JavaBean includes methods to

- Add a product to the shopping cart
- Delete a product from the shopping cart
- Return the number of items in the cart
- Calculate the total cost of the purchase
- Empty the shopping cart

```
ShoppingCart
1  import java.util.*;
2
3  public class ShoppingCart
4  {
5  Vector products = new Vector();
6
7      public void addProduct(Product i)
8      {
9          boolean productFound = false;
10         Enumeration productEnum = getProducts();
11         while(productEnum.hasMoreElements())
12         {
13             Product product = (Product)productEnum.nextElement();
14             if(product.getId().equals(i.id))
15             {
16                 productFound = true;
17                 product.quantity += 1;
18                 break;
19             }
20         }
21         if (!productFound)
22         {
23             products.addElement(i);
24         }
25     }
26
27     public void deleteProduct(String id)
28     {
29         Enumeration productEnum = getProducts();
30         while(productEnum.hasMoreElements())
31         {
32             Product product = (Product)productEnum.nextElement();
33             if(product.getId().equals(id))
```

1. Import the java.util.* package. This package contains the Vector class.

2. Define a class called ShoppingCart.

3. Create a new instance of the Vector class called products. The products vector will store all the items added to the shopping cart.

TIP

If you don't feel comfortable using vectors, why not return to Chapter 5, "Working with Strings and Arrays," for a brief refresher?

```
ShoppingCart                                                    _ □ X
 7        public void addProduct(Product i)
 8        {
 9               boolean productFound = false;
10               Enumeration productEnum = getProducts();
11               while(productEnum.hasMoreElements())
12               {
13                      Product product = (Product)productEnum.nextElement();
14                      if(product.getId().equals(i.id))
15                      {
16                             productFound = true;
17                             product.quantity += 1;
18                             break;
19                      }
20               }
21               if (!productFound)
22               {
23                      products.addElement(i);
24               }
25        }
26
27        public void deleteProduct(String id)
28        {
29               Enumeration productEnum = getProducts();
30               while(productEnum.hasMoreElements())
31               {
32                      Product product = (Product)productEnum.nextElement();
33                      if(product.getId().equals(id))
34                      {
35                             products.removeElement(product);
36                             break;
37                      }
38               }
39        }
18:39   INS
```

4. Create a public addProduct method. This method will add a Product object to the products vector. If the product is already in the shopping cart, it simply increases the quantity instance variable by one.

5. Create a deleteProduct method. This method will delete the product from the products vector. The product ID must be passed to the deleteProduct method. The product ID locates the product that must be deleted.

```
ShoppingCart                                                    _ □ X
27        public void deleteProduct(String id)
28        {
29               Enumeration productEnum = getProducts();
30               while(productEnum.hasMoreElements())
31               {
32                      Product product = (Product)productEnum.nextElement();
33                      if(product.getId().equals(id))
34                      {
35                             products.removeElement(product);
36                             break;
37                      }
38               }
39        }
40
41        public void emptyCart()
42        {
43               products = new Vector();
44        }
45
46        public int getNoProducts()
47        {
48               return products.size();
49        }
50
51        public Enumeration getProducts()
52        {
53               return products.elements();
54        }
55
56        public double getTotal()
57        {
58               Enumeration productEnum = getProducts();
59               double total = 0;
18:39   INS
```

6. Create an emptyCart method. This method removes all items from the shopping cart by declaring the products vector. If a vector that contains data gets declared, its content is deleted.

7. Create a getNoProducts method. This method will return the number of products that are in the shopping cart. The size method returns the number of elements stored in a vector.

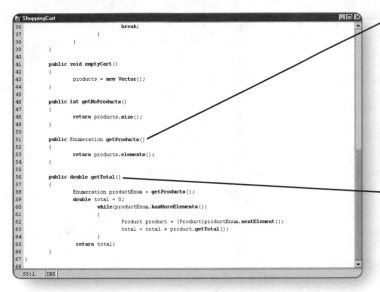

```
ShoppingCart
36                          break;
37                 }
38            }
39       }
40
41       public void emptyCart()
42       {
43              products = new Vector();
44       }
45
46       public int getNoProducts()
47       {
48              return products.size();
49       }
50
51       public Enumeration getProducts()
52       {
53              return products.elements();
54       }
55
56       public double getTotal()
57       {
58              Enumeration productEnum = getProducts();
59              double total = 0;
60                  while(productEnum.hasMoreElements())
61                  {
62                         Product product = (Product)productEnum.nextElement();
63                         total = total + product.getTotal();
64                  }
65              return total;
66       }
67 }
68
55:1    INS
```

8. Create the getProducts method. This method will return all of the products stored in the shopping cart as an enumeration. You will use the returned enumeration to list the contents of the shopping cart on the ViewCart.jsp page.

9. Create a getTotal method. This method tallies the product prices by looping through each element stored in the vector and adding the price to the total.

Displaying the Product Catalog

The product catalog displays the products that the user can purchase. The ProductCatalog table contains the list of products. You will need to connect to the OnlineStore MySQL database, retrieve the products, and display a product list in a table. If you have hundreds of products, categories will become important and you will need a search facility as well. Each product must contain a link or button that the user can click to add the product to the shopping cart.

```
Product Catalog - Microsoft Internet Explorer
File  Edit  View  Favorites  Tools  Help
Links  Best of the Web  Channel Guide  Customize Links
Address  http://127.0.0.1:8100/OnlineStore/DisplayCatalog.jsp           Go

Product Catalog
                                                              View Shopping Cart
ProductID  Title                          Author    Description                        Price
1          Macromedia Dreamweaver UltraDev Fast  Aneesha   Learn to create dynamic Web sites.   $25.99  BUY
           and Easy Web Development        Bakharia
2          Macromedia Dreamweaver UltraDev 4     Aneesha   Learn to create dynamic Web sites    $29.99  BUY
           Fast and Easy Web Development   Bakharia  even faster.
5          JavaServer Pages Fast and Easy Web    Aneesha   Leverage the power of Java and create $29.99  BUY
           Development                     Bakharia  interactive Web applications.

                                                              Internet
```

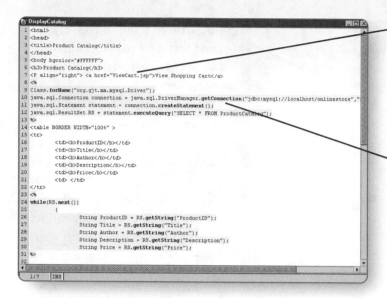

1. Insert a link to the ViewCart.jsp page. This link is usually found in the upper-right corner. The user will click on this link to view the contents of the cart.

2. Create a connection to the OnlineStore MySQL database. You will need to specify org.gjt.mm.mysql.Driver as the JDBC driver to access MySQL databases.

NOTE

The connection URL is slightly different. You need to specify the path to the MySQL server and not the DSN for the database. If your database is password-protected, you will need to pass the password and user name to the getConnection method as well.

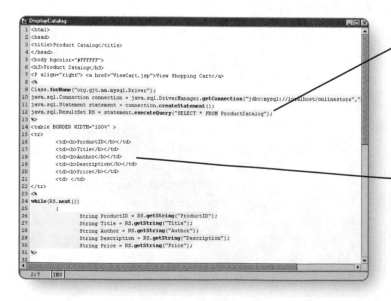

3. Query the ProductCatalog database and store the returned records in a ResultSet object. For the sake of simplicity in this example, all the products will be selected.

4. Display the products in a table. The ProductID, Title, Author, Description, and Price fields should be displayed.

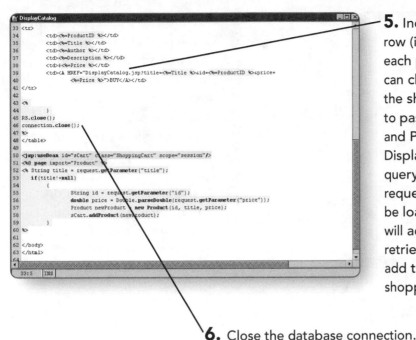

```
DisplayCatalog
33 <tr>
34        <td><%=ProductID %></td>
35        <td><%=Title %></td>
36        <td><%=Author %></td>
37        <td><%=Description %></td>
38        <td>$<%=Price %></td>
39        <td><A HREF="DisplayCatalog.jsp?title=<%=Title %>&id=<%=ProductID %>&price=
40            <%=Price %>">BUY</A></td>
41 </tr>
42
43 <%
44        }
45 RS.close();
46 connection.close();
47 %>
48 </table>
49
50 <jsp:useBean id="sCart" class="ShoppingCart" scope="session"/>
51 <%@ page import="Product" %>
52 <% String title = request.getParameter("title");
53    if(title!=null)
54        {
55            String id = request.getParameter("id");
56            double price = Double.parseDouble(request.getParameter("price"));
57            Product newProduct = new Product(id, title, price);
58            sCart.addProduct(newProduct);
59        }
60 %>
61
62 </body>
63 </html>
64
33:5    INS
```

5. Include a link in each table row (in other words, a link for each product) on which the user can click to add the product to the shopping cart. You will need to pass the ProductID, Title, and Price fields to the DisplayCatalog.jsp page in the query string. You are basically requesting that the same page be loaded again. In Step 9, you will add some JSP script to retrieve the query string and add the product to the shopping cart.

6. Close the database connection.

```
DisplayCatalog
33 <tr>
34        <td><%=ProductID %></td>
35        <td><%=Title %></td>
36        <td><%=Author %></td>
37        <td><%=Description %></td>
38        <td>$<%=Price %></td>
39        <td><A HREF="DisplayCatalog.jsp?title=<%=Title %>&id=<%=ProductID %>&price=
40            <%=Price %>">BUY</A></td>
41 </tr>
42
43 <%
44        }
45 RS.close();
46 connection.close();
47 %>
48 </table>
49
50 <jsp:useBean id="sCart" class="ShoppingCart" scope="session"/>
51 <%@ page import="Product" %>
52 <% String title = request.getParameter("title");
53    if(title!=null)
54        {
55            String id = request.getParameter("id");
56            double price = Double.parseDouble(request.getParameter("price"));
57            Product newProduct = new Product(id, title, price);
58            sCart.addProduct(newProduct);
59        }
60 %>
61
62 </body>
63 </html>
64
33:5    INS
```

7. Insert a useBean tag with sCart as its ID. You must set the class attribute to ShoppingCart, which is the class name of the JavaBean. The scope of the JavaBean must be set to session because the contents of the cart must be stored for the duration of the user's visit to the Web site.

8. Import the Product class. The Shopping Cart JavaBean uses the Product class when creating product objects.

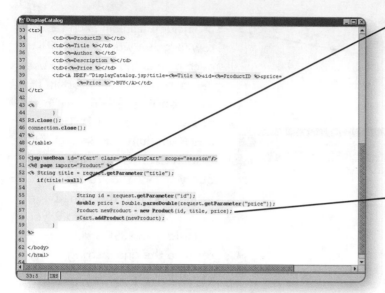

```
DisplayCatalog

33  <tr>
34      <td><%=ProductID %></td>
35      <td><%=Title %></td>
36      <td><%=Author %></td>
37      <td><%=Description %></td>
38      <td>$<%=Price %></td>
39      <td><A HREF="DisplayCatalog.jsp?title=<%=Title %>&id=<%=ProductID %>&price=
40              <%=Price %>">BUY</A></td>
41  </tr>
42
43  <%
44      }
45  RS.close();
46  connection.close();
47  %>
48  </table>
49
50  <jsp:useBean id="sCart" class="ShoppingCart" scope="session"/>
51  <%@ page import="Product" %>
52  <% String title = request.getParameter("title");
53     if(title!=null)
54         {
55             String id = request.getParameter("id");
56             double price = Double.parseDouble(request.getParameter("price"));
57             Product newProduct = new Product(id, title, price);
58             sCart.addProduct(newProduct);
59         }
60  %>
61
62  </body>
63  </html>
64
33:5    INS
```

9. If a query string is present, it means that the user clicked on a link to add a product to the shopping cart. You need to extract the title, ID, and price of the product that must be added from the query string. Use the getParameter method to do this.

10. Create the newProduct object by calling the Product constructor. You will need to pass the values retrieved from the query string to the constructor method.

```
DisplayCatalog

33  <tr>
34      <td><%=ProductID %></td>
35      <td><%=Title %></td>
36      <td><%=Author %></td>
37      <td><%=Description %></td>
38      <td>$<%=Price %></td>
39      <td><A HREF="DisplayCatalog.jsp?title=<%=Title %>&id=<%=ProductID %>&price=
40              <%=Price %>">BUY</A></td>
41  </tr>
42
43  <%
44      }
45  RS.close();
46  connection.close();
47  %>
48  </table>
49
50  <jsp:useBean id="sCart" class="ShoppingCart" scope="session"/>
51  <%@ page import="Product" %>
52  <% String title = request.getParameter("title");
53     if(title!=null)
54         {
55             String id = request.getParameter("id");
56             double price = Double.parseDouble(request.getParameter("price"));
57             Product newProduct = new Product(id, title, price);
58             sCart.addProduct(newProduct);
59         }
60  %>
61
62  </body>
63  </html>
64
33:5    INS
```

11. Call the addProduct method and pass the newProduct object to it. The addProduct method is in the Shopping Cart JavaBean. It will add a Product object to the vector that is used to store the contents of the shopping cart. If the product has already been added to the shopping cart, the addProduct method will simply increase the product quantity by one.

Viewing the Shopping Cart

The shopping cart stores all of the items that the user wishes to purchase. The contents of the shopping cart are stored in a session variable, but this is all taken care of behind the scenes.

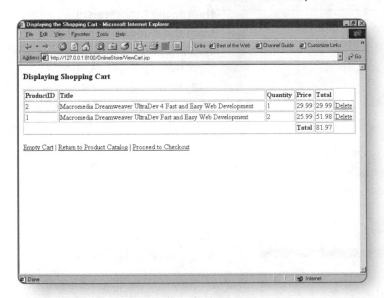

The contents of the cart can be retrieved at any time and displayed. The user will be allowed to remove items from the cart as well as completely empty the cart. Luckily, all of this functionality has already been encapsulated in the Shopping Cart JavaBean.

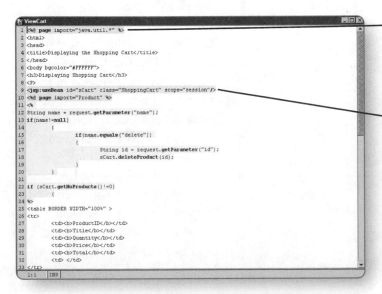

1. Import the java.util.* package. This will be required to use an enumeration to display the contents of the cart.

2. Insert a useBean tag with sCart as its ID. You must set the class attribute to ShoppingCart, which is the class name of the JavaBean. The scope of the JavaBean must be set to session because the contents of the cart must be stored for the duration of the user's visit to the Web site.

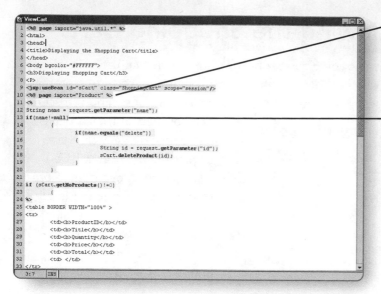

```
ViewCart                                                    _ □ ×
1  <%@ page import="java.util.*" %>
2  <html>
3  <head>
4  <title>Displaying the Shopping Cart</title>
5  </head>
6  <body bgcolor="#FFFFFF">
7  <h3>Displaying Shopping Cart</h3>
8  <P>
9  <jsp:useBean id="sCart" class="ShoppingCart" scope="session"/>
10 <%@ page import="Product" %>
11 <%
12 String name = request.getParameter("name");
13 if(name!=null)
14         {
15                 if(name.equals("delete"))
16                 {
17                         String id = request.getParameter("id");
18                         sCart.deleteProduct(id);
19                 }
20         }
21
22 if (sCart.getNoProducts()!=0)
23         {
24 %>
25 <table BORDER WIDTH="100%" >
26 <tr>
27         <td><b>ProductID</b></td>
28         <td><b>Title</b></td>
29         <td><b>Quantity</b></td>
30         <td><b>Price</b></td>
31         <td><b>Total</b></td>
32         <td> </td>
33 </tr>
3:7    INS
```

3. Import the Product class. The Shopping Cart JavaBean uses the Product class when creating product objects.

4. If a query string is present, it means that the user clicked on a link to delete a product from the shopping cart. You need to extract the ID of the deleted product from the query string. The getParameter method is used to do this.

```
ViewCart                                                    _ □ ×
1  <%@ page import="java.util.*" %>
2  <html>
3  <head>
4  <title>Displaying the Shopping Cart</title>
5  </head>
6  <body bgcolor="#FFFFFF">
7  <h3>Displaying Shopping Cart</h3>
8  <P>
9  <jsp:useBean id="sCart" class="ShoppingCart" scope="session"/>
10 <%@ page import="Product" %>
11 <%
12 String name = request.getParameter("name");
13 if(name!=null)
14         {
15                 if(name.equals("delete"))
16                 {
17                         String id = request.getParameter("id");
18                         sCart.deleteProduct(id);
19                 }
20         }
21
22 if (sCart.getNoProducts()!=0)
23         {
24 %>
25 <table BORDER WIDTH="100%" >
26 <tr>
27         <td><b>ProductID</b></td>
28         <td><b>Title</b></td>
29         <td><b>Quantity</b></td>
30         <td><b>Price</b></td>
31         <td><b>Total</b></td>
32         <td> </td>
33 </tr>
21:1   INS
```

5. Call the deleteProduct method and pass the product ID to it. The deleteProduct method will remove the product from the shopping cart.

6. Call the getNoProducts method. This method returns the number of products in the shopping cart. If this method returns zero, you don't want to display a blank shopping cart table—it would just look unprofessional. Instead, inform the user that the cart is currently empty, using the else clause of the if statement.

7. Include a table that has columns to display the product ID, title, quantity, price, and total.

8. Call the getProducts method and store the result in an enumeration object. The getProducts method returns all products in the shopping cart. Everything that is stored in the vector will be returned.

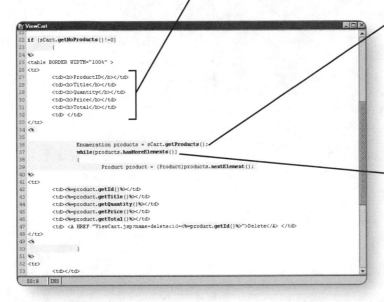

```
 ViewCart                                                        _ □ ×
21
22  if (sCart.getNoProducts()!=0)
23           {
24  %>
25  <table BORDER WIDTH="100%" >
26  <tr>
27          <td><b>ProductID</b></td>
28          <td><b>Title</b></td>
29          <td><b>Quantity</b></td>
30          <td><b>Price</b></td>
31          <td><b>Total</b></td>
32          <td> </td>
33  </tr>
34  <%
35
36              Enumeration products = sCart.getProducts();
37              while(products.hasMoreElements())
38              {
39                      Product product = (Product)products.nextElement();
40  %>
41  <tr>
42          <td><%=product.getId()%></td>
43          <td><%=product.getTitle()%></td>
44          <td><%=product.getQuantity()%></td>
45          <td><%=product.getPrice()%></td>
46          <td><%=product.getTotal()%></td>
47          <td> <A HREF "ViewCart.jsp?name=delete&id=<%=product.getId()%>">Delete</A> </td>
48  </tr>
49  <%
50              }
51  %>
52  <tr>
53          <td></td>
   50:9    INS
```

9. Use a while loop to print each product to a new table row. You will have to call the get accessor methods of the Product class to return the product ID, title, quantity, price, and total.

10. Include a link in each table row (in other words, a link for each product), on which the user can click to remove the product from the shopping cart. You will need to pass the product ID to the ViewCart.jsp page in the query string. You are basically requesting that the same page be loaded again. In Step 4, you already inserted the JSP code to retrieve the query string and delete the product from the shopping cart.

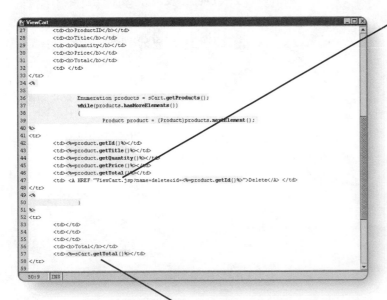

```
 ViewCart                                                        _ □ ×
27          <td><b>ProductID</b></td>
28          <td><b>Title</b></td>
29          <td><b>Quantity</b></td>
30          <td><b>Price</b></td>
31          <td><b>Total</b></td>
32          <td> </td>
33  </tr>
34  <%
35
36              Enumeration products = sCart.getProducts();
37              while(products.hasMoreElements())
38              {
39                      Product product = (Product)products.nextElement();
40  %>
41  <tr>
42          <td><%=product.getId()%></td>
43          <td><%=product.getTitle()%></td>
44          <td><%=product.getQuantity()%></td>
45          <td><%=product.getPrice()%></td>
46          <td><%=product.getTotal()%></td>
47          <td> <A HREF "ViewCart.jsp?name=delete&id=<%=product.getId()%>">Delete</A> </td>
48  </tr>
49  <%
50              }
51  %>
52  <tr>
53          <td></td>
54          <td></td>
55          <td></td>
56          <td><b>Total</b></td>
57          <td><%=sCart.getTotal()%></td>
58  </tr>
59
   50:9    INS
```

11. Call the getTotal method to return the total cost of all products that are in the shopping cart.

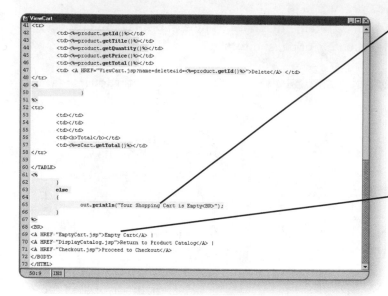

```
ViewCart                                                      _ □ ×
41 <tr>
42          <td><%=product.getId()%></td>
43          <td><%=product.getTitle()%></td>
44          <td><%=product.getQuantity()%></td>
45          <td><%=product.getPrice()%></td>
46          <td><%=product.getTotal()%></td>
47          <td> <A HREF="ViewCart.jsp?name=delete&id=<%=product.getId()%>">Delete</A> </td>
48 </tr>
49 <%
50                  }
51 %>
52 <tr>
53          <td></td>
54          <td></td>
55          <td></td>
56          <td><b>Total</b></td>
57          <td><%=sCart.getTotal()%></td>
58 </tr>
59
60 </TABLE>
61 <%
62          }
63          else
64          {
65                  out.println("Your Shopping Cart is Empty<BR>");
66          }
67 %>
68 <BR>
69 <A HREF="EmptyCart.jsp">Empty Cart</A> |
70 <A HREF="DisplayCatalog.jsp">Return to Product Catalog</A> |
71 <A HREF="Checkout.jsp">Proceed to Checkout</A>
72 </BODY>
73 </HTML>
   50:9    INS
```

12. Display a message to inform the user that the shopping cart is empty.

13. Include a link to EmptyCart.jsp. The user will click on this link to empty the contents of the cart.

```
ViewCart                                                      _ □ ×
41 <tr>
42          <td><%=product.getId()%></td>
43          <td><%=product.getTitle()%></td>
44          <td><%=product.getQuantity()%></td>
45          <td><%=product.getPrice()%></td>
46          <td><%=product.getTotal()%></td>
47          <td> <A HREF="ViewCart.jsp?name=delete&id=<%=product.getId()%>">Delete</A> </td>
48 </tr>
49 <%
50                  }
51 %>
52 <tr>
53          <td></td>
54          <td></td>
55          <td></td>
56          <td><b>Total</b></td>
57          <td><%=sCart.getTotal()%></td>
58 </tr>
59
60 </TABLE>
61 <%
62          }
63          else
64          {
65                  out.println("Your Shopping Cart is Empty<BR>");
66          }
67 %>
68 <BR>
69 <A HREF="EmptyCart.jsp">Empty Cart</A> |
70 <A HREF="DisplayCatalog.jsp">Return to Product Catalog</A> |
71 <A HREF="Checkout.jsp">Proceed to Checkout</A>
72 </BODY>
73 </HTML>
   50:9    INS
```

14. Include a link back to the DisplayCatalog.jsp page. This will allow the user to return to do more shopping.

15. Include a link to Checkout.jsp. This user will click on this link to purchase the products in the shopping cart.

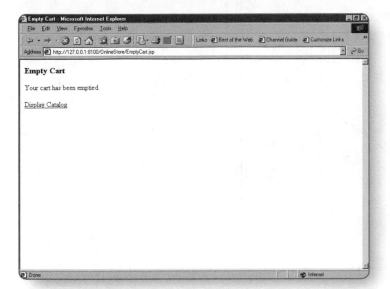

Emptying the Shopping Cart

After shopping, the user might not be happy with any of the products that have been added to the cart. Rather than deleting products individually, the user can click on the Empty Cart link and delete all products from the cart at once.

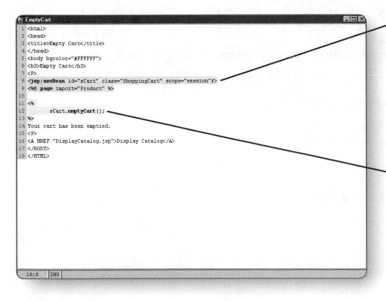

1. Insert a useBean tag with sCart as its ID. The class attribute must be set to ShoppingCart, which is the class name of the JavaBean. The scope of the JavaBean must be set to session.

2. Call the emptyCart method. This method will delete all products stored in the shopping cart.

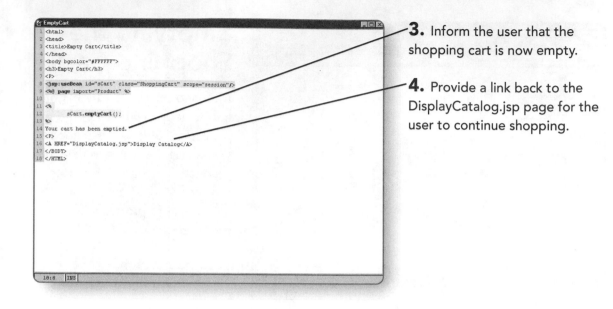

```
1  <html>
2  <head>
3  <title>Empty Cart</title>
4  </head>
5  <body bgcolor="#FFFFFF">
6  <h3>Empty Cart</h3>
7  <P>
8  <jsp:useBean id="sCart" class="ShoppingCart" scope="session"/>
9  <%@ page import="Product" %>
10
11 <%
12     sCart.emptyCart();
13 %>
14 Your cart has been emptied.
15 <P>
16 <A HREF="DisplayCatalog.jsp">Display Catalog</A>
17 </BODY>
18 </HTML>
```

3. Inform the user that the shopping cart is now empty.

4. Provide a link back to the DisplayCatalog.jsp page for the user to continue shopping.

Building the Checkout Page

The checkout page needs to display the products that are being purchased and their total cost. Displaying the shopping cart again easily inserts these details. The checkout page must also include a form to collect the user's name, address, and credit card details.

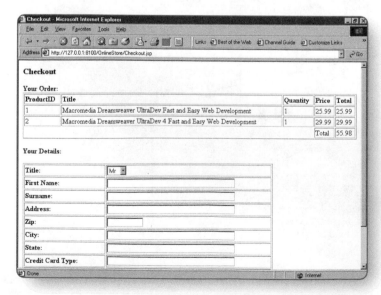

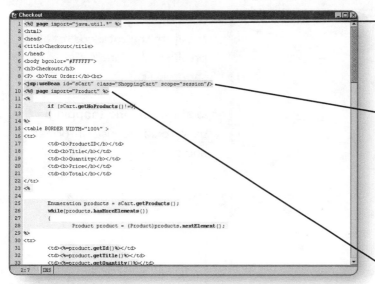

1. Import the java.util.* package. This will be required when using an enumeration to display the contents of the cart.

2. Insert a useBean tag with sCart as its ID. The class attribute must be set to ShoppingCart, which is the class name of the JavaBean. The scope of the JavaBean must be set to session.

3. Import the Product class. The Shopping Cart JavaBean uses the Product class.

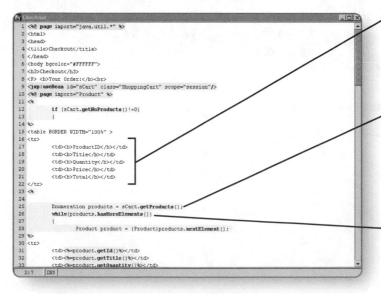

4. Include a table that has columns to display the product ID, title, quantity, price, and total.

5. Call the getProducts method and store the result in an enumeration object. The getProducts method returns all products in the shopping cart.

6. Use a while loop to print each product to a new table row. You will have to call the get accessor methods of the Product class to return the product ID, title, quantity, price, and total.

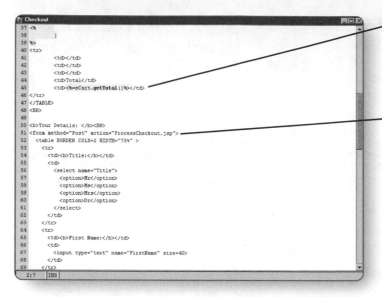

7. Call the getTotal method to return the total cost of all products that are in the shopping cart.

8. Insert a form that will be used to collect user information and payment details. The ProcessCheckout.jsp page will process the form.

NOTE

You should never send credit card information over the Internet without a secure connection to your Web server. You will need to purchase and install a secure certificate on your Web server. A secure certificate allows data to be encrypted to and from your server. 128-bit encryption is currently supported. Visit the VeriSign Web site for more information, at http://www.verisign.com.

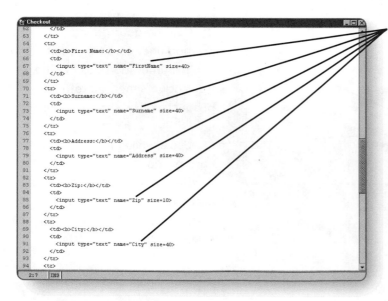

9. Include form fields to collect the information you require from users. This will usually include their name, address, and credit card details. The form must also have a submit button.

> ### NOTE
> It would also be worthwhile to validate the data entered by the user to ensure that data has been entered and is in the required format. You could do this with client-side JavaScript or JSP. Chapter 10, "Retrieving Information from a User," introduced a few useful validation methods.

Processing the Purchase

You will need to retrieve the details entered into the form by the user and store them in the Orders table. The OrderID field will contain the unique ID for the order. This field is automatically generated by the database. Calling the getLastInsertID method will retrieve the unique ID for the order. Each product in the shopping cart will then need to be stored in the OrderDetails table. The unique order ID, product ID, and quantity need to be stored in the OrderDetails table.

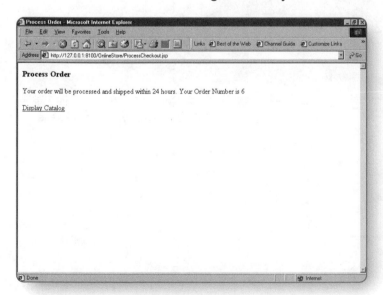

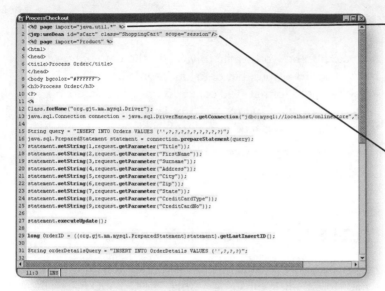

1. Import the java.util.* package. This will be required when using an enumeration to retrieve products from the shopping cart and add them to the OrderDetails table.

2. Insert a useBean tag with sCart as its ID. The class attribute must be set to ShoppingCart, which is the class name of the JavaBean. The scope of the JavaBean must be set to session.

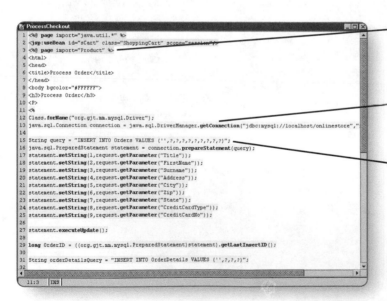

3. Import the Product class. The Shopping Cart JavaBean uses the Product class.

4. Create a connection to the OnlineStore MySQL database.

5. Create a parametized INSERT query to insert the user information and payment details into the Orders table.

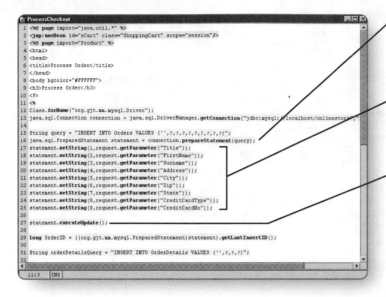

```
ProcessCheckout                                                    _ □ X
 1  <%@ page import="java.util.*" %>
 2  <jsp:useBean id="sCart" class="ShoppingCart" scope="session"/>
 3  <%@ page import="Product" %>
 4  <html>
 5  <head>
 6  <title>Process Order</title>
 7  </head>
 8  <body bgcolor="#FFFFFF">
 9  <h3>Process Order</h3>
10  <P>
11  <%
12  Class.forName("org.gjt.mm.mysql.Driver");
13  java.sql.Connection connection = java.sql.DriverManager.getConnection("jdbc:mysql://localhost/onlinestore");
14
15  String query = "INSERT INTO Orders VALUES ('',?,?,?,?,?,?,?,?,?)";
16  java.sql.PreparedStatement statement = connection.prepareStatement(query);
17  statement.setString(1,request.getParameter("Title"));
18  statement.setString(2,request.getParameter("FirstName"));
19  statement.setString(3,request.getParameter("Surname"));
20  statement.setString(4,request.getParameter("Address"));
21  statement.setString(5,request.getParameter("City"));
22  statement.setString(6,request.getParameter("Zip"));
23  statement.setString(7,request.getParameter("State"));
24  statement.setString(8,request.getParameter("CreditCardType"));
25  statement.setString(9,request.getParameter("CreditCardNo"));
26
27  statement.executeUpdate();
28
29  long OrderID = ((org.gjt.mm.mysql.PreparedStatement)statement).getLastInsertID();
30
31  String orderDetailsQuery = "INSERT INTO OrderDetails VALUES ('',?,?,?)";
32
 11:3     INS
```

6. Create a PreparedStatement object and pass the query to the prepareStatement method.

7. Use the setString method to insert the data retrieved from the form into the query.

8. Execute the query.

NOTE

In this example, the payment details are stored and must be processed manually. You will need to check to determine whether they are valid and have the required balance. You can also use a third-party service to validate the credit card and transfer the payment in real time. VeriSign offers a payment processing service. You should also evaluate CyberCash (http://www.cybercash.com) and Authorize.Net (http://www.authorizenet.com).

```
ProcessCheckout                                                    _ □ X
22  statement.setString(6,request.getParameter("Zip"));
23  statement.setString(7,request.getParameter("State"));
24  statement.setString(8,request.getParameter("CreditCardType"));
25  statement.setString(9,request.getParameter("CreditCardNo"));
26
27  statement.executeUpdate();
28
29  long OrderID = ((org.gjt.mm.mysql.PreparedStatement)statement).getLastInsertID();
30
31  String orderDetailsQuery = "INSERT INTO OrderDetails VALUES ('',?,?,?)";
32
33  Enumeration products = sCart.getProducts();
34  while(products.hasMoreElements())
35      {
36              Product product = (Product)products.nextElement();
37              statement = connection.prepareStatement(orderDetailsQuery);
38              statement.setLong(1,OrderID);
39              statement.setInt(2,Integer.parseInt(product.getId()));
40              statement.setInt(3,product.getQuantity());
41              statement.executeUpdate();
42      }
43
44  statement.close();
45  connection.close();
46
47  sCart.emptyCart();
48  %>
49  Your order will be processed and shipped within 24 hours. Your Order Number is <%=OrderID %>
50  <P>
51  <A HREF="DisplayCatalog.jsp">Display Catalog</A>
52  </BODY>
53  </HTML>
 25:1     INS
```

9. Cast the statement object to org.gjt.mm.mysql. PreparedStatement and call the getLastInsertID method. This method will return a unique ID for the order. Store this value in an integer variable.

10. Create a parametized INSERT query to insert the products being purchased into the OrderDetails table.

```
ProcessCheckout                                                    _ □ ×
22  statement.setString(6,request.getParameter("Zip"));
23  statement.setString(7,request.getParameter("State"));
24  statement.setString(8,request.getParameter("CreditCardType"));
25  statement.setString(9,request.getParameter("CreditCardNo"));
26
27  statement.executeUpdate();
28
29  long OrderID = ((org.gjt.mm.mysql.PreparedStatement)statement).getLastInsertID();
30
31  String orderDetailsQuery = "INSERT INTO OrderDetails VALUES ('',?,?,?)";
32
33  Enumeration products = sCart.getProducts();
34  while(products.hasMoreElements())
35          {
36                  Product product = (Product)products.nextElement();
37                  statement = connection.prepareStatement(orderDetailsQuery );
38                  statement.setLong(1,OrderID);
39                  statement.setInt(2,Integer.parseInt(product.getId()));
40                  statement.setInt(3,product.getQuantity());
41                  statement.executeUpdate();
42          }
43
44  statement.close();
45  connection.close();
46
47  sCart.emptyCart();
48  %>
49  Your order will be processed and shipped within 24 hours. Your Order Number is <%=OrderID %>
50  <P>
51  <A HREF="DisplayCatalog.jsp">Display Catalog</A>
52  </BODY>
53  </HTML>

28:1    INS
```

11. Call the getProducts method and store the result in an enumeration object. The getProducts method returns all products in the shopping cart.

12. Use a while loop to insert each product into the OrderDetails table. You need to insert the unique order ID, the product ID, and the quantity. You will use a Prepared Statement.

NOTE

You must use the setLong method to insert the unique order ID into the query. The setInt method must be used to insert the product ID into the query.

```
ProcessCheckout                                                    _ □ ×
22  statement.setString(6,request.getParameter("Zip"));
23  statement.setString(7,request.getParameter("State"));
24  statement.setString(8,request.getParameter("CreditCardType"));
25  statement.setString(9,request.getParameter("CreditCardNo"));
26
27  statement.executeUpdate();
28
29  long OrderID = ((org.gjt.mm.mysql.PreparedStatement)statement).getLastInsertID();
30
31  String orderDetailsQuery = "INSERT INTO OrderDetails VALUES ('',?,?,?)";
32
33  Enumeration products = sCart.getProducts();
34  while(products.hasMoreElements())
35          {
36                  Product product = (Product)products.nextElement();
37                  statement = connection.prepareStatement(orderDetailsQuery );
38                  statement.setLong(1,OrderID);
39                  statement.setInt(2,Integer.parseInt(product.getId()));
40                  statement.setInt(3,product.getQuantity());
41                  statement.executeUpdate();
42          }
43
44  statement.close();
45  connection.close();
46
47  sCart.emptyCart();
48  %>
49  Your order will be processed and shipped within 24 hours. Your Order Number is <%=OrderID %>
50  <P>
51  <A HREF="DisplayCatalog.jsp">Display Catalog</A>
52  </BODY>
53  </HTML>

28:1    INS
```

The query will be executed for each product in the shopping cart.

13. Close the database connection.

```
ProcessCheckout                                                        _ □ X
22 statement.setString(6,request.getParameter("Zip"));
23 statement.setString(7,request.getParameter("State"));
24 statement.setString(8,request.getParameter("CreditCardType"));
25 statement.setString(9,request.getParameter("CreditCardNo"));
26
27 statement.executeUpdate();
28
29 long OrderID = ((org.gjt.mm.mysql.PreparedStatement)statement).getLastInsertID();
30
31 String orderDetailsQuery = "INSERT INTO OrderDetails VALUES ('',?,?,?)";
32
33 Enumeration products = sCart.getProducts();
34 while(products.hasMoreElements())
35           {
36                  Product product = (Product)products.nextElement();
37                  statement = connection.prepareStatement(orderDetailsQuery );
38                  statement.setLong(1,OrderID);
39                  statement.setInt(2,Integer.parseInt(product.getId()));
40                  statement.setInt(3,product.getQuantity());
41                  statement.executeUpdate();
42           }
43
44 statement.close();
45 connection.close();
46
47 sCart.emptyCart();
48 %>
49 Your order will be processed and shipped within 24 hours. Your Order Number is <%=OrderID %>
50 <P>
51 <A HREF="DisplayCatalog.jsp">Display Catalog</A>
52 </BODY>
53 </HTML>

28:1      INS
```

14. Call the emptyCart method. After the products have been purchased, you can empty the shopping cart.

15. Inform the user that the order has been processed and display a unique order number. The user might want to use this as a reference.

Testing the Online Store

You should now test your the shopping cart. In this set of steps, you will

- Browse the product catalog and add products to the shopping cart

- View the shopping cart, remove items, and return to the product catalog to do some more shopping

- Add more products to the cart

- View the shopping cart and proceed to the checkout

- Enter postage and payment details

- Receive a unique order ID, which can be used to trace the order

1. Open the DisplayCatalog.jsp page. The product catalog will be displayed.

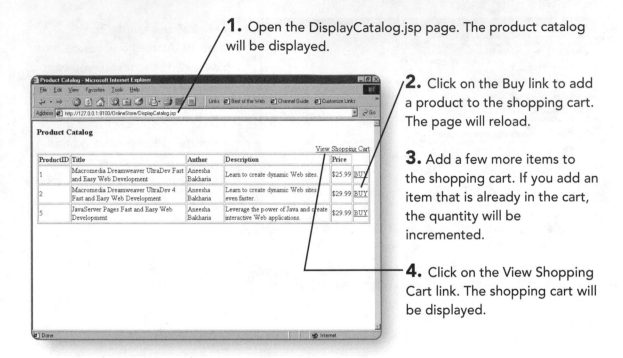

2. Click on the Buy link to add a product to the shopping cart. The page will reload.

3. Add a few more items to the shopping cart. If you add an item that is already in the cart, the quantity will be incremented.

4. Click on the View Shopping Cart link. The shopping cart will be displayed.

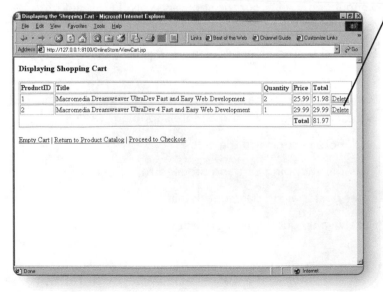

5. Click on the Delete link to remove an item. The page will reload.

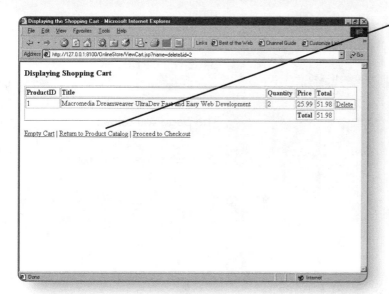

6. Click on the Return to Product Catalog link to continue shopping. The Product Catalog will be displayed again.

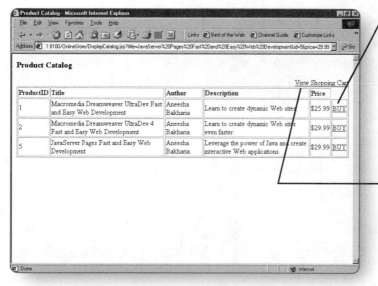

7. Add more items to the shopping cart.

8. Click on the View Shopping Cart link. The shopping cart will be displayed.

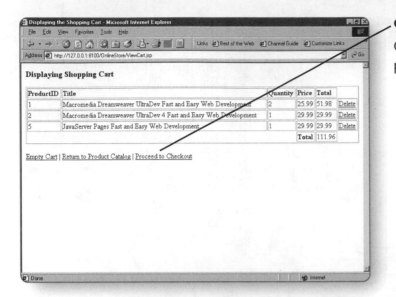

9. Click on the Proceed to Checkout link. The Checkout page will be displayed.

10. Enter your name, address, and payment details.

11. Click on Checkout. Your information will be stored in the OnlineStore database.

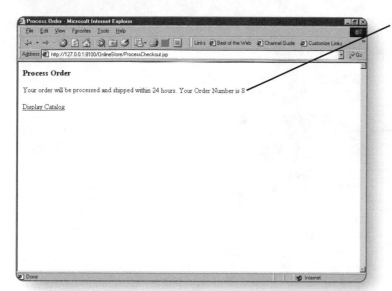

The unique order ID will be
displayed.

Now use MySQLGUI to view
the online transactions. You
could also build a Web interface
to view the transactions.

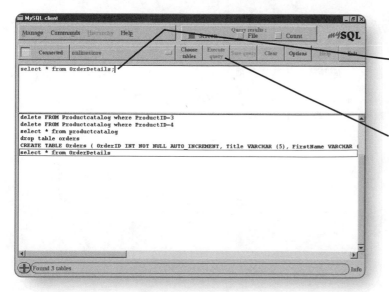

12. Open MySQLGUI.

13. Type in a SELECT query
to retrieve all records in the
OrderDetails table.

14. Click on Execute Query.
The MySQL results window will
open. A list of orders will be
displayed.

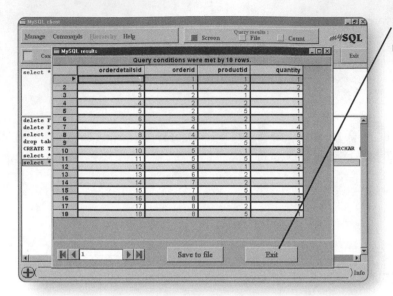

15. Click on Exit. The MySQL results window will close.

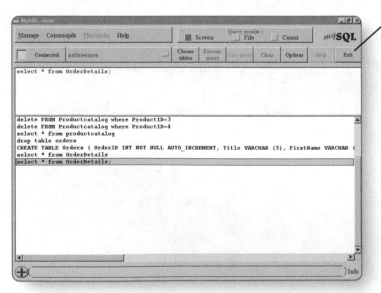

16. Click on Exit. MySQLGUI will close.

A

HTML Quick Reference

The purpose of this appendix is to provide you with a list of commonly used HTML tags. These tags will help you create a Web page into which you can insert JSP code. The list is by no means comprehensive, as this book assumes a prior knowledge of building static Web pages in HTML.

To	Use These Tags
Create a basic HTML page	`<HTML>`
	`<HEAD>`
	`<TITLE>Insert Page Title Here</TITLE>`
	`</HEAD>`
	`<BODY>`
	Insert text here
	`</BODY>`
	`</HTML>`
Specify page properties	`<BODY bgcolor="backgroundcolor" text="textcolor" link="linkcolor" vlink="visitedlinkcolor" alink="activelinkcolor">`
	Note: All colors need to be specified in hexidecimal (For example: `<BODY bgcolor="#FF0099" text="#333333" link="#330099" vlink="#FF0033" alink="330099">`)
Create a heading	There are six heading levels.
	`<H1>Insert Heading Here</H1>`
	`<H2>Insert Heading Here</H2>`
	`<H3>Insert Heading Here</H3>`
	`<H4>Insert Heading Here</H4>`
	`<H5>Insert Heading Here</H5>`
	`<H6>Insert Heading Here</H6>`
Make text bold	`<B>Insert text here</B>`
Make text italic	`<I>Insert text here</I>`
Set font, font color, and font size	`<FONT font="fontname" color="fontcolor" size="fontsize">` (For example: `<FONT font="Arial,Helvetica,Sans-serif" color="#333333" size="5">`)
Insert a horizontal rule	`<HR>`
Insert a line break	` `
Insert a paragraph break	`<P>Insert a paragraph break</P>`

To	Use These Tags
Create a table	<TABLE width="pixelvalue or percentage" border="bordersize">
	<TR>
	<TD>row 1 column 1</TD>
	<TD>row 1 column 2</TD>
	</TR>
	<TR>
	<TD>row 2 column 1</TD>
	<TD>row 2 column 2</TD>
	</TR>
	</TABLE>
Create an unordered list	<UL>
	<LI>Insert list item here</LI>
	<LI>Insert list item here</LI>
	</UL>
Create an ordered list	<OL>
	<LI>Insert list item here</LI>
	<LI>Insert list item here</LI>
	</OL>
Insert an image	<IMG scr="imagename.gif" width="pixelwidth" height="pixelheight">
Create a link	<A HREF="filename">Insert link text here</A>

NOTE

HTML closing tags always include a / after the < tag delimiter.

TIP

HTML is not a case-sensitive markup language. Tags may be in uppercase, lowercase, or both. However, uppercase HTML tags are easier to read.

B

JSP Quick Reference

Throughout the book, you have learned how to use JSP tags and page directives to create dynamically-generated content. This appendix provides you with an easy place to locate tag syntax and view practical examples.

To	Use This Tag
Comment your code	<%-- place your comment here --%>
Declare variables and methods	<%! Type variableName = value %> (For example: <%! String text = "Hello"; %>)
Print the result of an expression	<%=expression %> (For example: <%=new jave.util.Date() %>)
Insert Java code	<%
	place your code here
	%>
	For example:
	<%
	for (i=0; i<10; i++)
	{
	out.println(i + " ");
	}
	%>
Include a file	<%@ include file=filename.jsp" %>
Import packages	<%@ page import="package.*" %> (For example: <%@ page import="java.util.*" %>)
Create a custom error page	<%@ page isErrorPage="true" %>
Insert error handling	<%@ page errorPage="filename.jsp" %>
Change the content type	<%@ page contentType="mime-type" %>
	For example: Generating a Microsoft Excel Spreadsheet
	<%@ page contentType="application/vnd.ms-excel" %>
Load a custom tag library	<%@ taglib uri="taglib.tld" prefix="tagPrefix" %>
Use a Bean	<jsp:useBean name="id" parameters />
Setting Bean properties	<jsp:setProperty name="name" property="propName" value="value" />
Getting Bean properties	<jsp:getProperty name="name" property="propName" />

C

Additional Resources

So you've come to the end of this book. Creating dynamic Web applications should no longer be a mystery to you, but there will always be a need to enhance your knowledge. You need to challenge yourself and continually improve your JSP code. This appendix presents some resources that will help you become an expert JSP developer. In this appendix, you'll find:

- JSP resources
- Servlet resources
- Java-related technologies
- JSP application servers

JSP Resources

Site	URL
Sun's JSP Web Site	http://java.sun.com/products/jsp/index.html
The JSP Resource Index	http://www.jspin.com
JSPTags.com	http://jsptags.com
JSP Insider	http://www.jspinsider.com
JavaServer Pages (JSP) FAQ	http://www.jguru.com/jguru/faq/faqpage.jsp?name=JSP
ServerPages.com	http://www.serverpages.com/Java_Server_Pages

Servlet Resources

Site	URL
Sun's Servlet Web Site	http://java.sun.com/products/servlet
CoolServlets.com	http://www.coolservlets.com
ServletSource.com	http://www.servletsource.com

Java-Related Technologies

Site	URL
Sun's JDBC Tutorial JDBC Database Access	http://java.sun.com/docs/books/tutorial/jdbc/index.html
Java Technology and XML	http://java.sun.com/xml
JavaMail API	http://java.sun.com/products/javamail/index.html
JavaBeans	http://java.sun.com/beans/glasgow.jaf.html

Application Servers

Site	URL
BEA WebLogic Server	http://www.bea.com
The Jakarta Project	http://jakarta.apache.org
IBM WebSphere	http://www-4.ibm.com/software/webservers/appserv/index.html
Allaire JRun Application Server	http://www.jrun.com

What's on the CD-ROM

The CD-ROM that accompanies this book has everything you need to start building dynamic JSP-driven Web sites, including

- Source code for all JSP examples in the book

- Allaire JRun Developer Edition—an application server licensed for development use only, perfect for testing your JSP code locally

- A trial version of Allaire JRun Studio—a JSP editor that is based on HomeSite, the popular HTML editor

- A trial version of Allaire Kawa—a Java IDE for developing server-side Java applications

- A trial version of Macromedia Dreamweaver UltraDev—a visual environment for the drag-and-drop creation of JSP, ASP, and ColdFusion-based applications

- A trial version of Macromedia Fireworks—an ideal tool for creating and manipulating Web graphics

- A trial version of Macromedia Dreamweaver—a robust Web development application, ideal for creating dynamic Web pages

- Appendix C from the book—a list of links that you can click on to visit many helpful JSP sites

Running the CD-ROM with Windows 95/98/2000/Me/NT

The CD-ROM's content requires no installation and can be viewed from a Web browser. You only need to copy files you want to use to your hard drive, and install those applications that you want to use. To access the CD's contents, follow these instructions.

1. Insert the CD into the CD-ROM drive and close the tray.

2. Open Windows Explorer and double-click on the CD-ROM drive icon. The CD's contents will be displayed.

3. Double-click on the start_here.html file. Your default Web browser will open and load the Prima License Agreement.

The Prima License Agreement is the first thing that appears in the browser window. Before installing anything from the CD-ROM, you must read and accept the licensing agreement. Click on I Agree to accept the license and proceed with installation. If you do not accept the licensing agreement, click on I disagree to cancel installation, then remove the disc from your computer.

The Prima User Interface

The opening screen of the Prima user interface contains a two-panel window. The left panel contains a directory of the programs and files on the CD. The right panel displays a description of the entry selected in the left panel.

Using the Left Panel

Click on one of the options in the left panel: Programs, Examples, Appendix C, or Main. The right panel of the interface will display the appropriate information for the selected option.

Using the Right Panel

The right panel describes the entry you choose in the left panel. The information provided tells you about your selection, as the functionality of an installable program. When you select Programs from the left panel, the right panel will display information about how to download the trial versions from the CD.

Resizing and Closing the User Interface

To resize the window, position the mouse over any edge or corner, and click and hold the mouse while dragging the edge or corner to a new position. Release the mouse button when the window has been sized to your requirements.

To close and exit the user interface, select File, Close.

Index

License Agreement/Notice of Limited Warranty

By opening the sealed disc container in this book, you agree to the following terms and conditions. If, upon reading the following license agreement and notice of limited warranty, you cannot agree to the terms and conditions set forth, return the unused book with unopened disc to the place where you purchased it for a refund.

License:

The enclosed software is copyrighted by the copyright holder(s) indicated on the software disc. You are licensed to copy the software onto a single computer for use by a single concurrent user and to a backup disk. You may not reproduce, make copies, or distribute copies or rent or lease the software in whole or in part, except with written permission of the copyright holder(s). You may transfer the enclosed disc only together with this license, and only if you destroy all other copies of the software and the transferee agrees to the terms of the license. You may not decompile, reverse assemble, or reverse engineer the software.

Notice of Limited Warranty:

The enclosed disc is warranted by Prima Publishing to be free of physical defects in materials and workmanship for a period of sixty (60) days from end user's purchase of the book/disc combination. During the sixty-day term of the limited warranty, Prima will provide a replacement disc upon the return of a defective disc.

Limited Liability:

THE SOLE REMEDY FOR BREACH OF THIS LIMITED WARRANTY SHALL CONSIST ENTIRELY OF REPLACEMENT OF THE DEFECTIVE DISC. IN NO EVENT SHALL PRIMA OR THE AUTHORS BE LIABLE FOR ANY OTHER DAMAGES, INCLUDING LOSS OR CORRUPTION OF DATA, CHANGES IN THE FUNCTIONAL CHARACTERISTICS OF THE HARDWARE OR OPERATING SYSTEM, DELETERIOUS INTERACTION WITH OTHER SOFTWARE, OR ANY OTHER SPECIAL, INCIDENTAL, OR CONSEQUENTIAL DAMAGES THAT MAY ARISE, EVEN IF PRIMA AND/OR THE AUTHOR HAVE PREVIOUSLY BEEN NOTIFIED THAT THE POSSIBILITY OF SUCH DAMAGES EXISTS.

Disclaimer of Warranties:

PRIMA AND THE AUTHORS SPECIFICALLY DISCLAIM ANY AND ALL OTHER WARRANTIES, EITHER EXPRESS OR IMPLIED, INCLUDING WARRANTIES OF MERCHANTABILITY, SUITABILITY TO A PARTICULAR TASK OR PURPOSE, OR FREEDOM FROM ERRORS. SOME STATES DO NOT ALLOW FOR EXCLUSION OF IMPLIED WARRANTIES OR LIMITATION OF INCIDENTAL OR CONSEQUENTIAL DAMAGES, SO THESE LIMITATIONS MAY NOT APPLY TO YOU.

Other:

This Agreement is governed by the laws of the State of California without regard to choice of law principles. The United Convention of Contracts for the International Sale of Goods is specifically disclaimed. This Agreement constitutes the entire agreement between you and Prima Publishing regarding use of the software.